St. Patrick's Day, 2005

To Andy,

My hero priest...

May God and Mary
and St. Patrick
bless you!

The "Preferential Option for the Poor" in Catholic Social Thought from John XXIII to John Paul II

With great esteem,
admiration
and affection
for the gift of your
outstanding priesthood.

All the best, in Christ,

Gerry

THE "PREFERENTIAL OPTION FOR THE POOR" IN CATHOLIC SOCIAL THOUGHT FROM JOHN XXIII TO JOHN PAUL II

Gerald S. Twomey

Roman Catholic Studies
Volume 22

The Edwin Mellen Press
Lewiston•Queenston•Lampeter

Library of Congress Cataloging-in-Publication Data

Twomey, Gerald S. (Gerald Sean)
The preferential option for the poor in Catholic social thought from John XXIII to John Paul II / Gerald S. Twomey.
p. cm. -- (Roman Catholic studies ; v. 22)
Includes bibliographical references and index.
ISBN 0-7734-6213-9
1. Church work with the poor--Catholic Church--History--20th century. 2. Church work with the poor--South America--History--20th century. 3. Christian sociology--Catholic Church--History of doctrines--20th century. 4. John XXIII, Pope, 1881-1963. 5. John Paul II, Pope, 1920- I. Title. Series.

BX2347.8.P66T86 2005
261.8'325--dc22

2004061104

This is volume 22 in the continuing series
Roman Catholic Studies
Volume 22 ISBN 0-7734-6213-9
RCS Series ISBN 0-88946-240-X

A CIP catalog record for this book is available from the British Library

Front cover photo: Statue of the "Virgin of the Poor" outside the Cervini Chapel on the grounds of Xavier University in Cagayan de Oro, Mindanao, Philippines
Back cover: Author photo by Philip Saccio of Saccio Studios

Copyright © 2005 Gerald S. Twomey

All rights reserved. For information contact

The Edwin Mellen Press
Box 450
Lewiston, New York
USA 14092-0450

The Edwin Mellen Press
Box 67
Queenston, Ontario
CANADA L0S 1L0

The Edwin Mellen Press, Ltd.
Lampeter, Ceredigion, Wales
UNITED KINGDOM SA48 8LT

Printed in the United States of America

For Paul & Carol Ann

and Tom

Table of Contents

Foreword

> The option for the poor was first proclaimed for Christians in the 25th Chapter of Saint Mathew's Gospel: "I was hungry and you fed me, I was thirsty and you gave me drink, I was naked and you clothed me . . ." (MT 25: 35).

If this vision of the Christian vocation is heard against the background of the *favelas* (shanty town slums) of Rio de Janiero – or any other South American City – the challenge to those who are really listening becomes enormous. How can a Christian be silent in the presence of such suffering among the "least of these brothers and sisters?"

For Catholic Christians the challenge becomes even more pressing. The Catholic imagination has always been communal. As Michael Schuck observed in his study of the papal encyclicals between 1740 and 1987, the underlying image was always *the community* – whether it was the village in 1740 or the world community in 1987. Hence, those who lived in places like the shanty towns of Rio were part of the Catholic community. They simply could not be ignored.

Only they *had* been ignored for most of the history of Catholicism in South America. The Church had identified itself with the ruling oligarchy because it feared the revolutionary forces of "Liberalism" and later of Marxism. It has become the Church of the rich. Was it not time for it to take the side of the poor if it were to be true to what it believed? Liberation theology, which sought to take the side of the poor, proclaimed that it was time and long past time.

In this study, the Reverend Gerald Twomey, Ph.D., traces the development of this revolutionary slogan of the "preferential option for the poor" – in the South American context it can be called nothing else – to its present place as an undisputed component of Catholic Social Teaching.

In the process the "option" has changed somewhat. It is no longer revolutionary. Catholic social theory cannot accept class conflict as basis for social order. There may well be competition among the classes, but at the end of the day they cannot survive without one another. Thus, while in its origins there was perhaps a hint of Marxism in this exposition – and even occasional citations from Marxist analysis – in its present form it no longer calls for the Church to support revolutionary movements.

For some this development has "tamed" the option. This mindset held that only revolution can solve the problems of South America – or of the poor in any other part of the world. Unfortunately, the truth that revolution creates even more concentration of wealth and power was proven again and again in the twentieth century. Marxist regimes never really worked. Castro's Cuba offers a classic example of the ultimate failure of revolutions.

Moreover, it is not yet clear how one transforms a society from oligarchy to democracy, from a horrendous gap between the rich and the poor to some form of equitable distribution of wealth. Oil-rich countries like Mexico and Venezuela should be able to reduce poverty, but have not, largely because they lack the social and political structures and the civic cultures which would be required for such change. If such a government existed in South America that is concerned about the poor, it is the current "Worker's Party" in Brazil. Yet, its leaders realize that they must balance their goals against Brazil's obligations to the world community because the failure to meet the latter would plunge the country into economic disaster.

As Dr. Twomey observes, progress comes slowly. It is not enough to denounce the obvious injustice in a country. It is not enough to attack the complacent oligarchy (with which parts of the Church are still allied, especially the membership and leadership of some of the "new movements" in the Church are allied). Nor will it help the poor very much if the wealth of the oligarchs is taken away and distributed to the poor. In most places where this has been tried, the wealth goes to others but not to assist the poor directly.

Many of those who proclaim the option for the poor – especially in the North American context – don't seem to realize that attempts to reform the civic cultures (where one even exists) and the economic structures of a country are essential before one can expect any progress to be made against poverty. If the Catholic Church is to make any contribution toward these goals it will need cadres of trained economists and sociologists who can detail the concrete changes that are required. Such men and women must be committed to the poor, but they must also be skilled in knowing what they are talking about. Enthusiasm and commitment are no substitutes for professional skill. Zeal and a confidence in one's virtue are not enough to change society.

Unfortunately, Catholic social theorists have not only failed, as Dr. Twomey makes clear in this study, to present their teaching in terms that ordinary folk can understand. But they have also failed to articulate the means and the methods of social reform which will convert those theories into practical programs with some prospects for success.

None of these observations should detract from the importance of Dr. Twomey's study. Rather, they expressed the hope of an intransigent empiricist and social scientist that when Dr. Twomey writes his next book on the option for the poor, he will be able to cite the work of Catholic scholars and activists who have been able to apply that critical option into concrete and practical programs.

It is, I believe, time for the Church to realize that the abstract – and frequently idealized – paradigms of Eurocentric theology (even if spoken with an Hispanic accent) represent only half of the struggle to help and empower the poor, – and perhaps the *easier* half. If the Church really wishes to commit itself to be on the side of the poor, it must do much more than proclaim this fact.

Unfortunately, Catholicism has yet to learn how to do that sort of thing. Now that the option has become a solid and permanent part of the tradition of Catholic Social Teaching, it is time to challenge the Church with the question: "What are you going to do next?" Just talk about it? I'm afraid that won't do.

Reverend Andrew M. Greeley, Ph.D.
The University of Chicago
The University of Arizona

Acknowledgments

The late Reverend Alfred T. Hennelly, S.J., of Fordham University, supplied the impetus for this study. The Reverend Vincent E. Keane, Ph.D., offered hospitality during three summers of research at the libraries of Princeton University and Princeton Theological Seminary. The assistance of the library staff at the Maryknoll Theological Center is gratefully acknowledged. Doctor John Morgan of the Graduate Theological Foundation oversaw this work's completion as a doctoral dissertation in historical theology. The ongoing interest and support of the Reverends Walter J. Burghardt, S.J., professor *emeritus* of patrology at the Catholic University of America and Andrew M. Greeley, noted sociologist and prolific author, regularly inspire, along with the friendship of my old mentors, Distinguished University Professors at SUNY – Geneseo, Doctors William R. Cook and Ronald B. Herzman.

The interest of Joseph Carrieri, Esq. and Thomas William Patrick Dillon spurred the completion of this work, along with the generosity of Carol and Paul Tonna and Thomas Anthony Dillon. The encouragement of the parish staffs and parishioners of St. Anne's Church, St. John Nepomucene Church, St. James Church, St. Pius X Church, and Our Lady of the Miraculous Medal Church on Long Island instilled in me a predilection for the "preferential option for the poor." Special thanks to Ruth Koheil, Publisher, Dr. John Rupnow, Director of Author Services, Toni Tan, Director of Marketing and my fellow Geneseo State alumna, Patricia Schultz, Production Editor at the Edwin Mellen Press, for their interest, guidance and professionalism. Sylvia Macey and Rosalind Zayas provided expert advice and I.T. support when vexing computer problems stumped me.

Introduction

In a classic study on the development of Roman Catholic social theory and practice, Richard L. Camp concluded: "The historical development of Vatican social theory is one of the most significant chapters of modern social history."[1] Ironically, some astute observers have characterized the tradition of Catholic social teaching as its "best kept secret": "The Church has developed a body of teaching on social, economic, political and cultural matters, and *what* that body says seems to have been forgotten – or have never been known – by a majority of the Roman Catholic community in the United States... Catholic social teaching still remains outside the mainstream of ordinary parish life."[2] In an intervention during the Second Vatican Council, missionary Bishop Samuel Carter, S.J., of Jamaica, British West Indies lamented that while everyone seemed acquainted with the Church's teachings on abortion and contraception, very few seemed to be conversant with its social teaching: "Why? Because of the language we employ. Our documents are written in a style that makes them incomprehensible."[3]

On the level of official ethical reflection, concern for the "social question" came to dominate the modern era of Catholic social doctrine from the papacy of Leo

---

[1]Richard L. Camp, "The Development of the Social Conscience of the Vatican," in *The Papal Ideology of Social Reform: A Study in Historical Development, 1878-1967* (Leiden, Belgium: E. J. Brill, 1969), p. 1.

[2]Peter J. Henriot, S.J., Edward DeBerri, and Michael J. Schulteis, "Our Best Kept Secret," in *Catholic Social Teaching: Our Best Kept Secret/Centenary Edition* (Maryknoll, NY: Orbis Books, 1992 revision), p. 3.

[3]Cited in John F. X. Harriott, S.J., "The Difficulty of Justice," in *The Month* (January, 1972), p. 11.

XIII until the present day.[4] Properly speaking, as J. Bryan Hehir posits, the phrase "social teaching" in Catholic theology refers to "the body of papal, conciliar, and synodal teaching which extends from Pope Leo XIII, who died in 1903, to John Paul II... [It was] the Twentieth Century effort relating the social vision of the faith to the concrete conditions of the Twentieth Century."[5]

The 1994 *Catechism of the Catholic Church* promulgated by Pope John Paul II stressed that Catholic social teaching "proposes principles for reflection; it provides criteria for judgment; it gives guidelines for action" (no. 2423).[6] This authorative text emphasized that certain elements of the Church's social justice tradition are timeless while others develop organically: "the development of the doctrine of the Church on economic and social matters attests the permanent value of the Church's teaching at the same time as it attests the true meaning of her Tradition, always living and active" (no. 2421).[7] The catechism taught that the task of Catholic social teaching is "to mobilize resources toward objectives of moral, cultural, and economic development, 'redefining the priorities and hierarchies of values'" (no. 2438).[8] It offered the observation that: "The decisive point of the social question is that the goods created by God for everyone should in fact reach everyone in accord with justice and with the help of charity" (no. 2459).[9]

---

[4]See Franz H. Mueller, "The Church and the Social Question," in Joseph N. Moody and Justus George Lawler, *The Challenge of Mater et Magistra* (NY: Herder & Herder, 1963), pp. 13-154.
[5]J. Bryan Hehir, "John Paul II: Continuity and Change in the Social Teaching of the Church," in John W. Houck and Oliver F. Williams, C.S.C. (eds.), *Co-Creation and Capitalism* (Washington, DC: University Press of America, 1983), pp. 124-125.
[6]*Catechism of the Catholic Church* (NY: Doubleday Image Books edition, 1995), p. 641 See also Roger Heckel, S.J., *The Social Teaching of John Paul II: General Aspects of the Social Catechesis of John Paul II: The Use of the Expression "Social Doctrine of the Church"* (Rome: Pontifical Commission *Iustitia et Pax*, 1980).
[7]Ibid.
[8]Ibid., p. 645, citing Pope John Paul's 1991 social encyclical, *Centesimus Annus* (no. 28).
[9]Ibid., p. 650.

In the modern era, as Catholicism moved to embrace the "preferential option for the poor," it struggled through a protracted and at times contentious process. Advancements occurred incrementally and reflected new theories and methodologies embodied in such official magisterial documents as Pope Paul VI's 1971 Apostolic Exhortation, *Octogesima Adveniens* (no. 7): "It is to all Christians that we address a fresh and insistent call to action... it is not enough to recall principles, state intentions, point to crying injustices and utter prophetic denunciations; these words will lack real weight unless they are accompanied for each individual by the livelier awareness of personal responsibility and by effective action."[10] The writings that marked the tradition of Catholic social teaching were often viewed as an exercise in catching up with a world that bypassed the Church during much of the nineteenth and early twentieth Centuries.[11] The advent of industrialization, coupled with the rise of capitalism, yielded a profound and rapid transformation of traditional economic and social structures and values, particularly those that impacted upon workers. In the face of the loss of the working classes in Europe, the Church sought to cope with a new set of issues, both at the level of direct social service and through the elaboration of ethical norms tailored to meet the needs of the new economic realities.[12] Poverty came to be viewed in a new way, when for perhaps the first time in history humanity developed the capacity to escape from its deleterious effects. The nucleus of Nineteenth Century social Catholicism was pioneered in Mainz, Germany, under the

---

[10]Cited in David J. O'Brien and Thomas A. Shannon (eds.), *Catholic Social Thought: A Documentary Heritage* (Maryknoll, NY: Orbis Books, 1992), p. 267.
[11]On this point, see Liam Ryan, "The Modern Popes as Social Reformers," in *The Furrow* XLII (February, 1991), p. 99.
[12]See Norbert Mette, "Socialism and Capitalism in Papal Social Teaching," in John Coleman and Gregory Baum (eds.), *Rerum Novarum: A Hundred Years of Catholic Social Teaching* (London: SCM Press, 1991), pp. 24-35.

direction of Bishop Wilhelm von Ketteler,[13] who organized a circle to awaken the German Catholic Church to the need for social action. After 1870, the Catholic social movement spread rapidly throughout Europe, not only in Germany, but in France, Italy, Switzerland, Belgium, Great Britain, and in the United States of America, Canada and Australia as well.[14]

As Peter Hebblethwaite remarked, the foremost fruit of the pontificate of Pope Leo XIII was his great social encyclical, issued in 1891: "*Rerum Novarum* was the first pontifical document to pay any attention to the industrial revolution... Nearly fifty years after *The Communist Manifesto*, the Church was trying to recover lost ground."[15] In the document, he produced for the first time a papal, comprehensive view of the social issues of the times. Leo attempted to formulate the principles of a just solution, bearing in mind the particular situation of the workers who were alienated from the Church in Western Europe following the Industrial Revolution. In the Nineteenth Century, the Church began to develop social organizations in order to direct social reform into the right venues. *Rerum Novarum* emerged as a

---

[13]In *Rerum Novarum*, Leo XIII referred to von Ketteler as: "Our great predecessor from whom I have learned." See Etienne Gilson (ed.), *The Church Speaks to the Modern World: The Social Teaching of Pope Leo XIII* (NY: Doubleday Image, 1954), pp.248-275. Leo previously strove to put Ketteler's theories into practice while bishop of Perugia. On von Ketteler, see John Laux, *Christian Social Reform: Program Outlined By Its Pioneer, William Emmanuel Baron von Ketteler, Bishop of Mainz* (Philadelphia: The Dolphin Press, 1912), and William Hogan, *The Development of Bishop William Emmanuel von Ketteler's Interpretation of the Social Problem* (Washington, DC: Catholic University of America Press, 1946).

[14]See Antonio Gambasin, *Il movimento social nell'Opera dei Congressi* (Rome: Gregorian University Press, 1958); Hervé Carrier, S.J., *The Social Doctrine of the Church Revisited: A Guide for Study* (Rome: Pontifical Council *Iustitia et Pax*, 1990); along with Joseph Joblin, S.J., "*Doctrine et Action Sociale: Reflexion sur l'Evolution du Mouvement Social Chrétien, avant et après Rerum Novarum,*" in *Rerum Novarum/Laborem Exercens 2000: Symposium* (Rome: Pontifical Commission *Iustitia et Pax*, 1982), pp. 89-114.

[15]Peter Hebblethwaite, "The Popes and Politics: Shifting Patterns in Catholic Social Doctrine," in Charles E. Curran and Richard McCormick, S.J., *Readings in Moral Theology No. 5*, p. 266. See also George Weigel and Robert Royal (eds.), *A Century of Catholic Social Thought: Essays on "Rerum Novarum" and Nine Other Key Documents* (Washington, DC: Ethics and Public Policy Center, 1991).

watershed document of the social doctrine of the Church and set the agenda and the pattern for future Catholic social teaching. Pope Leo XIII brought Catholic social teaching up-to-date with the best thought of his era (which in the wake of his reactionary immediate predecessors loomed as a major achievement).

Marie-Dominique Chenu, O.P. remarked of *Rerum Novarum*: "This was where the talk of the Church's social doctrine began."[16] Pope Leo XIII set the tone for this new thrust in the unfolding tradition. As Leo wrote in *Rerum Novarum*: "Some opportune remedy must be found quickly for the misery and wretchedness pressing so unjustly upon the majority of the working class" (no. 3).[17] Pope Leo XIII pre-saged the "preferential option for the poor" within the text of his renowned social encyclical: "...When there is a question of protecting the rights of individuals, the poor have a claim of special consideration" (no. 29). *Rerum Novarum* broke new ground and established its teaching as a foundation and point of departure within the unfolding Catholic social tradition that sought to champion human rights and advance which is necessary for authentic human development.[18] As the British historian of the papacy E. E. Y. Hales wrote:

---

[16]Marie-Dominique Chenu, O.P., "The Church's 'Social Doctrine,'" in Dietmar Mieth and Jacques Pohier (eds.), *Christian Ethics and Economics: The North-South Conflict* (NY: Seabury Press, 1980), p. 71. Note that Chenu placed a negative "spin" on the use of the term "social doctrine," and criticized John Paul II's retrieval of the term in the opening address at Puebla in 1979. For the text of the Pope's address of January 28, 1979, see John Eagleson and Philip Sharper (eds.), *Puebla and Beyond* (Maryknoll, NY: Orbis Books, 1979), pp. 47-71. On Chenu's reaction, see M.-D. Chenu, *La 'Doctrine Sociale' de l'Eglise Comme Ideologie* (Paris: Editions du Cerf, 1979), especially p. 13. Chenu argued that the Council Fathers at Vatican II deliberately substituted the phrases "the social teaching of the Gospel" and "the Christian doctrine about society" in place of the term "social doctrine," which he viewed as static and suggestive of a corpus of immutable teaching inappropriate to Third World settings that tended to impose western categories and values not well suited to local situations in the developing countries.

[17]Pope Leo XIII, *Rerum Novarum*, in Michael J. Walsh and Brian Davies (eds.), *Proclaiming Justice & Peace*, p. 18.

[18]For an excellent treatment of this theme, see Joseph Joblin, S.J., "*La Chiesa e i diritti umani: quadro storico e prospettive future*," in *La Civilta Cattolica* 3334 (May 20, 1989), pp. 326-341.

> It was in extending the realm of human rights into the economic field that Leo was original... He was really saying that the economic order, ecclesiastical or governmental, existed for the sake of man, that the ultimate purpose was to enable man, in freedom, to live his own life and to save his soul.[19]

Leo's successors recognized that in its social doctrine and actual practice, the Church was often justly accused of "siding with the rich against the proletariat," as Pope Pius XI noted in his famous1931 encyclical, *Quadragesimo Anno* (cf. no. 44), or of encouraging dull resignation to the *status quo*, as reflected in a *Motu propio* issued on December 18, 1903 in which Pope Pius X claimed that "in conformity with the order established by God that there should be in human society, princes and subjects, patrons and proletariat, rich and poor, learned and ignorant, nobles and plebians."[20] In a letter to the French hierarchy, dated August 25, 1910, Pope Pius X asserted that "a Christian democracy 'should maintain the distinction of classes which is proper to a well-constituted city, and should seek, for human society, the character that God, its author, has given it.'"[21] (In contrast, Pope John XXIII offered a critique of this position in *Mater et Magistra* (no. 16): "Before approaching the social question, the Church [appeared to have] confined itself to preaching resignation to the poor and generosity to the rich").

Quadragesimo Anno, Pope Pius XI's celebrated social encyclical that marked the fortieth anniversary of *Rerum Novarum*, devoted its entire second section to "*doctrina de re sociali et oeconomica*" ("doctrine pertaining to social and economic

---

[19]E. E. Y. Hales, *Pope John and His Revolution* (London: Cox & Wyman, Ltd., 1965), p. 42.
[20]For an English version of the text, see Thomas O'Dea, *The Catholic Crisis* (Boston: Beacon Press, 1968), p. 78.
[21]Ibid., p. 78.

matters").[22] His successor, Pope Pius XII, often made use of the term the "social doctrine of the Church"[23] in his writings and public discourses. As Pope John XXIII added in 1961, in *Mater et Magistra*: "It is not enough merely to publicize a social doctrine. It has to be translated into action... this is particularly true of Christian social doctrine, whose light is truth, whose objective is justice, and whose driving force is love" (no. 226). With the advent of the papacy of John XXIII, a new phase emerged in Catholic social teaching. Pope John XXIII moved from the deductive to the inductive method. He took as his point of departure the "signs of the times" in the historical moment, to be scrutinized under the lens of the Gospel. In the view of Richard McCormick, S.J.: "This led to a complete re-evaluation of lay persons *vis-à-vis* social teaching, a re-evaluation completed by Vatican II. Lay persons do not simply share in the Church's social teaching; they must share in its very construction."[24]

---

[22]See especially nos. 15-20. The source for the English language translations for the various papal and conciliar documents cited herein is Michael Walsh and Brian Davies (eds.), *Proclaiming Justice & Peace: Papal Documents From Rerum Novarum Through Centesimus Annus* (Mystic, CT: XXIII Publications, 1991 revision).

[23]See, for instance, the following elocutions of Pius XII: "Address to Italian Catholic Action Members" (September 7, 1947), in *A.A.S.* 39 (1947), p. 428; "Address to the Delegates of the International Union of Catholic Women's Leagues" (September 11, 1947), in A.A.S. (1947), p. 487; "Address to the Delegates of the World Health Organization" (June 27, 1949), in *Osservatore Romano* (June 29, 1949), p. 1.

[24]Richard A. McCormick, S.J., "*Laborem Exercens* and Social Morality," in Richard A. McCormick, S.J. and Charles E. Curran (eds.), *Readings in Moral Theology No. 5: Official Catholic Social Teaching*, p. 227. McCormick makes a similar point in *Readings in Moral Theology No. 11*, p. 65, citing *Gaudium et Spes* nos. 44 and 43, respectively: "It is the task of the entire People of God, especially pastors and theologians, to hear distinguish and interpret the many voices of our age, and to judge them in the light of the Divine Word"; and, "Let the layperson take on his own distinctive role."

At the end of Vatican II a young theologian named Joseph Ratzinger,[25] reflected upon the "limitations of the methodology of the older, "manual"-based approach to Catholic social doctrine. He noted that the "return to the sources" of the ancient Christian writers known collectively as the "Fathers of the Church" and the biblical renewal that marked Catholicism in the post-war era made possible:

> ...a move beyond a narrow way of doing theology that might be defined, a little abusively, as "encyclical theology," toward broader theological horizons. By "encyclical theology" is meant a kind of theology in which tradition seemed to be gradually identified with the most recent statements of papal magisterium. Many theological works before and even during the Council could be seen as efforts to reduce theology to a record – and perhaps even a systematization – of magisterial statements.[26]

This approach was presaged long before the Council by promoters of the "Catholic Action" movement inspired by Canon (late, Cardinal) Joseph Cardijn of Belgium. The "Catholic Action" movement spearheaded in the pre-World War II Europe pioneered a new methodology that centered upon the famous three steps of "see," "judge" and "act."[27] The "Jocist" model radically departed from the abstract and totally deductive approach characteristic of the earlier, classicist worldview. The older, prevailing model that emphasized immutable and unchanging truths based in the natural law was enlarged and expanded to take into account biblical data and

---

[25]At 35, the later Prefect for the Congregation of the Doctrine of the Faith and Dean of the College of Cardinals was a protégé of Karl Rahner, S.J., and taught systematic theology at the seminary in Cologne. He served as a *wünderkind* theological *peritus* to Cardinal Josef Frings at the first session of the Second Vatican Council.

[26]Josef Ratzinger, *Il nuovo Popolo di Dio* (Brescia: Editrice Queriniana, 1977), pp. 310-311.

[27]See Georges Garrone, *L'Action Catholique, son Histoire, sa Doctrine, son Panorama* (Paris: *Editions du Cerf*, 1958), and M. Walckiers, *Sources Inédites Relatives aux Debuts de la J.O.C.* (Louvain: Catholic University of Louvain Press, 1970), pp. 34-53.

ongoing Revelation within the tradition.[28] From the Reformation era onwards to the time of the Second Vatican Council, the Roman Catholic Church endeavored to embrace the quest for a more just social order. But pre-conciliar Catholicism tended to view this movement more in terms of conformity to natural law than as a response to the mandates of the Gospel. As Dom Helder Câmara commented:

> ...specialized Catholic Action went much further: it took us right into the midst of the workers, peasants, students, and so on, operating on the basis of Cardijn's trilogy – see, judge, act. Long before the phrase was invented [by the Brazilian pedagogue Paulo Freire in the late 1950's], we were busy with the task of "consciousness raising."[29]

Along this line, a 1988 Vatican document on the study and teaching of the Church's social doctrine in seminaries and theologates heartily embraced this new approach and sought to promote:

> ...a better understanding [of] the dynamic inductive-deductive process of the methodology which, although already followed in the earlier documents in a general way, is better specified in the encyclical *Mater et Magistra*, and taken on decisively in the Pastoral Constitution *Gaudium et Spes* and in subsequent documents. This method is developed in three phases: seeing, judging, and acting.[30]

---

[28]See Charles E. Curran, "Official Catholic Social Teaching and Conscience," in *Tensions in Moral Theology* (Notre Dame, IN: University of Notre Dame Press, 1988), p.168-169.

[29]Cited in José de Broucker, *Dom Helder Câmara: The Conversions of a Bishop* (London: Collins, 1979), p. 116.

[30]Congregation for Catholic Education, *Guidelines for the Study and Teaching of the Church's Social Doctrine in the Formation of Priests* (Rome: Congregation for Education, 1988), p. 12.

These guidelines concluded: "It is up to the real Christian to follow this doctrine and make it 'the foundation of his wisdom and of his experience in order to translate it concretely into forms of action, participation, and commitment.'"[31]

Departing from a prior tendency that might colloquially be described as ecclesiastical "pie in the sky when you die," the "Pastoral Constitution on the Church in the Modern World," *Gaudium et Spes*, dramatically shifted the focus towards an understanding of the Church as a pilgrim people that shares the concerns and destiny of the entire human race (no. 1) and serves as the sign and safeguard of the transcendence of the human person (no. 76) and defender and advocate of authentic human rights (no. 41). As Jesuit theologian Avery Cardinal Dulles noted: "In a dynamically evolving world (GS, 4), social and political liberation pertains integrally to the process of redemption and hence is not foreign to the Mission of the Church... The Church's concern for human solidarity, peace and justice, therefore, is not confined to the sphere of supernatural salvation in a life beyond."[32]

As Gustavo Gutiérrez, the "godfather of liberation theology" and popularizer of the term the "preferential option for the poor," reflected: "[T]he expression 'preferential option for the poor' had an important and significant predecessor... [in] John XXIII's statement, a month before the opening of Vatican II, that the Church is called to be a Church of the poor."[33] As Gutiérrez suggested, with "good Pope John" one begins to trace clearly the outlines of the "preferential option for the poor" within contemporary Roman Catholicism.[34] Pope John XXIII opened the windows of the

---

[31]Ibid., p. 13, echoing the words of Pope Paul VI in his 1975 Apostolic Exhortation, *Evangelii Nuntiandi* (no. 38). See also the 1994 *Catechism of the Catholic Church*, (no. 2423), p. 641.
[32]Avery Dulles, S.J., "The Gospel, the Church, and Politics," cited in *Origins* 16 (1987), p. 641.
[33]Gustavo Gutiérrez, "Expanding the View," p. 13.
[34]One could point to other antecedent events and factors, such as the World Council of Church's Bandung Conference of 1955 that first promoted the notion of the "Third World." See Monika Hellwig, "Liberation Theology: An Emerging School," in *The Scottish Journal of Theology* 30 (1976), pp. 137-138.

Church to the modern world, and paved the way for a renewed self-awareness of the Church's role, *vis à vis* the world. As M.-D. Chenu suggested:

> We are here involved in one of the consequences of the "Copernican revolution" realized by the council: the world is not made for the Church which supplies the blueprints of its construction and the laws of its transformation in some magisterial and authoritative way, but the Church is made for the world, which is where it exists and which in its self-determination brings to the Church the raw material of its enterprise of divinization. Just as the incarnate Christ consented to becoming completely human, the Church, the body of Christ, finds its sole existence, *raison d'être*, and power in its involvement with the world.[35]

A catalyst that ushered in this new reality was the growing, mid-Twentieth Century contrast between the industrialized, wealthy northern world, and the underdeveloped, poor southern one. In the words of Irish theologian Donal Dorr:

> The new Catholic ethos which developed as a result of the work of John XXIII and Vatican II prepared the ground for a truly remarkable shift in the relationship between the Church and the dominant powers in society... This shift is summed up in the term "option for the poor." The first full-fledged commitment to such an option came at Medellín, when Latin American Church leaders pledged themselves to side with the poor in the struggle for justice.[36]

In an essay on "The Influence of Liberation Theology," its foremost North American proponent and interpreter, Alfred Hennelly, S.J., suggested: "The Latin American Church made the most important decision in its entire history at Medellín (1968) and even more decisively at Puebla (1979) when it turned away from what had been its major commitment to the wealthy classes in order to embrace the cause

---

[35]Marie-Dominique Chenu, O.P., "The Church's Social Doctrine," p. 72.
[36]Donal Dorr, *Option for the Poor*, p. 357.

of the poor."[37] The kernel seeds of the "preferential option for the poor" were implicitly planted at the Latin American bishops' conference at Medellín, Colombia, in 1968, and explicitly formulated at their next meeting at Puebla, Mexico, in 1979.

The "preferential option for the poor" subsequently appeared in documents of the authentic papal magisterium, such as the later social encylicals of John Paul II: *Sollicitudo Rei Socialis* (1988) and *Centesimus Annus* (1991). This progression framed the backdrop of a renewed commitment by the Church to look upon society from the viewpoint of the materially poor, the weak, and the marginalized and lent support to the struggle aimed towards their integral liberation. As the final report of the Extraordinary Synod of Bishops held in 1985 acknowledged: "Following the Second Vatican Council, the Church became more aware of its Mission in the service of the poor, the oppressed, and the outcast. In this preferential option, which must not be understood as exclusive, the true spirit of the Gospel shines forth" (no. 11).[38]

As Avery Dulles commented on this synodal document in an incisive essay:

> With John XXIII and Vatican II, the emphasis shifted. The apostolate of peace and social justice came to be seen as intrinsically connected with the Church's Mission to carry on the work of Christ, who had compassion on the poor and oppressed... Seeking to carry out the Council's mandate to discern the signs of the times in the light of the Gospel (*Gaudium et Spes*, no. 4), Popes and episcopal conferences have given increasingly concrete directives concerning matters of public policy. The theme of the Church's solidarity with the poor, already broached at Vatican II (*Gaudium et Spes*, no. 1), has given rise in Latin America to the idea of a "preferential option" for the poor.[39]

---

[37]Alfred T. Hennelly, S.J., "The Influence of Liberation Theology," in Edward Cleary, O.P. (ed.), *Born of the Poor: The Latin American Church Since Medellín* (Notre Dame, IN: University of Notre Dame Press, 1990), p. 38.

[38]Synod of Bishops, "Final Report", in *Origins* 15 (December 15, 1985), p. 450.

[39]Avery Dulles, S.J., "The Church According to Vatican II," in *Vatican II and the Extraordinary Synod: An Overview* (Collegeville, MN: The Liturgical Press, 1986), p. 20.

Various theologians and social ethicists pointed to a discernible break between the early phases of this teaching, from Leo XIII to Vatican II, and its post-conciliar forms of expression. Gregory Baum identified this subsequent, identifiable shift as:

> ...bolder and more incisive, beginning with Vatican II and from 1971 on, reflecting the influence of the liberationist perspective adopted by the Latin American Bishops' Conference (1968) held at Medellín. Although the moment of discontinuity between the two phases and the radical nature of the second phase has not always been fully appreciated.[40]

As Jon Sobrino commented years afterwards, Medellín remained:

> ...despite its "outdated" texts – the unsurpassed symbol of the new evangelization.... that has produced the most radical change in the history of the Latin American Church, changing it from an evangelically watered-down and historically imported to a Christian and Latin American Church.[41]

At Vatican II, and especially after Medellín, Catholic social teaching adopted, amended, and integrated a number of progressive, modern ideas, among them the "preferential option for the poor." As Joseph Gremillion noted:

> Before the *aggiornamento* [of Vatican II], Catholic social teaching addressed itself almost exclusively to the North Atlantic region, the nations that first experienced the Industrial Revolution. Indeed, original reflection on the Gospel, Church, and modern economic power was concentrated within a small oblong diamond whose points

---

[40]Gregory Baum, "The Originality of Catholic Social Teaching," in John Coleman and Gregory Baum (eds.), *Rerum Novarum*: *A Hundred Years of Catholic Social Teaching*, p. 55.
[41]Jon Sobrino, S.J., "The Winds in Santo Domingo and the Evangelization of Culture," in Alfred T. Hennelly, S.J. (ed.), *Beyond Santo Domingo*, p. 168.

reached approximately Paris, Brussels, Munich, and Milan.[42] The Latin American bishops who emerged from the Medellín Conference forged a new vocabulary that included three key concepts: the preferential option for the poor; integral liberation; and social sin. The Medellín documents argued that the Church must be "poor, paschal, and missionary" ("Document on Poverty," no. 15).[43] The Puebla "Final Document" sought to extend further upon this vision: "Bit by bit, the Church has been dissociating itself from those who hold economic or political power, freeing itself from various forms of dependence, and divesting itself of privileges" (no. 623).[44] As Edward L. Cleary remarked, "This bold language was astounding to those who remembered the Latin Americans' restive silence during the Council."[45]

Peruvian theologian Gustavo Gutiérrez adverted further to this development:

Medellín had already spoken of "giving preference to the poorest and most needy sectors and to those segregated for any cause whatever" ("Poverty," no. 9)... During the difficult decade of the 1970's this attitude gave rise to many experiences and resultant theological reflections in the Latin American Church. In the process, formulas intended to express commitment to the poor and oppressed proliferated. This became clear at Puebla, which chose the formula "preferential option for the poor" (see the Puebla Final Document, part 4, chapter 1). It was a formula that theologians in Latin America

---

[42]Joseph Gremillion, "Overview and Prospectus," in *The Gospel of Peace and Justice: Catholic Social Teaching Since Pope John* (Maryknoll, NY: Orbis Books, 1976), p. 35.

[43]For the text of the Medellín documents, see Louis Michael Colonnese (ed.), *The Church in the Present Day Transformation of Latin America in the Light of the Council: Volume II, Conclusions* (Washington, DC: Secretariat for Latin America, National Conference of Catholic Bishops, 1979 revision).

[44]All citations from the Puebla Final Document are taken from John Eagleson and Philip Sharper (eds.), *Puebla and Beyond.*

[45]Edward L. Cleary, O.P., "The Journey to Santo Domingo," in Alfred T. Hennelly, S.J. (ed.), *Santo Domingo and Beyond: Documents and Commentaries From the Fourth General Conference of Latin American Bishops* (Maryknoll, NY: Orbis Books, 1993), p. 3.

> had already begun to use in preceding years. The Puebla Conference thus gave it a major endorsement and importance.[46]

The specific notion of the "preferential option for the poor" was coined in a succession of terms linked together by the writings of Gutiérrez in 1968. He reflected in a much later interview:

> The phrase comes from the experience of the Latin American church. The precise term was born somewhere between the Latin American Bishops' Conference in Medellín (1968) and in Puebla (1979). In Medellín, the three words (option, preferential, poor) are all present, but it was only in the years immediately following Medellín that we brought these words into a complete phrase. It would be accurate to say that the term 'preferential option for the poor' comes from the Latin American church, but the content, the underlying intuition, is entirely biblical. Liberation theology tries to deepen our understanding of this core biblical conviction. The preferential option for the poor has gradually become a central tenet of the church's teaching.[47]

Over the course of the previous hundred years, by "reading the signs of the times" and retrieving the core evangelical notion of the "option for the poor," the Church sought to incorporate the option for the poor as an integrative metaphor within its teaching and practice. The documents of Medellín, Puebla, and later, the developing thought of Pope John Paul II all came to incorporate this outlook. In one of the earliest documents of his pontificate, Pope John Paul II reaffirmed his concern for the social question:

---

[46]Gustavo Gutiérrez, "Expanding the View," in *A Theology of Liberation* (Maryknoll, NY: Orbis Books, 1988 revision), p. 12.

[47]Daniel Hartnett, "Remembering the Poor: An Interview with Gustavo Gutiérrez," in *America* (February 3, 2003), p. 14.

> It is not to be thought that this dimension of catechesis is altogether new... Since *Rerum Novarum* especially, social concern has been actively present in the catechetical teaching of the Popes and the Bishops. Many synod fathers [in 1971] rightly insisted that the rich heritage of the Church's social teaching should, in appropriate forms, find a place in the general catechetical education of the faithful (no. 29).[48]

Pope John Paul stood squarely in the line of this tradition in the quest for integral liberation, greater solidarity, and implementation of the values of justice and peace in the modern world. In his opening address delivered at Puebla, he remarked that "the complete truth about human beings is the basis for the Church's social teaching, even as it is the basis of authentic liberation."[49] Initially, however, Pope John Paul remained skeptical about the methods and goals of liberation theology as expounded in Latin America. During the papal flight to Mexico in 1979, he derided its Marxist-Leninist underpinnings and dismissed it as "not a true theology" at all.[50] John Paul II significantly modified this position in an address to the Roman Curia in 1984, in which he appropriated the term, the "preferential option for the poor" and affirmed: "I have made and continue to make this 'option' my own. I identify with it... It is an option which is unwavering and irreversible."[51] He further articulated this stance in his 1986 Encyclical, *Sollicitudo Rei Socialis*:

---

[48]John Paul II, *Catechesis tradendae*, p. 26.
[49]John Paul II, "Opening Address at Puebla," in John Eagleson and Philip Sharper (eds.), *Puebla and Beyond* (Maryknoll, NY: Orbis Books, 1979), p. 64. For a full explanation of the use of this term in the early years of John Paul II's pontificate, see Roger Heckel, S.J., *The Social Teaching of John Paul II: General Aspects of the Social Catechesis of John Paul II: The Use of the Expression "Social Doctrine of the Church"* (Rome: Pontifical Commission *Iustitia et Pax*, 1980).
[50]On this point, see the interesting discussion of Darcy O'Brien, *The Hidden Pope: The Untold Story of a Lifelong Friendship That Is Changing the Relations Between Catholics and Jews/The Personal Journey of John Paul II and Jerzy Kluger* (NY: Daybreak Books, 1998), p. 28.
[51]John F. O'Brien, C.Ss.Sp., "Poverty," in Judith A. Dwyer (ed.), *New Dictionary of Catholic Social Thought*, p. 776.

> The Church's social doctrine... constitutes a category of its own... [It is] the accurate formulation of the results of a careful reflection on the complex realities of human existence, in society and in the international order, in the light of faith and of the Church's tradition. Its main aim is to interpret these realities, determining their conformity with or divergence from the lines of the Gospel teaching on the human person and his or her vocation, a vocation that is both earthly and transcendent; its aim is thus to guide Christian behavior (no. 41).

The 1988 Vatican guidelines on the Church's social doctrine acknowledged the need to stress the element of ongoing development within the Church's social teaching, and underscored its requirement for ongoing refinement within the tradition. It noted that while Catholic social teaching preserves "a substantial identity as a doctrinal 'corpus' with great coherency, it has not been reduced to a closed system. [It] has shown itself attentive to evolving situations, and capable of responding to new problems, or to their new ways of being raised."[52] This study noted that while the crux of the Church's social doctrine was formed during the Nineteenth Century as a complement to the tract on morality dedicated to the virtue of justice, "it soon acquired a notable autonomy due to the ongoing organic and systematic development of the Church's moral reflection on the new and complex social problems."[53] But, as John Coleman remarked in a speech commemorating tradition of modern Catholic social teaching, "The logical unity of the teaching still needs to be shown."[54] The present study seeks to identify the concept of the

---

[52]Congregation for Catholic Education, *Guidelines for the Study and Teaching of the Church's Social Doctrine in the Formation of Priests*, p. 16.

[53]Congregation for Catholic Education, *Guidelines for the Study and Teaching of the Church's Social Doctrine in the Formation of Priests*, p. 88. Interestingly, in this document, the phrase "preferential option for the poor" never appears, while the phrase "preferential love of the poor" is substituted, for example, on p. 74.

[54]John A. Coleman, "Development of Church Social Teaching," in Charles E. Curran and Richard A. McCormick, S.J. (eds.), *Readings in Moral Theology No. 5: Official Catholic Social Teaching* (NY: Paulist Press, 1986), p. 176.

"preferential option for the poor" as an integrative metaphor to provide linkage for such a "logical unity."

The great impetus for change along this line emanated from the Church in Latin America. In an essay originally published in Spanish in 1973, Gustavo Gutiérrez wrote: "...theology in Latin America today will be a reflection in, and on, faith as a liberation praxis. It will be an understanding and a commitment."[55] In an essay published in *Concilium* the following year, Gutierréz stated: "...an authentic and effective 'option for the poor'... is the axis on which turns the new way of being human and being a Christian in Latin America... [and requires] a demand for the construction of a new social order."[56]

While the term, the "preferential option for the poor" was originally coined by the partisans of liberation theology to bolster their own theological enterprise, it was soon gained currency as both episcopal and papal teaching offices sought to legitimize its use within mainstream Catholic social thought. The protracted conflicts that shadowed the option for the poor revolved around its modes of interpretation and proper implementation. Ironically, at the turn of the twenty-first Century it has been argued by some that "the phrase 'church of the poor' and its

---

[55]Gustavo Gutiérrez, "Liberation Praxis and Christian Faith," in *The Power of the Poor in History* (Maryknoll, NY: Orbis Books, 1983), p. 60. In a 1978 paper on "The Voice of the Poor in the Church," Gutiérrez asserted: "How are we doing on the point of the liberation process, the grassroots classes, liberation praxis? How are we doing on the point of the presence of the Gospel? Is liberation theology at the service of the liberation process and of the preaching of the Gospel?... What is important is the liberation of oppressed people and the announcement of the Gospel from among the poor," in the *Proceedings of the Catholic Theological Society of America* 33 (1978), pp. 30-31.

[56]Gustavo Gutiérrez, "Liberation, Theology, and Proclamation," in Claudé Geffre and Gustavo Gutiérrez (eds.), *The Mystical and Political Dimension of the Christian Faith* (NY: Herder & Herder, 1974), p. 59. This essay represents the *first documentable usage* of the term the "option for the poor," as Gutiérrez indicted in a telephone interview with me on July 19, 1993. In the same essay, on p. 59, Gutiérrez traced the roots of this idea to the texts of various sectors of the Latin American Church contained in *Signos de renovación* (Lima: CEP, 1969), *Signos de liberación* (Lima: CEP, 1973), as well as in Ronaldo Muñoz, *Nueva conciencia de la Iglesia en América Latina* (Santiago de Chile: Ediciones Paulinas, 1973).

companion phrase 'option for the poor' may be the only survivors of what by today's standards was the radical language of theologians, popes and bishops in the 1960s and 1970s."[57] Paradoxically, the option for the poor served both to unite and divide the Church. As Gustavo Gutiérrez wrote, this new thrust drew upon "the Gospel and the experiences of men and women committed to the process of liberation in the oppressed and exploited land of Latin America... [which] is now an essential element in the understanding that the Church as a whole has of its task in the present world."[58] In spite of this claim, one of Gutiérrez's principal North American exponents, Robert McAfee Brown, urged reticence and deliberation in the appropriation and usage of the term the "preferential option for the poor":

> It would be misleading to distill an "organizing principle" for liberation theology, giving the impression that liberation theology is believing in certain things rather than living in certain ways. But if we bear the warning in mind, we can acknowledge coherence as a theological virtue that becomes a vice only when too much is claimed for it.[59]

The liberation theologians who fostered this new option sought to propel the Church to work in solidarity with the poor, and to empower the oppressed to become the protagonists of their own history. As George Pixley noted, this movement constituted the "*formal* novelty of the option for the poor, which aimed to challenge "the system from the standpoint of the popular struggle, of disassociating oneself from works on the social-institutional level and moving to works on the popular-

---

[57]Denis Murphy, "Is 'Church of the Poor' Just Rhetoric?," in *America* (January 6-13, 2003), p. 12.
[58]Gustavo Gutiérrez, "Introduction," in *A Theology of Liberation* (Maryknoll, NY: Orbis Books, 1990 revision), pp. xiii, xxviii.
[59]Robert McAfee Brown, *Gustavo Gutiérrez: An Introduction to Liberation Theology* (Maryknoll, NY: Orbis Books, 1990), p. 106.

organizational level."[60] The option for the poor demonstrated a dramatic shift in theological emphasis. Marie-Dominique Chenu hailed the direction that it signaled as both part of the "new birth" of theology and theologians in the developing world, and as the catalyst for the emergence of a "new paradigm."[61] Johannes Baptist Metz echoed this assessment,[62] while Hans Küng volunteered similar reflections in a paper delivered at an international theological symposium in Tübingen in 1983.[63]

M.-D. Chenu argued that the new paradigm of the "Church of the Poor" neatly summarized:

> [The] one feature of the face of the Church [it] sought to adopt at the Vatican Council, in an effort to be true to itself and have a livelier awareness of its true nature... It was therefore not just a matter of pastoral exhortation to a more or less romantic evangelism: it was the very essence of the Church that was in question.[64]

Enrique Dussel added to this assessment that the post-Conciliar Church sought to become:

> ...a Church from out of the poor. This is the history of its people, this is its self-awareness, this is its struggle. There has been a change from a commitment to the poor, to being, as a Church, the people of

---

[60]George V. Pixley, "The Option for the Poor During a Thousand Years of Church History," in Clodovis Boff and George V. Pixley, *The Bible, The Church and the Poor* (Maryknoll, NY: Orbis Books, 1989), p. 183.
[61]Marie-Dominique Chenu, O.P., "Vatican II and the Church of the Poor," in Norbert Greinmächer and Alois Müller (eds.), *The Poor and the Church* (NY: Seabury Press, 1977), p.57.
[62]Johannes Baptist Metz, *Un nuevo modo de hacer teologia: tres breves tesís*," in *Vida y reflexión. Aportés de la teologia de la liberación al pensamiento teologico actual* (Lima: CEP, 1983), pp. 45-56. See also Titus F. Guenther, *Rahner and Metz: Transcendental Theology as a Political Ideology* (Lanham, MD: University Press of America, 1993).
[63]Hans Küng, "*Paradigmawechsel in der Theologie. Versuch einer Gründladenerklarung*," in Hans Küng and David Tracy (eds.), *Theologie: wohin? Auf dem Weg zu einem neuen Paradigma* (Cologne: Gerd Mohn, 1983), pp. 37-53. For an approach critical of this tack, see Rosino Gibellini, "*Un novo paradigma in teologia*?," in *Il Regno Attualitá* 14 (1983), pp. 328-330.
[64]Marie-Dominique Chenu, O.P., "Vatican II and the Church of the Poor," p. 56.

> the poor. This was the most profound fruit of the Council, the most authentic reformation, a return to its origins in the first three centuries.[65]

In the immediate aftermath of the Second Vatican Council, the Church placed stronger emphasis on the defense of human rights.[66] Within the context of the Church in Latin America, the focus of theological reflection shifted markedly. As Gustavo Gutiérrez reflected:

> ...doing theology is an expression of the rights of the poor. In this connection, more and more in Latin America we prefer to speak of the rights of the poor, not of human rights. That is to say, we do not wish to speak of rights in the liberal and bourgeois sense, but in terms more biblical, and more conflictual...[67]

By the early 1990s, as social ethicist Stephen Pope remarked: "The preferential option for the poor has become a major theme in contemporary Catholic ethics, [though] like many significant theological innovations, it is highly contested."[68] His colleague, Patrick Byrne asserted likewise that the "preferential option for the poor" became "something of a watchword in conversations among Christians throughout the world as they endeavor to comprehend what sorts of actions they are called to by their faith."[69]

---

[65]Enrique Dussel, "The Church of the Poor and the Anti-Conciliar Movement, 1972-1979," in Adrian Hastings (ed.), *Modern Catholicism: Vatican II and After* (NY: Oxford University Press, 1991), p. 322.

[66]On this point, see David Hollenbach, S.J., *Justice, Peace & Human Rights: American Catholic Social Ethics in a Pluralistic Context* (NY: Crossroad, 1988); Alfred T. Hennelly, S.J. and John Langan, S.J. (eds.), *Human Rights in the Americas: The Struggle for Consensus* (Washington, DC: Georgetown University Press, 1982); and, David Hollenbach, S.J., *Claims in Conflict: Retrieving and Renewing The Catholic Human Rights Tradition* (NY: Paulist Press, 1979).

[67]See Gustavo Gutiérrez, "The Voice of the Poor in the Church," p. 31.

[68]Stephen J. Pope, "Proper and Impartial Partiality and the Preferential Option for the Poor," in *Theological Studies* 54 (June, 1993), p. 242.

[69]Patrick H. Byrne, "*Ressentiment* and the Preferential Option for the Poor," in *Theological Studies* 54 (June, 1993), p. 213.

The term the "preferential option for the poor" merited a major entry in the third supplement to *The New Catholic Encyclopedia*[70] published under the auspices of the Catholic University of America, as well in as contemporary "First World"[71] and Latin American[72] lexicons and dictionaries of theology. Although Latin American in its origins, in its earliest extra-regional expansion, North American theologians such as Philip Land,[73] J. Bryan Hehir,[74] Gregory Baum,[75] Peter Henriot,[76] Edward Cleary,[77] and Rembert G. Weakland[78] all identified the term "option for the poor" as a key theme in the theology and practice of the Universal Church today. Similarly, the concept gained currency in many recent, official publications of the United States Catholic Conference: *Economic Justice for All: Pastoral Letter on Catholic Social Teaching the U.S. Economy*;[79] *A Century of Social Teaching: A Common Heritage, A Continuing Challenge*;[80] *Principles, Prophecy and a Pastoral*

---

[70]Paul Surlis, "Option for the Poor," in *The New Catholic Encyclopedia* Vol. 17 (NY: McGraw-Hill, 1991), pp. 339-340.

[71]"Option for the Poor," in Gerald O'Collins, S.J., and Edward G. Farrugia, S.J., *A Concise Dictionary of Theology* (NY: Paulist Press, 1991), pp. 163-164.

[72]Gustavo Gutiérrez, "The Poor: Object of a Basic Option," in Ignacio Ellacuría, S.J., Jon Sobrino, S.J. *et al.* (eds.), *Mysterium Liberationis: Fundamental Concepts of Liberation Theology* (Maryknoll, NY: Orbis Books, 1993), pp. 559-620.

[73]Philip Land, S.J., "Catholic Social Teaching: 1891-1981," in *Center Focus* 43 (May, 1981), p. 3.

[74]J. Bryan Hehir, "Christians and New World Disorders," in Richard John Neuhaus and George Weigel (eds.), *Being Christian Today: An American Conversation* (Washington, DC: Ethics and Public Policy Center, 1992), pp. 237-238.

[75]Gregory Baum, "Liberation Theology and the Supernatural," in *The Ecumenist* 19:6 (September-October, 1981), pp. 19-20.

[76]Peter J. Henriot, *et al.*, *Catholic Social Teaching: Our Best Kept Secret/ Centenary Edition*, p. 19.

[77]Edward Cleary, O.P., "The Theology of Liberation," in *The Church and Change* (Notre Dame, IN: University of Notre Dame Press, 1985), p. 88.

[78]Archbishop Rembert George Weakland, O.S.B., "The Kingdom of God and This World," in *Faith and the Human Enterprise: A Post-Vatican II Vision* (Maryknoll, NY: Orbis Books, 1992), p. 34.

[79]National Conference of Catholic Bishops, *Economic Justice for All: Pastoral Letter on Catholic Social Teaching and the U.S. Economy* (Washington, DC: United States Catholic Conference, 1986), pp. x, xi, 28, 45.

[80]A *Century of Social Teaching: A Common Heritage, A Continuing Challenge/ A Pastoral Message of the Catholic Bishops of the United States on the 100th Anniversary of Rerum Novarum* (Washington, DC: United States Catholic Conference, 1990), pp. 6-7.

Response: An Overview of Modern Catholic Social Teaching;[81] *Sharing the Tradition, Shaping the Future: A Christian Community Sharing Experience*;[82] *Political Responsibility: Revitalizing American Democracy*;[83] "Putting Children and Families First: A Challenge For Our Church, Nation and World";[84] as well as the 1983 pastoral letter on the economy of the Canadian Conference of Catholic bishops, *Ethical Reflections on the Economic Crisis*.[85] The 2003 quadrennial statement of the Administrative Committee of the United States Conference of Catholic Bishops, "Faithful Citizenship: A Catholic Call to Political Responsibility," identified the "option for the poor and vulnerable" as one of seven key "themes of Catholic Social Teaching": "The Church calls on all of us to embrace this preferential option for the poor and vulnerable… A fundamental measure of our society is how we care for and stand with the poor and vulnerable."[86]

While the formal concept of the "preferential option for the poor" emerged in church discourse from within the Latin American context only in the early 1970s, it quickly spread and became more widely embraced as an apt metaphor to focus attention on the official teaching of the Church as a defense of the poor and powerless in society and an encouragement to them in the struggle for justice. The

---

[81] Joseph R. Hacala, S.J. and James R. Jennings (eds.), *Principles, Prophecy and a Pastoral Response: An Overview of Modern Catholic Social Teaching* (Washington, DC: Campaign for Human Development, 1991), pp. 7-9.
[82] Jude Heinz, O.F.M. Conv. (ed.), *Sharing the Future, Shaping the Tradition: A Christian Community Sharing Experience* (Washington, DC: Campaign for Human Development, 1991), pp. 3-5.
[83] USCC Administrative Board/1992 Elections, *Political Responsibility: Revitalizing American Democracy* (Washington, DC: United States Catholic Conference, 1991), pp. 4, 7.
[84] National Conference of Catholic Bishops, "Putting Children and Families First: A Challenge for Our Church, Nation and World," in *Origins* 21 (November 28, 1991), pp. 397, 399.
[85] Canadian Conference of Catholic Bishops, *Ethical Reflections on the Economic Crisis* (Ottawa, Ontario: Episcopal Commission on Social Affairs, 1983). For relevant excerpts, see *The [Toronto] Globe and Mail* (January 1, 1983), p. T-15.
[86] Administrative Board, United States Conference of Catholic Bishops, *Faithful Citizenship: A Call to Catholic Responsibility* (Washington, DC: USCCB Publishing, 2003), p. 15, citing Pope John Paul II, *Novo millennio ineunte* (January 6, 2001), no. 38.

notion of the preferential option for the poor advanced and became, in the assessment of Leonardo Boff and Virgil Elizondo, "an option of the Universal Church" that sought to catalyze "nothing short of a Copernican revolution for the Church."[87]

The Church's appropriation of the "preferential option for the poor" occurred as an outgrowth of the dynamic renewal unleashed at Vatican II, and intensified by way of post-conciliar renewal movements within the Latin American Church. As Brazilian Bishop Pedro Casadáliga posited: "Today the option for the poor is timelier than ever. There are two reasons: There are more of them, both in Latin America, and in all of the Third World; and, they are ever-poorer."[88] The foremost exponent of the preferential option for the poor, Gustavo Gutiérrez counseled that this movement was not restricted to a regional phenomenon:

> My main reason for being committed to the poor is not because I am Latin American but because I am *Christian*. This is my main reason... The preferential option for the poor is not a Latin American issue. It is a biblical, evangelical question. All of us in the Church must find our way in this preferential option for the poor...[89]

Edward Schillebeeckx emphasized the biblical roots of the "preferential option for the poor":

> The option for the poor is a *datum of revelation*. The basis for that option is the Christian faith in the God of Jesus Christ, who himself gives witness to this partisan option. That option for the poor is thus

---

[87]"Editorial," in Leonardo Boff and Virgil Elizondo (eds.), *Option for the Poor: Challenge to the Rich Nations* (Edinburgh: T. & T. Clark, Ltd., 1986), p. ix.

[88]Cited in Jon Sobrino, S.J., "Preface to the English Edition," in Ignacio Ellacuría, S.J. and Jon Sobrino, S.J. (eds.), *Mysterium Liberationis*: *Fundamental Concepts of Liberation Theology* (Maryknoll, NY: Orbis Books, 1993), p. xiv.

[89]Gustavo Gutiérrez, "Church of the Poor," in Edward Cleary, O.P. (ed.), *Born of the Poor: The Latin American Church Since Medellín* (Notre Dame, IN: University of Notre Dame Press, 1991), pp. 19, 24.

> a question of Christian orthodoxy; it touches all the belief statements of the Christian credo... Only within this perspective can we now speak of the concrete universality of ecclesiastical Christianity, insofar as it walks in the footsteps of Jesus. It is therefore a matter of "concrete universality"... [which] has therefore a universal meaning: *a meaning for all* – also for the rich and powerful as a summons to solidarity.[90]

The option for the poor irrupted as a theocentric option, centered upon God. Gustavo Gutiérrez revealed this awareness in an interview conducted by Italian theologian and editor Rosino Gibellini: "...The ultimate and most important reason for liberation theology, the preferential option for the poor, is not to be found in social analysis, but in God in whom we believe in the communion of the Church."[91] Elsewhere, Gustavo Gutiérrez insisted:

> The ultimate reason for commitment to the poor and oppressed is not to be found in the social analysis we use, or in human compassion, or in any direct experience we ourselves may have of poverty. These are all doubtless valid motives that play an important part in our commitment. As Christians, however, our commitment is grounded, in the final analysis, in the God of our faith. It is a theocentric, prophetic option that has its roots in the unmerited love of God and is demanded by this love.[92]

---

[90]Edward Schillebeeckx, O.P., "The Religious and the Human *Ecumene*," in Marc H. Ellis and Otto Maduro, *Expanding the View*, p. 137.

[91]"We Cannot Do Theology in a Dead Corner of History: A Conversation with Gustavo Gutiérrez," in Rosino Gibellini, *The Liberation Theology Debate* (Maryknoll, NY: Orbis Books, 1988), p. 87. The interview appeared originally in *Il Regno Attualitá* 8 (1984), pp. 189-192. See also the assessment of James Nickoloff that "the Church functions in nearly all [Gutiérrez's] writings as a paramount source, locus, hermeneutical principle, and chief beneficiary of [his] theological reflection." Cited in "Church of the Poor: The Ecclesiology of Gustavo Gutiérrez," in *Theological Studies* 54 (September, 1993), p. 512.

[92]Gustavo Gutiérrez, "Expanding the View," p. 14.

What, then, is meant by the phrase, the "preferential option for the poor?" First, it is *preferential*. In a seminal essay, Gustavo Gutiérrez notes: "The very term *preference* obviously precludes any exclusivity; it simply points to who ought to be the first – not the only – objects of our solidarity."[93] As Robert McAfee Brown asserted of the first official use of the term by the third Latin American bishops' [CELAM] conference at Puebla in 1979: "In their 'Final Document,' the option for the poor is preferential in the sense that it is more central or enjoys a higher pastoral priority than other pastoral options proposed at Puebla."[94] Albert Nolan, O.P., echoed this sentiment: "The option for the poor is not a choice about the *recipients* of the gospel message, *to whom* we must preach the Gospel; it is a matter of *what Gospel* we preach to anyone at all. It is concerned with the *content* of the Gospel message itself."[95]

Perhaps the best clarification of the adjectival qualifier "preferential" is contained in the writings of Leonardo Boff:

> Preferential is not a synonym for "more" or "special," alone "exclusive" or "divisive." The meaning here is more radical and is apparent when one analyzes the causes that generate social poverty. The poor person does not stand alone: he or she stands in relation to the rich person who is the exploiter, and with allies from the other classes who offer support in the struggle. Therefore, to opt preferentially for the poor means: to love the poor first, as Jesus did, then starting from the poor to love all others, inviting them to liberate themselves from the mechanisms of the production of riches on the one hand and poverty on the other... The Church loves the poor

---

[93]Gustavo Gutiérrez, "Option for the Poor," in Ellacuría and Sobrino, *Mysterium Liberationis*, p. 239.
[94]Robert McAfee Brown, *Gustavo Gutiérrez*, p. 36. Brown failed to note that at Puebla, the bishops made *two* explicit "preferential options," for the *poor*, and for *youth*. See the Puebla "Final Document," nos. 1166-1205, especially no. 1186, along with nos. 33, 71, 95, and 127.
[95]Albert Nolan, O.P., "The Option for the Poor in South Africa," in *Cross Currents* 36 (1986), p. 18.

inasmuch as it combats, not rich persons, but the socio-economic mechanisms which make them rich at the expense of the poor.[96]

As Gustavo Gutiérrez noted: "The entire Bible... mirrors God's predilection for the weak and abused of history. This *preference* brings out the *gratuitousness* or the unmerited character of God's love."[97] As he suggested elsewhere, the God of Judeo-Christianity orients history towards the establishment of justice and right: "He is more than a provident God. He is a God who takes the side of his people and who liberates them from slavery and oppression... In the liberation of the poor is given the true 'theophany,' the revelation of God."[98] Gutiérrez argued that "the poor deserve preference not because they are morally or religiously better than others, but because God is God, in whose eyes 'the last are first.' This statement clashes with our narrow understanding of justice; this very preference reminds us, therefore, that God's ways are not ours."[99]

Gutiérrez eventually refined his view of how God manifested God's own actual preference for the poor. He recognized that while the option for the poor offered a special preference to the materially poor, it was not intended to be in an exclusive or class-conscious way.[100] For Gutiérrez, the preferential option imitates the love of God both in its *partiality* as well as in its *universality*.[101] In his later years, Gutiérrez concluded:

---

[96]Leonardo Boff, *Do Lugar do Pobre* (Petropolis, Brazil: Editores Vozes, 1984), p. 37.
[97]Gustavo Gutiérrez, "Expanding the View," pp. 29, 31.
[98]Gustavo Gutiérrez, "*Revelación y Anuncio de Dios en la Historia*," in *Páginas* 2 (marzo, 1976), pp. 3-4.
[99]Gustavo Gutiérrez, "Introduction," in *A Theology of Liberation*, p. xxviii.
[100]See, especially, Gutiérrez's discussion regarding the use of the term, the "preferential option for the poor" at Puebla, in *The Power of the Poor in History*, pp. 126-130. As the subsequent chapters of the present study shall indicate, this clarification is frequently insisted upon in the official pronouncements of Pope John Paul II, and of the Congregation for the Doctrine of the Faith, along with the "Final Report" of the 1985 Synod.
[101]Gustavo Gutiérrez, *A Theology of Liberation*, p. 130.

> Some people feel, wrongly, I believe, that the word *preferential* waters down or softens the option for the poor, but this is not true. God's love has two dimensions, the universal and the particular; and while there is a tension between the two, there is no contradiction. God's love excludes no one. Nevertheless, God demonstrates a special predilection toward those who have been excluded from the banquet of life. The word *preference* recalls the other dimension of the gratuitous love of God – the universality.[102]

Second, it is an *option*. Gutiérrez developed the notion of the preferential option for the poor as essential to Christian morality, in light of the position previously articulated by Pope Paul VI in *Octogesima Adveniens*: "In concrete situations, and taking account of solidarity in each person's life, one must recognize a legitimate variety of possible options..." (no. 50). Gutiérrez extended upon this notion to claim that the option for the poor "is not 'optional' in the sense that a Christian is free to make or not make this option, or commitment, to the poor, just as the love we owe to all human beings without exception is not 'optional.'"[103] In his entry on "The Poor: Object of a Basic Option" in the authoritative omnibus of liberation theology, *Mysterium Liberationis*, Gutiérrez added:

> The word "option" has not always been well interpreted. Like any slogan, it has its limits. What it seeks to emphasize is the free commitment of a decision. The "option for the poor" is not "optional" in the sense that a Christian need not necessarily make it, any more than the love we owe every human being, without exception, is optional. It is a matter of deep, ongoing solidarity, a voluntary, daily involvement with the world of the poor.[104]

---

[102]Daniel Hartnett, "Remembering the Poor: An Interview with Gustavo Gutiérrez," in *America* (February 3, 2003), p. 14.
[103]Gustavo Gutiérrez, "Introduction," in *A Theology of Liberation* (Maryknoll, NY: Orbis Books, 1988 revision), p. xxvi.
[104]Gustavo Gutiérrez, "The Poor: Object of a Basic Option," pp. 584-585.

Elsewhere, Gutiérrez likewise asserted: "Participation in the process of liberation is an obligatory and privileged locus for Christian life and reflection" in which will be heard "nuances of the Word of God that are imperceptible in other existential situations and without which there can be no authentic and fruitful faithfulness to the Lord."[105]

Gutiérrez's contemporary, the former Brazilian Franciscan friar Leonardo Boff, reflected on the meaning of the term "*option*":

> ...we must be careful not to fall into a semantic trap of endowing the same word with several very different meanings... Liberation Christology takes the side of the oppressed, feeling that it is compelled to do so by its faith in the historical Jesus. In our present historical situation, noncommitment would signify acceptance of the existing situation and a subtle stand in favor of those already oppressed.[106]

Many years later, Gutiérrez told a North American interviewer:

> In some ways *option* is perhaps the weakest word in the sentence. In English, the word merely connotes a choice between two things. In Spanish, however, it evokes the sense of commitment. The option for the poor is not optional, but is incumbent upon every Christian. It is not something that a Christian can either take or leave. As understood by Medellín, the option for the poor is twofold: it involves standing in solidarity *with* the poor; but it also entails a stance *against* inhumane poverty.

The preferential option for the poor is ultimately a question of friendship. Without friendship, an option for the poor can easily become commitment to an abstraction (to a social class, a race, a culture, an idea)... As Christians, we are called

---

[105]Gustavo Gutiérrez, *A Theology of Liberation*, p. 29.
[106]Leonardo Boff, *Jesus Christ Liberator: A Critical Christology for Our Times* (Maryknoll, NY: Orbis Books, 1978), p. 275.

to reproduce this quality of friendship in our relationships with others. When we become friends with the poor, their presence leaves an indelible imprint on our lives, and we are much more likely to remain committed."[107]

Finally, the preferential option finds its *raison d'être* in its orientation *for the poor*. By the poor, the framers of the theology of liberation meant those who are poor in the biblical sense, the *anawim*, those bent over and heavily burdened by the weight of their misfortune.[108] As the noted exegete, Joachim Jeremias, declared: "The 'poor' are those who are oppressed in quite a general sense: the oppressed who cannot defend themselves, the desperate, the hopeless."[109] In his earlier writings, such as his seminal 1973 essay on "Liberation Praxis and Christian Faith," Gustavo Gutiérrez sounded a note reminiscent of classical Marxism:

> The poor, the oppressed, are members of one social class that is being subtly (or not so subtly) exploited by another social class. This exploited class, especially in its most clear-sighted segment, the proletariat, is an active one. Hence, an option for the poor is an option for one social class against another. It means taking sides with the dispossessed. It means entering into the world of the exploited social class, with its values, its cultural categories. It means entering into solidarity with its interests and its struggles... The first and main question here is a radical one. It is a question of the prevailing social order... Hence, we speak of social revolution, not reform; of

---

[107]Daniel Hartnett, "Remembering the Poor: An Interview with Gustavo Gutiérrez," in *America* (February 3, 2003), pp. 14-15.

[108]For excellent surveys of this theme, see Juan Alfaro, S.J., *Theology of Justice in the World* (Rome: Pontifical Commission *Iustitia et Pax*, 1973), pp. 12-37, as well as the relevant paragraphs composed by the Jesuit scripture scholar, John R. Donahue, (nos. 28-52) in *Economic Justice for All: Pastoral Letter on Catholic Social Teaching and the U.S. Economy* (Washington, DC: United States Catholic Conference, 1986), pp. 15-30.

[109]Joachim Jeremias, *New Testament Theology* (NY: Scribners, 1971), p. 113.

liberation, not development; of socialism, not modernization of the prevailing system.[110]

The implications of such theological reflection understandably aroused the suspicion and ire of the more conservative factions within the Vatican and beyond, who detected and reacted against a perceived Marxist-socialist tinge undergirding the theology of liberation.[111] However, as Clodovis Boff stated, "To pretend to 'discuss liberation theology' *without seeing the poor* is to miss the whole point, for one fails to see the central problem of the theology being discussed. For the core and kernel of liberation theology is not theology, but liberation."[112]

The entire methodology of liberation theology takes the poor as its starting point. Gustavo Gutiérrez asserted that the option for the poor must extend from the standpoint of the poor,[113] and seek to be "an expression of love, is solidarity *with the poor*[,] ...a protest against poverty."[114] Elsewhere, Gutiérrez posited: "Christ makes himself present precisely through those who are 'absent' from history, those who are

---

[110]See Gustavo Gutiérrez, "Liberation Praxis and Christian Faith," p. 45, as well as the interesting introductory comment of Jon Sobrino, S.J., in *Mysterium Liberationis*, p. xvi: "... historic socialism had no part in the origin of the theology of liberation nor was it essential in its development, even though it[s methodology] proved helpful (as is evidently the case even in some encyclicals of John Paul II) in the critique of capitalism... The origin, impulse and direction of the theology of liberation did not come from socialism, but from the experience of God in the poor of this world, an experience at once of grace and challenge."
[111]Note the charge made by the Congregation for the Doctrine of the Faith that Gutiérrez combined a reductionist Marxism with Pelagianism to distort the mission of the Church and abuse it as a "mobilizing factor at the service of the revolution," cited in the Congregation for the Doctrine of the Faith's "*Observaciones sobre la teologia de la liberación de Gustavo Gutiérrez*," in *Misión abierta* 1 (1985), p. 35. Note that in an even-handed way, the *Catechism of the Catholic Church* (no. 2425), published in 1994, devotes equal criticism to the excesses of both "socialism" and liberal capitalism. See p. 642 of the original Doubleday Image Books edition.
[112]Clodovis Boff, "Introduction," in Clodovis and Leonardo Boff, O.F.M., *Liberation Theology: From Dialogue to Confrontation* (NY: Orbis Books, 1988), p. xxii.
[113]Gustavo Gutiérrez, *Teologia del reverso de la historia* (Lima: CEP, 1977), published in English as *The Power of the Poor in History* (Maryknoll, NY: Orbis Books, 1983).
[114]Gustavo Gutiérrez, *A Theology of Liberation*, pp. 300-301.

not invited to the banquet... The poor are not a 'category,' but real persons."[115] Previously, Gutiérrez reflected upon the evangelizing potential of the poor, whom he took to "reveal the presence of the Church in the 'nobodies' of history."[116]

In the post-Conciliar Church, largely due to Latin American influences, the poor came to be considered as a privileged locus, a basic source for authentic Christian theology.[117] Ignacio Ellacuría, one of the Jesuit martyrs of El Salvador's University of Central America (U.C.A.) argued:

> Is it not true that this decisive turning towards the poor is the mission of the Church in Latin America, and of the Latin American Church within the Universal Church? In a real sense, they define what Latin America is: poor in health, poor in education, poor in living standards, poor in having a say in their own destiny. By virtue of the universal call of the Gospel and by virtue of the historical summons specific to the region in which the Latin American Church lives, it must be the Church of the poor. If it were to be that in truth, then it would give new impetus to a new historical form of Christianity that should be transmitted to the Universal Church. And this new form will be transmitted, if it acquires the necessary drive and tension.[118]

Elsewhere in the same text, Ellacuría asserted: "The full and integral salvation of the Third World, of the world of the poor, is a great historical challenge. Responding to this challenge should be regarded as the fundamental charisma of the Latin American Church."[119]

---

[115]Gustavo Gutiérrez, *The Truth Shall Make You Free* (Maryknoll, NY: Orbis Books, 1990), p. 157.
[116]Ibid., p. 152.
[117]See Ignacio Ellacuría, "*La Iglesia de los pobres, sacramento histórico de liberación*," in *Estudios Centroamericanos* (October-November, 1977), pp. 707-721, as well as "*Iglesia de los pobres: presencia y anuncio de una Iglesia nueva*," in *Cruz y Resurección* (Mexico City: CRT, 1978), pp. 47-273.
[118]Ignacio Ellacuría, S.J., *Freedom Made Flesh: The Mission of Christ and His Church* (Maryknoll, NY: Orbis Books, 1976), p. 146.
[119]Ibid., p. 148.

Pope John Paul II himself eventually came to align himself explicitly with the "preferential option for the poor" when he declared that God requires of all believers "a call to have a special openness with the small and weak, those that suffer and weep, those that are humiliated and left on the margin of society, so as to help them win their dignity as human persons and children of God."[120] He articulated this position even more clearly and forcefully in his Apostolic Exhortation, "*Ecclesia in America*," which he signed on the first day of a pastoral visit to Mexico, citing Pope Paul VI's first encyclical, *Mysterium Fidei*:

> We must not neglect a third place of encounter with Christ, the persons, especially the poor, with whom Christ identifies himself. At the close of the Second Vatican Council, Pope Paul VI recalled that 'on the face of ever human being, especially when marked by tears and sufferings, we can and must see the face of Christ'" (no. 12).[121]

In a section of this same papal document entitled, "Preferential Love for the Poor and Outcast," John Paul II remarked: "The goal of the Church is to ensure that no one is marginalized... Concern for those most in need springs from a decision to love the poor in a special manner. This is a love which is not exclusive and thus cannot be interpreted as a sign of partiality or sectarianism" (no. 58). Even its crafter and principal exponent, Gustavo Gutiérrez, acknowledged that the term the "preferential option for the poor" was not always correctly understood and retained certain definite limitations.[122] In his later years, he expounded on the meaning of the term, "for the poor":

> The term *poverty* refers to the real poor... The poverty to which the option refers is material poverty. Material poverty means premature

---

[120]Cited in *Revista Eclesiastica Brasileira* 47 (June, 1987), p. 356.
[121]Pope John Paul II, "*Ecclesia in America*," in *Origins* (February 4, 1999), p. 571.
[122]See Gustavo Gutiérrez, "Expanding the View," p. 12.

> and unjust death. The poor person is someone who is treated as a non-person, someone who is considered insignificant from an economic, political and cultural point of view. The poor count as statistics. They are the nameless. But even though the poor remain insignificant within society, they are never insignificant before God.[123]

Other theologians such as George Pixley also warned that "the very phrase... can lead to a paternalistic understanding of its object... [whereby] the poor are reduced to the status of *objects* of Christians' love."[124] Despite such caveats, Gutiérrez continued to insist that the option for the poor constituted "the nub and core of a new way of being human and Christian in Latin America today."[125]

The "preferential option for the poor" helped to craft a new awareness of what it meant to be human and Christian in the world today. It presented the poor as both the privileged recipients of the Gospel, as well as its messengers.[126] It furnished Christian theology with a privileged hermeneutical perspective in order to observe and analyze reality, and as a spur to action. The preferential option for the poor, with all of its practical difficulties and its pastoral and theological implications, emerged as one of the most important contributions to the life of the Roman Catholic Church that eminated from the theology of liberation and from the Church in developing lands. Gutiérrez accorded its rise to prominence to a variety of factors:

> [B]etter understanding of the depth and complexity of the poverty and oppression experienced by most of humanity; our perception of the economic, social, and cultural mechanisms that produce that poverty;

---

[123]Daniel Hartnett, "Remembering the Poor: An Interview with Gustavo Gutiérrez," in *America* (February 3, 2003), p. 14.

[124]George V. Pixley, "Practical Aspects of the Option for the Poor," p. 221.

[125]Gustavo Gutiérrez, "From Medellín to Puebla," in *The Power of the Poor in History* (Maryknoll, NY: Orbis Books, 1984), p. 44.

[126]See Gustavo Gutiérrez, "Liberation and the Poor," in *The Power of the Poor in History*, p. 151.

> and before all else, due to the new light that the Word of the Lord sheds on that poverty.[127]

The present study traces and elucidates the development of the concept of the "preferential option for the poor" in official Catholic social teaching spanning the period of the pontificate of Pope John XXIII until the Fourth General Meeting of the Latin American Bishops' Conference at Santo Domingo, Dominican Republic in October, 1992,[128] and culminating especially in the pronouncements made during the final years of the papacy of Pope John Paul II in the early years of the New Millennium.

---

[127]Gustavo Gutiérrez, "The Poor: Object of a Basic Option," pp. 559-560.

[128]See United States Catholic Conference Secretariat, "Bishops' Committee for the Church in Latin America," *Santo Domingo: Conclusions/New Evangelization, Human Development, Christian Culture* (Washington, DC: U.S.C.C. Publications Office, 1993), and Alfred T. Hennelly, S.J. (ed.), *Santo Domingo and Beyond* (Maryknoll, NY: Orbis Books, 1993).

Chapter One

Pope John XXIII and the "Church of the Poor"

Some discernible movements in favor of the calling of an Ecumenical Council stirred during the early pontificate of Pope Pius XII, in the aftermath of World War II. Cardinal Alfredo Ottaviani, Prefect of the Holy Office, proposed the concept to Pius, at the behest of Cardinal Ernesto Ruffini of Palermo.[129] Sixty-five bishops were hand-picked and an exploratory commission was established. Beginning in 1948, the Holy Office worked in secret to produce schemas on such topics as communism, war, missiology, and mariology. However, in 1951, Pope Pius XII abruptly suspended all preparatory work. He evidently concluded that he could do anything that a Council could do, – better, more efficiently, and more economically. To many observers, it seemed that the age of the councils was definitively past.[130] The Church in the immediate post-World War II era was concerned with three main elements: preoccupation with the spread of communism; dramatic progress and rapid evolution within various social and sacred sciences; and, an intramural clash over church life and structure between its progressive and conservative elements. As Edward Schillebeeckx noted, Pius XII sought to maintain the *status quo ante*:

---

[129]For the background on this abortive idea, see Peter Hebblethwaite, *Paul VI*: *The First Modern Pope* (NY: Paulist Press, 1993), pp. 226-227, along with the more detailed chronicle of "the Council that never was" by Giovanni Caprile,S.J., "*Pio XII e un nuovo projetto di concilio oecumenico*" in *La Civilta Cattolica*, August 6, 1966, pp. 209-227.

[130]See Giovanni Caprile, S.J., *Il Concilio Vaticano II: Annunzio e preparazione/ 1959-1960* (Rome: *La Civilta Cattolica*, 1965), pp. 16-24.

> Neither [he] nor the Curia had any intention at the time of shaking the firm position of the Roman Curia by calling in outsiders. Everything points to the fact that 'the Pentagon,' as five cardinals were called (Cardinals Canali, Micara, Pizzardo, Mimmi and Ottaviani), were furious opponents of a council, and did everything possible to stem the breakthrough...[131]

Vladimir d'Ormesson, The French ambassador to the Vatican, in his dispatches to the foreign office desk in Paris complained of "the reactionary gang which had more power and influence over Pius XII as he grew older, weaker, more and more obsessed by communism."[132] In fact, as Yves Congar asserted, "Pius XII was, it seems, thinking of resuming and completing Vatican I, whereas John XXIII made it clear that his council would be Vatican II."[133]

Some commentators such as Yves Congar went so far as to suggest that November 20, 1962, the date when the council fathers voted to reject Cardinal Alfredo Ottaviani's original schema on the two sources of Revelation, Scripture and Tradition, marked the end of the Counter-Reformation, sometimes nick-named the "Pian era."[134] The perceived need for radical change within church life and structures seemed transparently obvious to many reform-minded thinkers within the Church.

---

[131]Edward Schillebeeckx, O.P., "John Is His Name: Twenty-five Years After the Death of John XXIII," in *For the Sake of the Gospel* (New York: Crossroad, 1990), p. 131.

[132]Cited in John G. Clancy, *Paul VI: Apostle for Our Time* (London: Collins, 1964), p. 74. Despite his later touted "opening to the left," John XXIII was hardly soft on Marxist Communism. In an October 28, 1947 diary entry, he noted: "Between Karl Marx and Jesus Christ, an agreement is impossible." He was fully in accord with the assertion of Pius XI's encyclical, *Divini redemptoris* that: "Communism is intrinsically evil and no collaboration with it can be allowed." See Mario Benigni and Godfreddo Zanchi, *Pope John XXIII: The Official Biography* (Boston, MA: Daughters of St. Paul, 2001), p. 234. As Archbishop of Venice, Roncalli wrote in a pastoral letter dated August 12, 1956: "It is an error to... to be in league with an ideology, Marxism, which is a denial of Christianity and whose applications cannot mesh with the premises of the Gospel of Christ" Cited *ibid.*, p. 266.

[133]Yves Congar, O.P., "A Last Look at the Council," in Alberic Stacpoole, O.S.B. (ed.), *Vatican II Revisited*, p. 339.

[134]See Robert Roguette, S.J., "*Bilan du Concile*," in *Etudes* (January, 1963), p. 104, along with Yves Congar, *Martin Luther: sa Foi, sa Réforme* (Paris: Cerf, 1983).

In many respects, Pius XII was the last Roman Pontiff to stand in the pre-conciliar tradition critiqued by Walbert Bühlmann:

> In recent centuries, the Church has always been on the side of monarchical authority and has, in principle, supported efforts to suppress the democratic movement at birth. Only during Vatican II did she decisively move out of the castles of princes and renounce, as a matter of principle, the privileges deriving from the alliance between altar and throne.[135]

As Cardinal Leon-Josef Suenens noted:

> It had become necessary to free ourselves from a theology that limited and restricted the mystery of the Church. What we were about to experience was not a "theology of liberation," but rather "liberation from a particular theology"... We were about to experience the end of an era, heir to the legacies of a long past – from Constantine in the Fourth Century, to Vatican I in the Nineteenth, by way of the Council of Trent in the Sixteenth. There would be continuity, certainly, in the essence; but there would also be new perspectives, and these would bring forth a vision of the Church enriched by a return to the sources.[136]

The winds of change swirled by time of the 1958 conclave that elected Cardinal Angelo Roncalli, Patriarch of Venice, as Pope John XXIII in the aftermath of Pius XII's death.

---

[135]Walbert Bühlmann, O.F.M. Cap., *The Coming of the Third Church: An Analysis of the Present and the Future of the Church* (Maryknoll, New York: Orbis Books, 1977), p. 178.

[136]Leon-Josef Cardinal Suenens, *Memories and Hopes* (Dublin: Veritas, 1992), pp. 75-76. Suenens' ecclesiology was heavily derivative from Henri de Lubac, S.J.'s great work, *Meditation sur L'Eglise* (Paris: Cerf, 1953). On de Lubac's contribution to the theology of Church at the Council, see Karl Heinz Neufeld, S.J., "In the Service of the Council: Bishops and Theologians at the Second Vatican Council (for Cardinal Henri de Lubac on His Ninetieth Birthday)," in René Latourelle, S.J. (ed.), *Vatican II: Assessment and Perspectives* Vol. I, pp. 74-105. On the vital concept of the "return to the sources," see John O'Malley, S.J., "Reform, Historical Consciousness and Vatican II's *Aggiornamento*," in *Theological Studies* 32 (1971), pp. 573-601.

In an assessment critical of the prior epoch, Carlo Falconi suggested that during Pope John XXIII's pontificate:

> The expressions most frequently heard and most typical were precisely those which under his predecessor were the most strongly disapproved: "*dialogo*" and "*apertura*" – dialogue and opening. But his dialogue with the world was never abstract and theoretical like those classic dialogues with cultural pretensions which, pronounced in a void, never succeed in establishing communication.[137]

Along this line, a noted churchman, Don Primo Massolari, told the Italian periodical *Adesso* upon learning of the death of Pope Pius XII that it would not be totally strange if the Lord were pleased "to give his Church a poor and humble pontiff, concerned only with protecting the helpless and dissipating darkness from people's minds and terror from their hearts. We are weary of too much learning, too much power. We are weary of greatness, prestige... words.[138] In his final days, Pope John reflected this desire as he identified himself with the poor of the world and reverted to his humble origins in Bergamo: "I want the Lord to find me as I am in reality: poor and with nothing."[139] During his first public radio message of October 29, 1959, he scored the unchecked arms' race and its impact upon "all classes of citizens, particularly of the poor[.] Turn your gaze toward the people entrusted to you and listen to their voices. What are they asking? What are they begging of you?"[140] Pope John echoed this concern in his most famous radio address of September 11,

---

[137]Carlo Falconi, *Pope John and His Council: A Diary of the Second Vatican Council/September-December, 1962* (London: Weidenfeld and Nicolson, 1964), p. 25.

[138]Cited in Peter Hebblethwaite, *Pope John XXIII: Shepherd of the Modern World* (New York: Doubleday, 1985), p. 270.

[139]Bishop Loris V. Capovilla, *Quindici letture* (Rome, Storia e Letteratura, 1970), p. 483.

[140]*Discursi, Messagi, Colloqui di S. S. Giovannni XXIII*, vol. I (Rome: Vatican Polyglot Press, 1960), pp. 8-9.

1962: "Confronted by the underdeveloped nations, the Church must present itself as it is and wants to be – - the Church of everyone, especially the Church of the poor."[141]

As the American social ethicist, Sulpician Father John Cronin, observed:

> More than any other modern pontiff, Pope John asked the Christian to become a part of the world, so that he might humanize or Christianize it. Earlier papal social teachings seemed to embody detached, aloof, and impartial judgments passed upon the problems of the day.[142]

Yves Congar pointed out that the *Dictionnaire de Théologie Catholique*, published in fifteen volumes between 1903 and 1950, contained no entries of social, political, scientific, or economic themes but had 103 columns on "the power of the Pope in the temporal order."[143] Walbert Bühlmann commented further:

> The theological background of this attitude lies in the anxious quest for the "eternal verities," which, the old theology manuals taught, had been called into question by the findings of psychological studies and new theological interpretations. Rome preferred to withdraw to the bunker, instead of confronting the new age.[144]

As Bernard Häring reflected:

---

[141]*Discursi, Messagi, Colloqui di S. S. Giovanni XXIII*, vol. IV (Rome: Vatican Polyglot Press, 1964), p. 523. In the official biography prepared for his beatification, Mario Begnini and Godfreddo Zanchi note: "... with [t]his message the pope opened new perspectives that kindled outstanding initiatives among the Council Fathers and paved – not without difficulty – the way that would lead to *Gaudium et Spes*," in *John XXIII: The Official Biography* (Boston, MA: Daughters of St. Paul, 2001), p. 389.
[142]John F. Cronin, S.S., "A Commentary on *Mater et Magistra*," in The Staff of the Pope Speaks Magazine (eds.), *The Encyclicals and Other Messages of John XXIII* (Washington: TPS Press, 1964), p. 241.
[143]Yves Congar, O.P., "Moving Towards A Pilgrim Church," in Alberic Stacpoole, O.S.B., (ed.), *Vatican II Revisited: By Those Who Were There* (Minneapolis, MN: Winston Press, 1986), p. 144.
[144]Walbert Bühlmann, O.F.M. Cap., *Dreaming About the Church* (Kansas City, MO: Sheed & Ward, 1987), p. 31.

> Were the Church to use the power structures of this world to conserve its unity and integrity of faith – inquisition, temporal power and privilege are essentially not service but a means of being served – it would be weak; it would also obscure its Mission. The Church of [John XXIII] has firmly set aside all of these trappings and legal usages which no longer seem appropriate for spreading its message in the world today.[145]

By the mid-twentieth century, Catholicism continued to embody a defensive, seige mentality. The Church often reacted as though the world was conspiring against it, and therefore seemed closed to most currents that emanated from without.[146] Under John's pastoral guidance, the seemingly-ossified features of the pre-councilar Church became transformed precisely in the realms most frequently impinged upon before by church authorities: freedom of conscience, freedom of religion, ecumenical openness, democracy, concern with the social question and increased attention to the role of the laity.[147] Vatican II both broke with the past and developed and fulfilled aspirations that were already gaining ground, even if not at the center, but in the peripheral areas of church life.

Pope John envisioned the Church to be poised for a dramatic outpouring of the Holy Spirit that would be, in his term, a "New Pentecost."[148] In his Apostolic Exhortation, *Sacrae Laudes* (January 6, 1962), John stated that the Council

---

[145]Bernard Häring, *Vatican II in the Sign of Unity* (London: Geoffrey Chapman, 1963), pp. 23-24.
[146]On this point, see Yves Congar's insightful essay, "Moving Towards a Pilgrim Church," in Alberic Stacpoole, O.S.B. (ed.), *Vatican II Revisited*, pp. 129-152.
[147]Note the comment of Pope John Paul II in his 1999 Apostolic Exhortation, "*Ecclesia in America*, no. 44, who asserted that any renewal in Catholic life is impossible without "the active presence of the laity… they are largely responsible for the future of the Church." This document was signed and promulgated during his pastoral visit to Mexico City.
[148]This phrase constituted a favorite theme of Pope John. See his address on May 17, 1959, in *La Documentation Catholique* [*D.C.*] (1959), pp. 759-760; his address on Pentecost, 1960, in *D.C.* (1960), p. 806; "The Proclamation of the Second Vatican Council," *Humanae Salutis*, December 25, 1961, in The Staff of the Pope Speaks Magazine (eds.), *Encyclicals and Other Messages*, p. 389; and, his discourse at the close of the first session of the Council, December 7, 1962, in The Staff of the Pope Speaks Magazine (eds.), *Encyclicals and Other Messages*, p. 439.

represented a "New Epiphany,"[149] awaited not only by Catholics, but by other persons of good will throughout the entire world[150], and that the Church stood on the threshold of a new era.

In one of the great ironies of history, the burly Venetian Patriarch, Angelo Giuseppe Roncalli, emerged as a near-perfect match for the description contained in the speech "On Choosing a New Pope" delivered by the Dean of the College of Cardinals, Antonio Bacci, on October 25, 1958. As the conclave's veil of secrecy descended, Cardinal Bacci offered a "wish list" of a Pope who would be:

> ...[a] pastor of souls... [with] heart [imbued] with particular tenderness especially for those peoples oppressed by totalitarian persecution and those in great poverty... May the new Vicar of Christ form a bridge between all levels of society... Rather than someone who has explored and experienced the subtle principles belonging to the art and discipline of diplomacy, we need a pope who is above all holy, so that he may obtain from God what lies beyond natural gifts...[151]

This profound shift in emphasis resonated in the words of the then-Cardinal Giovanni Battista Montini, the future Pope Paul VI, on December 2, 1962:

---

[149]Cited in Giacomo Martina, S.J., "The Historical Context in which the Idea of a New Ecumenical Council Was Born," in René Latourelle, *et al.* (eds.), *Vatican II: Assessment and Perspectives/Twenty-Five Years After (1962-1967)* (New York: Paulist Press, 1988), p. 4.

[150]A further indication of this tendency can be seen in the fact that John addressed his 1963 Encyclical, "*Pacem in Terris*," to "all persons of good will."

[151]Cited in J. Derek Holmes, *The Papacy in the Modern World* (New York: Crossroad, 1981), p. 200. In his book, *Con il Latino a servizio do quattro papi* (Rome: Studium, 1964), p. 89, Cardinal Bacci noted: "Some wrote that I had clearly and precisely drawn the portrait of John XXIII. In fact I had simply presented to the cardinals the ideal figure of a pope that the age demanded. So the merit was not mine." Note that Pope John, himself, would later define his role within the papacy in precisely these terms: "The new Pope, let us repeat, first of all expresses in himself that shining image of the Good Shepherd... we wish to make this clear, that we cherish as dearest to our heart our task as shepherd of the whole fold. The other human qualities – learning, intelligence, diplomatic tact and organizing skill, may serve as an adornment and completion of papal rule, but can never be substitutes." Cited in Ernesto Balducci, *John: The Transitional Pope* (NY: McGraw-Hill, 1964), pp. 38-39.

> Yesterday, the theme of the Church seemed to be confined to the power of the Pope. Today, it is extended to... the whole body of the Church. Yesterday, we spoke of the rights of the Church, by transferring the constitutive elements of civil society to the definition of perfect society. Today, we have discovered other realities in the Church... which cannot be defined by purely juridical ideas. Yesterday, we were above all interested in the external history of the Church. Today, we are equally concerned with its inner life, brought to life by the hidden presence of Christ in it.[152]

In Pope John XXIII, a new style of Catholicism emerged, that appeared determined to abandon the defensive and exclusive methods of the past in order to bring the Church in line with modern culture, and which sought to free it from the climate of juridicism, triumphalism, and clericalism that characterized it during the pre-conciliar era.[153] Pope John reflected upon this trajectory: "The idea of an ecumenical council was not the ripe fruit of long, drawn out deliberations, but occurred to us like the amazing blossoming of an unexpected spring."[154] In an address to the clergy of Venice, he noted that the Council's arrival was "the consequence of a spontaneous idea, which we felt in the simplicity of our heart as an unforeseen and unexpected shock."[155] The new stance ushered in by Pope John moved even the socialist leader Pietro Nenni to remark, "In place of the hieratical papal figure who intimidates there came the pastor who touches the heart."[156] As

---

[152]Cardinal Giovanni Battista Montini, "*Il mistero della chiesa nella luce di S. Ambrogio*," in *Osservatore Romano* (December 10/11, 1962), p. 6.

[153]These three items were denounced as sinful attitudes by Bishop Emile-Joseph De Smedt of Bruges on December 2, 1962, in one of the most memorable interventions at Vatican II. The text of his speech is contained in *Acta Synodalia Concilii Vaticani* II I:4 (Rome: Vatican Polyglot Press, 1970), p. 142.

[154]Pope John XXIII, *Motu Propio "Suaperno Die nutu,"* (Pentecost, 1960), in *A.A.S.* 52 (1960), p. 609.

[155]Pope John XXIII, "*Exhortatio* to the Clergy of Venice," (April 21, 1959) in *A.A.S.* 51 (1959), p. 680.

[156]Cited in Paul Johnson, *Pope John XXIII* (Boston: Little, Brown & Company, 1974), p. 134.

John told the Benedictine monks at the Roman basilica of St. Paul's Outside the Walls on January 25, 1959, the very same date of his surprise announcement of the Second Vatican Council: "The new Pope hopes to bring to the attention of the world the ancient truth reflected under new forms... Though the Church has great respect for what is ancient, beautiful, and good, her first concern is souls."[157]

Pope John's announcement of his intention to call the ecumenical council had the effect of a theological bombshell. "Good Pope John" felt somewhat naively that he could conclude the work of the Council in a single session before Christmas, 1962, in conjunction with the four hundredth anniversary of the Council of Trent. Since he learned on September 21, 1962 that he had inoperable intestinal cancer, Pope John longed to see the Council through to an expedited end. As Cardinal Agostino Casaroli recalled, "Pope John thought that all the conciliar problems could be solved in the space of a month."[158] Cardinal Pericle Felici's assessment modified this view slightly: "[John] thought the Council could be finished in a single session – two months – or, at the very most, given the difficulties that had emerged in the preparatory commission, two sessions."[159]

In contrast to the dualistic perspective often reflected by the encyclicals of Pope Pius XII, John had learned much from the forward-looking, optimistic model of pastoral leadership personified by Emmanuel Cardinal Suhard of Paris,[160] whom he admired while serving as the Papal Nuncio in France. He realized that by simply maintaining the *staus quo ante*, the Church was doomed to lose many modern men

---

[157]Cited in James I. Tucek and James C. O'Neill, "John XXIII," in Zsolt Aradi, James I. Tucek, and James C. O'Neill, *Pope John XXIII: An Authoritative Biography* (New York: Farrar, Straus and Cudahy, 1959), p. 294.
[158]Cited in Carlo Cremona, *Paolo VI* (Milan: Rusconi, 1991), p. 195.
[159]Cited ibid., p. 195.
[160]On the contrast of Cardinal Suhard's theological optimism with the more pessimistic worldview of Pope Pius XII, see J. Vinatier, *Le Cardinal Suhard, L'Evêque du Renouveau Missionnaire 1874-1949* (Paris: Cerf, 1983).

and women, much as the working classes were lost in Europe in the prior century, and to quench any likelihood of true renewal in light of the Gospel. In Pope John's judgment, the contemporary Church needed to speak not only *ad intra*, in and of itself, – its faith and internal affairs, – but also *ad extra*,[161] in relationship to the world, in order to demonstrate that it both shared in and cared for humanity and longed to be immersed in its most urgent problems: respect for human dignity and the inviolability of human rights; concern for social justice; attention to the gaps between the developing and the industrialized nations; evangelization of the poor; and, issues of war and peace.

On May 19, 1962, Pope John directed Cardinal Amleto Cicognani to distribute photocopies of Suenens' plan to a select, influential group of Cardinals who were on the Central Preparatory Commission for the Council: Julius Doepfner, Giovanni Battista Montini, Giuseppe Siri, and Achille Lienart.[162] All agreed that the Council should deal with the doctrinal issues during the first session, and then focus on the more pastoral ones during one or more subsequent sessions. In John's famous

---

[161]In response to a meeting with Suenens in March, 1962, John asked him to prepare a plan for the schemata on the Church at the Council. He soon presented John with a "Note on the Subject of the Council," which dealt with a "double range of issues," concerning the Church *ad extra* and *ad intra*. See L.-J. Cardinal Suenens, *Memories & Hopes*, p. 79. In his intervention of December 4, 1962 during the first session of the Council, Suenens defined *ad extra* as "the heading under which we would examine the Church in its dialogue with the world of today," and *ad intra* as pertaining to "the Church within herself, again with a view to assisting her to fulfill her Mission in the world." His remarks were echoed over the course of the next two days by two other leaders of the progressive bloc, Cardinals Giovanni Battista Montini and Giacomo Lercaro. See Henri de Reidmatten, O.P., "History of the Pastoral Constitution," in Group 2000 (eds.), *The Church Today: Commentaries on the Pastoral Constitution on the Church in the Modern World* (Westminster, MD: Newman Press, 1968), p. 3.

[162]For Montini's account of these meetings and the topics discussed, see Giovanni Battista Montini, *Discorsi e scritti sul concilio (1959-1963)* (Rome: Quaderni dell'Instituto, 1983), pp. 225-232. Note the contrast between this inner circle of advisors hand-picked by John XXIII and the powerfully entrenched curial cardinals whom he felt at the time conspired to undercut his authority: Angelo Dell'Acqua, Carlo Confalonieri, Alfredo Ottaviani and Domenico Tardini. On this point, see the Pope's letter cited in Mario Benigni and Goffredo Zanchi, *John XXIII: The Official Biography* (Boston, MA: Daughters of St. Paul, 2001), p. 325.

radio broadcast of September 11, 1962, he claimed as his own the distinction between the Church *ad intra* and *ad extra* on which the Suenens' plan hinged. This thrust received the potent approval of one of the Council's prime movers, Cardinal Montini, who embraced it and extended further upon its themes.

In a letter intended for John XXIII, dated October 18, 1962, the Archbishop of Milan asked for greater structure and coherence in the organization of the Council.[163] Montini felt that while Pope John provided the Council with due inspiration, a substantial plan of organization was required. As Montini's letter noted:

> The Council... does not have any organic program; nor can one see a plan emerging, based on some particular idea or logic... Without some organic structure, the lofty aims by which the Holy Father has justified the celebration of this extraordinary event cannot be realized... The material already prepared is not a harmonious and well thought out piece of architecture, nor can it reach the height needed to be a lighthouse casting its beams on the world and time.[164]

Montini stressed in this letter that the central theme of the Council should be the nature of the Church, which he believed could be dealt with in a first session. In the second session, he foresaw treatment of the Mission of the Church, what it actually does. Finally, he proposed a third session, in order to deal with the Church's relationships *vis à vis* other human groupings, in light of its renewed self-understanding. As Peter Hebblethwaite observed:

> That was uncannily close to what actually happened at the Council... Montini took over the Suenens' plan, reflected and prayed about it over the summer, re-imagined it and made it workable... It was a

---

[163]The letter was actually addressed to Cardinal Amleto Cigognani, but was clearly intended for the ailing Pope John. Cited in L.-J. Suenens, *Memories & Hopes*, p. 86.
[164]Cited in Peter Hebblethwaite, *Paul VI*, pp. 306-307.

> remarkable foreshadowing of the way he would run the Church when he became Pope... [B]y proposing three sessions he was in effect raising the question of succession, since Pope John clearly could not be expected to last that long.[165]

During the Council's first session, in the public eye Cardinal Montini of Milan, Pius XII's "Substitute Secretary of State" and the presumed heir apparent to John as a *papa di passagio*, struck a remarkably quiet posture.[166] He spoke publicly in the *Aula*, the knave of St. Peter's Basilica that served as the Council chamber, only twice. The task remained for Suenens to serve as the standard-bearer of *aggiornamento*. With the subsequent approval of Pope John, Suenens plunged ahead:

> Thus I had no moral qualms as I made my speech, *in Aula*, on December 4, 1962, proposing the central theme which the Council immediately approved. The unanimous endorsement of the Council was further reinforced on the following day, when Cardinal Montini – who remained somewhat reserved during the first session of the Council – spoke with enthusiasm in favor of my proposal, as did Cardinal Lercaro.[167]

In that same speech, under the heading of *ad extra*, Suenens listed four topics that required the Council's attention: a). things concerned with "human dignity," including the population explosion; b). social justice; c). the Church and poor; d). war and peace. He went on to suggest that this program "involves us in a three-fold dialogue: with the faithful; with our separated brothers; with the world."[168] Suenens emphasized that he stood in continuity with the program of the Council already laid

---

[165]Ibid., p. 308.

[166]Suenens pointed out that Montini "remained very reserved during [the first session of] the Council," in *Aux Origines de Vatican II*, p. 5.

[167]Suenens, *Memories & Hopes*, p. 87.

[168]The text is contained in *Acta Synodalia Concilii Vaticani Secundi* Vol. I, No. 4, p. 224.

out by John XXIII in his radio address of September 11, 1962 ("*Lumen Christi, Ecclesia Christi*") along with his opening address at the Council of October 11, 1962 ("*Gaudet Mater Ecclesia*"[169]): "...there is nothing here [*viz.*, in Suenens' intervention] that was not already contained in the speech [of Pope John of October 11] already mentioned."[170] But, in fact, Suenens took a further step and on the advice of Dom Helder Câmara of Recife, Brasil, advocated for the permanent establishment of a "Secretariat for the Problems of the Contemporary World."[171] On December 5, 1962, Montini, representing the mind of John XXIII,[172] endorsed the Suenens' plan put forth on the previous day. At this point, the preparatory phase of the Council appeared hopelessly gridlocked. Bishop James Griffiths, Auxiliary Bishop of New York, cited John's Gospel in his intervention: "Up until now, we have labored all night and have caught nothing."[173] According to journalist Peter Hebblethwaite, the Montini intervention proved to be crucial: "This was the key. It unlocked the Council."[174] For good measure, Cardinal Giacomo Lercaro extended upon this agenda in his speech of December 6, 1962, in which he echoed Pope John's memorable September 11th broadcast that "the Church presents herself as she is and as she wishes to be, as the Church of all, and especially, the Church of the poor."[175]

When Pope John arose from his sickbed to close the first session of the

---

[169]For the background on this key address, see Alberto Melloni, "*Formazione, contenuto e fortuna dell'allocuzione Gaudet mater ecclesia,*" in Giuseppe Alberigo and Alberto Melloni, *Fede, Tradizione, Profezia*, pp. 187-222.

[170]*Acta Synodalia Concilii Vaticani II*, I:4, p. 247.

[171]Cited in *Acta Synodalia Concilii Vaticani II*, I:4, p. 224.

[172]See Jan Grootaers, "*L'Attitude de l'Archevêque Montini au Cours de la Première Periode du Concile,*" in *Giovanni Battista Montini di Milano e il Concilio Ecumenico Vaticano* II, *Preparazione e Primo periodo* (Brescia: Arcivescovo, 1985), p. 276.

[173]The full text of Griffiths' intervention is contained in *Acta Synodalia Concilii Vaticani* II I:3, p. 181. See also Xavier Rynne, *Letters from Vatican City*, p. 232, and Peter Hebblethwaite, *Paul VI: The First Modern Pope*, p. 311.

[174]Peter Hebblethwaite, *Paul VI*, p. 312.

[175]*Acta Synodalia Concilii Vaticani II* I:4, p. 330.

Council on December 8, 1962, he appeared to affirm the progressive tenor set by Suenens, Montini, and Lercaro. The end of the first session signaled the intensification of work on the Council's agenda, rather than its conclusion. In late December, 1962, Pope John empowered a committee of cardinals to supervise the preparatory work for the overall schemas and to provide him with advice on the content of the documents presently being drafted. A new "Coordinating Commission" met from January 21-31, 1963 that was heavily influenced by the lines set out in Montini's letter and memorandum of October 18, 1962.

To Suenens, Pope John entrusted both the schema *ad intra*, which became the Dogmatic Constitution on the Church, *Lumen Gentium*, as well as the final schema *ad extra*, – which became the "Pastoral Constitution on the Church in the Modern World," *Gaudium et Spes*. As Suenens commented: "It was an engrossing task, since these two were in fact the key documents of the Council. Pope John had deliberately assigned them to me so that I would incorporate, as much as possible, the suggestions I had made in my plan for the Council."[176] Suenens attempted to incorporate all seventy-two of the draft texts into the two-fold plan on the theme, *De Ecclesiae Christi Mysterio* that he already set out to organize *ad intra* and *ad extra*.[177] He re-ordered the drafts in light of Montini's memorandum (which Hebblethwaite judged to be "the decisive moment in the history of the Council").[178] Suenens' outline proved to be remarkably close, both in content and form, to the final shape of the sixteen council documents. The last schemata proposed by Suenens, "Schema XVII," was entitled, *De ecclesiae principiis et actione ad bonum societatis promovendum* ("On the Principles of the Church's Action in Promoting the

---

[176]Suenens, *Memories & Hopes*, p. 106.
[177]See L.-J. Suenens, "*Aux Origines du Vatican II*," in *Nouvelle Revue Theologique* 107 (1985), pp. 1-21, and *Memories & Hopes*, pp. 78-100.
[178]Peter Hebblethwaite, *Paul VI*, p. 314.

Betterment of Society"). It retained the working title, "Schema XVII," until the fourth and final session of the Council, when in common parlance its revised working title conformed to the new arrangement of the proposed documents, as "Schema XIII." This working text formed the basis of the ensuing "Pastoral Constitution on the Church in the Modern World," commonly known by its Latin title derived from the opening words of its text, *Gaudium et Spes*, which proved to be among the Council's most novel and enduring contributions.

Initially, John seemed destined to be a "*papa di passaggio*," a transitional pope destined to stay the course of the "Barque of Peter" until a sufficiently-groomed, long-term successor could be elected (the presumptive heir-apparent and John XXIII's own choice for his successor was Archbishop Giovanni Battista Montini of Milan). John's style stood in marked contrast to the style of Pius XII, as reflected in his address to the Jesuit Order issued on September 17, 1946:

> Let no one seek to change what cannot be changed. Much has been said about the "new theology," which, along with everything that evolves, is itself in evolution, always on the way, but never arriving. If such an opinion were to be embraced, what would become of never-to-be-changed Catholic dogmas, what would happen to unity and stability?[179]

In the wake of Pius XII's death, the old order began to pass away, and the possibility emerged for a sudden and fruitful flourishing of a new horizon, dubbed by Nicholas Cheetham, a British historian of the papacy, as "a turning point, if not a revolution, in the life of the Church."[180]

---

[179]*A. A. S.* 38 (1946), pp. 384-385, 387.

[180]Nicholas Cheetham, *Keepers of the Keys: A History of the Popes From St. Peter to John Paul II* (New York: Scribners, 1983), p. 292. Papal historian E. E. Y. Hales seized upon this theme, and entitled his biography of John XXIII, *Pope John and His Revolution* (London: Catholic Book Club, 1965).

John reflected upon his impact on the modern papacy in his private journal, in an entry dated August 10, 1961:

> ...at seventy-seven years of age, everyone was convinced that I would be a provisional and transitional Pope. Yet here I am, already on the eve of the fourth year of my pontificate, with an immense program of work in front of me to be carried out before the eyes of the whole world, which is watching and waiting.[181]

Pope John made the concept of *aggiornamento* (the desire to bring the Church "up-to-date" and to make it effective in the contemporary world) the watchword for his own papacy, as well as the pervasive theme of the Council. As Patriarch of Venice, he wrote a pastoral letter to the people of the archdiocese: "You've probably heard the word *aggiornamento* repeated so many times. Well, Holy Church who is ever youthful wants to be in a position to understand the diverse circumstances of life, so that she can adapt, correct, improve, and be filled with fervor."[182] In his first encyclical, *Ad Petri Cathedram,* he returned to this theme, and called for "the adjustment of Christian discipline to the exigencies of modern day living."[183] He likewise stressed in the opening address at the Council that church doctrine "should be studied afresh and reformulated in contemporary terms."[184] John outlined the task of the Council in his allocution opening the first session, on October 11, 1962, as that

---

[181]Pope John XXIII, *Journal of a Soul* (New York: McGraw-Hill, 1965), p. 303.

[182]Pope John XXIII, "Pastoral Letter" (October 8, 1957), cited in Giuseppe and Angelina Alberigo, *Giovanni XXIII, Profezia nella fedelta* (Brescia: Editrice Queriniana, 1978), p. 248. The original text is contained in Cardinal Angelo Giuseppe Roncalli, *Scritti e discorsi* (Rome, Edizione Paoline, 1959), vol. III, p. 264.

[183]Pope John XXIII, "Truth, Unity, and Peace: The Encyclical '*Ad Petri Cathedratum*'" (June 29, 1959), in The Staff of the Pope Speaks Magazine (eds.), *Encyclicals and Other Messages*, p. 55. Club, 1965).

[184]Pope John XXIII, "Opening Address to the Council" (October 11, 1962), in The Staff of the Pope Speaks Magazine (eds.), *Encyclicals and Other Messages*, p. 430. Cf. Dom Christopher Butler, O.S.B., "The Aggiornamento of Vatican II," in John H. Miller, C.S.C. (ed.), *Vatican II: An Interfaith Appraisal* (Notre Dame: University of Notre Dame Press, 1966), pp. 3-13.

of introducing "ways and means of expounding truths in a manner more consistent with a predominantly pastoral view of the Church's teaching office."[185] In a statement dictated to Cardinal Amleto Cicognani, the Vatican Secretary of State, on May 24, 1963, just days before his death, Pope John reflected:

> Today's world, the needs made plain in the last fifty years, and a deeper understanding of doctrine have brought us to a new situation... Those who have lived as long as I have were faced with new tasks in the social order at the start of the century; those who, like me, were twenty years in the East and eight in France, were able to compare different cultures and traditions, and know that the moment has come to discern the signs of the times, to seize the opportunity and to look far ahead.[186]

In this respect, Pope John repeated a theme struck at the beginning of the Council:

> The Church must keep in mind new situations, new forms of life that open up new ways... Our duty is not just to guard this treasure, as though it were some museum-piece and we the curators, but earnestly and fearlessly to dedicate ourselves to the work that needs to be done in this modern age of ours."[187]

As Pope, John XXIII wasted no time to mark out the "defense of the poor" as one of the primary concerns of his new pontificate. He identified the poor as "one of the most beautiful jewels of the Catholic Church."[188] Yet the imprint of his own personal journey and his own experience of poverty exerted profound influence upon his expressed concern for the poor. Indeed, as two of his foremost biographers

---

[185]Pope John XXIII, "Opening Address at the Council," p. 431.

[186]Cited in Bishop Loris Capovilla, *Ite, Misa Est* (Padua: Messagero, 1983), p. 212. See also Loris Capovilla, *The Mind and Heart of John XXIII* (NY: Hawthorn Books, 1964).

[187]Pope John XXIII, "Opening Address to the Council," *Encyclicals and Messages*, p. 430.

[188]Pope John XXIII, "Radio Message for the Opening of the 'World Refugee Year'" (28 June 1959), in Permanent Observer Mission of the Holy See to the United Nations, *Paths to Peace: A Contribution* (Brookefield, WI: Liturgical Publications, 1987), p. 433.

asserted, one cannot ignore "the inseparability of Roncalli's personal journey from the events of the pontificate of John XXIII."[189] As Pope, he wrote to his brother, Zaverio: "At my death I shall not lack the praise which did so much honor to the saintly Pope Pius X: 'He was born poor and died poor.'"[190] In an undated diary entry from 1962, Pope John mused:

> Having come forth from the poverty and littleness of Sotto il Monte [in the hills of Bergamo], I tried never to separate myself from it. What a great grace the Lord has granted me... a poverty that was serene and contented... I want to die without knowing whether I own anything of my own. Poverty has often embarrassed me, especially when I was not able to help my own who were poor. But I have never regretted it![191]

As papal nuncio in Turkey and Greece, he wrote to his sisters, Ancilla and Maria: "[Your brother] loves the poor, and Providence comes to his aid. He willingly gives away what others give to him. But he is always poor, and will die poor."[192] Earlier, as papal nuncio in Bulgaria, he wrote to his cousin, Sofia: "...[God] likes to be called the Lord of poor folk, and he knows how to come to our help in one way or another."[193] John did not romanticize poverty, nor did he accept it uncritically. In a letter to his brother, Zaverio, composed during World War I, he complained of the food situation, both in Austria and in Italy, where bread, meats, sugar, and olive

---

[189]Giuseppe and Angelina Alberigo, *Giovanni XXIII, profezia nelle fedelta*, p. 105.
[190]Letter to his brother, Zaverio, dated from the Vatican, 3 December 1961, in Loris Francesco Capovilla (ed.), *Pope John XXIII: Letters to His Family: 1901-1962* (London: Geoffrey Chapman, 1970), p. 829. As an example of his personal poverty, when he died, John was able to leave his family only 10,000 *lire*, or the equivalent of $17.50. See E. E. Y. Hales, *Pope John and His Revolution*, p. 9.
[191]Cited as "Diary Pages and Final Reflections," reprinted from *Osservatore Romano* in The Staff of the Pope Speaks Magazine (eds.), *Encyclicals and Other Messages*, p. 497.
[192]To his sisters, Ancilla and Maria, from Constantinople, 29 April 1943, in Loris Capovilla (ed.), *Letters to His Family*, p. 464.
[193]Letter to his cousin, Sofia Ravasio, from Sofia, Bulgaria, 21 March 1929, ibid., p. 137.

oil were rationed, and two days a week were declared "meatless."[194] After World War II, he wrote to his sisters, from Paris: "Our families are still poor. I too am sometimes made uncomfortable by my poverty, but we must not complain... But this does not mean that we need not do our best to improve our material conditions."[195]

As a young priest, he was deeply influenced by his diocesan bishop, Giacomo Maria Radini Tedeschi, of Bergamo, who greatly furthered the agenda of the "Catholic Action" movement in Italy after World War I.[196] As early as 1909, in an article in the diocesan newspaper, *La Vita Diocesana*, he defended Radini Tedeschi's social activism with a solid treatise on the right and necessity of the Church to "intervene in politics." He denounced the notion that "a bishop should not embrace the cause of the oppressed," and concluded that this direction would ignore the biblical injunction that, "Christ's *preference* goes to the disinherited, the weak, and the oppressed."[197] Few knew that young Don Angelo Roncalli joined the diocesan fraternity of the "Priests of the Sacred Heart," and professed a vow of poverty that became perpetual in 1917,[198] nor that as a junior papal diplomat in Bulgaria after World War I, he fed 250 refugee children each day: "I shall soon be opening another refectory for the poor children – I have chosen to make them my special care."[199] As

---

[194]Letter to his brother Saverio, from Bergamo, 17 April 1918, in Loris Capovilla (ed.), *Letters to His Family*, p. 47. For a comprehensive analysis of the situation in Italy at the time, see Christopher Seton-Watson, *Italy from Liberalism to Fascism* (New York: Barnes & Noble, 1967), p. 487.

[195]Letter to his family, from Paris, 26 September 1948, in Loris Capovilla (ed.), *Letters to His Family*, p. 605.

[196]See Angelo Roncalli, *Mons. Giacomo Maria Radini Tedeschi, vescovo di Bergamo* (Rome: Vatican Polyglot Press, 1963), pp. 63-74, as well as Giacomo Lercaro and Gabriele De Rosa, *John XXIII: Simpleton or Saint?* (Chicago: Franciscan Herald Press, 1967), pp. 43-46.

[197]Msgr. Loris Capovilla included the entire text of this article in *Pasqua di Risurrezione Con Papa Giovanni XXIII* (Rome: Storia e Letteratura, 1976), pp. 17ff. The English translation is found in Peter Hebblethwaite, *Pope John XXIII*, p. 64.

[198]See the correspondence of John XXIII with the fraternity, in Giambattista Busetti (ed.), *Giovanni XXIII, il Pastore* (Padua: Messagero, 1980), p. 43.

[199]Letter to his sister Ancilla, dated Sofia, Bulgaria, 31 January 1926, in Loris Capovilla (ed.), *Letters to His Family*, p. 91.

papal nuncio in Turkey and Greece at the outbreak of World War II, he wrote to his family: "Here in Constantinople there is an alarming dearth of foodstuffs of all kinds. If you could only see how many poor people I have around me! And how many poor people there are who are unknown to me and who hide their sufferings away in hunger and grief."[200]

The events of the Second World War affected him profoundly. As papal nuncio in Paris, he witnessed the return to France of the survivors of death camps and prisoners-of-war, and commented: "[W]e live among tragic spectacles of suffering and death, and the hope of new life."[201] Beginning in the 1930's, and increasingly after the close of the Second World War, Roman Catholicism was influenced by a current of French theological and philosophical thought called "integral humanism," or "Social Christianity." Its principal exponent was the lay philosopher Jacques Maritain,[202] and its prime institutional incarnation was the organization "Catholic Action." A ferment of new ideas and approaches of theology emerged in Europe, known as "*nouvelle théologie*," and set the stage for the unfolding "anthropological turn" later validated by Pope John XXIII.[203] In 1948, Albert Camus addressed the Paris Dominicans, and implored them to seek Christ "in the blood-stained face of the history of our age."[204] Claude Geffré identified three features of this movement of renewal in post-war France: a return to biblical and patristic sources; a heightened interest in ecclesiological research; and, a decidedly pastoral and ecumenical

---

[200]Ibid., letter to his family, from Constantinople, 25 December 1939, pp. 367-368.
[201]Angelo Giuseppe Roncalli, *Mission to France 1944-1953* (London: Geoffrey Chapman, 1966), p. 36.
[202]See the principal work of Jacques Maritain, *Humanisme Integral: Problèmes Temporels et Spirituels d'une Nouvelle Chrétientè* (Paris: *Aubier*, 1936), for the text that sparked this movement.
[203]Pope Paul VI further articulated this theme often, and it finds concise expression in the *Catechism of the Catholic Church* (no. 2459): "Man is himself the author, center and goal of all economic and social life."
[204]Cited in Peter Hebblethwaite, *Pope John XXIII*, p. 218.

orientation.[205] The outbreak of World War II and its subsequent post-war developments (political, economic, and social) wrought a new set of issues in France that catalyzed change and development in the arena of the Church's social teaching. The renaissance of Catholic thought that flourished in Paris during the post-war era profoundly affected John's outlook, and helped to shape his evolving social thought.[206]

As Patriarch of Venice, Cardinal Roncalli later wrote to his sister Ancilla: "The Venetians are indeed very good... but there is also great poverty here... In Paris I had plenty of work, but it was nothing compared with here... I'm like the mother of a poor family who is entrusted with so many children."[207] While serving as Patriarch of Venice, he preached a magnificent Ascension Day sermon in 1958 on the meaning of the paschal candle, with its threefold acclamation: "*Lumen Christi, Deo Gratias*." He concluded this threefold exegesis with the final assertion that Christ is the Light "for the social order which finds in the Gospel and the teaching of the Church immortal principles leading to progress, prosperity, and peace."[208]

Within the first two months of his election as Pope, John put flesh on this vision, as he paid a Christmas visit to the children in the *Gesú Bambino* Hospital, welcomed orphans from the Villa Nazareth, and visited the inmates at *Regina Coeli* Prison and washed their feet on Holy Thursday. During Lent, he visited "stational churches" throughout Rome, and later continued to visit parish churches in the slum

---

[205]Claude Geffré, "*Silence et Promesses de la Théologie, Catholique Francaise*," in *Revue de Théologie et de Philosophie* Vol. 114 (1982), pp. 227-245.
[206]This fact was equally true of Archbishop Giovanni Battista Montini, later Pope Paul VI. See Peter Hebblethwaite, *Paul VI*, pp. 85, 221-222, 245-246.
[207]Letter to his sister Ancilla, Fietto, Treviso, 15 May 1953, in Loris Capovilla (ed.), *Letters to His Family*, pp. 742-743.
[208]Cited in Giuseppe and Angelina Alberigo, *Giovanni XXIII*, p. 261.

districts that were communist strongholds.[209] The words and deeds of Pope John exerted profound impact upon the masses, who felt that he understood and loved them, and chose to be near to them. His simple language and unshaken optimism touched them. They greatly appreciated his human gestures toward the lowly, the poor, and the sick in Rome.

In the sweep of John's life, one can readily discern in advance the history of the future. In his Christmas, 1959 radio broadcast, on "True Christian Peace," he applied this vision of social morality to the present-day conditions of humanity:

> It will be necessary again and again to remove the obstacles erected by human malice... [reflected] in social injustice, in involuntary unemployment, in poverty contrasted with the luxury of those who indulge in dissipation, in the dreadful lack of proportion between the technical and moral progress of nations, and in the unchecked arms race, where there has yet to be a glimpse of a serious possibility of solving the problem of disarmament.[210]

Pope John affirmed his openness to the modern world in a speech delivered on June 20, 1961: "The [forthcoming] Council is not an assembly for speculation but a living, vibrant organism which surveys and embraces the whole world... it is the Church that calls all people to itself."[211] In the Apostolic Constitution *Humanae Salutis* issued on December 25, 1961, John formally proclaimed advent of the Second

---

[209]On this point, see Alden Hatch, *A Man Named John: The Life of Pope John XXIII* (New York: Hawthorne Books, 1963), pp. 202-203. Cf. also J. Derek Holmes, *The Papacy in the Modern World*, p. 203.

[210]Pope John XXIII, "True Christian Peace: The 1959 Christmas Broadcast," in The Staff of the Pope Speaks Magazine, *Encyclicals and Other Messages*, pp. 205-206.

[211]Cited in Carlo Falconi, *Pope John and His Council: A Diary of the Second Vatican Council: September-December, 1962* (London: Wiedenfeld and Nicolson, 1964), p. 19.

Vatican Council, and within this address he stressed the need "to recognize the signs of the times,"[212] by which:

> ...in the midst of all the hideous clouds and darkness [one can] perceive a number of things that seem to be omens portending a better day for the Church and for humankind... I would rather recognize the hidden guidance of divine providence in the present course of events.[213]

John expressed the desire for the Church to be renewed "in this age of ours through a new Pentecost, as it were,"[214] in order to "show itself better and better fitted to solve the problems of people of this age,"[215] and thus to strive "to make a little more human the lives of individual people... helping them to know themselves better. For [the Church] leads them to understand what they really are, what dignity they enjoy, what goal they must pursue."[216] He further expressed:

> [The Church] is well aware of the precise benefit that can be conferred on immortal souls by whatever seeks to make a little more human the lives of individual people, as it is helping them to know themselves better. For it leads them to understand what they really are, what dignity they enjoy, what goal they must pursue.[217]

---

[212]This key phrase would reappear in 1965 within the text of the Pastoral Constitution on the Church in the Modern World, *Gaudium et Spes*, which stressed the duty of the Church as "scrutinizing the signs of the times and of interpreting them in the light of the Gospel" (no. 4). For an excellent treatment of the use of the term in conciliar thought, see M.-D. Chenu, O.P., "The Signs of the Times," in Group 2000, *The Church Today*, pp. 43-59.

[213]Pope John XXIII, "Proclamation of the Second Vatican Council, The Apostolic Constitution *'Humanae salutis*,'" in The Staff of the Pope Speaks Magazine (eds.), *Encyclicals and Other Messages*, p. 387.

[214]Pope John XXIII, "Proclamation of the Second Vatican Council," p. 394.

[215]Ibid, p. 389.

[216]Ibid., p. 392.

[217]Ibid.

In his broadcast delivered on September 11, 1962, one month prior to the opening of the Council, Pope John sought to present to the Church "...a further luminous point: confronted with the underdeveloped countries, the Church presents herself as what she is, and wants to be, as the Church of all, and particularly, as the Church of the poor... [in order to redress] the miseries of social life that cry out for vengeance in the sight of God..."[218] In this speech, for the first time John introduced the theme of the "Church of the Poor," a topic that stirred considerable reflection and debate within the *Aula*, especially during the framing of the "Pastoral Constitution on the Church in the Modern World," *Gaudium et Spes*.

On October 4, 1962 (the first time a Pope officially left Rome since 1870) Pope John travelled by rail to Assisi to celebrate the feast of St. Francis. He went to the shrine of the "Little Poor Man" not only to pray for the success of the Council, but also to commend his plea for the realization of the "Church of the poor" expressed within the September 11 broadcast to the patronage of St. Francis.[219] In a similar vein, John extended upon this line of thought in his renowned opening address to the Council of October 11, 1962.[220] As he formally convoked the Council, Pope John emphasized the this-worldly nature of church life: "The major interest of the Ecumenical Council is this: that the sacred heritage of Christian truth be safeguarded and expounded with greater efficacy. That doctrine embraces the whole

---

[218]Cited in Giuseppe and Angelina Alberigo, *Giovanni XXIII*, pp. 357-358. This speech was largely inspired by a pre-conciliar working memorandum submitted to John by Cardinal Suenens. See Henri DeReidmatten, O.P., "*Histoire de la Constitution Pastorale*," in *L'Eglise dans le Monde de ce Temps, Schema XIII*, Commentaires (Paris: Mame, 1967), p. 53, along with Peter Hebblethwaite, *Pope John XXIII*, p. 424. Adrian Hastings points out in *Modern Catholicism: Vatican II and After* (New York: Oxford University Press, 1991), p. 30: "This [sentence] provided the impetus for the opening sentence of *Gaudium et Spes*."

[219]See Peter Hebblethwaite, *Pope John XXIII*, pp. 425-426.

[220]See Giuseppe Alberigo and Alberto Melloni, "*L'allocuzione 'Gaudet Mater Ecclesia' di Giovanni XXIII (11 ottobre 1962)*'" in *Fede, Tradizione, Profezia. Studi su Giovannni XXIII e sul Vaticano II* (Brescia: Editrice Queriania, 1984), pp. 185-283.

person, body and soul. It bids us to live as pilgrims here on earth, as we journey onwards towards our heavenly homeland."[221] His inaugural address to the council fathers set out the main lines of the Council's agenda, and emphasized the need for dialogue with humanity. It stressed that the purpose of the Council was to be pastoral rather than dogmatic, not to restate and defend past doctrines, but:

> ...to make a leap forward in doctrinal insight and the education of consciences in ever greater fidelity to authentic teaching... this authentic doctrine has to be studied in light of the research methods and the literary forms of modern thought. For the substance of the ancient deposit of faith is one thing, and the way it is presented is another.[222]

John maintained his basic optimism, and took issue with the nay sayers "who see nothing but calamity and disaster in the present state of the world... the prophets of doom, who are always forecasting worse disasters..."[223] In his closing address at the end of the first session of the Council, on December 8, 1962, he extended upon these themes:

> It is right to conclude that a good beginning has been made. It will then be a question of extending to all departments in the life of the Church, social questions included... It will be a new Pentecost indeed, which will cause the Church to renew its interior riches and to extend its care in every sphere of human activity. It will be a new advance of the Kingdom of Christ in the world, an elevated and persuasive reaffirmation of the good news of redemption, a clarion call of God's kingship, of human bonds in charity, of the peace promised on earth to persons of good will in accordance with God's good pleasure.[224]

---

[221]Pope John XXIII, "Opening Address to the Council," p. 428.
[222]Ibid., p. 430.
[223]Ibid., pp. 426, 427.
[224]John XXIII, "Toward a New Pentecost: An Address of Pope John XXIII at the Close of the Council's First Session," in The Staff of the Pope Speaks Magazine (eds.), *Encyclicals and Other Messages*, pp. 444-445.

Of the Johannine encyclical tradition, David Hollenbach observed that "the thread that ties all these documents together is their common concern for the protection of the dignity of the human person."[225] In his first great social encyclical, *Mater et Magistra,* John outlined as the Church's "immense task, to humanize and to Christianize this modern civilization of ours" (no. 256).[226] In a speech delivered on May 14, 1961 that previewed the publication of *Mater et Magistra,* John emphasized that the entire sweep of the modern tradition of Catholic social teaching "is always dominated by one basic theme – an unshakable affirmation and vigorous defense of the dignity and rights of the human person."[227] He expounded on this thread more clearly within the text of the encyclical itself:

> The cardinal point of this teaching is that individual persons are necessarily the foundation, cause and end of all social institutions. We are referring to human beings, insofar as they are social by nature, and raised to an order of existence which transcends and subdues nature. Beginning with this very basic principle whereby the dignity of the human person is affirmed and defended, Holy Church, especially during the last century... has arrived at clear social teachings whereby the mutual relationships of men and women are ordered (nos. 219, 220).

Michael Walsh and Brian Davies correctly asserted that in practice, "*Mater et Magistra* marked a quite decisive break with the past... Pope John was the first Roman pontiff to raise a subject which has since become a major element in papal

---

[225]David Hollenbach, S.J., "The Development of Roman Catholic Rights Theory," in *Claims in Conflict: Retrieving and Renewing the Catholic Human Rights Tradition* (New York: Paulist Press, 1977), p. 42.

[226]John XXIII, *Mater et Magistra,* in Michael Walsh and Brian Davies (eds.), *Proclaiming Justice and Peace: Papal Documents from Rerum Novarum Through Centesimus Annus* (Mystic, CT: Twenty-Third Publications, 1991 revision), p. 122.

[227]Pope John XXIII, "A Preview of *Mater et Magistra,* in The Staff of the Pope Speaks Magazine (eds.), *Encyclicals and Other Messages,* p. 233.

social teaching: aid to underdeveloped countries."[228] Some of the most original thoughts contained therein treated the demands of justice and of the common good in the relations between nations at varying stages of economic development. International questions tended to dominate the encyclical.[229] In this encyclical, John explored the theme of "development":

> Probably the most difficult problem today concerns the relationship between political communities that are economically advanced and those that are in the process of development. Whereas the standard of living is high in the former, the latter are subject to extreme poverty. The solidarity which binds all people together as members of a common family makes it impossible for wealthy nations to look with indifference upon the hunger, misery, and poverty of other nations whose citizens are unable to enjoy even elementary human rights. The nations of the world are becoming more and more dependent on one another and it will not be possible to preserve a lasting peace so long as glaring economic and social imbalances exist (no. 157).

John gathered around himself an expert staff of theological consultants who assisted in the writing of this Encyclical, such as Pietro Pavan and Agostino Ferrari Toniolo of the Lateran University, in order to link systematically new aspects of the social question. But, as Peter Hebblethwaite pointed out, by virtue of the "new tone" struck in *Mater et Magistra*, the Holy Father "had found his own voice."[230] In his 1963 Easter message, John identified a special linkage between *Mater et Magistra* and the forthcoming encyclical, *Pacem in Terris*, both of which "offer new reasons for serious reflection on socio-economic and political problems with a view to

---

[228]Michael Walsh and Brian Davies (eds.), *Proclaiming Peace and Justice*, p. 81.
[229]See Donald R. Campion, S.J., "The World-Wide Response," in Joseph N. Moody and Justus George Lawlor (eds.), *The Challenge of Mater et Magistra* (NY: Herder & Herder, 1963), pp. 155-205.
[230]Peter Hebblethwaite, *Pope John XXIII*, p. 386.

reaching solutions based on respect and love for those immutable and universal laws written in the heart of every person."[231]

Pope John expounded further upon this theme in his last great encyclical, *Pacem in Terris*, addressed to all humanity, with a call to "a more human standard, based, as it must be, on truth, tempered by justice, motivated by mutual love, and holding fast to the practice of freedom" (no. 149). In *Pacem in Terris*, John moved beyond the greeting of *Mater et Magistra* "to the clergy and faithful of the entire Catholic world," and extended the thrust of his teaching to "all people of good will." In a diary entry for May 24, 1963, written several weeks before his death, John noted: "Today, more than ever, we must be concerned to serve man and woman as such, and not just Catholics, and to defend the rights of everyone, and not just of the Catholic Church."[232] In *Pacem in Terris,* John set out to advance the cause of humanity in terms of value judgments and social dynamics (nos. 36-37) along the lines already laid down in *Mater et Magistra.* In his final encyclical, John expressed the hope "that the poorer countries, in as short a time as possible, will arrive at that degree of economic development which will enable every citizen to live in conditions more in keeping with his or her dignity" (no. 121). He added emphatically that the aid offered to these peoples "should be effected with the greatest respect for the liberty of the countries being developed, for these must realize they are the principal artisans in the promotion of their own economic development and social progress" (no. 123).[233]

---

[231]Pope John XXIII, "1963 Easter Message," in The Staff of the Pope Speaks Magazine (eds.), *Encyclicals and Other Messages*, pp. 376-377.

[232]Diary entry for May 24, 1963, cited in Giuseppe and Angelina Alberigo (eds.), *Giovanni XXIII: Profezia nella Fedelta*, p. 494.

[233] On the theme of development and the progression of John's thought in relationship to capitalism and socialism, see Jean Yves Calvez, S.J., *The Social Thought of John XXIII: Mater et Magistra* (London: Burns & Oates, 1964), pp. 64-66.

John based his methodology for arriving at the sources of ethical wisdom and knowledge that grounded his social teaching almost exclusively on the principles of natural law.[234] He demonstrated this posture throughout the text of *Mater et Magistra*, in the line of Popes Leo XIII (no. 15), Pius XI (no. 30) and Pius XII (no. 42). His methodology was inductive, not based on biblical sources nor drawn from the insights of contemporary social or behavioral sciences. As David Hollenbach suggested:

> [Pope John] adopted a normative framework for a pluralistic world. This move amounts to a definitive shift in Catholicism from a social ethic which proposed a concrete model of society as demanded by the natural law to a social ethic in which all social models are held accountable to the standards of human rights.[235]

Within the framework on the natural law tradition, *Pacem in Terris* yielded the most detailed statement in the papal social tradition of human rights. John issued this Encyclical during Holy Week, 1963, less than two months prior to his death. In David Hollenbach's assessment, it comprised "the most complete and systematic list of... human rights in the modern Catholic tradition,"[236] based on the inherent dignity of the person, and additional corresponding duties. This newly-placed emphasis represented a significant shift in Catholic self-understanding, since the older tradition

---

[234]On this point, see Charles E. Curran, "A Significant Methodological Change in Catholic Social Ethics," in Charles E. Curran, *Directions in Catholic Social Ethics* (Notre Dame, IN: University of Notre Dame Press, 1985), pp. 43-69.

[235]David Hollenbach, S.J., "Global Human Rights: An Interpretation of the Contemporary Catholic Understanding," in Alfred Hennelly, S.J. and John Langan, S.J., *Human Rights in the Americas: The Struggle for Consensus* (Washington: Georgetown University Press, 1982), pp. 12-13. See also Michael J. Schuck, *That They May Be One: The Social Teaching of the Papal Encyclicals* (Washington, DC: Georgetown University Press, 1991), p. 166 nn. 72, 73, along with Peter Hebblethwaite, *Pope John XXIII: Shepherd of the Modern World*, p. 485.

[236]David Hollenbach, S.J., *Claims in Conflict*, p. 66. On this point, see John Langan, S.J., "Human Rights in Roman Catholicism," in Charles E. Curran and Richard A. McCormick, S.J. (eds.), *Readings in Moral Theology No. 5: Official Catholic Social Teaching*, pp. 110-129.

emphasized duties, not rights. In John's line of reasoning, the primary concern of social rights is the preservation of human dignity in social interdependence: "It is generally accepted that the common good is best safeguarded when personal rights and duties are guaranteed" (no. 60). Peter Hebblethwaite concurred: "...to start from the dignity of the human person was not to introduce a new element into 'Catholic social doctrine;' the novelty lay in the way it was applied."[237]

Within the body of *Pacem in Terris*, Pope John asserted:

> Any human society, if it is to be well ordered and productive, must lay down as a foundation this principle, namely, that every human being is a person; that is, his or her nature is endowed with intelligence and free will. Indeed, precisely on account of this personhood, he or she has rights and obligations flowing directly from his or her very nature. And as these rights are universal and inviolable, so they cannot in any way be surrendered (no. 9).

In both *Mater et Magistra* and *Pacem in Terris* John publicly exerted his own voice and committed the Church to a policy of social reform in favor of the poor and deprived, both within individual nations and transnationally. *Mater et Magistra*'s teaching on private property reflected this stance: "Our predecessors have constantly taught that inherent in the right to have private property there lies a social role and responsibility" (no. 119). Each successive twentieth century Pope in turn laid greater stress than his predecessor on the social obligations attached to private property,[238] but John placed new emphasis upon the social responsibilities incurred by such ownership. He extended upon this line of thought to insist that human needs and the common good take priority over any individual's or group's right to private property.

---

[237]Peter Hebblethwaite, *Pope John XXIII*, p. 485.

[238]See Matthew H. Habiger, *Papal Social Teaching on Private Property: 1891-1991* (Washington: The Catholic University of America Press, 1987).

Pope John resisted the objections of certain influential members of the Roman Curia to denounce the "opening to the left" ("*apertura a sinestra*") created by the Socialist-Christian Democrat coalition government formed by Prime Minister Amintore Fanfani in February, 1962.[239] He outlined this new posture in a speech when he received Prime Minister Fanfani at the Vatican on April 11, 1961 (in what became commonly known as the "Wider Tiber Speech)."[240] As John asserted: "We must blow off the dust from the chair of Constantine which has been lying too long on the chair of Peter."[241] Without referring explicitly to Communism, in *Pacem in Terris* the Pope went so far as to claim that:

> Catholics, who in order to achieve some external good, collaborate with unbelievers or with those who in error lack the fullness of faith in Christ, may possibly provide the occasion or even the incentive for their conversion to the truth... It can happen, then, that meetings for the attainment of some practical end, which formerly were deemed inopportune or unproductive, might now or in the future be considered opportune or useful. (nos. 158, 159, 160).

The proponents of the *status quo ante*, both within and beyond the pale of the Church, sought to block John's liberal reformist agenda with obstructionist tactics. Pope John came to appreciate (as later recounted by Cardinal Suenens in his memorial eulogy delivered in the *Aula* on October 28, 1963) that "[his] personal part

---

[239]One might agree with the assessment on Donald Dorr: "Perhaps the most accurate way to sum up the effect of that encyclical [*Mater et Magistra*], and of Pope John's social teaching in general, would be to call it not so much an opening to the left as a decisive move away from the right." Cited in *Option for the Poor: A Hundred Years of Vatican Social Teaching* (Maryknoll, NY: Orbis Books, 1983), p. 114. Parenthetically, Fanfani, a devout Catholic, previously published his *Catechism of Catholic Social Teaching* (Westminster, MD: Newman Press, 1960).

[240]See Pope John XXIII, *Discorsi, messagi, colluqui del Santo Padre Giovanni XXIII, 1958-1963* III (Rome: Vatican Polyglot Press, 1967), p. 205.

[241]The text of this speech is cited in Yves Congar, O.P., *Power and Poverty in the Church*, p. 127. See also Paul Johnson, *Pope John XXIII*, p. 134.

in the preparation of the Council... [would] be suffering."[242] John's first Secretary of State, Cardinal Domenico Tardini, told a right wing Roman publication he believed John had taken leave of his senses.[243] Curial insiders like Cardinal Eugene Tisserant wrongly caricaturized John to be a dim-witted, dangerous innovator.[244] Cardinal Giuseppe Siri of Genoa complained that John's pontificate "was the greatest disaster in recent ecclesiastical history."[245] In June, 1962, Cardinal Alfredo Ottaviani, Pro-Prefect of the Holy Office, was overheard to say, "I pray to God that I may die before the end of the Council – in that way I can die a Catholic."[246] Pope John himself duly noted the attempts of the Roman Curia to undercut his influence. He commented in a journal entry about a current piece of disdainful humor that circulated about the corridors of the Vatican: "*Angelo regna, Carlo informa, Alfredo sorveglia, Domenico governa, Giovanni bendice.*" ["Angelo (Dell'Acqua, the Substitute) rules, Carlo (Confalonieri, Secretary of the Congregation for Seminaries and Christian Education) spies, Alfredo (Ottaviani, Prefect of the Holy Office) watches over, Domenico (Tardini, Secretary of State) governs, and John (XXIII, the Pope), merely blesses!]".[247] Among the Catholic laity, some conservative elements

---

[242]L.-J. Cardinal Suenens, *"A Man Sent From God": A Homily Delivered at the Opening of the Second Session of Vatican Council II, in Memory of Pope John XXIII*, (Dublin: Veritas, 1992), p. 6.
[243]See "*Lo Svizzero* [pseudonym]" *La Chiesa dopo Giovanni* (Rome: Editrice del Borghese, 1963), p. 15.
[244]See Peter Hebblethwaite, *Pope John XXIII*, p. 337.
[245]Cited in Peter Hebblethwaite, *Pope John XXIII*, p. 328. Years later, Cardinal Siri recanted this view, in a brief submitted during John XXIII's beatification process.
[246]Reported by Giancarlo Zizola, in "*Rapporti tra Moro e Giovanni*, in the Italian periodical *Panorama* (May 10, 1982), p. 257.
[247]Cited in Peter Hebblethwaite, *Pope John XXIII*, p. 344, where the author notes, additionally, "the fact that it went into the pope's private notebook suggests that he knew how the balance of forces in his curia was perceived in Rome." John XXIII commented on this ditty: "Strong words, cutting deed," in Bishop Loris F. Capovilla (ed.), *Lettere ai familiari* (Rome: Storia e Letteratura, 1968), p. 518. In reference to this rift, Mario Benigni and Godfreddo Zanchi state: "Though it was true that he exercised his role with great discretion – carefully avoiding heated conflicts – John XXIII followed the events of the Church closely and never failed to give direction or to intervene authoritatively," in *Pope John XXIII: The Official Biography* (Boston, MA: Daughters of St. Paul, 2001), p. 325.

bristled at the Church's renewed social consciousness, and greeted this development with a resounding: "*Mater, si, magistra, no*!"[248]

As the cancer in John's intestines metastasized, he felt compelled to solidify his positions. The fullest expression of his social thought took form in *Pacem in Terris*. On February 9, 1963, John confided to Roberto Tucci, S.J., and editor of *Civilta Cattolica*: "I don't have very long to live. I must therefore be very careful to weigh every move. Otherwise, the conclave that will take place after my death may be a conclave *against me* and make a choice that would destroy what I've begun to build.'"[249] As Peter Hebblethwaite suggested, "*Pacem in Terris* became his last will and testament."[250]

As John prepared the way for the Second Vatican Council, he gave it the task of opening the Church to the world, of finding an appropriate theological language, and of bearing witness to a Church both *of* and *for* the poor. The council fathers appropriated this theme in their "Message to Humanity" issued on October 20, 1962, just eight days after John's memorable opening address to the Council:

> Like Christ, we would have pity on the multitude weighed down with hunger, misery, and lack of knowledge. We want to fix a steady gaze on those who still lack the opportune help to achieve a way of life worthy of human beings... so that man's life can become more human according to the standards of the Gospel.[251]

---

[248]This phrase was first used by William F. Buckley, Jr., in a series of editorials commenting on *Mater et Magistra*. For a fuller description of his reaction, see National Review 11/6 (August 12, 1961), p. 77, along with the editorials in the prior and subsequent issues: 11/4 (July 29, 1961), p. 38, and 11/8 (August 26, 1961), p. 114-115.

[249]Cited in Giancarlo Zizola, *L'utopia di Papa Giovanni* (Cittadella Editrice, 1973), p. 247. See also Sandro Magister, *La politica vaticana e l'Italia 1954-1978* (Rome: Reuniti, 1975), p. 294 and Mario Begnini and Goffredo Zanchi, *Pope John XXIII: The Official Biography* (Boston: Daughters of St. Paul, 2001), p. 420.

[250]Peter Hebblethwaite, *Pope John XXIII*, p. 484.

[251]"Message to Humanity, Issued at the Beginning of the Second Vatican Council by Its Fathers, with the Endorsement of the Supreme Pontiff," cited in Walter Abbott, S.J., *The Documents of Vatican II* (NY: America Press, 1966), pp. 5, 6. Later, some theologians criticized the language of this text as

The direction undertaken by Pope John greatly influenced the themes and outlook of the Pastoral Constitution on the Church in the Modern World, *Gaudium et Spes*, promulgated in December, 1965. This movement reflected John's abiding desire to engage the Church in the social question. As Peter Hebblethwaite observed:

> …in death, John's abiding influence in the framing of the pastoral constitution bore fruit in the Church's identification: ...in the profoundest sense, [as] "the Church of the Poor" (no. 1). The Council could have arrived at these conclusions unaided; but it was helpful to have the example of Pope John to prove that such attitudes were found at the highest level of the Church. In that sense, Pope John's example was much more immediately influential than his encyclical, *Mater et Magistra*.[252]

John's personal witness taught the Church how to approach the problems of the contemporary world, and how to respect the sweep of the tradition while being faithful to its continuity with the spirit of the Gospel along with that of the ancient Church, while remaining open to the action of the Holy Spirit in the modern age. John's untimely death cut short his program of reform. In an interview in *Le Figaro* published on June 2, 1963, French theologian René Laurentin mused on John's unfinished agenda:

> John XXIII did not have time to fathom, to bring into action, another idea, more specifically Christian, which he brought up many times: the Church's Mission to the poor, which the Gospel tradition, obscured in the XIX Century, has always defended against the rigid principles of Roman law. For many bishops, one of the major problems of the Council is for the Church to become once more the Church of the poor, on a large scale. Here she will find her true Mission, which is not to accomplish a clerical enterprise in the world,

---

static and uninvolved, *viz.*, Dorr, *Option for the Poor:* "...the Fathers say they want to 'fix a steady gaze' on the poor; it is as though they are looking at the poor from the outside," p. 135.

[252]Peter Hebblethwaite, *Pope John XXIII*, pp. 368-369.

> but to animate prophetically the good will of the masses immersed today in the problems of wretchedness, hunger, and demographic explosion.[253]

Pope John's one-time adversary and later close collaborator, Cardinal Giacomo Lercaro, described him after his death as "the man chosen by Providence to be the great Doctor of the Church in the new era he himself inaugurated."[254] The American Vatican insider, Redemptorist Father Francis X. Murphy,[255] likewise noted that history will record that what John did for the Church in the Twentieth Century was "similar to what Leo the Great did for it in the Fifth, Gregory the Great in the Seventh, and Gregory VII in the Eleventh Centuries. Above all, he desired to return the Church to the spirit which animated the earliest Christian communities."[256] His successor, Cardinal Giovanni Battista Montini of Milan, neatly captured John's contribution: "Perhaps never before in our time has a human word – the word of a master, a leader, a prophet, a Pope – rung out so loudly and won such affection throughout the world."[257] In a stirring display of Latin oratory directed to the council fathers, Cardinal Suenens depicted the heart of John's legacy:

---

[253]René Laurentin, "An Appreciation of John XXIII," in *Le Figaro* (June 2, 1963), p. 1.
[254]Giacomo Lercaro and Gabriele De Rosa, *John XXIII: Simpleton or Saint?*, p. 28. See the text of his speech, "*Linee per una ricerca su Giovanni XXIII,*" in Cardinal Giacomo Lercaro, *Giovanni XXIII, Linee per una ricerca storica* (Rome: Storia e Letteratura, 1965), p. 32.
[255]The later self-confessed "Xavier Rynne" whose dispatches from Rome printed in *The New Yorker* and subsequently published in four volumes by Farrar, Strauss & Giroux (1963-1967) raised eyebrows and brought acclaim. See his extensive admission of authorship of the four volumes, in Francis X. Murphy, C.Ss.R., *Synod Extraordinary* (Wilmington, DE: Michael Glazier, 1987).
[256]F. X. Murphy, C.Ss.R., "Introduction and Biography," in The Staff of the Pope Speaks Magazine (eds.), *Encyclicals and Other Messages*, p. 6.
[257]Cardinal Giovanni Battista Montini, "Eulogy for Pope John XXIII," in Loris F. Capovilla, *Ite, Misa Est*, p. 225.

> History will surely judge that he opened a new era for the Church and that he laid the foundations for the transition from the Twentieth to the Twenty-first century... The tomb of John XXIII will not be able to confine his heritage... His life was a grace for the world... People recognized his voice, a voice speaking to them of God, but also of human solidarity, of the re-establishment of social justice, of a peace to be established throughout the whole world... The poor wept for him; they knew he was one of them, and that he was dying poor like them, thanking God for the poverty that had been for him such a grace... At his departure, he left people closer to God, and the world a better place for men and women to live.[258]

Pope John was a visionary innovator, though no raging liberal. While he did not specifically commit the Church to a "preferential option for the poor" in the strict sense of the term, he sowed the seeds for this unfolding doctrine, as evidenced in the directions taken in his principal social encyclicals, *Mater et Magistra* and *Pacem in Terris.*[259] Commentators like Donal Dorr assessed that John's teaching "made a major contribution towards putting the Church on the side of the poor," and affirmed that he was "deeply concerned about the plight of poor people."[260] John XXIII's social teaching and analysis launched the process by which the "preferential option for the poor" began to take shape in Latin America in the second half of the twentieth century. As Dorr suggested, "For the ability to see the need for such option, the Church owes much to John XXIII and especially to the social teaching of *Mater et Magistra.*"[261] Clodovis Boff and George Pixley concurred that Pope John XXIII's legacy:

---

[258]Cardinal Leon-Josef Suenens, "*A Man Sent From God*," pp. 3, 8, 9, 13.

[259]See, for example, nos. 124, 150, 154, 157-174 and 185 of *Mater et Magistra*, and nos. 88, 95, 96, 101, 103-107, and 121-125 of *Pacem in Terris*.

[260]Donal Dorr, *Option for the Poor*, p. 102.

[261]Donal Dorr, *Option for the Poor*, p. 116. For a more extensive treatment of this theme, see also Donal Dorr, "John XXIII and the Option for the Poor," in *Irish Theological Quarterly* 47 (1980), pp. 247-271.

> ...was still not a clear *option* for the poor" since in Europe many of the working classes were already "lost" to the Church and sufficiently secularized that it was impossible for the Church to make a clear option for them. It was only in Latin America, where the oppressed masses were also believers that the bishops pronounced clearly in favor of a preferential option for the poor, at Puebla in 1979.[262]

In Latin America during the late 1960s the groundwork laid by Pope John XXIII began to bear fruit, and the momentum advanced in favor of a "Church of the Poor." A new social locus of the Church emerged, a movement "from the center to the margin."[263] This shift was anticipated by the great systematic theologian, Karl Rahner:

> We do know, however, that the Church of the future will be characterized by the marks of the local community: poverty, few in number, diaspora. In other words, the future ecclesial experience is anticipated already by the ecclesial experience of the local community. For the person of the future will encounter the Church of the future only when he or she sees in the Church the presence of Christ realized and experienced in the legitimate proclamation of the Gospel and in the remembrance of Christ's death and resurrection in the Eucharist. This is where the Christian of tomorrow will apprehend the actual nature of the Church, for this is where the most original religious and theological experience of the Church will take place: in the community.[264]

This transformational movement found resonance, also, in the "Dogmatic Constitution on the Church," *Lumen Gentium*, which stressed that the Universal Church exists only through expression in local churches: "In these communities, though frequently small and poor... Christ is present" (no. 26).

---

[262]Clodovis Boff and George V. Pixley, *The Bible, the Church, and the Poor*, p. 187.
[263]Archbishop José María Pires popularized this phrase in his work of the same title, "from the center to the margins": *Do centro para a margem* (João Pessoa, Brazil: Editora Acaua, 1970).
[264]Karl Rahner, S.J., *The Church After the Council* (New York: Herder & Herder, 1966), p. 49.

In essence, John's contribution to the unfolding doctrine of the preferential option for the poor was partial and transitional. He prompted the stirrings of a new paradigm within the realm of official Catholic social teaching. John longed to initiate "*un balzo in avanti*" ("a leap forward"), and succeeded admirably in launching his program of renewal, despite his limited tenure. Two of Pope John XXIII's most astute chroniclers, Giuseppe and Angelina Alberigo, captured his essence: "To study John is to have the exhilarating experience of writing the history of the future."[265] John provided the Church and the world with a pre-glimpse of what the shape of the Church and of humanity might be. As Cardinal Leon-Joseph Suenens spoke in his encomium to John that he delivered in the *Aula*:

> On the dawn of his election Pope John may have seemed to be a "transitional Pope." And this he certainly was, but in an unexpected way which the expression, in its habitual meaning, does not suggest. When history has been set in its proper perspective, people will undoubtedly be able to say that he opened a new era for the Church, and prepared the passage from the Twentieth to the Twenty-First Century.[266]

John XXIII longed for the realization of "the Church of the poor," and set the stage for its unfolding teaching and practice over the course of the ensuing decades. By embracing the notion of the "Church of the Poor," Pope John became the embodiment of his "last will and testament" that he shared on May 24, 1963 with two of his closest curial collaborators during his final days, Cardinal Amleto Cicognani and Archbishop Angelo Dell'Aqua, less than two weeks prior to his death:

> Now more than ever, and certainly more than in centuries past, we intend to serve man as he is, not just Catholics; to defend above all

[265]Giuseppe and Angelina Alberigo, *Giovanni XXIII, profezia nella fedelta*, p. 108.
[266]Cardinal Leon-Joseph Suenens, *A Man Sent From God*, p. 6.

> and everywhere the rights of all human beings, not only those of the Catholic Church. Contemporary circumstances, the needs of the last fifty years, doctrinal deepening, have placed a new reality before our eyes. As I said in my discourse at the opening of the Council, it is not that the Gospel has changed, it is we who begin to understand it better… the moment has arrived to recognize the signs of the times, to seize the opportunities, and to look far beyond.[267]

"Good Pope John" seized the opportunity in the world arena to advocate for the poor and downtrodden. He scrutinized the "signs of the times," availed himself of opportunities, and afforded the Church the vision to look far beyond.

---

[267]Recounted by Pope John's personal secretary and confidant, Bishop Loris F. Capovilla, in *Ite, Misa Est* (Bergamo: Grafica e Arte), p. 212. See also Loris F. Capovilla, *The Heart and Mind of John XXIII* (NY: Hawthorn Books, 1964), pp. 130-139 for a first-hand account of the last days of "good Pope John."

Chapter Two

Vatican II, Pope Paul VI and *Populorum Progressio*

In January, 1963, Cardinal Giovanni Battista Montini discoursed on the aim of the Second Council of the Vatican with a group of young priests from the Archdiocese of Milan:

> At the Council, the Church is looking for itself. It is trying, with great trust and at great effort, to define itself more precisely and to understand what it is. After twenty centuries of history, the Church seems to be submerged by secular civilization, and absent from the contemporary world. It is therefore experiencing the need to be recollected and purified and to recover itself so as to be able to set off on its own path again with great energy... While it is undertaking the task of defining itself in this way, the Church is also looking for the world and trying to come into contact with [it]... How should that contact be established? By engaging in dialogue with the world, discerning the needs of the society in which it acts, observing the shortcomings, the needs, the aspirations, the sufferings that lie within human hearts.[268]

Montini later refined this view on the day of his papal coronation, when he stressed the aspect of the Church's solidarity with the poor: "We will strive to preserve and augment the Church's pastoral action, as she presents it, free and poor..."[269]

Pope John XXIII previously declared that the essential object of the Council was "not to discuss one or another of the Church's fundamental articles," not to be

---

[268]Cited in Cardinal Giovanni Battista Montini, *Discorsi al Clero, 1957-1963* (Milan: Messagero, 1963), pp. 78-80.
[269]Pope Paul VI, "Homily at Mass of Coronation," in *La Documentation Catholique* (1963), p. 932.

doctrinal or juridical, but to be "above all pastoral in character."[270] Later, as Pope Paul VI, he further delineated the aims of the Council as:

> ...to spread light upon those places and institutions where people are working for union, for social peace, for the welfare of the poor, for progress, for justice, for liberty... This event will be important for the Church and for the whole of humanity. It will be the greatest Council the Church has ever held in the whole of its twenty centuries of history... Before our eyes, history is opening up enormous prospects for centuries to come.[271]

For Roman Catholicism, Vatican II represented a recovery of directions, neglected but not abandoned, that were profoundly embedded in the Christian tradition, a retrieval of a dynamic theology nourished by the Scriptures and the works of the Fathers of the Church. Among the principal themes of Vatican II, concern for social and pastoral involvement came to the fore only at the end of the first session of the Council. Some hesitation and tentativeness inevitably emerged at the beginning of its work, but the Council began to direct its attention resolutely toward the world, with its problems of poverty and hunger and its hopes for development and peace. By identifying itself concretely with humanity, after the manner of Christ, the Council came to a clearer awareness of the challenges that awaited it. It gradually evolved towards the landmark document, "Schema XIII," that emerged as one of the

---

[270]Pope John XXIII, "Opening Address at the Council (October 11, 1962)," p. 431. On September 21, 1965, Archbishop Gabriel-Marie Garrone noted that the title "Pastoral" Constitution had been approved by the coordinating commission in order to make the document in accordance with "the supreme intention and purpose of the Council, as defined by Pope John XXIII." See Xavier Rynne, *The Fourth Session*, p. 57.

[271]Discourse delivered at a public audience on November 18, 1965. Cited in *La Documentation Catholique* LXII (1965), col. 2046. Paul VI made this observation on several occasions, and declared that no other council had such breadth and scope. In this sense, he once remarked in correspondence to the schismatic Archbishop Marcel Lefebvre (June 29, 1975) that Vatican II "has no less importance, and in certain respects is more important than Nicaea." See also Yves Congar, O.P., "A Last Look at the Council," in Alberic Stacpoole, O.S.B. (ed.), *Vatican II Revisited*, p. 355 n.24., and "*La Condamnation Sauvage*," in *Itinéraires* (September, 1976), p. 45.

most enduring contributions, the document known as "The Pastoral Constitution on the Church in the Modern World," often called by its Latin title, *Gaudium et Spes*.[272]

In the final pastoral letter that he issued as Archbishop of Milan entitled "The Christian and Comfort," Cardinal Montini wrote: "The gospel design is perpetuated in the Church of the poor, as John XXIII pointed out to the Ecumenical Council when suggesting this great subject of meditation and reform... We must have a special respect, a great solicitude for the poor. The poor person is the image of Christ, a living sacrament of Christ, as it were..."[273] In the theological purview of Pope Paul VI, everything was contained within the mystery of Christ. Likewise, in his address of September 29, 1963, he expressed the notion that the Church is first and foremost a mystery, "a reality imbued with the hidden presence of God."[274] For Paul VI, the Church was a kind of fundamental sacrament of Christ, just as Christ is the fundamental, or primordial sacrament of God.[275] This sacramental principle undergirded the principal documents on the Church at Vatican II. *Gaudium et Spes* described the Church as "the universal sacrament of salvation simultaneously manifesting and realizing the mystery of the love of God for man" (no. 45).[276] This sacramental understanding of Church presented the practical consequence that the

---

[272]For treatments of the history and background of *Gaudium et Spes*, see C. Moeller, "History of the Constitution," in Herbert Vorgrimler (ed.), *Commentary on the Documents of Vatican II*, Vol. V, pp. 1-76, along with Henri de Riedmatten, O.P., "Introduction: History of the Pastoral Constitution," in Group 2000, *The Church Today*, pp. 1-40.

[273]Cited in Desmond O'Grady, "Towards a Church of the Poor," p. 40. For the full text, see *La Documentation Catholique* (1963), pp. 688-690. The notion of the sacramentality of the Church, a key theme developed by both Edward Schillebeeckx and Karl Rahner, achieved fuller stature by its inclusion in the "Dogmatic Constitution on the Church" at Vatican II.

[274]Cited in Richard McBrien, "The Church (*Lumen Gentium*)," in Adrian Hastings, *Modern Catholicism*, p. 88.

[275]This concept is largely derived from the seminal work of Edward Schillebeeckx, O.P., *Christ: The Sacrament of the Encounter With God* (NY: Sheed & Ward, 1963).

[276]"Pastoral Constitution on the Church in the Modern World," in Walter Abbott, S.J. (ed.), *The Documents of Vatican II*, p. 247.

Church must attempt to effect and signify what it aspires to be.[277] *Lumen Gentium* spoke of the Church as "a kind of sacrament or sign of intimate union with God, and of the unity of all mankind" (no. 1).[278] In his address to the Council on September 29, 1963, Paul VI reiterated that the aim or the Council encompassed its desire to speak "to all humanity."[279]

Pope Paul believed that humanity could only be finally understood and explained in terms of Jesus Christ and that in Christ human beings are properly revealed to one another. Paul was a proponent of the new Christology that came into vogue in the post-World War II era. He solidified the link between theology and anthropology, and presented Christ as the fulfillment of what it means to be human. In an address on September 29, 1963, during the second session of the Council, entitled, "Christ the Beginning, Way, and Goal of the Council," Paul VI identified the Risen Lord as:

> ....both the Road we travel and our guide on the way; ...our hope and our final end... Christ is our Founder and Head... We receive everything from him, and constitute with him the whole Christ... If we recall this, we shall be better able to understand the main objectives of this Council. For reasons of brevity and understanding, we enumerate here those objectives in four points: 1). The self-awareness of the Church; 2). Its renewal; 3). The bringing together of all Christians in unity; 4). The dialogue of the Church with the contemporary world.[280]

---

[277]On this point, see the incisive analysis of the later Cardinal Avery Dulles, S.J., in *Models of the Church* (NY: Doubleday, 1974), especially chapter IV.

[278]"Dogmatic Constitution on the Church," in Walter J. Abbott, S.J. (ed.), *The Documents of Vatican II*, p. 15.

[279]Paul VI, "Allocution to the Council" (September 29, 1963), in *A.A.S.* 55 (1963), pp. 847, 854.

[280]Cited in Hans Küng, *et al.* (eds.), *Council Speeches of Vatican II* (Glen Rock, NJ: Paulist Press, 1964), pp. 19-20.

Of these four points articulated by Paul VI, the one that received the most extensive and profound treatment throughout the sessions of the council was the necessity of "dialogue with the world." This central thrust accounted for the shift of focus at the end of the first session and opened up pathways along which the work of the Council would advance, culminating in the promulgation of *Gaudium et Spes* and also reflected in *Lumen Gentium*: "Christ is the light of the world, from whom we go forth, in whom we live, and toward whom our journey leads us" (no. 3).[281] *Gaudium et Spes* treated this theme as well, and suggested that "only in the mystery of the incarnate Word does the mystery of humanity truly become clear... Christ the Lord... reveals man to himself and brings to light his most high calling" (no. 22).[282] The council fathers acclaimed the Risen Lord in *Gaudium et Spes* as both "Lord of human history as well as of salvation history" (no. 42). Pope Paul VI returned to this theme in his closing address on the religious value of the Council at the conclusion of the final session. On December 7, 1965, Pope Paul suggested that the turn toward the service of humanity did not require a turning away from God, but instead, required a turning toward God.[283] In the poor, Christians recognized the face of Christ, the face of God:

> Our humanism becomes Christianity though the face of every person – especially when tears and sufferings have made it more transparent

[281]"Dogmatic Constitution on the Church," in Walter Abbott, S.J., *The Documents of Vatican II*, p. 16.

[282]"Pastoral Constitution on the Church in the Modern World," in Walter Abbott, S.J., *The Documents of Vatican II*, p. 220. On this text, see Josef Ratzinger, "The Dignity of the Human Person," in Herbert Vorgrimler (ed.), *Commentary on the Documents of Vatican II*, Vol. IV (NY: Herder & Herder, 1969), p. 159: "...here for the first time in an official document of the magisterium a new type of completely Christocentric theology appears. On the basis of Christ, this dares to present theology as anthropology and only becomes radically theological by including man in discourse about God by way of Christ, thus manifesting the deepest union of theology." For Karl Rahner's understanding of the relationship between anthropology and Christology, see his "Christian Humanism," in *Theological Investigations*, Vol. IX (NY: Herder & Herder, 1967), pp. 187-204.

[283]See *A.A.S.* 58 (1966), pp. 55-59,

> – we can and must recognize the face of Christ... [The task of the Council] is nothing other than a friendly and pressing appeal, urging humanity to rediscover God through the path of fraternal love.[284]

In this same closing address, Paul asked rhetorically whether or not the Council may have "deviated" by accepting the "anthropocentric positions of modern culture." He immediately responded, "Deviated, no; diverted, yes."[285] As Pope Paul indicated in his closing address on December 7, 1965:

> At the Council the Church has been concerned not just with herself and her relationship of the union with God, but with man – man as he really is today, living man, man wrapped up all in himself, man who makes himself not only the center of his every interest but dares to claim that the is the principle and explanation of all reality.[286]

The council fathers echoed this approach in this observation in *Gaudium et Spes* that "We are witnesses of the birth of a new humanism, one in which man is defined first of all by his responsibility toward others and toward history" (no. 55). The process by which the council fathers approached the drafting of *Gaudium et Spes* was "more biblical, more historical, more vital, and more dynamic" than prior papal and conciliar documents.[287] Concern with the notion of scrutinizing "signs of the times" that emerged as one of Vatican II's most characteristic orientations (*Gaudium*

---

[284]Pope Paul VI, "Closing Address on the Religious Value of the Council" (December 7, 1965), in *Documenti: Il Concilio Vaticano II* (Rome: Vatican Polyglot Press, 1966), p. 1080. The council fathers extended upon this theme in *Ad Gentes*: "Since this Mission continues and, in the course of history, unfolds the Mission of Christ, who was sent to evangelize the poor, then the Church, urged on by the Spirit of Christ, must walk the road Christ himself walked, a way of poverty..." (no. 5), cited in Walter Abbott, S.J., "Decree on the Church's Missionary Activity," in *The Documents of Vatican II*, p. 590.

[285]Pope Paul VI, "Closing Address on the Religious Value of the Council" (12/7/65), in *Documenti: Il Concilio Vaticano II* (Rome: Vatican Polyglot Press, 1966), p. 1079.

[286]Pope Paul VI, *Insegnamenti*, Vol. III, p. 720.

[287]Avery Dulles, S.J., "The Church," in Walter Abbott, S.J., *The Documents of Vatican II*, p. 11.

et Spes no. 4; cf. no. 44), as the council fathers sought to direct their attention to social, cultural, economic and political dimensions of the contemporary world. Although John XII's favored the term, "*signa temporum*," the expression "signs of the times" appeared only once in the council documents [i.e., in the introduction to *Gaudium et Spes*]. Nevertheless, yet the concept held sway, and served as a benchmark during the deliberations on the schema on the "Church in the Modern World." As M.-D. Chenu noted: "...it might well be considered as one of the three or four most important formulas used by the Council, one which served as a source of its inspiration and guided its progress."[288]

The special drafting sub commission headed by Bishop Marcos McGrath, C.S.C. of Panama City met in September, 1964, and defined the "signs of the times" as: "The phenomena which occur so frequently and so pervasively that they characterize a given epoch and seem to express the needs and aspirations of contemporary humanity."[289] In his speech of October 9, 1964, Dom Manuel Larrain of Chile told the assembly:

> Excessive institutionalism can pose the danger of lessening charity. The world moves too fast sometimes, and institutions cannot keep up the pace – especially if their structures have become too rigid. We must listen not only to the scholars, but also to events themselves if we are to read the signs of the times.[290]

As Yves-Marie Congar pointed out in his commentary on the council's third session:

> It is plainly a matter of recognizing the historicity of the world and of the Church itself which, though separated from the world, is also bound to it. The events of the world must have an echo in the Church, at least to the extent that they raise questions for the Church.

---

[288]M.-D. Chenu, "The Signs of the Times," p. 43.
[289]Cited ibid., p. 48.
[290]Cited ibid., p. 54.

> It will not have adequate and ready-made answers for every question, but it will realize that the answers of a given moment cannot be simply repeated over and over again. When we speak of the signs of the times, we are saying that the times themselves have something to teach us.[291]

At times, this approach had the sobering effect of toning down the extraordinary optimism displayed in some of Pope John's documents and prouncements. A careful reading of the "signs of the times" also contrasted the ideal with reality, – a reality often marred by social evil.[292]

On November 22, 1962, the Council announced "the creation of another extra-Conciliar commission... on 'peace and the poor'... [to address] the Council's response to the problems of the modern world, and the authentic response of the Church."[293] Work began at the end of December, 1962, with a small group of *periti*, including the principal drafters of *Mater et Magistra* and *Pacem in Terris*: Bishops Pietro Pavan and Agostini Ferrari Toniolo. A first draft was drawn up in March, 1963, and at the behest of Cardinal Suenens it was reworked completely over the summer, with input from Yves Congar, Karl Rahner, and Jean Daniélou. In July, 1963, at the insistence of Cardinal Suenens, the general commission decided to work up a new document. In February, 1964, the commission and its periti met at the Jesuit residence in Zurich to amend the revised draft. Its first paragraph survived nearly intact as the opening words of *Gaudium et Spes* (no. 1). Pope John's primary theme of the "signs of the times" stressed by Paul VI in his address to the observers to the Council on October 17, 1963 was taken as integral to the mission of the Church in the world. The first discussion of the schema occurred during the

---

[291]Yves Congar, O.P., *Le Concile au Jour le Jour: Troisième Session* (Paris: Cerf, 1965), p. 84.
[292]For instance, *Gaudium et Spes* (no. 63) served as a reminder that economic progress often brings the by-product of disdain and contempt for the poor.
[293]In *La Documentation Catholique* LIX (1962), column 1613.

Council's 105th general assembly on October 20, 1964, and in mid-November, 1964 during three additional three meetings. The draft was reworded into coherent form, including "Part II" devoted to political life, culture, socio-economic order, and peace.

While Cardinal Suenens brought the idea of a document on the Church in the modern world before the Council on December 4, 1962, there was no pre-existing draft of such a schema, although certain themes had been touched on in the work of the preparatory commissions on social action and on the Christian moral order. The motive force behind the decision to compose this new document rested with John XXIII, Helder Câmara, Leon-Josef Suenens, and Cardinals Paul-Emile Leger of Montreal and Giovanni Battista Montini of Milan. In the main, two groups of bishops supported the schema from the very beginning: the French and the Belgians, along with the bishops from the underdeveloped countries.

One of the defining moments of the first session of the Council came on December 6, 1962. In an intervention dubbed as "the *'Magna Carta'* of the Church of the Poor,"[294] Cardinal Giacomo Lercaro stated:

> If we treat this subject of winning the poor for the Gospel as just another one of the many themes which must occupy the attention of the Council we shall not satisfy the most real and the most profound exigencies of our day (including our great hope of furthering the unity of all Christendom) – indeed, we shall make it impossible for us to do so... The Church herself is in truth the theme of the Council [especially insofar as] she is above all "the Church of the poor."[295]

---

[294]Desmond O'Grady, "Towards a Church of the Poor," in *Perspectives* X (March-April, 1964), p. 38.

[295]The full text of Lercaro's intervention is printed in English translation in Paul Gauthier, *Christ, the Church and the Poor* (London: Geoffrey Chapman, 1964), pp. 153-157. The relevant selection cited is on page 153.

Cardinal Lercaro, the Archbishop of Bologna, was a close advisor to John XXIII, and made a firm stand on stressing the connection between poverty and the Church as a vital theme of the Council. He grounded this emphasis in both the mystery of Christ and the mystery of the Church: "The Mystery of Christ in the Church is always, but particularly today, the Mystery of Christ in the poor, since the Church, as our Holy Father Pope John XXIII has said, is truly the Church of all, but is particularly the 'Church of the poor.'"[296] Lercaro added an eloquent plea:

> We shall not be doing our task sufficiently well, and our spirit will not be sufficiently responsive to God's design and our expectation unless we place the Mystery of Christ in the poor and the preaching of the Gospel to the poor at the heart and center of our doctrinal and legislative work at this Council. This, in fact, is an obvious, practical, topical and urgent task for our day. Certainly by comparison with other epochs, it seems that in our day the poor have the Gospel less preached to them, their hearts seem farther away from and foreign to the Mystery of Christ in the Church. At the same time, ours is an epoch in which, by agonizing and almost dramatic questions, the spirit of man turns to and closely examines the mystery of poverty and the condition of the poor, both the condition of the individual and that of whole peoples who live in destitution, and yet are newly becoming conscious of their proper rights. This is an epoch in which the poverty of the majority (two-thirds) of mankind is outraged by the immense riches of a minority, in which poverty inspires a greater horror among the masses each day, and in which the worldly man is plagued by the unslaked thirst for riches.[297]

Cardinal Lercaro returned to this theme in a television interview on December 22, 1962,[298] as well as in a later lecture at the College of the Apostles in Lebanon during August, 1964, wherein he stated that the absence of this essential aspect of the

---

[296]Cardinal Giacomo Lercaro, cited in Paul Gauthier, *Christ, the Church and the Poor*, p. 153.
[297]Ibid., p. 154.
[298]As reported in *Civilta Cattolica* 114 (1963), pp. 285-286.

Christian message was a serious defect in the provisional schemata presented to the Council. He indicated further that a serious reading of the "signs of the times" required making the theme of the "Church of the poor" one of the Council's central concerns.[299] Despite the sustained applause which greeted Lercaro's famous intervention at the Council, the session closed without the insertion of a schema devoted to the world's problems, and without any alteration of the original program of work prepared by the Council's preparatory commissions.

At the close of the first session of the Council, on December 6, 1962, Cardinal Franz Koenig of Vienna stated: "We have certainly not done everything... [But] despite our differences, we have maintained the charity of Christ, and have prepared ourselves for the presentation to the world of the truth and love of Christ that we daily hope to accomplish in the next session."[300] On this same date, Cardinal Lercaro expressed his agreement with the view previously put forth by Cardinals Giovanni Battista Montini and Leo-Josef Suenens that the Council should confront directly the problems of social justice, poverty, overpopulation, war and peace. Bishop George Hakim of Nazareth invoked the theme of the "Church of the poor" advanced by John XXIII on September 11, 1962, and implored the council fathers to produce a document that spoke to the needs of their contemporaries:

> Let them speak another language to us, the language of our age... Let them speak the language of John XXIII and the language of the Gospel to us... If they presented papal primacy to us as a service and

---

[299]Lercaro refined this text and included it as the "Preface" to *Eglise et Pauvretè* (Paris: Editions du Cerf, 1965), pp. 9-21. For reaction to Lercaro's speech of December 6, 1962, see the comments of Robert Roquette, S.J.: "This intervention by the Cardinal of Bologna is the boldest and most reforming to have been made during the first session: it may well open up a whole new path," cited in *Etudes* (February, 1963), p. 265.

[300]Cited in Xavier Rynne, *Letters From Vatican City*, p. 232.

as the answer to Christ's three-fold question of love to Peter, such a language would be understood by all Christians.[301]

The Council appeared to be experiencing the throes of frustration and chaos when a series of planned interventions approved by John XXIII restored order and hope. As a prelude to these key council speeches, on October 2, 1963 Cardinal Valerian Gracias of Bombay told the assembled council fathers that the draft schema, "*De Ecclesia*" should take care not to present the Church as a community closed in on itself, but rather, as being open to the world: "The Church exists in itself, but not for itself; it exists for service, not for privilege or domination... The Church seeks to expand not as a means for increasing its power, but rather in order to increase the scope of its service."[302] On October 4, 1963, the feast of St. Francis, Cardinal Pierre-Marie Gerlier of Lyon endorsed the proposal of thirteen East African bishops that the introduction of the proposed document on the Church should say something about the place of the poor in the Church.[303]

During a press conference on October 8, 1963, under the aegis of the Council's documentation center, Cardinal Suenens gave the first indication of work on the draft declaration then known as "Schema XVII," the first information to be made public on that working document.[304] At the end of the first session, under Suenens' direction, a new overall program for the Council was outlined, in order to

---

[301]Cited in Henri Fesquet, *The Drama of Vatican II*, pp. 95-96. Hakim was greatly influenced by the presence within his diocese of the French worker-priest, Paul Gauthier, who exercised disproportionate influence at the Council. See also Paul Gauthier, *Nazareth Diary* (London: Geoffrey Chapman, 1966).

[302]Cited in Floyd Anderson (ed.), *Council Daybook: The Ecumenical Council / June, 1962 – December, 1965* (NY: Random House, 1965), p. 157.

[303]See Xavier Rynne, *The Second Session: The Debates and Decrees of Vatican Council II, September 29 to December 4, 1962* (New York: Farrar, Straus & Giroux, 1964), p. 65.

[304]See Floyd Anderson (ed.), *Council Daybook: Vatican II/ Session 1, Oct. 11 to Dec. 18, 1962; Session 2, Sep. 29 to Dec. 4, 1963* (Washington, DC: National Catholic Welfare Conference, 1965, p. 173.

reduce the number of topics and give some direction to its work. This program envisioned the overall plan as concentrating on the subject of the Church, with the first objective to deal with the Church's intramural problems and the second phase to concentrate on the Church's relationship with the outside world. The immediate impetus for the drafting of the pastoral constitution came with Suenens' speech on the floor of the *Aula* of December 4, 1962, ratified on successive days by the interventions of Cardinals Montini and Lercaro. Suenens noted the irony of the lack of church teaching on social justice:

> The Church should speak of social justice. Moralists have written so many volumes on the sixth commandment that no domain is still unexplored on that subject, but they are almost silent when it comes to concretely settling the social duty of private property. More than that, what the fine encyclicals say on the subject is not widely taught in the schools, nor as fully as it should be in books. How should we fix the bounty which should go to the poor? What is the theological and practical duty of wealthy nations towards the poor, and the hungry nations? The Church should speak of the evangelization of the poor, and of the conditions required on our part for our testimony to reach them and to be acceptable... The Council will pursue a triple dialogue: that of the Church with her children; ecumenical dialogue with others not visibly united; a dialogue with the world of today.[305]

Suenens modeled his address on John XXIII's speech of October 11, 1962, and listed four topics that called for attention under the *ad extra* heading: the population explosion; social justice; "the Church of the poor"; and war and peace.

During the Council's second session, on October 26, 1963, Bishop Pierre Boillon of Verdun spoke on the issue of the Church and poverty:

---

[305]Cited in Giovanni Caprile, S.J., *Il Concilio Vaticano II: Annunzio e preparazione, 1961-1962* (Rome: Civilta Cattolica, 1966), p. 247. For the full text of Suenens' intervention, see in *La Documentation Catholique* IX (1963), columns 46-62.

> The Church is a stranger to the poor. Marxism has captured the attention of the poor because it speaks to them of their human dignity. Why is the Church not heard? Because the exterior signs of wealth deceive the poor... Let the Council declare that the poor have a divine right to first place in the Church. Let the Church be poor and appear poor. Vatican II cannot be silent on this question.[306]

The voices of council fathers from many developed nations, from France and Belgium in particular, exhorted the Church to relinquish wealth and privilege in order to retain freedom of witness, of judgment, and of action, along with the active participation of the hierarchy of Brazil. Dom Helder Câmara typified this new direction. He stated: "Since every deep reform in the Church has always begun with poverty... let us remove the things which separate us from the spirit of our time, especially the poor and the workers."[307] Archbishop Emile Guerry of Cambrai, in a Lenten pastoral letter in 1963, commented on the incongruity of a Church ensconced in the trappings of wealth delivering a message of poverty:

> ...we for our part have to deliver this message from the height of our marble altars and episcopal "palaces," in the incomprehensible baroque idiom of our pontifical masses, with their strange mitered ballet, in the still stranger circumlocutions of our ecclesiastical language; and we go out to meet our people clad in purple, in a car of the latest model... and our people come to us calling us "Your Eminence," and genuflecting to kiss the stone in our ring! It is not easy to struggle free of all this weight of tradition.[308]

These sentiments were previously expressed by Bishop Dammert Bellido of Peru:

---

[306]Cited in Henri Fesquet, *The Drama of Vatican II*, p. 193.
[307]Cited in Marcel Gérard, S.J., (ed.), "Documentation to Direct Religious Education Towards The Service of the Poor and of All Mankind: Words and Actions of the Church in Council," in *Lumen Vitae* XVII (December, 1963), p. 704.
[308]Cited in Yves Congar, *Power and Poverty in the Church* (Baltimore, MD: Helicon Press, 1965), pp. 155-156.

> One area in which, with the best of intentions, we still provoke scandal in some and disgust in others is in the lack of simplicity in the decoration of our churches and the riches with which we surround our ceremonies. In all innocence, we stretch our resources to obtain the costliest ornaments, which are in doubtful taste to begin with, while at the same time children of God are suffering from hunger, sickness, and misery. This is a true cause for scandal in the Church today. Sumptuosity is not in accord with the poverty of our age.[309]

A working group of council fathers and *periti* arose spontaneously to espouse the theme of the "Church of the poor" contained within the speeches of John XXIII and of Cardinal Lercaro. Archbishop George Hakim of Nazareth and Bishop Charles-Marie Himmer[310] of Tournai circulated a brief working paper of the French priest, Paul Gauthier, a well-known worker-priest at Nazareth and former seminary professor at Dijon, entitled, *Christ, the Church, and the Poor*.[311] In one of his earlier works, Gauthier wrote:

> ...the Eucharist is the very sacrament of Christ the poor man. Behind the ornamentation and richness of the tabernacle... there lies Christ hidden under the appearance of a poor piece of bread, the food of the poor. He is just as little and humble as he was on in the manger and on the Cross, waiting to serve the lowly...[312]

309Cited in Xavier Rynne, *Letters from Vatican City*, pp. 63-64. Many of the bishops of the "Belgian College Study Group" donated their pectoral crosses at a Mass in the catacombs, to be sold to the poor. Paul VI shed the tiara during a concelebrated Mass at St. Peter's on November 14, 1964, and later donated it to Cardinal Francis Spellman of New York to be sold for charity. He made numerous comparable gestures, as when he donated his Lincoln limousine to a then-unknown nun in Calcutta named Mother Teresa. See also Henri Fesquet, *The Drama of Vatican II*, pp. 516, 517, 800, 801, 811.
310On October 27, 1964, during an intervention at the Council, Bishop Himmer asserted that "Poverty is the key to the whole schema (XIII)." See Xavier Rynne, *The Third Session: The Debates and Decrees of Vatican Council II: September 14 to November 21, 1964* (New York: Farrar, Straus & Giroux, 1965), p. 144.
311Paul Gauthier, *Christ, the Church, and the Poor* (London: Geoffrey Chapman, 1964).
312Ibid., pp. 159-160.

Dom Helder Câmara and Dom Manuel Larrain were the motive forces behind two groups that met during the Council that provided a locus of encounter among bishops and theologians from all over the world, particularly from developing countries, as well as those others interested in socio-cultural problems.[313] They typified the spirit of the mimeographed writings of Paul Gauthier that circulated among the council fathers:

> In addition to the anguish felt over this lost modern world, there is that of seeing the sociological structure of the Church so far removed from it. There is the painful knowledge of the gulf separating the Church, seemingly on the side of the wealthier classes, from the working class and sub-working class population.[314]

Without a doubt, the presence of bishops from the underdeveloped nations increased the sensitivity of the council fathers to issues pertaining to the poor. In a press conference on November 25, 1962, Helder Câmara noted:

> A valuable benefit of this Council has been the meeting of bishops from all over the world... Formal sessions have been followed up by informal meetings where bishops have engaged each other in friendly conversation... These informal meetings have resulted in something that is, as it were, a response to *Mater et Magistra*. A demand has been made that a special commission be created within the Council, charged with the task of studying current world problems in a concrete way. Among these we might note particularly the relationship between industrialized nations and the underdeveloped countries, and also the problem of world peace.[315]

---

[313]See René Laurentin, *L'Amèrique Latine a l'Heure du l'Enfantement* (Paris: Editions de Seuil, 1969).
[314]Paul Gauthier, *Nazareth Diary*, p. 173.
[315]Cited in *La Documentation Catholique* LIX (1962), column 1613.

The informal reflection groups that sprung up during the Council were popularly known by their French titles: "*Le Christ et l'Eglise Servante et Pauvre*," and "*L'Eglise et l'Aide aux Pays en Voi de Développement: Conditions d'une Action Efficace*" (known more colloquially, as "The Church of the Poor Group" and the "Friday Meetings of the Vatican Group," respectively).[316] In a message that circulated among the members of the Council's preparatory commission in the fall of 1962, Father Paul Gauthier warned:

> The hierarchy... seems a stranger to two thirds of humanity lacking bread for body and soul, and forced to labor hard for a meager profit. The rift between the Church and poor is a more serious scandal, a deeper wound. A rift between the Church and the poor is as serious as the division among churches, for that means a schism, a rent in the body of Christ. Yet Christ is indissolubly identified with the Church and with the poor.[317]

During the second session, the vigor displayed by Cardinal Lercaro concerning the Church's attitude toward the poor was echoed in an intervention of Cardinal Pierre-Marie Gerlier of Lyon, on October 4, 1963. Gerlier referred to the speech of Paul VI at the opening of the second session, which affirmed that "'...the poor, the needy, the afflicted, the hungry... belong to the Church, by the right which the Gospel gives her'... The presence of the poor signifies the presence of Christ in our midst. We will be judged on our attitude toward them."[318] Later that day, Bishop Charles-Marie Himmer of Tournai stressed that if the Church wanted to reveal its true face to the poor, it must strive more forcefully to serve the poor: "Christ wanted

---

[316]On the evolution of these two groups see José de Broucker, *Dom Helder Câmara: The Conversions of a Bishop*, pp. 165-168.
[317]Cited in Marcel Gérard, "Documentation," in *Lumen Vitae* XVII:4 (December, 1963), pp. 686-687.
[318]Cited in Henri Fesquet, *The Drama of Vatican II*, p. 140. See the further comments of Xavier Rynne, in *The Second Session*, p. 65.

to be identified with the poor... We shall be judged with regard to the charity we have shown to the poor, because of the presence of Christ in them."[319] On the same date (not coincidentally, the feast of St. Francis of Assisi), Bishop Mercier of the Sahara distributed a declaration through the "White Fathers Information Center" in Rome that read:

> The Christian world on the whole is rich. The Church is in danger of losing in the future the "two thirds" of the world that is poor as she lost the working classes in the past. Only the Church is capable of removing the scandalous character and the threat of revolt from the shocking inequality in the human condition.[320]

This movement prompted an intervention at the Council in early October, 1963 by Bishop C.-M. Himmer, who stated: "If the Church does not give the poor first place, she is not showing her true countenance."[321]

On October 26, 1963, a group of ten council fathers met at the Belgian College for the first time, in order to reflect on questions posed in an essay to the council fathers by Paul Gauthier on the question of poverty in the Church ("the Church that is poor") and of outreach and evangelization to the poor ("the Church of the poor"). The group's ranks swelled as they frequently gathered to hear influential theologians such as François Houtart, a Belgian sociologist, and Yves-Marie Congar, who delivered a powerful lecture to them in November, 1962 entitled "The Historical Development of Authority,"[322] wherein he argued that all authority in the Church was

---

[319]Cited in Henri Fesquet, *The Drama of Vatican II*, pp. 141-142, and Xavier Rynne, *The Second Session*, pp. 65-66.

[320]Cited in Fesquet, *The Drama of Vatican II*, p. 142.

[321]In *La Libre Belgique* (October 5, 1963), cited in Marcel Gerard, S.J., "Documentation to Direct Religious Education Towards the Service of the Poor and of Mankind," in *Lumen Vitae* XIX (March, 1964), pp. 68-69.

[322]The text of this lecture is contained in Yves Congar, O.P, *Power and Poverty in the Church*, pp. 40-79. For an understanding of the key role played by Congar in the formation of the group's identity and consciousness of the attendant theological issues, see his work included as the appendix, "*Le*

for service. The "Church of the Poor" group played a pivotal role in furthering the Church's rediscovery of Christ in the poor of the world. Though it held no official status, the group remained in continual contact with influential council figures through its *ad hoc* president, Cardinal Pierre-Marie Gerlier. Gerlier served as an able spokesperson for the movement, and observed:

> It is essential that the Church, which does not want to be rich, should be set free from the appearance of riches. The Church must appear as she is: the Mother of the poor, whose first care it is to give the bread of the body and the bread of the soul to her children... As bishops, we must keep in the forefront of the Council's preoccupations the problem of preaching the Gospel to the poor, of the apostolate among the workers. The present Council must be the opportunity of asserting this.[323]

Per Pope John XXIII's request, the "Church of the Poor" group kept in regular contact with Cardinal Lercaro, who acted as its liaison with him.[324] At the same time, Dom Helder Câmara suggested to Cardinal Suenens that he should initiate a new dialogue between the developed and the underdeveloped nations. Suenens wasted no time in acting on this suggestion, and organized an informal meeting between the bishops of the wealthy and poor countries.[325]

In a newspaper interview on November 14, 1962, Paul Gauthier noted:

> Poverty was not included in the Council's agenda; yet John XXIII spoke these prophetic words: "The Church is for all people, and especially the poor." The first session made this serious shortcoming

---

Fondement du Mystère des Pauvres dans le Mystère de Dieu et du Christ," in Paul Gauthier, "*Consolez mon Peuple." Le Concile et l'Eglise des Pauvres* (Paris: Seuil, 1965).

[323]Cited in *Equipes Enseignantes*, special number, 2e trimestre 1963-1963, p. 89.

[324]For an interesting history of this group, from Gauthier's perspective, see "*Consolez mon Peuple." Le Concile et l'Eglise des Pauvres* (Paris: Editions Universitaires, 1965).

[325]On this point, see José de Broucker, *Dom Helder Câmara: The Conversions of a Bishop*, pp. 164-167.

> clear. Subsequently, much work has been done in special meetings [principally of the "Church of the poor" group]... Schema XIII can be the map of rediscovery for the Church and the poor... I make mine these words of Father [Bernard] Häring: "The Archimedes' fulcrum" of Schema XIII is poverty.[326]

On November 22, 1963, Cardinal Valerian Gracias of Bombay made a strong plea that Schema XVII (revised to "Schema XIII" later, during the third session) be considered at the beginning of the third session, since the proposed draft schema on the Church did not emphasize the battle against misery or that "the poor are the images of Christ, the living sacrament of Jesus," to echo the phrase of Pope Paul VI.[327] A week later, Chilean Bishop Bernardino Pinera Carvallo echoed this appeal for an overhaul in lifestyle within the Church:

> Let us abandon our episcopal way of living. Let us shun the exterior trappings of wealth – ostentatious ceremonies, insignia, and honorific titles. Let us live according to evangelical simplicity. Without that, no witness is possible. For we are judged on it. Let us strive with all our strength to be humble. Immediately. Our wealth is in the treasure of the poor.[328]

On December 11, 1962, in an interview in *Croix*, Jean Guitton, a professor at the University of Paris and the only Catholic layman invited to attend the first session of the Council, expressed the hope that the preparatory work would bring out fully one of the hopeful aims of the Vatican Council, namely, "to find Christ more than ever in the poor. We know that this Council wishes to restore in the Church this 'sacrament' of poverty, the presence of Christ in the guise of those who suffer."[329]

---

[326]Cited in Henri Fesquet, *The Drama of Vatican II*, p. 519.
[327]Cited ibid., p. 260.
[328]Cited in ibid., p. 265.
[329]Cited in Marcel Gérard, "*Documentation*," in *Lumen Vitae* XVII (December, 1963), p. 685.

Debate on Schema XIII finally closed on November 10, 1964, at the 119th general congregation, and the attendant issues were taken up again during the fourth (and final) session, in the autumn of 1965. In reply to Cardinal Suenen's challenge to the Church to speak both *ad intra* (to its own concerns) and *ad extra* (in its dialogue with the world), Vatican II attempted to fashion its reply in *Gaudium et Spes*. Father Gerald Mahon, a major religious superior (and head of the English-based missionary Order, the Mill Hill Fathers) later suggested during an intervention on November 10, 1964:

> [Vatican I] said nothing about social justice or the undeserved misery of workers... I propose that what is said on hunger and misery be clearer and that it become one of the most important parts of Vatican II. There is a duty to educate all Christians to the responsibility of social justice between nations. It is scandalous that our plea to rich nations to help poor countries is in vain.[330]

The fourth and final session of Vatican II began on September 14, 1965. It served as a last chance, wrap-up session. At the conclusion of the Council, in November, 1965, a document issued from the Belgian College Study Group circulated among the council fathers when some forty bishops concelebrated Mass in the catacombs of St. Domitila at the invitation of the Belgian Bishop Charles-Marie Himmer. This text received the euphemistic nickname, "Schema XIV," a reference to its extension beyond the lacunae and omissions of *Gaudium et Spes* on the question of poverty. Although no separate schema on poverty emanated from the Council, the circulation of the unofficial draft of "Schema XIV" served to advance dialogue among the council fathers pertaining to social concerns. In part, the paper read:

---

[330]Cited ibid., pp. 500-501.

> We will give as much of our time as possible to... workers, the economically deprived, and the underdeveloped, without prejudice to other groups... We will support laity, religious, deacons or priests whom the Lord calls to evangelize the poor by sharing in their lives, whose economic situation is one of weakness or underdevelopment... We commit ourselves to sharing... our lives with our sisters and brothers in Christ... in order that our ministry will be a true service.[331]

As Clodovis Boff and George Pixley pointed out:

> Schema XIV could be described as one of the strongest links between Vatican II and the Medellín and Puebla Conferences, which, on a continental level, developed the potential of the theme of the evangelical perspective of the poor, springing from its concentrated expression – like the grain of mustard seed – in *Lumen Gentium* (no. 8).[332]

For six months, the editorial committee charged with revising the text of the pastoral constitution subjected it to a final major revision, beginning with an extensive week spent at Ariccia in early February, 1965. On May 11, 1965, the completed text was distributed to the council fathers as *De Ecclesia in mundo huius temporis*, "On the Church in the Modern World." It was identified as a "*Constitution Pastoralis*," as a pastoral counterpart to the Dogmatic Constitution on the Church, *Lumen Gentium*. The text was subjected to intensive criticism and further alteration, with the hope that that approval of the schema would come before the end of the fourth session. On October 5, 1965 Cardinal Joseph Cardijn gave an impassioned

---

[331]Cited ibid., p. 800. It is worth pointing out that this brief statement contained thirty-six biblical references, a shift away from traditional, natural law-based methodology to a more biblically-based critique.

[332]Clodovis Boff and George V. Pixley, *The Bible, the Church and the Poor*, p. xiv.

speech on the needs and problems of workers,[333] two days after he spoke eloquently about young people in developing nations. On the same day, Bishop Manuel Larrain, President of CELAM, the Latin American bishops' conference which first met in plenary session in 1955 in Rio de Janiero, offered a summary of development problems in Central and South America and the Caribbean.

American Catholic layman James Norris, executive director of the "National Council of Catholic Men," was one of eleven non-clerics invited to attend the second session of the Council as a lay auditor.[334] He served as assistant to Bishop Edward Swanstrom, then-executive director of the U.S.-based Catholic Relief Services, who was also president of the International Catholic Migration Commission. Towards the close of the second session, on November 5, 1964, Norris was invited (on six hours' notice) to introduce the topic of poverty contained in the draft of article 24 in Schema XIII, on the theme of solidarity among peoples. The content of his historic intervention merits citation:

> In the last decade, the problem of poverty – one of the oldest and deepest that confronts the Christian conscience – has taken on a new shape, new dimensions, and a new urgency... The gap between the rich and the poor is rapidly widening- side by side, the rich grow richer and the poor grow poorer, in a single world community. This is a wholly unprecedented historical fact, and it presents that Christian conscience of the western nations with a challenge, because

---

[333]See Xavier Rynne, *The Fourth Session*, p. 101, as well as Henri Fesquet, *The Drama of Vatican II*, p. 674. Canon Joseph Cardijn was responsible for the "See/Judge/Act" methodology made famous through the Young Christian Students and Young Christian Workers movements exported from Belgium and popularized through Latin America by Helder Câmara.

[334]In a later commentary on *Gaudium et Spes*, Norris noted: "Why is it that our document stresses so frequently the problem of poverty and misery in the world?... the great emphasis on the gap between rich and poor nations occurs in the Council document so frequently because of the large number of bishops from underdeveloped areas of the world. They are the 'Lazarus Church' begging crumbs from the table of the 'Dives Church.' This is the unreported story of Vatican II." Cited in James J. Norris, "International Order," in John H. Miller, C.S.C. (ed.), *Vatican II: An Interfaith Appraisal*, p. 503.

> for the first time in history it is accepted as a fact that, given time, the western nations have the means to wipe out poverty in the rest of the world... From this Ecumenical Council could come a clarion call for action which would involve the creation of a structure that could devise the kind of institutions, contacts, forms of cooperation and policy, which the Church can adopt, to secure full Catholic participation in the world-wide attack on poverty.[335]

Cardinal Josef Frings of Cologne immediately seconded Norris' proposal, and called for the establishment of episcopal committees, on national and international levels, to promote projects designed to alleviate world hunger.[336] Cardinal Suenens lent his prestige to the suggestions of Dom Helder Câmara[337] and Norris, and offered a dramatic new proposal:

> Like the secretariat for ecumenical questions, I think there should be a similar one, within the Council, for social questions, or at least, a

[335]Cited in Xavier Rynne, *The Third Session*, pp. 180-181. The ecumenical counterpart of the Pontifical Commission [later, Council] *Iustitia et Pax*, which it sponsored jointly with the World Council of Church's "Church and Society" department was "The Committee on Society, Development, and Peace" (SODEPAX), which held its first meeting on the issue of world development in Beirut in 1968. For information on the founding of this joint committee, see M. Kohnstamm, "Report to the General Secretariat of the World Council of Churches," in *La Documentation Catholique* (September 1, 1968), cols. 1507-1503.

[336]See Henri Fesquet, *The Drama of Vatican II*, p. 489.

[337]Câmara suggested that the impetus for the establishment of the Secretariat, the Pontifical Commission Justitia et pax, came from a dialogue among the "Church of the Poor Group": "One result of such meetings had been the idea of setting up a body to implement *Mater et Magistra.* It has been suggested that there should be a special commission with the task of studying the problems raised by the modern world, especially world peace and the relationship between the industrialized and underdeveloped countries." Cited in Henri De Riedmatten, O.P., "*Histoire de la Constitution Pastorale," in L'Eglise dans le Monde de ce Temps, Schema XIII, Commentaires* (Paris: Mame, 1967), pp. 60-61. See also Xavier Rynne, *The Third Session*, pp. 180-181. The ecumenical counterpart of the Pontifical Commission [later, Council] *Iustitia et Pax*, which it sponsored jointly with the World Council of Church's "Church and Society" department was "The Committee on Society, Development, and Peace" (SODEPAX), which held its first meeting on the issue of world development in Beirut in 1968. For information on the founding of this joint committee, see M. Kohnstamm, "Report to the General Secretariat of the World Council of Churches," in *La Documentation Catholique* (September 1, 1968), cols. 1507-1503. See Henri Fesquet, *The Drama of Vatican II*, p. 489.

> special section of a new commission, whose task would be to make easier and arrange the work of other commissions. In our first message, our desire for dialogue was made clear to the world; the creation of this secretariat would be the practical and concrete expression of this expressed desire.[338]

The proposal for the secretariat for world peace and justice at the fourth session was inspired by a paper drawn up by Msgr. Joseph Gremillion, Msgr. Luigi Ligutti, Fr. Arthur McCormack, and James Norris.[339] The impetus for the Pontifical Commission *Iustitia et Pax* stemmed largely from the efforts of voluntary groupings of bishops and *periti* who formed three clusters to promote within the Council their special concerns for the poor, for peace, and for world justice and development. These groups planned, coordinated, and promoted their overlapping agenda and causes both within the drafting committees and during open discussions at the Council, as well as behind the scenes. Apart from bringing the Church's social doctrine up to date, they aimed to institutionalize follow-up on these issues after Vatican II, by means of a social ministry secretariat within the Roman Curia and an ecumenical network of cooperation operating among church bodies worldwide. The most active participants in this dialogue included Helder Câmara of Brazil; Bishop Angelo Fernandes of India; Bishop Edward Swanstrom of the United States; Cardinal Leo-Josef Suenens of Belgium; Cardinal Raul Silva of Chile; and Father Gerald Mahon. On October 5, 1965, Bishop Swanstrom and three other speakers intervened on behalf of the creation of the proposed secretariat. Bishop Swanstrom stated:

---

[338]For the dialogue between Suenens and Câmara, and the Belgian Cardinal's ultimate response, see Marcel Gérard, "Documentation," in *Lumen Vitae* XVIII:4 (December, 1963), pp. 688-689, as well as the report contained in José de Broucker, *Dom Helder Câmara: The Conversions of a Bishop*, pp. 165-166.

[339]See Joseph Gremillion, "Justice and Peace," in Adrian Hastings, *Modern Catholicism,* p. 188.

> There is a great gulf between our accepting the Church's teaching and our putting it into practice. Hence I propose concretely that the Church launch a deep and long-term campaign of education, inspiration and moral influence to promote among Christians and all people of good will a live understanding and concern for world poverty and to promote world justice and development in all their facets.[340]

On December 7, 1965, the last voting day of Vatican II, the council fathers approved the text of the "Pastoral Constitution on the Church in the Modern World," *Gaudium et Spes*. The texts were revised right up to the last possible moment, and the draft text was submitted to a conciliar vote on December 4 and 6, 1965. On December 7, 1965, 2,309 of the council fathers voted in favor of it, with 75 opposed. Pope Paul VI immediately promulgated the text under the title of the "Pastoral Constitution on the Church in the Modern World."[341] The text indicated:

> Taking into account the immensity of the hardships which still afflict a large section of humanity, and with a view to fostering everywhere the justice and love of Christ for the poor, the Council suggests that it would be most opportune to create some organization of the Universal Church whose task it would be to arouse the Catholic community to promote the progress of areas which are in want, and to foster social justice among nations (no. 90).

On January 6, 1967, Pope Paul VI established the Pontifical Commission *Iustitia et Pax*, with Cardinal Maurice Roy as its President and Monsignor Joseph Gremillion of Pennsylvania as its Secretary. Pope Paul charged it to animate the

---

[340]Cited in Xavier Rynne, *The Fourth Session*, p. 98. See also Henri Fesquet, *The Drama of Vatican II*, p. 661.

[341]For two excellent summaries of the evolution of *Gaudium et Spes*, see Louis J. Lebret, O.P., "Economic and Social Life: the Community of Nations," in Group 2000, *The Church Today*, pp. 168-191, as well as Henri de Riedmatten, O.P., "Introduction: History of the Pastoral Constitution," in the same work, pp. 3-40.

Church's mission for promoting social justice and development, peace and human rights.[342] He compared the commission to a weathervane poised on the steeple of the Church "as a symbol of watchfulness," in order to "keep the eye of the Church alert, her heart open, and her hand outstretched for the work of love she is called upon to do."[343] As the council's lay observer James Norris later declared:

> The document called for the creation of an organism of the Universal Church which would have the role of educating the Catholic community about the problems of the poor nations of the world, stimulate development in poor countries and promote social justice among nations. Why had so many bishops spoken on the subject of poverty and misery in the world in a forum like the Council, if they did not want some such action at the highest level of the Church? If the Secretariat had not been called for, the hundreds of statements on the subject would have had little meaning and would have been without response on the part of the Council.[344]

In spite of this progress, one of the most valid criticisms of the shortcomings of Vatican II's social teaching appeared in a work of a Sri Lankan theologian, Tissa Balasuriya, O.M.I.:

> [Vatican II's] inadequacy was due partly to its lack of adequate social analysis of what was going on in the world at the time. It had no real sense of the struggles of the poor, the working class, of women, of oppressed racial groups... There was no deep dialogue with other religions, cultures, and ideologies as offering alternative analyses and worldviews to the white, western, capitalist, male mindset that still dominated Catholicism. Some of the main theologians of the Council – Congar, Rahner, Ratzinger, Küng – rendered valuable service as far

---

[342]Pope Paul VI, "*Motu propio Catholicam Christi Ecclesiam,*" *in La Documentation Catholique* (February 5, 1967), no. 1487, cols. 193-196. For additional details on the creation of the Commission, see René Laurentin, *L'Enjeu du Synode* (Paris: *Seuil*, 1967), p. 196.

[343]Pope Paul VI, *Insegnamenti di Paolo VI*, Vol.V (Rome: *Libreria editrice Vaticana*, 1968), p. 171.

[344]James Norris, "International Order," in John H. Miller, C.S.C., *Vatican II: An Interfaith Appraisal*, p. 504.

> as they went, but their experience was European and Church-centered... [The Council] did not propose relevant practical goals in the real world and strategies for transforming mentalities and structures. Its relationship to the world order and human development remained within the framework of "aid" to the poor by the rich.[345]

Gaudium et Spes presaged the new tack to be adopted by the Church *vis à vis* society that indicated a shift in the offing concerning the relationship between the Church and civil authorities:

> The Church... does not rest its hopes on privileges offered to it by civil authorities; indeed, it will even give up the exercise of certain legitimately acquired rights in situations where it has been established that their use calls in question the sincerity of its witness, or where new circumstances require a different arrangement (no. 76).

This passage was greeted by many in the Church of Latin America as an invitation to adopt a very different posture – to distance itself from the comfortable embrace of the ruling elites, and to challenge structural injustice. As Donal Dorr suggested, "In this sense it was *Gaudium et Spes* that provided the foundation on which was built, three years later at Medellín, the Latin American Church's formal commitment to taking 'an option for the poor.'"[346]

In *Lumen Gentium*, the council fathers asserted that "the Church recognizes in those who are poor and suffer, the image of her poor and suffering founder. She does all in her power to relieve their need and in them she strives to serve Christ"

---

[345]Tissa Balasuriya, O.M.I., *Planetary Theology* (Maryknoll, New York: Orbis Books, 1984), p. 148. [Balasuriya became something of a *cause celébré* a decade later, when he was excommunicated for theological views deemed unacceptable by the Congregation for the Doctrine of the Faith, but was reconciled to his priestly ministry in May, 1999, due to the intervention of his superior general with Vatican officials of the Congregation for the Doctrine of the Faith].

[346]Donal Dorr, *Option for the Poor*, p. 138.

(no. 8). Jon Sobrino, S.J. noted that this text demonstrated that "the Church is *partisan*; this is perhaps the greatest novelty in the present-day Church... [which] proclaims that its duty is to cultivate solidarity with the poor in which it will make their problems and struggles its own."[347] The council fathers extended upon this notion in the decree on Missions, *Ad Gentes*:

> The Mission of the Church... is a continuing one. In the course of history it unfolds the Mission of Christ himself, who was sent to preach the Gospel to the poor. Hence, prompted by the Holy Spirit, the Church must walk the same road which Christ walked: a road of poverty and obedience, of service and self-sacrifice... (no. 5).

Gaudium et Spes trumpeted the desire of the Church to become engaged with the concerns of the poor in its very opening lines:

> The joys and the hopes, the griefs and the anxieties of the people of this age, especially those who are poor or in any way afflicted, these too are the joys and hopes, the griefs and anxieties of the followers of Christ. Indeed, nothing genuinely human fails to find an echo in their hearts (no. 1).

Peter Hebblethwaite discerned within this text the petal notes of the Church's later articulated "preferential option for the poor":

> *Gaudium et Spes* picks up this emphasis in its opening sentence which expresses a willingness to share in the joys and hopes of all mankind, but "especially those who are in any way poor or afflicted." This was the starting point for liberation theology with its "option for the poor." It was "post-conciliar," but it carried forward what the

[347]Jon Sobrino, S.J., *The True Church and the Poor*, pp. 240-241.

> Council had promised and applied it to Latin America where... the future of the Church is being played out.[348]

Situated within the rich biblical and patristic tradition,[349] *Gaudium et Spes* advocated "solidarity in action at this turning point in history [as] a matter of urgency" in *Gaudium et Spes* (no. 10). The documents of Vatican II considered the theme of poverty within a variety of the sixteen texts: (nos. 4, 8); *Perfectae Lumen Gentium* (nos. 8, 41); *Gaudium et Spes* (nos. 1, 69. 81, 88, 90); *Apostolicam Actuositate Caritatis* (nos. 1, 13, 30); Ad Gentes (nos. 3, 5); and, *Presbyterorum Ordinis* (no. 17). However, as Donal Dorr suggested, a lack of cohesion and synthetic wholeness marked this approach, since "none of these documents offers a developed spirituality of poverty which integrates the Christological and evangelical aspects with the economic and social reality."[350]

In an insightful analysis on the shortcomings of the Council's approach to the problem of poverty, Gustavo Gutiérrez noted:

> John XXIII gave the Council the task of opening the Church to the world, finding an appropriate theological language, and bearing witness to a Church for the poor. After it had overcome its initial difficulties, the Church fulfilled the first of these two demands... The third task given by John XXIII to the Council barely appears in its texts. The theme of poverty, "Schema XIV" as it was called in the Council corridors, knocked at the Council's door, but only got a glimpse inside. However many Christians have recently been becoming more and more aware that if the Church wants to be faithful to the God of Jesus Christ, it has to rethink itself *from below*,

---

[348]Peter Hebblethwaite, *Synod Extraordinary: The Inside Story of the Rome Synod, November – December, 1985* (NY: Doubleday, 1986), p. 12.

[349]For an interesting assessment of the impact of patristic influences on the revitalized approach to the Church and the poor taken at Vatican II, see Ermenegildo Lio, "*Povertá (Theologia morale)*," in Salvatore Garofalo (ed.), *Dizionario del Concilio Ecumenico Vaticano Secondo* (Rome: Vatican Polyglot Press, 1969), Col. 1646.

[350]Donal Dorr, *Option for the Poor*, p. 299 n. 70.

> from the position of the poor of this world, the exploited classes, the despised races, the marginal cultures. It must descend into the world's hells and commune with poverty, injustice, the struggles and hopes of the dispossessed, because of them is the Kingdom of Heaven. Basically it means the Church living as a Church the way many of its own members live as human beings... The aim is to be faithful to the Gospel, and the constant renewal of God's call. Gradually people are realizing that in the last resort it is not a question of the Church being poor, but of the poor of this world being the People of God, the disturbing witness to the God who sets free.[351]

To its credit, and in light of its accompanying limitations, Vatican II sought to represent and embrace the members of the universal Church in the fullest sense. As the council fathers declared in their "Message to Humanity" of October 20, 1962, "the Church is supremely necessary for the modern world if injustices and unworthy inequalities are to be denounced, and if the true order of affairs and of values is to be restored, so that man's life can become more human according to the standards of the Gospel."[352] Unfortunately, as Yves Congar suggested, "Vatican II stopped halfway, setting forth compromise solutions not only as to the formulas used, but also as the ecclesiastical content behind these statements."[353]

In the assessment of Juan Alfaro, S.J.:

> ... the Church will lack the moral authority required for its mission, as long as it cooperates with the economic and social structures

---

[351]Gustavo Gutiérrez, "The Poor in the Church," in Norbert Greinbächer and Alois Müller (eds.), *The Poor and the Church* (NY: Seabury Press, 1977), pp. 12-13.

[352]"Message to Humanity Issued at the Beginning of the Second Vatican Council By Its Fathers, With the Endorsement of the Supreme Pontiff," in Walter Abbott, S.J., *The Documents of Vatican II*, p. 6. For an incisive commentary on this text, see M.-D. Chenu, "*Le Message au Monde des Pères Conciliares (octobre, 1962)*," in Y.-M. Congar and M. Peuchmaurd (eds.), *L'Eglise dans le Monde de ce Temps: Constitution Pastoral 'Gaudium et Spes': Tome III, Reflections et Perspectives* (Paris: *Cerf*, 1967), pp. 191-193.

[353]Cited in Angel Antón, S.J., "Postconciliar Ecclesiology: Expectations, Results, and Prospects for the Future," in René Latourelle, S.J. (ed.), *Vatican II: Assessment and Perspectives Vol. I*, p. 423.

> oppressing the needy classes. The Church will have to win its own true freedom and liberation, by committing itself to the freedom of the oppressed. Nowadays, Christian hope demands from the entire Church and from each of its members a task that is both difficult and urgent: opting for the poor and the second-class citizens of society. In the words of Vatican II, Christian hope today demands "universal changes in ideas and attitudes" (*Gaudium et Spes*, no. 63).[354]

Although the Church experienced difficulties in bringing this vision to fruition, Vatican II often declared that the present situation of the Church requires radical reform and renewal (cf. *Gaudium et Spes*, nos. 21, 42, 76, 88; *Lumen Gentium*, nos. 8, 15; *Unitatis Redintegratio*, no. 6). The council fathers acknowledged the difficulties inherent in living in the unrealized tension between the "now" and the "not yet" of the fullness of the Reign of God, that will be realized "when Christ hands over to the Father a kingdom eternal and universal: 'a kingdom of truth and life, of holiness and grace, of justice, love and peace.' On this earth, that kingdom is already present in mystery; when the Lord returns, it will enter into its fullness" (*Gaudium et Spes*, no. 39).[355]

One of the most manifest limitations of Vatican II's social teaching is reflected in its Eurocentric, or "First World" rootedness. Apart from *Gaudium et Spes'* treatment of economics, attention to the situation in developing nations was lacking at best. In the main, the contribution of the bishops from Latin America in direct interventions from the floor was virtually non-existent. Despite the Council's effort to divest itself of the formerly prevalent attitude seen in the oft-quoted phrase of Hilaire Belloc that, "The Faith is Europe, and Europe is the Faith,"[356] the vast

---

[354]Juan Alfaro, S.J., "Reflections on the Eschatology of Vatican II," in René Latourelle, S.J. (ed.), *Vatican II: Assessments and Perspectives*, Vol. II, p. 512.
[355]"Pastoral Constitution on the Church in the Modern World," in Walter Abbott, S.J., *The Documents of Vatican II*, pp. 237-238.
[356]Hilaire Belloc, *Europe and the Faith* (NY: Paulist Press, 1920), p. 261.

majority of the council fathers were Western Europeans, and reflected the cultural limitations and biases of persons educated and trained prior to World War II. At Vatican II, the 311 bishops from Africa comprised only eight percent of the total, and of them only sixty were native Africans. Too little awareness surfaced that reflected the real situation of the Church in the Southern Hemisphere. Over six hundred Latin American bishops attended the Council (22 percent of the total, though they represented nearly 40 percent of the total Catholic population of the world at the time). They were also disproportionately underrepresented on the study commissions and executive organs of the Council.[357] Some journalists even dubbed the Latin American bishops to be leaders of "a Church of silence."[358] But the presence of bishops like Manuel Larrain and Helder Câmara helped give voice to the needs of the poor and sensitized the Universal Church to global issues of social justice.[359] As one of the foremost early exponents of the theology of liberation, Gustavo Gutiérrez, suggested:

> It is not difficult to understand why the theme of the Church of the poor was largely neglected in Vatican II, despite the efforts of many bishops and other persons during the Council... in the process of Vatican II, the issue of poverty attained only a tiny presence... It is easy to understand (painful but easy): the majority of bishops and experts came from important countries, rich countries that had entered the modern world; they were citizens of the modern world.

---

[357]See Enrique Dussel, *History and the Theology of Liberation: A Latin American Perspective* (Maryknoll, NY: Orbis Books, 1976), p. 112.

[358]One might concur with the comment of Giuseppe Alberigo, "The Christian Situation After Vatican II," in Giuseppe Alberigo, *et al.* (eds.), *The Reception of Vatican II*, p. 11 n. 33, that although the Third World bishops at Vatican II "acted rather as supporters of the Central European leadership and were unable effectively to influence [the work and decisions of the Council], much less go beyond it. This does not mean that they participated passively; on the contrary, the experience of these bishops at the Council was the basis for the role that they and their churches are now playing in the final decades of the Twentieth Century."

[359]For a summary of the role that Câmara and Larrain played at Vatican II, see José de Broucker, *Dom Helder Câmara: The Conversions of a Bishop*, pp. 163-170.

> Poverty, in spite of the empathy and profundity of many who attended the Council, remained a distant question.[360]

Giuseppe Alberigo offered several reasons why the Council fell short in its treatment of the Church and the poor:

> Poverty and peace are economic and political problems, but they are more than that: they are also two dimensions that are keys to the very future of the human race. For this reason they are surely pregnant signs of the Gospel as a message of divine love for human beings. John XXIII had directed attention to this point; Vatican II could not summon up the energy needed to deal with these matters, but it did stimulate the churches to be sensitive to them.[361]

Alberigo observed further that while in the end Vatican II was reserved, if not silent, on these two key problems of contemporary Christian life and experience, in any event the fact of the breakthrough in the process of inquiry began to bear fruit: "In many cases the fruits are undeniably still bitter and unsatisfactory, but they light up the future and nourish hope to the extent that they are pledges of renewed fruitfulness in the womb of a Church that for centuries had produced nothing but stereotyped repetition."[362] Donal Dorr echoed this assessment:

> The treatment by Vatican II of the question of poverty is... deficient; a reason for this is that the perspective is not that of the masses of the world's poor... It was only in the few years *after* the Council that this new spirituality came to the fore... Within a decade it became evident that a notable lacuna had been left in Christian spirituality... It is not

---

[360]Gustavo Gutiérrez, "Church of the Poor," in Edward Cleary, O.P. (ed.), *Born of the Poor: The Latin American Church Since Medellín* (Notre Dame, IN: University of Notre Dame Press, 1990), pp. 12-13.
[361]Giuseppe Alberigo, "The Christian Situation After Vatican II," in Giuseppe Alberigo, *et al.* (eds.), *The Reception of Vatican II*, p. 20.
[362]Ibid., p. 21.

enough to be *for* the poor; one must discover what it means to be *with* the poor.[363]

In retrospect, a certain naive optimism marked the worldview of many of the council fathers and came to dominate the pastoral constitution *Gaudium et Spes*, which underestimated the complexities of the world economic order, and placed excessive confidence in the Church's own role and contribution in the development of humankind on the way to universal prosperity and well-being. Preoccupation with the *ad intra* concerns of the Church may have kept its focus from sufficient consideration of the problem of poverty. On November 21, 1965, a roundtable discussion on the subject of aid to underdeveloped countries held at Paul Gauthier's residence yielded the conclusion that the general public was disappointed in Vatican II because "the Council has attached such importance to problems within the Church and has given so little time to the question of world poverty. There was time to discuss indulgences in the *Aula*, but no time to inform bishops about the problems of underdeveloped nations."[364] As French journalist Henri Fesquet noted:

> On the social plane, Vatican II clearly affirmed the primacy of an equitable distribution of wealth over private property. This is a giant step forward. The episcopacies of underdeveloped countries must draw the practical consequences of this emphasis and vigorously denounce the scandalous injustice of societies that are pagan both in their structures and in their customs. Will the postconciliar Church take up the challenge of those who say, not without reason, that Christian governments serve Mammon more than God?[365]

---

[363]Donal Dorr, *Option for the Poor*, p. 135.
[364]Henri Fesquet, *The Drama of Vatican II*, pp. 780-781.
[365]Ibid., p. 814.

Latin American bishops at the Council issued their own special message to their peoples,[366] and the Mar de Plata, Argentina meeting of the Latin American bishops' conference held from October 9-16, 1966 signaled a continuation in this new direction.[367] Both of these events subsequently exerted great impact on the Medellín Conference convened in Colombia in 1968 by Dom Manuel Larrain, President of CELAM, in conjunction with the quadrennial Eucharistic Congress scheduled for that year that marked the first time that a Pope visited Latin America. CELAM II took as its theme: "The Transformation of the Church in Latin America in Light of the Council," a topic that will receive extensive attention in the subsequent chapter.

During a course on pastoral renewal given during the summer of 1960, Cardinal Montini delivered an address in Milan on the forthcoming "Ecumenical Council in the Life of the Church" He cited German historian Hubert Jedin's observation on the Council of Trent, and applied it to Vatican II: "The Council's deepest significance does not lie in any one doctrine defined, nor in any one reform it instituted: its importance consisted in the fact that it was the true and proper expression of the Catholic concept of the Church."[368] In a letter to dissident traditionalist Archbishop Marcel Lefebvre, dated June 29, 1975, Paul expressed the striking opinion that Vatican II "has no less authority, and, in certain respects, is more important than Nicaea."[369] Cardinal Suenens noted that in the aftermath of the Council, journalists asked him, "'Are you satisfied with the Council?', and I

---

[366]For an English translation of the text, see *Between Honesty and Hope*, pp. 3-12.
[367]See Helder Câmara, "The Church in the Development of Latin America," for the text of a major address at this conference reflecting the imprint of Vatican II, in *The Church and Colonialism: The Betrayal of the Third World*, pp. 112-130.
[368]Pope Paul VI, "*I Concilii Ecumenici nella vita della Chiesa,*" in *The Church* (Montreal: Palm Publishers, 1964), p. 141.
[369]Oddly, this letter was not included in the Vatican's official published collection of documents that contained Paul's teaching for the year 1975. The text is reproduced in "*La Condamnation Sauvauge,*" in *Itinéraires* (September, 1976), p. 45.

answered, 'Yes, it is a new springtime for the Church, but a late-February – early-March springtime; we are still having heavy showers and early morning frosts. But we're moving along."[370] Edward Schillebeeckx remarked that in Catholic circles during the early 1960s, something of a sense of naive optimism pervaded the pastoral constitution *Gaudium et Spes*, in which "the Church had given conciliar definition to its own role and contribution in the great development of humankind on the way to universal prosperity and well-being. But since the 1970s we have been confronted with a very different picture of the world, and we have to be careful and economize."[371]

In his address to a conference of the U.N. Food and Agriculture Organization in 1965, Paul VI displayed a more global consciousness as he noted with alarm that "more than half of the population of the world does not eat enough to appease hunger; entire populations are still undernourished; and from the financial mechanisms of the modern world, it would seem that the gap between the rich and the poor is growing instead of diminishing."[372] In his 1967 social encyclical, *Populorum Progressio*, Paul VI set out "to throw the light of the Gospel on the social questions of the age" (no. 2). By studying the "signs of the times," Pope Paul VI came to this realization as well, and reflected a new direction of social thought in the encyclical,[373] in which he attempted to provide leadership for the present with a sense of continuity for the past: Since the Church does dwell among humanity, it has the duty of "scrutinizing the signs of the times and interpreting them in the light of the

[370]L.-J. Cardinal Suenens, "*Memories & Hopes*," p. 150.

[371]Edward Schillebeeckx, *For the Sake of the Gospel*, p. 138.

[372]Pope Paul VI, "Address to the 13th Session of the Conference of the Food and Agriculture Organization," in The Permanent Observer Mission of the Holy See to the United Nations, *Paths to Peace*, p. 308.

[373]For commentaries on the encyclical, see Vincent Cosmao, *Le Développement des Peuples, Populorum Progressio* (Paris: Centurion, 1967), and Peter J. Riga, *The Church of the Poor: A Commentary on Paul VI's Encyclical "On the Development of Peoples"* (Techny, IL: Divine Word Publications, 1968).

Gospel" (no. 13). Paul observed that "local and individual undertakings are no longer enough. The present situation of the world demands concerted action, based on a clear vision of all economic, social, cultural and spiritual aspects" (no. 13).[374]

Paul issued *Populorum Progressio* on March 26, 1967, less than a year and a half after the promulgation of *Gaudium et Spes*, Cardinal Agostino Casaroli suggested that Pope Paul begin to compile a dossier on "development" upon return from his visit to India in 1964.[375] The appeal that he made in Bombay on December 3, 1964[376] was repeated verbatim in *Populorum Progressio,* "...to work together to build a common future for humanity" (no. 43). Following the tack taken in his address on "No More War" delivered at the United Nations General Assembly on the feast of St. Francis, October 4, 1965, Paul desired that his vision of the linkage between development and peace culminate in an explicit, authoritative document. He was also deeply influenced by the social thought of the French Dominican, Louis Lebret, who served at the Council as a *peritus*, and as a Vatican emissary on various missions connected with the United Nations.[377] Early in the text, Pope Paul cited Lebret authoritatively: "As an eminent specialist has very rightly and emphatically declared, 'We do not believe in separating the economic from the human, nor development from the civilization in which it exists. What we hold important is man, each man and each group of men, and we even include the whole of humanity'"

---

[374]In a message of Paul VI to Raul Prebisch, Secretary-General of the U.N. Conference on Trade and Development, dated January 29, 1968, the Pope noted: "The solutions must come from a moral drive to eliminate the inequalities between developing and developed nations. There is no magic formula for solving the extremely technical and complicated problems involved in restructuring world trade on equitable lines, but unwearying good will and determination to succeed should permeate the technical discussions." Cited in Permanent Observer Mission of the Holy See to the United Nations, *Paths to Peace*, p. 235.

[375]As noted in Cardinal Agostino Casoroli, "Sermon in Brescia Cathedral," September 24, 1984, cited in Peter Hebblethwaite, *Paul VI: The First Modern Pope*, p. 483.

[376]*A.A.S.* 57 (1965), p. 132.

[377]Following Father Lebret's death in 1966, Paul asserted that *Populorum Progressio* would be "a tribute to the memory of Père Lebret." See Peter Hebblethwaite, *Paul VI*, p. 483.

(no. 14).[378] As René Laurentin suggested, Pope Paul desired "to underline the connection between development and peace. It is expressed in the conclusion of the encyclical, 'development is the new name for peace.'" Paul VI borrowed the axiom from the pioneers of the development movement. He had already put the concept into words several months before issuing the encyclical – both in a letter to U.N. Secretary-General U Thant dated May 26, 1966, and during a Mass celebrated on October 4, 1966, in St. Peter's Square, when he commemorated the anniversary of his trip to New York.[379]

One of the key breakthroughs of *Populorum Progressio* was its aim to bring papal social teaching up-to-date, particularly in its international applications (cf. nos. 3, 5, 48-49, 58, 62, 77, 81). Pope Paul VI held that modern people will have to find more equitable and efficacious means to promote international social justice, founded directly on the principle of the solidarity of the human family (nos, 3, 5, 44, 48). In *Populorum Progressio*, he noted: "In communion with the greatest aspirations of men, and suffering from seeing them unsatisfied, the Church desires to help them attain their full stature, and this is why it proposes to them what is its fundamental possession: a global vision of man and humanity" (no. 13). In a turn of the phrase that echoed the anthropology of both John XXIII and *Gaudium et Spes*, the encyclical endorsed the "search of a new humanism... [that] will permit the fullness of authentic

---

[378]Louis J. Lebret, O.P., *Dynamique Concrete du Développement* (Paris: Les Editions Ouvrieres, 1961), p. 28. Note that this theme is enshrined in the universal *Catechism of the Catholic Church* (no. 2459), published in 1994: "Man himself is the author, center and goal of all economic and social life. The decisive point of the social question is that goods created by God for everyone should in fact reach everyone in accordance with justice and charity." Cited in the Doubleday Image translation, p. 650.

[379]See René Laurentin, *Liberation, Salvation and Development* (Maryknoll, New York: Orbis Books, 1972), p. 109. The phrase "development is the new name for peace" was coined by Cardinal Maurice Feltin at Geneva on October 28, 1960. For the full text of Feltin's presentation, see *La Documentation Catholique* (December 4, 1960), col. 1341. Dom Manuel Larrain also helped to popularize the phrase "development is the new name for peace," prior to Paul VI's letter to U.N. Secretary General U Thant of May 26, 1966.

development, a development which is for each and all the transition from less human conditions to those which are more human" (no. 20). Pope Paul stated that "Humanity can only realize itself by reaching beyond its limits," and by being open to God's plan, men and women could experience in "human life its true meaning" (no. 42). He further identified what he considered to be "less human conditions" (i.e., "selfishness, oppressive power structures... abuses of ownership or abuses of power, exploitation of workers or unjust transactions") and "conditions that are more human," (i.e., conditions that "increase esteem for the dignity of others... cooperation for the common good, and the will and the desire for peace" (no. 43). He endeavored to foster what he called "complete humanism" (no. 42) or "transcendent humanism" (no. 16). As Peter Riga commented: "What can be done, once again, progressively, to humanize this system? This is the great question the Pope addresses himself to in *Populorum Progressio*."[380]

In *Populorum Progressio,* the optimism and seeming naïveté of Pope John XXIII was tempered by Pope Paul's more realistic and nuanced perspective of how complicated the social question had become. The very first lines of the document reflected Paul's sober realism: "The development of peoples has the Church's close attention, particularly the development of those peoples who are striving to escape from hunger, misery, endemic diseases, and ignorance; of those who are looking for a wider share in the benefits of civilization" (no. 1). Paul graphically outlined his position: "The world is sick. Its illness consists less in the unproductive monopolization of resources by a small number of people than in the lack of brotherhood among individuals and peoples" (no. 66). In the encyclical, the Church renewed its commitment to the integral promotion of the poorest peoples, a point that was inadequately made at the Council. As Paul noted in its text, "Today the principal

---

[380]Peter Riga, *The Church of the Poor*, p. 44.

fact we must all recognize is that the social question has become worldwide" (no. 3). He concluded: "We want to be clearly understood: the present situation must be faced with courage and the injustice linked with it must be fought against and overcome. Development demands bold transformations, innovations that go deep. Urgent reforms must be undertaken without delay" (no. 32). This approach departed from the older, more fatalistic approach that encouraged the poor to await their reward in paradise, and to offer up their human miseries as a purgation incurred by life in this earthly "vale of tears" (cf. nos. 9 and 12). As Peter Hebblethwaite stated:

> ...previous social encyclicals, including *Mater et Magistra* of Pope John XXIII, had been written from a predominantly "European" point of view, with North Americans included as honorary Europeans. With *Populorum Progressio* the Church became truly Catholic, universal and planetary.[381]

Paul followed in the tradition of *Pacem in Terris*, and more directly, *Gaudium et Spes*, which without reservation condemned the arms race: "...extravagant sums are being spent for the furnishing of ever new weapons, [so that] an adequate remedy cannot be provided for the multiple miseries afflicting the modern world... it must be said again: the arms race is a treacherous trap for humanity, and one that injures the poor to an intolerable degree" (no. 81). In *Populorum Progressio,* Paul excoriated the fact of the "wasteful expenditures" of the "exhausting armaments race" to be "an intolerable public scandal" (no. 53).

As Hebblethwaite suggested further, "[*Populorum Progressio*'s] main theme was the interdependence of all the peoples of spaceship earth. It was a prophetic document in that it was ahead of most conventional wisdom of the 1960s. It anticipated that the North-South conflict would turn out to more important than that

---

[381]Peter Hebblethwaite, *Paul VI*, p. 483.

between East and West."[382] Paul began to acknowledge a shift away from the East-West conflict, and to view the division of the world more properly between rich and poor, between the industrially advanced and wealthy nations of the "North" (those situated above the Tropic of Cancer) and a still pre-modernized, pre-technological, poverty-ridden "South" which had been drawn into the vortex of the world economy, but could neither compete on equal footing, nor derive a fair share of its benefits: "Nations whose industrialization is limited are faced with serious difficulties when they have to rely on their plans for development. The poor nations remain ever poor, while the rich ones become still richer" (no. 57). As Barbara Ward pointed out in her commentary on *Populorum Progressio*: "...it is to these conflicts, product of a divided world, rooted in history, sustained by interest, resented by the 'South' and all too often ignorantly taken for granted in the 'North' that the whole encyclical is aimed."[383] Paul rejected unequivocally many of the basic tenets of capitalism, including unrestricted private property, the profit motive, and reliance on "free trade" within the global economy.

For Paul VI, "development" assumed social, as well as economic dimensions, since "economic growth depends in the first place upon social progress" (no. 35). The Pope noted within the body of the encyclical that people ought "to discover, themselves, in faithfulness to their own genius, the means toward their own social and human progress" (no. 64), and are entitled to share in a growing "world solidarity... [that] must allow all peoples to become themselves the artisans of their own destiny" (no. 65), and "have the prime responsibility to work for their own development" (no. 77). As Donal Dorr stated:

---

[382]Peter Hebblethwaite, "The Popes and Politics: Shifting Patterns in Catholic Social Doctrine," in Charles Curran and Richard McCormick, *Readings in Moral Theology No. 5*, p. 271.
[383]Barbara Ward, "Commentary," in *On The Development of Peoples* (New York: Paulist Press, 1967), p. 6.

> The encyclical has as a central theme the idea that every person and all peoples are entitled to be the shapers of their own destiny. This is one of the most important contributions of *Populorum Progressio* to the understanding of development: it is not possible to develop people; development is something people have to do for themselves.[384]

Barbara Ward observed a decade after the publication of the encyclical: "It is very striking reading *Populorum Progressio* again, to note how much this sense that *people* are at stake, dominates the encyclical; the reminder that development is for people, and, unless they are the actors in their own drama, there can be no true development."[385] In a similar vein, Dom Helder Câmara remarked: "Paul VI was courageous enough to say that what the developed countries gave with one hand they took away with the other."[386] It is no accident that Paul's harsh critique of the excesses of liberal capitalism within *Populorum Progressio*[387] aroused the ire of *The Wall Street Journal*, which charged that he was serving up "warmed-over Marxism."[388] Following in the tradition of *Quadragesimo Anno*, Paul echoed Pius XI's condemnation of "the international imperialism of money," in rejecting that a just economic order could be built on the principles and ideology of liberal capitalism, on "profit as the key motive for economic progress, competition as the supreme law of economics, and private ownership of the means of production as an absolute right that has no limits and carries no corresponding social obligation" (no.

---

[384]Donal Dorr, *Option for the Poor*, p. 152.

[385]Barbara Ward, "Looking Back on *Populorum progessio*," in Charles Curran and Richard McCormick (eds.), *Readings in Moral Theology No. 5: Official Catholic Social Teaching* (New York: Paulist Press, 1986), p. 133.

[386]José de Broucker, *Dom Helder Câmara: The Conversions of a Bishop*, p. 172.

[387]See nos. 7, 26, 34, 52, 54, 59, 63, 70.

[388]In fact, the encyclical explicitly rejected Marxist analysis: "The Christian cannot admit that which is based upon a materialist and atheist philosophy, which respects neither the religious orientation of life to its final end, nor human freedom and dignity" (no. 39).

26). Paul attempted to counter this mentality by asserting the duties of more developed nations:

> The obligations stem from a brotherhood that is at once human and supernatural, and takes on a three-fold aspect: first, the duty of human solidarity – the aid that the rich nations must give to developing countries; next, the duty of social justice – the rectification of inequitable trade relations between powerful nations and weak nations; finally, the duty of universal charity – the effort to bring about a world that is more human toward all men, where all will be able to give and receive, without one group making progress at the expense of the other. The question is urgent, for on it depends the whole future of the civilization of the world (no. 44).

By proposing the principle of solidarity of the rich and poor (nos. 48-49, 76-77) and of dialogue (nos. 54, 73), Paul set about to encourage cooperative planning on a global scale (nos. 50-52, 60-61, 64, 78). In the body of the text of *Populorum Progressio*, Paul made the bold claim: "One must recognize that it is the fundamental principle of liberalism [i.e., liberal capitalism], as the rule for commercial exchange, which is in question here" (no. 58). He spoke explicitly of "the reorganization which is required [that] will allow peoples still underdeveloped to break through the barriers that seem to enclose them" (no. 64). He further suggested:

> ...the superfluous wealth of rich countries should be placed at the service of poor nations. The rule which up to now held good for the benefit of those nearest to us, must today be applied to all of the needy of the world. Besides, the rich will be the first to benefit as a result. Otherwise, their continued greed will certainly call down on them the judgment of God and the wrath of the poor, with consequences no one can foretell" (no. 49).[389]

---

[389]Here, Paul VI extends beyond the teaching of *Gaudium et Spes*: "Advanced nations have a very serious obligation to help developing peoples" (no. 86).

In addition, Pope Paul noted that "every program, made to increase production, has, in the last analysis, no other *raison d'être* than the service of man" (no. 34). He denounced "stifling materialism" (no. 18) as the bane of the developed world, and warned against the temptations attendant to material prosperity (no. 41). In a later public address, Paul scored the imbalance between "overdeveloped means and underdeveloped ends."[390] Pope Paul decried "the scandal of glaring inequalities not merely in the enjoyment of possessions but even more in the exercise of power" (no. 9). He later returned to this theme in 1974, in a message delivered to the United Nations General Assembly on the problems of development:

> Convinced as we are that a new order of development will promote peace and serve he genuine advantages of all, we appeal to the developed nations to make greater efforts to forgo their own immediate advantages, and to adopt a new lifestyle that will exclude both excessive consumption and those superfluous needs that are often artificially engendered... One should not forget that a lifestyle based on ever greater consumption has deleterious effects on nature and the environment and finally on the moral fiber of man himself, especially the young.[391]

In Latin America, in particular, a sustained theological analysis of the root causes of poverty began to take place, which held profound implications for church life. In an influential work that appeared during the final session of the Council, *Desarrollo. Exito o fracaso en América Latina* ("Development: Success or Failure in Latin America?"), Dom Manuel Larrain pointedly commented: "Wretched conditions, hunger, and the sickness hunger brings with it lead every year to as many

---

[390]Pope Paul VI, "Address to the International Seminar of Catholic European periodicals and the African Society of Culture," October 2, 1969, in Permanent Observer Mission of the Holy See to the United Nations, *Paths of Peace*, p. 114.
[391]Pope Paul VI, "Message to Secretary-General Kurt Waldheim on the Occasion of the Extraordinary Session of the General Assembly on the Problems of Raw Materials and Development," April 4, 1974, in Permanent Observer Mission of the Holy See to the United Nations, *Paths of Peace*, p. 216.

deaths in the Third World as occurred in the four years of the Second World War... The history of the world has never seen a crueler struggle. The tax in blood that the underdeveloped world is paying is a scandal that cries out to the heavenly Father."[392] Gustavo Gutiérrez agreed with Larrain's analysis:

> In a continent like Latin America, the main challenge does not come from the non-believer but from the *non-human* – i.e., the human being who is not recognized as such by the prevailing social order. These are the poor and exploited people, the ones who are systematically and legally despoiled of their being human, those who scarcely know what a human being might be.[393]

A similar perspective was enunciated by Segundo Galilea:

> In Latin America we are dealing with the right to work, to earn a minimum wage, to be fed, to acquire a basic education, not to live in permanent insecurity, not to be systematically deprived and discriminated against and to have workers' organizations. In Latin America, the rights of man are the rights of the poor.[394]

By the end of the 1960s, the chasm between the rich and poor nations dramatically deepened, rather than decreased. The concept of "developmentalism" came to be seen by many to typify tokenism, exploitation, and paternalism.[395] The Prebisch report compiled by the Secretary-General of the United Nations Conference

---

[392]Manuel Larrain, *Desarrollo. Exito o fracaso en América Latina* (Santiago de Chile: Ediciones Mundo, 1965), p. 2. *Populorum Progressio* contains a strong echo of this final phrase: "There are certainly situations whose injustice cries to heaven" (no. 30); cf. also the opening lines of the Puebla "Final Document."

[393]Gustavo Gutiérrez, "Liberation Praxis and Christian Faith," in Rosino Gibbellini (ed.), *Frontiers of Theology in Latin America*, p. x.

[394]Segundo Galilea, "The Church in Latin America and the Struggle for Human Rights," in *The Church and the Rights of Man* (New York: Seabury, 1979,) pp. 104-105.

[395]See Gustavo Gutiérrez, *A Theology of Liberation* (Maryknoll, NY: Orbis Books, 1973), pp. 13-25, 49-57.

on Trade and Development conceded the disastrous results of the misnamed "Decade of Development." Gradually, the vapid, wide-ranging confidence in "development" was replaced by disappointment in and rejection of "developmentalism," when social and behavioral scientists and theologians began to espouse a different interpretation of "underdevelopment." This emerging point of view spurred the struggle for liberation forward, especially among progressive clergy and laity in Latin America.

As Dom Helder Câmara suggested of *Populorum Progressio*, "It was an impressive document that showed quite clearly how, under the cover of international solidarity, the rich were becoming richer and the poor poorer."[396] Câmara reflected the new direction undertaken in Latin America:

> We now prefer, in Brazil and in the rest of Latin America, to speak of "liberation," and... to ensure that this word does not become degraded as the word "development" became degraded. It didn't take long for people to forget the true definition of development, the one given by François Perroux and cited by Paul VI: "the development of the whole man and of all men."[397]

As a renewed anthropology and a heightened awareness of injustice began to take hold many Latin American Christians, in particular, reflected upon and interpreted their situations in terms of domination and colonialism, both internal and external. They undertook to analyze the structures of social and political injustice with new eyes. In time, the theme of "liberation" became the key idea for many to both ministry and theological reflection. Some church leaders revamped the traditional alliances with the ruling classes and began to distance themselves from those in power, while placing themselves closer to, or even among, the materially poor. Pope Paul VI augured this shift in the letter he sent to the Latin American

---

[396]Helder Câmara, *The Conversions of a Bishop*, p. 178.
[397]Ibid., p. 90.

episcopal conference meeting at Mar del Plata, Argentina in 1966: "Development must be integral if it is to be authentic, raising up the whole person and the whole of humanity... guided by the principle of unity."[398]

As Gustavo Gutiérrez noted, the position staked out by Pope Paul VI on "integral development" (cf. *Populorum Progressio*, no. 21) formed a bridge to the foundation of the liberation theology movement, and aided "to establish the distinction between the three levels of a single process of liberation... Paul VI thus threw significant light on the problems we were facing at that time in our pastoral activity."[399] This profound shift helped to launch the fledgling theology of liberation, as the next chapter demonstrates.

---

[398]Cited in Helder Câmara, *The Church and Colonialism: The Betrayal of the Third World* (Denville, New Jersey: Dimension Books, 1969), p. 170.

[399]Gustavo Gutiérrez, *The Truth Shall Make You Free/ Confrontations* (Maryknoll, New York: Orbis Books, 1990), pp. 119, 120.

Chapter Three

The Birth of Liberation Theology and Medellín

At the Second Vatican Council, the Roman Catholic Church embraced engagement in the social sphere and preached active involvement in solidarity with the poor and oppressed of the world.[400] Vatican II presented itself as the Church's response "to the outstanding problems of our time" (*Gaudium et Spes*, no. 10). As Latin American theologian Hugo Cabal indicated, Pope John XXIII "let fresh air into the Church; he opened the windows to our world, even doors and floodgates. 'John's revolution' found expression in Vatican II, which he conceived and prepared for the liberation of the dormant energies of the Church."[401] Pope John's much-heralded "New Pentecost" shifted the axis of theological reflection to the Third World, and gave rise to a "new paradigm" that redirected the Church's focus from "the center to the periphery" that began to recast the formulation of traditional theology to the grassroots and from the vantage point of the poor. However, Vatican II's thrust was limited by constraints of time and competing *agendas*. Gutiérrez noted that the proclamation of the Gospel to the poor was broached at Vatican II, especially by Pope John XXIII's September 11, 1962 radio address and the intervention in the *aula* by Cardinal Lercaro at the close of the First Session, but concluded: "At Medellín, however, it did become the main question: it was the context of the preferential option for the poor that inspired the main text of the [CELAM II] conference."[402] As

---

[400]See, especially, *Gaudium et Spes* (nos. 1, 69, and 88), and *Lumen Gentium* (no. 8).

[401]Hugo Cabal, *The Revolution of the Latin American Church* (Norman, OK: University of Oklahoma Press, 1978), p. 12.

[402]Gustavo Gutierrez, "Option for the Poor," in *Mysterium Liberationis*, p. 249.

Roberto Oliveros noted, the Latin American bishops at Vatican II were largely described as "the Church of silence" and the Council did not formally render issues relating to the "Church of the Poor" explicit, but rather "it stood at the door, beckoning."[403] Prior to calling the Council, Pope John expressed great concern about the social conditions of Latin America, and demonstrated his desire for the Church to insert itself as an agent of social change. In November, 1958, he directed a letter to the Latin American bishops in which he appealed for "an awakening to the grave situation of this continent, and of the challenges and demands to be confronted by the Church."[404] In November, 1961, Pope John made a dramatic appeal to the bishops of Latin America, with the example of Castro's recent revolution in Cuba very much in mind: "That the bishops should demonstrate to the governments and all those responsible the urgency of structural reforms and improvement for the underdeveloped masses; that the hierarchy and the Church, in a subsidiary fashion, should cooperate in this improvement and participate actively in it."[405]

Vatican II continued in this vein to reveal a deepening aspiration to "poverty" and structural change within the Church, largely due to the personal influence of Pope John; the leavening presence of Paul Gauthier, Helder Câmara, the "Church of the Poor" and "Belgian College" groups; and, the active participation of bishops from the developing nations. As Gustavo Gutiérrez points out: "The deep, demanding evangelical theme of the proclamation of the Gospel to the poor was broached at Vatican II but it did not become its central question; it was the context of the preferential option for the poor that inspired the major texts of the [Medellín]

---

[403]Roberto Oliveros, "History of the Theology of Liberation," in *Mysterium Liberationis*, pp. 14, 12.
[404]Cited in Alceu Amoroso Lima, *Joaõ XXIII* (Rio de Janeiro: Livraria José Olympio Editora, 1966), p. 114.
[405]Cited in Raimundo Caramuru de Barros, *Brasil: uma Ingreja em renovaçao* (Petropolis: Editorial Vozes, 1967), p. 24.

conference."[406] The heightened social consciousness of the Council also mirrored the mature development and appropriation of the methodology of the various Jocist movements that helped pave the way for a renewed consciousness of social theory and practice and set the stage for what was arguably the most important theological breakthrough in Latin American history: the "preferential option for the poor." But viewed from the perspective of the Church of Latin America, the agenda of Vatican II was incomplete. As Gustavo Gutiérrez pointed out:

> Pope John XXIII gave the Council the task of opening the Church to the world, finding an appropriate theological language, and bearing witness to a Church of the poor. After it had overcome its initial difficulties, the Church fulfilled the first of these two demands... The third task given by John XXIII to the Council barely appears in its texts. The theme of poverty, "Schema XIV" as it was called in the Council corridors, knocked at the Church's door, but only got a glimpse inside.[407]

As Karl Rahner suggested, a great transformation of Catholicism took place following the Second Vatican Council, a "transition from one historical and theological situation to an essentially new one," which resulted in a change from "a Christianity of Europe... to a fully world religion."[408] Rahner saw the Council as "the first major official event in which the Church actualized itself precisely as a world Church," and concluded that in the aftermath of Vatican II it entered a period "in which the sphere of the Church's life is in fact the entire world."[409] Rahner believed that the desire of the Church to embrace its universal character in the latter decades

---

[406]Gustavo Gutiérrez, "Option for the Poor," in Ellacuría and Sobrino (eds.), *Mysterium Liberationis*, p. 249.

[407]Gustavo Gutiérrez, "The Poor in the Church," in Norbert Greinbächer and Alois Müller (eds.), *The Poor and the Church* (NY: Seabury Press, 1977), pp. 12-13.

[408]Karl Rahner, S.J., "Towards a Fundamental Theological Understanding of Vatican II," in *Theological Studies* 40 (December, 1979), p. 722.

[409]Ibid., p. 717.

of the Twentieth Century could only be compared to its decision in the First Century to evangelize Gentiles. Johannes Baptist Metz echoed Rahner's view of the "coming of the Third Church." He viewed the post-conciliar Church as "a culturally polycentric genuinely universal Church whose first hints and beginnings showed themselves at Vatican II."[410] In region like Latin America, the pastoral challenges emanated not primarily from the non-believer, but from the "non-person," that is, from those who were marginalized and not treated as human by the dominant social order. As Gustavo Gutiérrez proposed, from a Latin American perspective, "... the question is not so much how to speak of God in a world come of age, as how to proclaim God in an inhuman world, the implications of what it means to tell the non-person that he or she is a child of God."[411]

The overarching spirit of the Council, coupled with the thrust of its sixteen documents, yielded several decisive end results. It officially legitimated a church renewal already well underway in parts of Latin America. As Clodovis Boff argued, before the emergence of liberation theology at the end of the 1960s, "a full-fledged liberation praxis was already underway in Latin America... A life *practice* was well underway even in the early 1960s. The *theology* of liberation, then, came in a 'second moment.' It came as the expression of this liberation praxis on the part of the Church."[412] The groundwork laid in liberation theology's "first movement" provided the impetus for the Church in Latin America to implement a creative acceptance of the Council from a point of departure different from that of the Council's own anticipation, conception, and realization, that is, from the viewpoint of the poor.

---

[410]See Johannes Baptist Metz, "Standing at the End of the Eurocentric Era of Christianity: A Catholic View," in Virginia Fabella, M.M. and Sergio Torres (eds.), *Doing Theology in a Divided World* (Maryknoll, NY: Orbis Books, 1985), pp. 85-90.
[411]Gustavo Gutiérrez, "*Prassi di liberazione, teología e annuncio*," in *Concilium* 6 (1974), pp. 87-88.
[412]Clodovis Boff, *Liberation Theology: From Confrontation to Dialogue* (San Francisco: Harper & Row, 1986), p. 9.

Another prime element in this transformation came as a direct response to the rise of Castro and the inroads of the communist revolution in Cuba. As Pablo Richard suggested, "the Cuban Revolution propelled the anti-Communist Latin American Church to go to the poor."[413] Gradually, the focus of the Church and its leadership shifted away from the desire to fight communism to seek to redress the root causes of social ferment: hunger, malnutrition, poverty, and exploitation. In Latin America, the Church redefined its Mission as a commitment to the liberation of the oppressed. The bishops and theologians of the region began to apply the social teaching of the Church to Latin American reality, and set out to enrich and expand upon the conciliar doctrine from a point of departure based in the reality of the poor and oppressed.[414]

Already by the time of the appearance of *Populorum Progressio* in 1967, the Universal Church was moving to embrace the poor of the developing world. The undergirding philosophy of the encyclical's guiding light, the French Dominican Louis Lebret,[415] favored a "developmental economics" that sought to move from a less human to a more human stage of integral human development. This approach embodied a dynamic and historical concept of the human person that looked toward the future, and evaluated present-day reality in order to shape a more promising lot for the oppressed of the world. What Pope Paul VI said of "integral development" in paragraphs 14-21 of *Populorum Progressio* began to inspire the concept of "integral liberation" or "total liberation" that took root within Latin America.[416]

---

[413]Cited in Christian Smith, *The Emergence of Liberation Theology* (Chicago: University of Chicago Press, 1991), p. 93.

[414]See Pablo Richard, *La Iglesia latino-americano entre el temor y la esperanza: apuntes teologicos para la decada de los años 80 (*San José, Costa Rica: Departamento Ecumenico de Investigaciones, 1981).

[415]See François Malley, *La Père Lebret: l'Economie au Service des Hommes* (Paris: Cerf, 1986).

[416]Gustavo Gutiérrez acknowledges his debt in developing his theology of liberation an the concept of the "preferential option for the poor" to *Populorum Progressio* in *A Theology of Liberation* (Maryknoll, NY: Orbis Books, 1973), pp. 36-37, 171-172, 176-178.

This new approach to theology linked the two elements of commitment to the poor, and the growth of the grassroots church communities. As Leonardo Boff suggested, the post-conciliar Church in Latin America moved from the model of the "Church in the world" to the "Church in the sub-world." This shift became possible only because of the renewal initiated at Vatican II. As Boff indicated:

> Medellín defined the position of the Church as being in the subworld of the poor. It abandoned a developmentalist discourse and began to speak of integral liberation and justice for all. It chose to take flesh in the subordinate classes and supported the base church communities, the natural locus of realization of the new face of the Church. The significance of Medellín was precisely in this turnabout in the Church. Medellín defined the new social locus from which the Church would henceforth organize its presence in the world. Now the door was open for a new historical enterprise. Now the gospel would be taken over by the poor and used by them for the purpose for which it is written... the integral liberation of the oppressed.[417]

Enrique Dussel noted similarly:

> Under the inspiration of the renewal of Vatican II... [the Church] modified its national and Latin American structures, the "spirit" of its institutions. It has taken on a new face towards the poor of the continent... It is no longer a distant, clerical body, churchy, exclusively inward-looking. It has gone into the streets and has won a place in Latin American civilization as perhaps never before, and this has not been "from above" but "from below." Liberation theology is the considered result of this profound renewal.[418]

In the years leading up to Medellín, a gradual intensification and more consistent shift in the focus of the Latin American Church occurred "from the center

---

[417]Leonardo Boff, *Faith on the Edge: Religion and Marginalized Experience* (San Francisco: Harper & Row, 1989), p. 13.

[418]Enrique Dussel, "Latin America," in Adrian Hastings (ed.), *Modern Catholicism*, p. 321.

to the margins," to employ the oft-cited term of Archbishop José María Pires.[419] Pope Paul VI helped to initiate this movement. In marking the tenth anniversary of CELAM (the Latin American bishops' conference), on November 23, 1965 Pope Paul VI delivered an address in the Vatican's Clementine Hall on the need for pastoral planning "on the continental level." He invited Bishops Manuel Larrain and Helder Câmara, the principal architects of CELAM, to contribute to the text, and noted that without proper attention to the widening gap between rich and poor in the developing nations, attraction to "the social message of Marxism" would grow, along with the propensity for 'violent revolution.'"[420] This ongoing development in church social teaching gave rise to what Leonardo Boff outlined as the three great "options," or choices confirmed at Medellín: "for the poor, for their integral liberation, and for the base church communities."[421]

In this context, many of the pastoral statements that emanated from Latin America following Vatican II reflected a new ideology. Echoing the address of Pope Paul VI at the close of the Second Vatican Council,[422] the Latin American bishops stated in the "Introduction to the Final Documents" at Medellín: "The Latin American Church... has in no way 'detoured from' but has actually 'returned to' humanity, aware that 'in order to know God it is necessary to know the human person'... [and move] from conditions of life that are less human to those that are more human" (no. 6).[423] Too often, the Church in Latin America appeared to be co-opted by a social order the pitted the powerful against the weak, and sided with the oligarchy against the masses. Gustavo Gutiérrez criticized this stance:

---

[419]José María Pires, *Do centro para a margem* (Petropolis, Brazil: Editorial Vozes, 1980).
[420]Pope Paul VI, *Insegamenti* 1965, pp. 656-657. See Peter Hebblethwaite, *Pope Paul VI*, p. 448.
[421]Leonardo Boff, *Faith on the Edge*, p. 13.
[422]Pope Paul VI, "Address of December 7, 1965," in *The Catholic Mind* (April, 1966), pp. 62-63.
[423]Documents of the Medellín Conference, "Introduction to the Final Document," p. 49.

> The protection which the Church receives from the social class which is the beneficiary and the defender of the prevailing capitalist society in Latin America has made the institutional Church into a part of the system and the Christian message into the dominant ideology. Any claim of non-involvement in politics... is nothing but a subterfuge to keep things the way they are.[424]

Increasingly, the Latin American Church began to take the side of the oppressed, and felt compelled to make this option for the poor on the basis of a new reading of the biblically-based claims of faith in the historical Jesus. For the Latin American Church, Medellín represented less of an application of Vatican II than a reformulation of the effects of the Council in light of the region's own theological and social experience and practice, which varied drastically from the realities of the First World. As Pablo Richard indicated:

> In Europe the theological challenge to the Church was the structure of modern atheism of modern society and its proclamation of the death of God. In Latin America, the theological challenge was exploitation and underdevelopment which was causing the death of the human being. As it dealt with the modern world, the European Church came to feel how far away it was from that world and sought to bring about reconciliation. The Latin American Church, by contrast, felt too identified with the modern world and sought to break away from it.[425]

Within the Latin American context, little discussion transpired concerning the notion of the "death of God," but rather, concern focused upon the "death of the people." As Leonardo Boff pointed out, a climate of despair was in full swing, at the hands of "a death-dealing social system that reduced men and women to the status

---

[424]Gustavo Gutiérrez, *A Theology of Liberation*, pp. 265-266.
[425]Pablo Richard, *Death of Christendoms, Birth of the Church* (Maryknoll, NY: Orbis Books, 1987), p. 5).

of sub-humans. The key question of the 1960s – and still the great question assailing the Christian conscience in Latin America today – was, 'What does it mean to be a Christian in the world of the oppressed?'"[426] Within the context of Central America, as Ignacio Ellacuría, the Jesuit sociologist later murdered at the El Salvador's University of Central America also observed:

> The underlying reality of this extreme situation is not the repression, but the structural injustice and the institutionalized violence, which, based on an immoral distribution in the ownership of resources, has created an economic, social, political and military structure that is ultimately responsible and the originating cause of what is currently happening...[427]

The encounter between the Church and the world in Latin America conspired to yield a new "*compromiso*," or "commitment" to the poor, who make up the vast majority of humankind. Although no English equivalent adequately rendered the phrase, "*pastoral de acompañamiento*," the "pastoral stance of accompaniment" suggested and required solidarity with the poor and witness to evangelical values of simplicity and concern for the oppressed. In the celebrated phrase of Mexican Bishop José María Gonzalez Ruíz, post-Vatican II Catholicism in Latin America required that "to believe is to be committed" ("*creer is comprometerse*").[428] A new focus evolved, directed toward the transformation of economic, social, political, and ideological structures. In this light, as Segundo Galilea observed, liberation theology was able to come to birth, rooted in three key assumptions about Latin America: that the vast majority of its inhabitants live in a state of underdevelopment and unjust dependence; that viewed from the lens of Christian morality, this reality constitutes

---

[426]See Leonardo Boff, *When Theology Listens to the Poor* (SF: Harper & Row, 1988), p. 10.
[427]Ignacio Ellacuría, S.J., "*Solución politica o solución militar para El Salvador?*," in *Revista UCA* (April/May, 1981), pp. 295-296.
[428]José María Gonzalez Ruíz, *Creer es comprometerse* (Barcelona: Fontanella, 1967).

a "sinful situation"; and, as a consequence, Christians have a duty in conscience to commit themselves to work to overcome this situation.[429] Gustavo Gutiérrez extended upon these points in an early essay entitled, "Freedom and Liberation":

> For years a growing number of Christians have shared in the revolutionary process in Latin America and thereby in the discovery of the world of the exploited people of the continent. This commitment is the major event in the life of the Latin American Christian community. It leads to a new way of being a person and a believer, to a new way of living and thinking the faith, to a new way of being gathered into the "*ecclesia.*" This commitment creates a dividing line between two experiences, two epochs, two worlds, two languages in Latin America and thus in the Church.[430]

Already during the course of the Council, Pope John XXIII recognized the necessity to "compare different cultures and traditions, and know that the moment has come to discern the signs of the times, to seize the opportunity, and to expand the view."[431] Pope Paul VI also seized on the notion of the "signs of the times." The groundwork laid by the *Gaudium et Spes'* application of the concept of the "signs of the times" prompted a new examination of present-day reality in Latin America that led in turn to renewed pastoral action. At the conclusion of the Council, Dom Manuel Larrain stated: "This has been a deeply moving experience, but unless we in Latin America are attentive to our own 'signs of the times,' the Council will pass our Church by, and who knows what will happen then?"[432] In 1968, in their "Message to the Peoples of Latin America," the bishops at Medellín stated: "In light of the faith

---

[429]See Segundo Galilea, "Liberation Theology and New Tasks Facing Christians," in Rosino Gibellini (ed.), *Frontiers of Theology in Latin America* (Maryknoll, NY: Orbis Books, 1979), p. 167.
[430]Gustavo Gutiérrez, "Freedom and Liberation," in Gustavo Gutiérrez and Richard Schaull, *Liberation and Change* (Atlanta: John Knox Press, 1977), p. 77.
[431]Pope John XXIII, "Statement of May 24, 1963," in Loris Capovilla (ed.), *Ite, Misa Est*, p. 212.
[432]Cited in Gustavo Gutiérrez, "The Church and the Poor: A Latin American Perspective," in Giuseppe Alberigo, *et al.* (eds.), *The Reception of Vatican II*, p. 184.

that we possess as believers, we have undertaken to discover the plan of God in the 'signs of the times.' We interpret the aspirations and clamors of Latin America as signs that reveal the direction of the divine plan."[433] At Medellín, the bishops further extended upon this theme:

> Many parts of Latin America are experiencing a situation of injustice which can be called institutional violence. The structures of industry and agriculture, of the national and international economy, the cultural and political life all violate fundamental rights. Entire peoples lack the bare necessities and live in a culture of such dependency that they can exercise neither initiative nor responsibility. Similarly, they lack all possibility of cultural improvement and of participation in social and political life. Such situations call for global, daring, urgent, and basically renewing change.[434]

In Latin American Catholicism, the slogan "to believe is to practice" gained increasing currency.[435] As Leonardo Boff asserted: "In our present historical situation noncommitment would signify acceptance of the existing situation and a subtle stand in favor of those already favored."[436]

Vatican II exerted enormous impact upon the Latin American Church. The six hundred assembled Latin American bishops learned to work together more collaboratively, and underwent a profound, collective educational and integrational process. The ties that they formed proved to be binding, and their four years at the

---

[433]Documents of the Medellín Conference are found in standard English translation in *The Church in the Present Day Transformation of Latin America in Light of the Council: Conclusions* Vol. III (Washington, DC: Latin American Division, United States Catholic Conference, 1970), p. 38.

[434]*Documentos Finales de Medellín* (Buenos Aires: Ediciones Paulinas, 1969), p. 50.

[435]Cf. Gustavo Gutiérrez: "Practice is the locus of verification of our faith in God, who liberates by establishing justice and right in favor of the poor... The only faith-life is the one the Scriptures call 'witness.' And witness is born in works. To believe is to practice," in *The Power of the Poor in History*, p. 17.

[436]Leonardo Boff, *Jesus Christ Liberator: A Critical Christology for Our Time* (Maryknoll, NY: Orbis Books, 1978), p. 275.

Council brought them together in a way that no other experience could have. This renewal continued in Latin America after the close of the Council, as noted by Enrique Dussel:

> In 1968 the bishops held their Second General Conference in Medellín, and this produced a dividing line: between a developmentalist Church and one committed to liberation. The theology of liberation was born at the same time as a widespread acceptance of political commitment to the cause of the "oppressed" – oppressed by "developmentalism," by dependent capitalism, and now by cruel and bloodthirsty dictatorships.[437]

The Church patterned on European lines at Vatican II began to be supplanted in Latin America in the late 1960's by a "Church of the Poor" model, which Dussel also described as, "intent on committing itself to the poor themselves, being with the poor, oppressed and starving people, and with them creating a new theology, a new pastoral strategy."[438] Prior to the Medellín Conference, the previous social agenda of the Latin American Church was remarkably lacking. For instance, no bishops from the region bothered to attend the first Catholic Inter-American Social Action Conference at Havana in 1945, where the most serious challenges discussed were the shortage of priests and the inroads of Protestant proselytism. Journalist Gary McEoin, who attended the meeting as an observer for the Archbishop of Trinidad, reported: "Nobody expressed concern about the need for land reform, the rapid population growth without a corresponding expansion of the economy, or the social issues raised by urbanization."[439] In 1952, Helder Câmara suggested to the then-Monsignor Giovanni Battista Montini (the Vatican Substitute Secretary of State) the

---

[437]Enrique Dussel, "General Introduction," in *The Church in Latin America: 1492-1962*, p. 15.
[438]Ibid., p. 16.
[439]Gary MacEoin, *Central America's Options: Death or Life* (Kansas City, MO: Sheed & Ward, 1988), p. 53.

idea of setting up a continent-wide conference, with a secretariat to serve all of the bishops of Latin America.[440] Later, at the 1955 Bandung Conference (where the phase, "Third World"[441] was coined), the term "development" began to be utilized in order to lend greater currency to the growing aspirations for more human conditions of life in the developing nations.[442] Even the first conference of the Latin American bishops held in Rio de Janiero in 1955 (when CELAM took form) had as its major ecclesial concerns the shortage of clergy and the aggressive inroads of Protestant proselytism.[443] In direct response to the rise to power of Fidel Castro in Cuba, some elements in the Church in Latin America undertook to construct a "theology of development."[444] The rise to prominence of progressive Latin American bishops like Helder Câmara, Manuel Larrain, Leonidas Proano, Enrique Angelelli, Enrique Alvear, Raul Silva, and Juan Landázuri Ricketts signaled the passing of the exclusively conservative tilt of the pre-conciliar Church. The leadership of Silva, Larrain, and Câmara in particular proved pivotal to this development. While Brazil led the field in this movement, a similar transformation occurred in Chile.[445] The text of Câmara's address on "The Church in Latin America" presented at the tenth convention of CELAM at Mar del Plata, Argentina, in 1966 mirrored this profound shift: "CELAM must direct the attention of episcopal conferences to the number one

---

[440]See Helder Câmara, *L'Evangile avec Dom Helder* (Paris: Editions du Seuil, 1985), and José DeBroucker, *Dom Helder Câmara: The Conversions of a Bishop*, p. 135.

[441]See Monika Hellwig, "Liberation Theology: An Emerging School," p. 138.

[442]ee Gustavo Gutiérrez, "Liberation Movements and Theology," in Edward Schillebeeckx and Bas van Iersel, *Jesus Christ and Human Freedom* (NY: Herder & Herder, 1974), p. 137.

[443]See Gary MacEoin and Nivita Riley, *Puebla: A Church Being Born* (NY: Paulist Press, 1980), p. 124.

[444]See Jiminéz Urresti, "*La Teología de liberación: antecedentes, causas, y contenidos*," in *Teología de la liberación* (Burgos, Spain: Diego de Siloe, 1973), p. 24.

[445]See Thomas G. Sanders, "The Chilean Episcopate: An Institution in Transition," in *American Universities Field Staff Reports* (West Coast South American Series) 15 (August, 1968), pp. 1-30, as well as Brian H. Smith, *The Church and Politics in Chile* (Princeton, NJ: Princeton University Press, 1982).

problem on this continent. *The number one problem is not priestly vocations*, as we have so often thought and said; *it is underdevelopment*."[446]

Medellín marked an explicit break and provided a qualitative leap from a world view tied to a "developmentalist" theory to one that espoused "liberation."[447] As Francisco Moreno Rejón comments: "Then came Medellín, with its sudden, powerful impulse for a period of fertile creativity and a dynamism both personal and theological."[448] Dependency theorists of the 1960s like Theotonio Dos Santos utilized the framework of Raul Prebisch's Report of the United Nations Economic Commission for Latin America to demonstrate that weaknesses in the regional economy in large measure derived from policies dictated from First World centers of financial power.[449] Theotonio Dos Santos defined "dependency" as: "a situation in which a certain group of countries have their economies conditioned by the development and expansion of another country's economy.[450] In 1968, the presiding officers of various Latin American episcopal conference social action commissions issued a joint document on "The Presence of the Church in Latin American Development," as a complement to the conclusions reached at CELAM's Mar del Plata meeting held in 1966. The statement concluded: "In large measure, the

---

[446]Dom Helder Câmara, "The Church and Modern Latin America," in the Peruvian Bishops' Committee for Social Action, *Between Honesty and Hope*, p. 40.
[447]See Peter Evans, *Dependency Development: The Alliance of Multinational, State, and Local Capital in Brazil* (Princeton: Princeton University Press, 1971), pp. 331-351, and C. Richard Bath and Dilmus Jones, "Dependency Analysis of Latin America," in *Latin American Research Review* 11 (1976), pp. 3-54.
[448]Francisco Moreno Rejón, "Fundamental Moral Theology in the Theology of Liberation," in Ellacuría and Sobrino (eds.), *Mysterium Liberationis*, p. 212.
[449]See Raul Prebisch, *Nueva política comercial para el desarrollo* (Mexico City: Fondo de Cultura Económica, 1964), and Werner Baer, "The Economics of Prebisch and the ECLA," in Charles T. Nisbet (ed.), *Latin America: Problems in Economic Development* (NY: The Free Press, 1969, pp. 203-219, along with Peter Evans, *Dependent Development: The Alliance of Multinational, State, and Local Capital in Brazil* (Princeton, NJ: Princeton University Press, 1972).
[450]Cited in Michael J. Francis, "Dependency: Ideology, Fad, and Fact," in Michael Novak and Michael P. Jackson (eds.), *Latin America: Dependency or Independence?* (Washington, DC: American Enterprise Institute, 1985), p. 89.

underdevelopment of Latin America is a *by-product* of capitalist development in the West... where the Latin American nations revolve as dependent, peripheral satellites around some center... Authentic development can come to Latin America only if we manage to throw over this *center-periphery* schema."[451] In 1971, the Peruvian bishops produced a similar statement:

> Like other nations of the Third World, we are victims of systems that exploit our natural resources, control our political decisions, and impose upon us the cultural domination of their values and consumer civilization. The situation that was denounced at Medellín is reinforced and supported by the internal structures of our nation. Economic, social, and cultural inequality is increasing, while politics are so perverted that instead of serving the common good, it favors a tiny minority.[452]

As the theological commission of the bishops of Northeastern Brazil later put it, "If the Church were to summarize the past decade of 'development' in Latin America, it would have to state that the result is more hunger."[453] Hugo Assmann echoed this assessment:

> Underlying liberation theology is the historical experience of the actual nature of *under*-development, as a form of dependence... If the historical situation of dependence and domination of two-thirds of humanity, with its thirty million deaths per year from hunger and malnutrition, does not now become the starting point for any Christian theology, in the rich and dominant countries as well, theology will no longer be able to locate and give specific historical expression to its basic themes. [The issue concerns] not merely

---

[451]"The Presence of the Church in Latin American Development," in The Peruvian Bishops' Commission for Social Action, *Between Honesty and Hope*, p. 21 [emphases in the original].
[452]Reprinted in *IDOC- North America 51* (March, 1973), p. 21.
[453]Cited in Penny Lernoux, "CELAM III: To Build or Tear Down?," in *National Catholic Reporter* (July 14, 1978), p. 1.

> underdeveloped peoples... but peoples "kept in a state of underdevelopment."[454]

As the decade of the 1960s wore on, the term "development" acquired a more pejorative connotation in Latin America. The concept of developmentalism was judged to perpetuate the prevailing economic structures, while the use of the term "liberation" came into increasing favor. As Dom Helder Câmara remarked:

> Paul VI was courageous enough to say that what the developed countries gave with one hand, they took away with the other... At the end of the first "decade of development," President Richard Nixon himself was forced to admit that the rich countries were emerging from the decade richer, and the poor countries poorer... This is why "development" was such a disappointment to us. We had such high hopes – Father Lebret, whom I chose as advisor at the Council, François Perroux, Paul VI. Now, we prefer to speak of "liberation."[455]

The Medellín Conference produced a dividing line of sorts, between a developmentalist Church, and one committed to liberation. In the "Introduction to the Final Document" at Medellín, the bishops noted: "[We] cannot cease to feel God's saving passage in view of 'true development,' which is the passage for each and all, from conditions of life that are less human, to those that are more human." Enrique Dussel observed that Medellín was the end of the preparatory stage for the evolving theology of liberation: "Its vocabulary was developmentalist (speaking of 'human promotion,' 'development') as well as liberationist ('international tensions and external neocolonialism,' 'the flight of capital,' 'international monopolies or the

---

[454]Hugo Assmann, *Theology for a Nomad Church* (Maryknoll, NY: Orbis Books, 1976), pp. 37-38, 49.

[455]Helder Câmara, "'Liberation' in Aid of 'Development,'" in José de Broucker, *Dom Helder Câmara: The Conversions of a Bishop*, pp. 172, 173, 175.

imperialism of money'). It was the fruit of a long process."[456] The Latin American bishops recognized this development in the "Introduction to the Medellín Documents:"

> Latin America is obviously under the sign of transformation and development; a transformation that, besides taking place with extraordinary speed, has come to touch and influence every level of human activity, from the economic to the religious... we are on the threshold of a new epoch in this history of Latin America. It appears to be a time of zeal for full emancipation, of liberation from every form of servitude, of personal maturity and of collective integration" (no. 4).

As Raul Vidales noted, Medellín marked a decisive moment in the development of the theology of liberation: "Although it is not quite true to say that it was born on that occasion, the future theological movement and its task received both official welcome and the impulse to move forward in the perspective of liberation."[457] As Jon Sobrino points out: "In Vatican II, the expression 'Church of the poor' was not well accepted, although it was advocated by John XXIII and personalities like Cardinal Lercaro – the Third World was not very present at the Council – but the emerging light of the Council was picked up in Latin America, and the Latin American reality put it to work."[458]

Indeed, the developmental model failed to produce the desired fruits, and the process of underdevelopment continued largely unabated throughout the decade of

---

[456]Enrique Dussel, "The Context of Liberation Theology," in Sergio Torres and Virginal Fabella, M.M., *The Emergent Gospel: Theology From the Developing World* (Maryknoll, NY: Orbis Books, 1978), p. 181.

[457]Raul Vidales, "Some Recent Publications in Latin America on the Theology of Liberation," in Claude Geffré and Gustavo Gutiérrez (eds.), *The Mystical and Political Dimension of the Christian Faith*, p. 127.

[458]Jon Sobrino, S.J., "Communion, Conflict and Ecclesial Solidarity," in Ellacuría and Sobrino (eds.), *Mysterium Liberationis*, p. 626.

the 1960s, as the gap increasingly widened between the rich and the poor. The study of Raul Prebisch undertaken by the United Nations Economic Commission on Latin America challenged the developmentalist view that international trade was mutually beneficial for all trading parties, and basically identified development and underdevelopment as two sides of the same coin. A series of failures in the development models led to complete disillusionment: the collapse of the "Alliance for Progress"; the manipulative control of aid organizations by First World governments, such as the United States-sponsored "Agency for International Development"; the militarization of the continent along with the rise of repressive dictatorships;[459] and, the massive outflow of raw materials, coupled with the lack of capital reinvestment within the local sphere. Whereas Vatican II spoke of "human promotion," in Latin America this concept was jettisoned and replaced with the phrase, "the liberation of the oppressed." In his famous paper presented at the SODEPAX conference, "In Search of a Theology of Development," delivered at Cartigny, Switzerland in November, 1969, Gustavo Gutiérrez asserted clearly that "developmentalism" had increasingly resulted in "*a state of dependence*... during the last few years there has been a significant changeover (although it is not always coherent) from the theme of development to the theme of liberation."[460] In time, the basis of the theology of development crumbled, as the theoretical foundations for the theology of liberation were set in place.

A significant by-product of the annual meetings of the Latin American bishops during the sessions of Vatican II was the issuance of the "Letter to Peoples of the Third World" dated July 31, 1966. The letter was signed by eighteen bishops

---

459On this point, see José Comblin, *The Church and the National Security State* (Maryknoll, NY: Orbis Books, 1979), especially chapter 4.

460Gustavo Gutiérrez, "Towards a Theology of Liberation," in Gerhard Bauer (ed.), *In Search of a Theology of Development* (Geneva: SODEPAX, 1970), p. 140.

from developing countries, including nine Brazilians and a Colombian.[461] This type of ongoing theological reflection in Latin America began to challenge the prevailing notions of "developmentalism," and pointed to the necessity of continent-wide structural liberation. Both Pope Paul VI's encyclical, *Populorum Progressio*, and the Helder Câmara-inspired "Letter to the Peoples of the Third World"[462] of the Latin American bishops served as a bridge to the Medellín Conference. The Medellín "Document on Peace" asserted that "Latin American underdevelopment, with its own characteristics in the different countries, constituted an unjust situation that promotes tensions that conspire against peace" (no. 1).[463] According to Gutiérrez, the "Letter to the Peoples of the Third World" represented the first comprehensive use of the terminology of liberation, whose language resonated at Medellín, and became one of CELAM's overarching concerns.[464]

The "Letter to the Peoples of the Third World" analyzed the structural injustices inherent in the capitalist system, and argued that "the moment a system fails to provide for the common good and shows favoritism to a particular few, the Church has the duty not only to denounce the injustice, but also to cut free from that unjust system, seeking to collaborate with some other system... The current social doctrine of the Church, reaffirmed by Vatican II, has already rescued it from the clutches of monetary imperialism – one of the forces to which it seemed bound for some time in the past."[465] The letter further expressed what later became ensconced as a key point in the theology of liberation then developing in Latin America: "From

---

[461]"Letter to the Peoples of the Third World," in *Between Honesty and Hope*, pp. 3-12, originally published in *Temoignage Chrétièn* (August 15, 1967).
[462]See Enrique Dussel, *Los Ultimos 50 Años (1930-1985) en la historia de la Iglesia en América Latina* (Bogotá: Indo-American Press Service, 1986), p. 36.
[463]Cited in Alfred T. Hennelly, S.J. (ed.), *Liberation Theology: A Documentary History*, p. 106.
[464]See Gustavo Gutiérrez, *A Theology of Liberation*, pp. 33-35.
[465]"A Letter to the Peoples of the Third World," in *Between Honesty and Hope*, p. 3, echoing the words of Pope Pius XI in *Qudragesimo anno* and Pope Paul VI in *Populorum Progressio*.

the viewpoint of doctrine, the Church knows that the Gospel calls for the first and most radical revolution: conversion, the thoroughgoing transformation from sin to grace, from egotism to love, from haughtiness to humble service."[466] The "Letter to the Peoples of the Third World" was soon affirmed by Bishop Eduardo Pironio of Argentina, then General-Secretary of CELAM: "Our Mission, like Christ's, consists of proclaiming the Good News to the poor, proclaiming the liberation of the oppressed."[467]

Taken together, the conjunction of three post-conciliar events, *Populorum Progressio*, the "Letter to the Peoples of the Third World," and the tenth assembly of the Council of Latin American Bishops at Mar del Plata, Argentina in 1966, all treated matters not sufficiently elaborated upon at the Second Vatican Council. They set out to analyze critically the economic and social order in a manner under-represented at Vatican II. At the same time, progressive priests' groups sprung up in almost every Latin American country. The most significant of these associations of priests included: "Priests for the Third World," in Argentina;[468] the "Group of Eighty," in Chile;[469] ONIS, in Peru;[470] the Golconda movement, in Colombia,[471] and

---

[466]"Letter to the Peoples of the Third World," in *Between Honesty and Hope,* p. 4.

[467]See Eduardo Pironio, "*Teología de la liberación,*" in *Criterio* (1970), pp. 1607-1608.

[468]*Social Activist Priests: Colombia, Argentina, LADOC Keyhole Series No. 6* (Washington, DC: United States Catholic Conference, n.d.).

[469]*Social Activist Priests: Chile, LADOC Keyhole Series No. 5* (Washington, DC: United States Catholic Conference, n.d.).

[470]Jeffrey Klaiber, S.J., *Religion and Revolution in Peru* (Notre Dame, IN: University of Notre Dame Press, 1977), and his *The Catholic Church in Peru: 1821-1985/ A Social History* (Washington, DC: Catholic University of America Press, 1992), pp. 291-197; Fernando Montes, "How the ONIS Movement Began and Grew," in *LADOC Keyhole Series No. 45* (Washington, DC: United States Catholic Conference, 1974). As Luís Pasara suggested, at the July, 1968 ONIS meeting, "It was Gustavo Gutiérrez who presented the first outline of what would come to be known as liberation theology. Over the following decade, the ONIS – with the tacit approval of Cardinal Juan Landázuri [Ricketts] – was to play a key role not only for radical Catholics but for the public image of the Peruvian Church itself," in "Peru: The Leftist Angels," in Scott Mainwaring and Alexander Wilde (eds.), *The Progressive Church in Latin America*, p. 280.

[471]*Social Activist Priests: Colombia, Argentina, LADOC Keyhole Series No. 6* (Washington, DC: United States Catholic Conference, n.d.).

ISAL, in Bolivia.[472] Nowhere was this progressive swing more clearly evident than in the post-conciliar Brazilian Church. This transformation showed itself most palpably in Brazil in the formation of thousands of basic Christian communities; by the inroads made by the educational methods pioneered by the pedagogue Paulo Freire (known as "conscientization"); and, within the universities, by the developing consciousness of ideologies employed by both the Church and state to legitimate oppression and injustice.[473]

Paulo Freire developed the techniques of "conscientization" in order to raise awareness among the poor of their plight, and for planning possible remedies for the misery of their situation.[474] Freire believed that even the most humble campesino could speak his or her own word, and become the artisan of his or her own destiny, since "there is no true word that is not at the same time a praxis... [and] to speak a true word is to transform the world."[475] The influence of Paulo Freire upon the new generation of liberation theologians, particularly in Brazil, can scarcely be overestimated.[476]

---

[472]See Michael Dodson, "The Christian Left in Latin American Politics," in Daniel H. Levine (ed.), *Churches and Politics in Latin America,* pp. 111-134; and, Ivan Vallier, "Radical Priests and Revolution," in Douglas Chalmers (ed.), *Changing Latin America: New Interpretations of Its Politics and Society* (Montpelier, VT: Capital City Press, 1972).

[473]See Alfred T. Hennelly, S.J., *Theology for a Liberating Church*, p. 28, as well as Juan Luís Segundo, S.J., "Two Theologies of Liberation," in *The Month* 17 (October, 1984), p. 10.

[474]See Paulo Freire, *Pedagogy of the Oppressed* (NY: Seabury Press, 1970), as well as Dennis Collins, *Paulo Freire: His Life, Works, and Thought* (NY: Paulist Press, 1977), and César Jerez, S.J. and Juan Hernandez Pico, "Cultural Action for Freedom," in *LADOC Keyhole Series 1* (Washington, DC: United States Catholic Conference, 1980), pp. 3-10.

[475]Pãolo Freire, "Cultural Freedom in Latin America," in Louis Michael Colonese (ed.), *Human Rights and the Liberation of Man in the Americas* (Notre Dame, IN: University of Notre Dame Press, 1970), p. 171. See also Pãolo Freire, "Conscientizing as a Way of Liberating," pp. 3-10.

[476]See Alfred T. Hennelly, S.J., "Pãolo Freire as a Liberation Theologian," in Alfred T. Hennelly, S.J., *Theology for a Liberating Church: The New Praxis of Freedom* (Washington, DC: Georgetown University Press, 1989), pp. 67-80, and Daniel Schipani, *Conscientization and Creativity: Pãolo Freire and Christian Education* (Lanham, MD: University Press of America, 1984).

In the decade immediately preceding Vatican II, concern for basic education and community evangelization dominated the pastoral plan of the Brazilian Catholic Church. This agenda became especially established in northeast Brazil. As Marina Bandeira notes: "We had been criticized by some bishops that the laity were getting too involved in social programs. Suddenly, the bishops of Medellín voted that this was exactly what the Church wanted. It certainly was an encouragement. Vatican II made official what was already happening in Brazil; we were living it."[477] The highlights of this movement included: the success of Jocist groups such as *Açio Operaria Catolica* ("Catholic Worker Action"), *Juventude Universitaria Catolica* ("Catholic University Youth"), and *Juventude Estudantil Catolica* ("Catholic Student Youth"); the experiment with popular catechesis in Bara do Pirai, in the state of Rio de Janiero; the Natal movement, in the state of Rio Grande do Norte, that aimed to overhaul religious, political, economic and social structures; the Basic Education Movement, which made use of radio schools and the pedagogical techniques pioneered by Paulo Freire; and, the Nizia Floresta pastoral experiment, which in 1962 laid the groundwork for evangelization through the grassroots faith communities [CEBs].[478]

The National Conference of Brazilian Bishops [CNBB] issued an "Emergency Pastoral Plan of 1962" that sparked wholesale renewal in parishes and within diocesan structures. It initiated massive re-thinking concerning approaches to ministry, education, and the role of the Church as actor in economic and social

---

[477]Interview conducted by Christian Smith, July 28, 1988, cited in his *The Emergence of Liberation Theology: Radical Religion and Social Movement Theory* (Chicago: University of Chicago Press, 1991), p. 99.

[478]On these developments, see Enrique Dussel, "From the Second Vatican Council to the Present Day," in Enrique Dussel (ed.), *The Church in Latin America: 1492-1992* (Maryknoll, NY: Orbis Books, 1992), p. 159, and Faustino Luiz Couto Teixeira, "Base Church Communities in Brazil," in Enrique Dussel (ed.), *The Church in Latin America: 1492-1992*, pp. 403-418.

life.[479] Already in 1962, the Central Committee of the CNBB declared: "No one can ignore the clamor of the masses who are being martyred by hunger."[480] The CNNB played a major role in pioneering changes in church life, and helped to create a receptive climate for the wide-ranging reforms anticipated in the Second Vatican Council, so as to awaken the Church in Brazil to the need for thorough renewal. Dom Helder Câmara and a group of bishops who were active pastorally in the northeast spearheaded the movement for social change within their dioceses.[481] In 1965, at the close of the Council, the Brazilian bishops met and confirmed a "Comprehensive Pastoral Plan." This strategy aimed to be "a first, firm application to the Brazilian Church of the main lines and decisions of the Council."[482] The five year plan enunciated as its goal: "To create means and conditions so that the Church in Brazil can adjust, as rapidly and as fully as possible, to the image of the Church of Vatican II."[483] The adoption of this plan stimulated a broader, more inclusive representation of the Church in Brazil, and helped to renew it structurally through the growth of new grassroots experiments.

Following the April 1, 1964 *coup d'etât* of General Joaõ Goulart, the pressure of the political situation also galvanized forces for renewal within the Brazilian Church.[484] Repression intensified within the church sector, as witnessed in the

---

[479]See Thomas C. Bruneau, *The Political Transformation of the Brazilian Catholic Church* (London: Cambridge University Press, 1974).
[480]Cited by Enrique Dussel, "From the Second Vatican Council to the Present Day," in *The Church in Latin America: 1492-1992*, p. 159.
[481]See Amaury de Souza, "*Março o Abril? Uma bibliografia commentada sobre o movimento politico de 1964 no Brasil*," in *Dados* 1 (1966), pp. 160-176, and Thomas Bruneau, The Political Transformation of the Brazilian Catholic Church), pp. 108-109.
[482]CNBB, "*Balanço do Plano de Pastoral de Conjuncto, janiero a junho de 1966*," in G. F. de Queiroga, *CNBB: comunhao e coresponsabilidade* (Sao Pãolo: Paulinas, 1977), p. 374.
[483]CNBB, *Plano de Pastoral de Conjuncto 1966-1970* (Rio de Janiero: Livraria Dom Bosco Editora, 1966), p. 25.
[484]See Godofredo Deelen, "*O Episcopado Brasileiro*," in *Revista Eclesiastica Brasileira* 27 (June, 1967), pp. 310-312.

"Institutional Act No. 5 of 1968," that aimed to imprison or silence many progressive, activist religious and political leaders. As Faustino Couto Teixeira suggests, "The Church, converted by the popular sectors, became little by little the 'voice' of this base, committed to its cause. The base communities were to emerge from this committed space."[485] Movements for pastoral renewal that promoted lay involvement proliferated, and accelerated the processes of critical reflection, theological analysis, and political commitment, especially in the grassroots communities.[486] The proceedings of the first national meeting of the base communities that took place in Brazil, published in 1975, demonstrated that while seeking to transform the faith of its members, the basic Christian communities [CEBs] caused dramatic changes in the model of the Church that prevailed in Brazil.[487] By the decade of the 1980s, more than 150,000 base communities emerged, and consisted in a membership of more than eight million, with Brazil having the largest number of groups.[488] As Leonardo Boff wrote in 1984:

> In the last thirty years, the [Brazilian] Church has endeavored to become more and more open to the people's participation... [T]housands of biblical reflection circles have sprung up, and many other small groups composed of Christians who want to live a life of

---

[485]Faustino Luiz Couto Teixeira, "Basic Church Communities in Brazil," in Enrique Dussel (ed.), *The Church in Latin America: 1492-1992*, p. 412. On this point, see also Marcello Azevedo, *Basic Ecclesial Communities in Brazil* (Washington, DC: Georgetown University Press, 1987), and Alfred T. Hennelly, S.J., "The Grassroots Church," in The Catholic Theological Society of America, *Proceedings of the 34th Annual Convention* (NY: Manhattan College, 1979), pp. 183-188.

[486]On the CEB's, see Alvaro Barreiro, S.J., *Basic Ecclesial Communities: The Evangelization of the Poor* (Maryknoll, NY: Orbis Books, 1982); José Maríns, "Basic Christian Communities in Latin America," in Claude Geffré and Gustavo Gutiérrez (eds.), *The Mystical and Political Dimension of the Christian Faith*, (NY: Herder & Herder, 1974), pp. 20-29; and, Thomas Bruneau, "Basic Christian Communities in Latin America: Their Nature and Significance (Especially in Brazil)," in Daniel H. Levine (ed.), *Churches and Politics in Latin America* (Beverly Hills, CA: Sage, 1981), pp. 225-237.

[487]CNBB, *Uma Igreja que Nasce do Povo* (Petropolis, Brazil: Editora Vozes, 1975). See also Frei Betto, *O Que e Comunidade Eclesial de Base* (Sao Pãolo: Editora Brasiliense, 1981).

[488]See Alan Riding, "Latin Church in Siege," in *The New York Times Magazine* (May 6, 1979), p. 40, along with José Maríns y Equipo, *Metodologia emergente de la CEB* (Quito: Don Bosco, 1980).

> shared faith have come into existence. In these groups, it is the people themselves who take responsibility for the key tasks of evangelization through newly evolving forms of ministry – always in communion with their pastors. We are seeing a marvelous convergence between these communities, which want their priests and bishops to be present with them, and the priests and the bishops who encourage and support the CEBs.[489]

These factors taken together conspired to create what has been described as "a major resonance in the base communities in the development of a new kind of theological thinking, in a common critique of the dominant social thinking, and in the hope shared, though at different historical moments, by the emerging popular movement, some as an aspiration, in the case of the base communities as a form of action already under way."[490] As Pablo Richard suggested, "There is a new doer, a new maker of history, in the Church, and this new active subject [CEBs] is doing theology, or at least inspiring new theological reflection in the Church... From here, liberation theology draws its power and its future."[491] The Brazilian hierarchy issued pastoral letters and documents that stressed this new identification with the poor and oppressed, which featured titles such as: "You Shall Not Oppress Your Brother,"[492] "I Have Heard the Cries of My People,"[493] and "Marginalization of a People, Cry of the Churches."[494] The Church in Brazil set the tone within the Latin American Church for this new direction. As Enrique Dussel suggested, in the aftermath of the

---

[489]Leonardo Boff, "Defense of His Book, *Church: Charism and Power*" (September 7, 1984)," in Alfred T. Hennelly, S.J. (ed.) *Liberation Theology: A Documentary History*, p. 433.
[490]Luiz Alberto Gomez de Sousa, "Preface," in Faustino Luiz Couto Teixeira, *A genese das CEBs no Brasil* (Sao Pãolo: Paulinas, 1988), p. 11.
[491]Pablo Richard, "Liberation Theology: A Difficult But Possible Future," in Marc H. Ellis and Otto Maduro, *Expanding the View*, p. 211.
[492]CNBB, "*Nao oprimas teu irmao*," in R. Azzi, "*A Igreja do Brasil na defesa dos Direitos Humanos*," *Revista Eclesiastica Brasileira* 37 (1977), pp. 106-142.
[493]CNBB, *Eu ouvi os clamores do meo povo* (Sao Pãolo: CNBB, 1974).
[494]CNBB, "*Marginalizaçao de um povo: grito das Ingrejas*," in *SEDOC* 22 (1973), pp. 607-627.

Council "there appears the 'theology of liberation' of the periphery and the oppressed, with whose onset the entire traditional theology begins its paschal movement into the perspective of the poor."[495]

The significant figure who keynoted this shift in doing theology was the Uruguayan Jesuit, Juan Luís Segundo.[496] Confronted with the reality of social sin, the Latin American Church of the 1960's was compelled to choose between siding with the victims of social injustice, or to continue to support and maintain the structures of the status quo that perpetuated the problem. With increasing clarity, the Latin American Church set out to analyze critically the socio-economic conditions of their continent. It embraced a commitment to the poor, and laid stress on the centrality of justice in the Scriptures and Christian tradition. Alfred Hennelly posited the "real beginning of liberation theology to be the presentation of a lecture on 'The Future of Christianity in Latin America' by Juan Luís Segundo, S.J. to a group of Catholic students in Paris in November, 1962."[497] Segundo's approach moved beyond the prevailing Eurocentric models and drew directly upon his own continent's experience of massive human misery and injustice.[498] Also in 1962, Segundo

---

[495]Enrique Dussel, "Domination – Liberation: A New Approach," in Claude Geffré and Gustavo Gutiérrez (eds.), *The Mystical and Political Dimension of the Christian Faith* (New York: Herder & Herder, 1974), pp. 53-54.

[496]See Alfred T. Hennelly, S.J., "Courage With Primitive Weapons," in *Cross Currents* (Spring, 1978), p. 14, as well as his *Theologies in Conflict: The Challenge of Juan Luís Segundo* (Maryknoll, NY: Orbis Books, 1979), and Anthony J. Tambasco, *The Bible for Ethics: Juan Luís Segundo and First World Ethics* (Lanham, MD: University Press of America, 1981). Note, however, the later assessment of Francisco Moreno Rejón in "Fundamental Moral Theory in the Theology of Liberation," in *Mysterium Liberationis*, p. 212: "The first intuitions sketched in this area by Juan Luís Segundo and H. C. de Lima Vaz had few repercussions. Then came Medellín, with its sudden, powerful impulse for a period of fertile creativity and a dynamism both pastoral and theological."

[497]Cited in Alfred T. Hennelly, S.J., *Liberation Theology: A Documentary History* (Maryknoll, NY: Orbis Books, 1990), p. 9.

[498]See Juan Luís Segundo, S.J., "*Derechos humanos, evangelización e ideologia,*" in *Christus* 43 (November, 1978), pp. 33-34.

published *Función de la Iglesia en la realidad Rioplatense*,[499] in which he reflected the distinctively indigenous ecclesiology that he utilized in a series of lectures he delivered in Uruguay in 1959.[500] In 1963 (some years before the first, formal appearance of the theology of liberation, generally accorded to Gutiérrez's 1968 conference paper "*Hacia una teologia de liberación*"[501] that first began to surpass the theology of development), Juan Luís Segundo presented his "The Future of Christianity in Latin America."[502] He completed another influential theological work in 1970, *De la sociedad a la teologia*.[503] In his own words:

> Contrary to the most common assumption, Latin American theology, without any precise title, began to have clearly distinctive features at least ten years before Gustavo Gutiérrez's well-known book, *A Theology of Liberation*. This was a kind of baptism, but the baby had already grown old. The real beginning came simultaneously from

---

[499]Juan Luís Segundo, S.J., *Función de la Iglesia en la realidad Rioplatense* (Montevideo, Uruguay: Barreiro y Ramos, 1962).

[500]Later published by Segundo as, *Etapas precristianos de al fe: Evolución de una idea de Dios en el Antiguo Testamento* (Montevideo, Uruguay: Cursos de Complementación Cristiana, 1962).

[501]Gustavo Gutiérrez, "Toward a Theology of Liberation (July, 1968)," in Alfred T. Hennelly, S.J. (ed.), *Liberation Theology: A Documentary History*, pp. 62-76. See the comment of Irish theologian Donal Dorr in "Preferential Option for the Poor," in Judith A. Dwyer (ed.), *The New Dictionary of Catholic Social Thought* (Collegeville, MN: Liturgical Press/A Michael Glazier Book, 1994), p. 756: "The concept of an option for the poor is a central element in liberation theology that emerged in Latin America during the 1960's. The Peruvian theologian Gustavo Gutiérrez is generally recognized as the father of liberation theology. His seminal book, *A Theology of Liberation*, devoted an important chapter to an analysis of the term 'poverty.'" In contrast, American Jesuit moral theologian James F. Keenan posited an interesting linkage within Roman Catholic Social Teaching, when he asserted that the by the turn of the Twenty-First Century, the Catholic tradition "has developed merciful concepts like distributive justice, the common good and the option for the poor." As cited in Jon Fuller, S.J. and James F. Keenan, S.J., "The International AIDS Conference in Bangkok: Two Views/ II. An Ethical Perspective," in *America* (August 30/September 6, 2004), p. 15.

[502]See Juan Luís Segundo, S.J., "The Future of the Church in Latin America," in *Lettre* 54 (Paris: Centurion, 1963), pp. 7-12, and *Función de la Iglesia en la realidad Rioplatense* (Montevideo, Uruguay, Barriero y Ramos, 1962), of which Enrique Dussel says: "If one were to point to a first text that marked the appearance of a properly Latin American theological reflection, still using functionalist sociology, this would have to be [it]," in "Recent Latin American Theology," *The Church in Latin America: 1492-1992*, p. 391.

[503]Juan Luís Segundo, S.J., *De la sociedad a la teología* (Buenos Aires: Carlos Lohle, 1970).

> many theologians working in countries and places in Latin America, even before the first session of Vatican II. In any case, these developments began some years before the [Pastoral] Constitution *Gaudium et Spes* in 1965, which, to a great extent, was used afterwards as an official support for the main views of this liberation theology.[504]

In March, 1964, the first group meeting that anticipated the theology of liberation was held in Petropolis, Brazil, at the invitation of the then-Monsignor Ivan Illich of Cuernavaca, Mexico. It featured papers presented by Gustavo Gutiérrez[505] of Peru, Juan Luís Segundo of Uruguay, and Lucio Gera of Argentina, and opened the way for a Latin American theology that became systematically framed in the expressions of liberation thought that it subsequently engendered. In his conference paper, Gutiérrez proposed as the new task of theology in Latin America to be "to carry out an analysis of forms of behavior from the religious point of view, from the point of view of salvation, to analyze what are the underlying options of the various types of persons."[506] At the Petropolis meeting, Gustavo Gutiérrez offered his definition of theology as "a critical reflection upon praxis."[507] In 1967, Enrique Dussel published his "Hypothesis for a History of the Church in Latin America," that augured the awareness that a new theological era was dawning.[508] These writings

---

[504]Juan Luís Segundo, S.J., *The Shift Within Latin American Theology* (Toronto: Regis College Press, 1983), p. 2.

[505]For a Latin American survey of the evolution of Gutiérrez's early thought, see Roberto Oliveros, *Liberación y teología: genesís y crecimiento de una reflexión, 1966-1976* (Lima: CEP, 1980), along with Miguel Manzanera, *Teología y salvación en la obra de Gustavo Gutiérrez* (Bilbao: Universidad de Deusto, 1978).

[506]Cited in Roberto Oliveros, *Liberación y teología: genesís y crecimiento de una reflexión 1966-1977* (Lima: Indo-American Press Service, 1977), p. 56.

[507]See Robert McAfee Brown, *Gustavo Gutiérrez: An Introduction to Liberation Theology* (Maryknoll, New York: Orbis Books, 1990), p. 34, and Roberto Oliveros, *Liberación y teología; genesís y crecimiento de una reflexión* (Lima: CEP, 1971).

[508]Enrique Dussel, *Hipótesis para una historia de la teología en América Latina* (Bogotá: *Paulinas*, 1967).

catalyzed an important opening moment, and a growing network of collaboration was cemented among the emerging cadre of theologians of liberation, who met in June, 1965 at Bogotá, Colombia, and in July, 1965 at Cuernavaca, Mexico and Havana, Cuba. Gutiérrez gave lectures in Montreal in July, 1967 and at Chimbote, Peru, in July, 1968 on the poverty of the Third World and the challenges it posed to the development of a pastoral strategy of liberation, which he dubbed for the first time a "theology of liberation."[509] He returned to this subject in November, 1969, at a meeting held in Cartigny, Switzerland, under the auspices of SODEPAX, the joint ecumenical peace and justice group of the World Council of Churches and the Pontifical Commission for Justice and Peace. The organizers of the consultation originally entitled Gutiérrez's presentation, "The Meaning of Development," but on the plane to Switzerland he renamed it, "Notes on a Theology of Liberation."[510] For his pioneering efforts, Gutiérrez is often credited as being "the father of liberation theology."[511] In an interview with Rosino Gibellini, Gutiérrez reflected:

> I was asked for a report on the theme which was at that time in fashion, again the theology of development, but I discussed the theology of liberation, giving quite a long lecture which was published the next year... This was a more developed treatment with a better structure... For me it was an occasion to think over the theme of liberation more thoroughly, associating it with the liveliest currents of contemporary theology, and also making a deeper study of some

---

[509]Gustavo Gutiérrez, *Hacía una teología de liberación* (Montevideo, Uruguay: MIEC, 1969), later published as "Toward a Theology of Liberation (July, 1968)," in Alfred T. Hennelly, S.J. (ed.), *Liberation Theology: A Documentary History*, pp. 62-76.
[510]Gustavo Gutiérrez, "*Notes pour une Théologie de la Liberation*," *IDOC* 30 (1970), pp. 54-78; later published as "Toward a Theology of Liberation," in Gerhard Bauer (ed.), *Beyond the Theology of Development* (Cartigny, Switzerland: SODEPAX, 1970).
[511]Alfred T. Hennelly, S.J., "Courage With Primitive Weapons," in *Cross Currents* (Spring, 1978), p. 14.

biblical themes like poverty. The text circulated widely in Latin America.[512]

In January, 1969, in Peru, the year after a military junta seized power, the national conference of Catholic bishops pointed to structural causes as the root of the nation's socio-economic woes: "This unjust situation... is the result of a world-wide process characterized by the concentration of economic and political power in the hands of very few and by the international imperialism of money, which operates in complicity with the Peruvian oligarchy."[513] The Peruvian hierarchy's position papers on the specified topics for the 1971 World Synod of Bishops, on "Justice in the World" and "The Ministerial Priesthood" proved equally instructive in this regard. Their preparatory document in advance of the Synod on "Justice in the World" stated:

> Building a just society in Latin America and in Peru means liberation from the present situation of dependency, or oppression, and of plunder in which the great majority of our people live. Liberation, on the other hand, will be a break with all that makes it impossible for humans to be fulfilled either personally or in community... For the Peruvian church community, this implies opting for the oppressed and excluded as a personal and community commitment. This choice excludes no one from our charity; rather, to opt for those who today are experiencing the most violent forms of oppression is for us an effective way of also loving those who, perhaps unconsciously, are oppressed by their situation as oppressors.[514]

---

[512]Rosino Gibellini, "'We Cannot Do Theology in a Dead Corner of History': A Conversation With Gustavo Gutiérrez," in Rosino Gibellini, *The Liberation Theology Debate* (Maryknoll, NY: Orbis Books, 1988), p. 81.

[513]The conclusions from the 26th Episcopal Assembly of the National Conference of Peruvian Bishops are cited in *Cronología Política* I, p. 54. See also Luís Pasara, "Peru: The Leftist Angels," p. 288.

[514]Social Action Department, "Justice in the World" (Lima: National Conference of Peruvian Bishops, 1977), p. 17. The Synod document famously stated that "action on behalf of justice" is a "constitutive element of the Gospel."

Spurred by the course charted in *Populorum Progressio*, a congress on "Faith and Development" was held in Mexico in November, 1969, and published its proceedings in two volumes.[515] Sergio Torres noted that "theologically the developmentalist period culminated in [this] meeting."[516] Paul VI's theology of development clamored for human progress and heightened social concern for people and nations, but its optimism and dynamism could not overcome the persistence of the underlying causes of poverty and injustice that were so engrained in the world.

The need for a shift to a new paradigm became evident less than a year later, when, as Enrique Dussel suggested, "The basic step [toward liberation theology] was still to be made."[517] The first Catholic conference on liberation theology was held in Bogotá in March, 1970, during which an international meeting on the theme, "Liberation: Option for the Church in the 1970s" was held, which produced two volumes of proceedings.[518] An early exposition of key themes of the theology of liberation that appeared in 1970 in the respected North American Jesuit journal, *Theological Studies* [its editor, Walter J. Burghardt, introduced the piece as "theological dynamite"[519]]. Gutiérrez wrote:

> In the 1960s a new attitude emerged. The developmental model has not produced the promised fruits. A pessimistic diagnostic has now

---

[515]*Memoria del primer Congreso Nacional de teología: Fe y desarollo* 2 Vols. (Mexico City: ESAC, 1970).

[516]Sergio Torres, "The Context of Liberation Theology," in Marc H. Ellis and Otto Maduro (eds.), *Expanding the View*, p. 182.

[517]Enrique Dussel, "Recent Latin American Theology," in *The Church in Latin America: 1492-1992*, p. 391.

[518]Juan A. Hernandez (ed.), *Aportés para la liberación* (Bogotá: Presencia, 1970), and Gustavo Gutiérrez (ed.), *Liberación: Opción de la Iglesia de la decada del 70* (Bogotá: Presencia, 1970).

[519]For additional comment on the impact of this article, see Richard McCormick, S.J., "Moral Theology 1940-1989: An Overview," in Charles E. Curran and Richard A. McCormick, S.J. (eds.), *The Historical Development of Fundamental Moral Theology in the United States/ Readings in Moral Theology No. 11* (NY: Paulist Press, 1999), p. 58.

> replaced the former optimistic one. Today we see clearly that the proposed model was an improper one. It was an abstract model, an ahistorical one, which kept us from seeing the complexity of the problem and the inevitably contradictory aspects of the proposed solution. The process of underdevelopment should be studied in historical perspective, i.e., contrasting it with the development of the great capitalist countries in whose sphere Latin America is situated... The reality so described is more and more obviously the result of a *situation of dependence*, i.e., the centers where decisions are made are located outside our continent – a fact that keeps our countries in a situation of neo-colonialism... [F]rom a variety of sources inside the Latin American Church, the term "development" is gradually being displaced by the term "liberation." The word and the idea behind it express the idea to get rid of the condition of dependence, but even more than that they underline the desire of the oppressed peoples to seize the reins of their own destiny and shake free from the present servitude... This liberation will only be achieved by a thorough change of structures.[520]

In May, 1971, Hugo Assmann chaired a groundbreaking symposium on "Liberation – Oppression: The Challenge to Christians," in Montevideo, Uruguay.[521] In December, 1971, Gutiérrez published the original Spanish version of his groundbreaking work, *Teología de liberación: perspectivas*,[522] the first systematic discussion of this emerging theology. The title of the liberation theology movement derived from this book. It further opened the path for the development of a theology from the margins that treated with the concerns of the marginalized, and posed an immense challenge to the evangelizing Mission and potential of the Church.[523] In the

---

[520]Gustavo Gutiérrez "Notes for a Theology of Liberation," in *Theological Studies* 31 (June, 1970), pp. 243, 257.

[521]See Leonardo Boff and Clodovis Boff, *Introducing Liberation Theology*, p. 70.

[522]Gustavo Gutiérrez, *Teología de liberación: perspectivas* (Lima: CEP, 1971).

[523]For a balanced critique of some of the shortcomings of Gutiérrez's early theology, see: José Luís Idigoras, S.J., "*Reflexiones sobre la teología en Peru,*" in *Revista de la Universidad Católica* [New Series] No. 7 (June, 1980), pp. 45-80, along with the works of two other Jesuits: Francisco Interdonato, S.J., "*¿Teología latinoamericana, teología de la liberación*? (Bogotá: Ediciones Paulinas, 1978), and Ricardo Durand Florez, S.J., *Observaciones a teología de la liberación* (Lima:

organizational plan of A Theology of Liberation, Gustavo Gutiérrez closely followed the structural arrangement of *Populorum Progressio*, and distinguished within the text three levels of liberation: a). political and social liberation of oppressed nations and social classes; b). liberation of humankind in the course of world history; c). liberation from sin and total reconciliation in communion with God through Jesus Christ.[524] This perspective propelled Gutiérrez in new directions. Further meetings on the liberation theme occurred in Bolivia and in Argentina in 1971, and featured a stable of aspiring young theologians such as Hugo Assmann, Juan Carlos Scannone, and Enrique Dussel.[525] Coupled with the publication of seminal works by Gustavo Gutiérrez and Rubem Alves.[526] With the paper on "The Theology of Liberation" presented by Bishop Eduardo Pironio at the annual convention of the Argentine Department of Education, liberation theology became established in Latin America as a factor with which to be reckoned on the theological landscape.[527]

In 1972, Leonardo Boff followed with his seminal work of Christology, *Jesus Christ Liberator*.[528] This formative period culminated in the meeting held at El Escorial, Spain in July, 1972, on the subject of "Christian Faith and the Transformation of Society in Latin America." The El Escorial conference focused international attention upon the infant theology of liberation. During this meeting,

---

Callao, 1985).

[524]See Gustavo Gutiérrez, *A Theology of Liberation* (Maryknoll, NY: Orbis Books, 1973), pp. 176-178, as well as Hugo Assmann, *Theology for a Nomad Church* (Maryknoll, NY: Orbis Books, 1976), p. 55.

[525]See Enrique Dussel, "*Recent Latin American Theology*," in *The Church in Latin America: 1492-1992*, p. 393.

[526]Gustavo Gutiérrez, *Teología de la liberación: Perspectivas* (Lima: CEP, 1971); Rubem Alves, *Theology of Hope* (Cleveland, OH: Corpus Books, 1969).

[527]See Eduardo Pironio, "*Teología de la liberación*," in *Teología* 8 (1970), pp. 7-28, as well as in *Criterio* (1970), pp. 1607-1608, along with his *En el espíritu de Medellín* (Buenos Aires: Editora Patria Grande, 1976).

[528]Leonardo Boff, *Jesus Christ Liberator: A Critical Christology for Our Times* (Maryknoll, New York: Orbis Books, 1978).

Gustavo Gutiérrez rose to prominence as the foremost articulator of the new theology of liberation. At the end of his lecture, he summarized what his conclusions signified for this project of theological reconstruction:

> Commitment to the process of liberation introduces Christians into a world quite unfamiliar to them and forces them to make what we have called a qualitative leap – the radical challenging of a social order and its ideology, and the breaking with old ways of knowing... But simultaneously, the buds of a new type of understanding of the faith are emerging within these same experiences. In them we have learned to link knowing and transforming, theory and practice. A re-reading of the Gospel forces itself upon us.[529]

In this same address, Gutiérrez noted: "To believe in God is not to limit ourselves to affirming his existence; to believe in God is to commit ourselves to him and to all people... [and to counter] oppressive structures created for the few and for the exploitation of peoples, races, and social classes."[530] He insisted further: "Christ's liberation is not reduced to political liberation, but Christ's liberation occurs in liberating historical events... in the concrete historical and political circumstances of today."[531] Gutiérrez concluded that this kind of liberating praxis requires "from within that process... identification with persons who suffer misery and exploitation," and the empowerment of the poor and oppressed so that they can "freely and creatively express themselves in society and among the people of God... and become the artisans of their own liberation."[532]

The liberation theology movement manifested its increasing *gravitas* with the dedication of an entire issue of *Concilium*, the international review of theology, to its

---

[529]Gustavo Gutiérrez, "The Hope of Liberation," in Gerald Anderson and Thomas F. Stranksy, C.S.P. (eds.), *Mission Trends No. 3*, p. 65.
[530]Ibid., p. 65-66.
[531]Gustavo Gutiérrez, "The Hope of Liberation," p. 68.
[532]Ibid., p. 69.

themes in June, 1974.[533] This volume featured a group of up-and-coming practicioners of the theology of liberation: Gustavo Gutiérrez, Leonardo Boff, Juan Luís Segundo, Enrique Dussel, Raul Vidales, Segundo Galilea, José Míguez Bonino, and Ronaldo Muñoz. In the early phases of the liberation theology movement, these theologians worked primarily with student intellectuals in university settings.[534] Their work was propelled by two principal factors: first, by the aspiration to poverty in and for the Church as envisioned at the Second Vatican Council, especially as articulated in *Lumen Gentium* (no. 8) and *Gaudium et Spes* (no. 1); and, second, by application of the theory and practice of Jocist-inspired groups that strove for a new understanding of Christian social and political life. By the early 1970s, the axes of theological reflection shifted away from the universities and intellectual centers toward popular pastoral work and the base communities [CEBs].

In a paper delivered at the Ecumenical Association of Third World Theologians [EATWOT] in Dar es Salaam in August, 1976, Gustavo Gutiérrez commented:

> From the start liberation theology has maintained that active commitment to liberation comes first, and theology develops from it. Theology is critical reflection on and from within historical praxis, and the historical praxis of liberation theology is to accept and live the word of God with faith... [L]iberation theology does not merely replace the deductive with the inductive method. Rather, liberation theology reflects on and from within the complex and fruitful relationship between theory and practice. Liberation theology's second central intuition is that God is a liberating God, revealed only

---

[533]Claude Geffré and Gustavo Gutiérrez (eds.), *The Mystical and Political Dimension of the Christian Faith* (NY: Herder & Herder, 1974).

[534]See Jon Sobrino, "*El conocimiento teológico en la teología europea y latinoamericana*," in *Resurrección de la verdadera Iglesia: Los pobres, lugar teológico de la eclesiologia* (Santander: Sal Terrae, 1981), pp. 21-53. For an analysis of some of the formative figures of liberation theology from a North American Perspective, see Philip Sharper, "The Theology of Liberation: Some Reflections," in *Catholic Mind* (April, 1976), p. 45.

> in the concrete historical context of the poor and oppressed. It is not enough to know that praxis must precede reflection; we must also realize that the historical subject of that praxis is the poor – the people who have been excluded from the pages of history. Without the poor as subject, theology degenerates into academic exercise. Theological discourse becomes true – is verified – in and through its engagement in the liberation of the poor.[535]

This presentation of Gutiérrez served as a powerful worldwide impetus toward the development of a pastoral strategy of the theology of liberation.

This new way of doing theology assimilated the spirit of Vatican II, mediated through *Populorum Progressio*, as a point of departure for future developments in the Church within Latin American society. In an early, formative text that anticipated the main lines of the theology of liberation, *La pastoral de la Iglesia en América Latina*, Gutiérrez defined theology as "a critical function of the pastoral action of the Church."[536] Later, in *A Theology of Liberation*, he described theology as "critical reflection on historical praxis in the light of the word."[537] Subsequently, he refined this definition even more precisely in *The Power of the Poor in History*: "Theology in this context will be a critical reflection both from within, and upon, historical praxis, in confrontation with the word of the Lord, as lived and experienced in faith."[538] In the preface to the same book, Gutiérrez said of the theology of liberation: "It is not so much a theology with a different *content*... as it is a theology with a different *method*, theology as the second act rather than the first."[539] By this, he

---

[535]Gustavo Gutiérrez, "Two Theological Perspectives: Liberation Theology and Progressive Theology," in Sergio Torres and Virigina Fabellla, M.M. (eds.), *The Emergent Gospel*, p. 247.

[536]Gustavo Gutiérrez, *La pastoral de la Iglesia en América Latina* (Montevideo, Uruguay: MIEC-JECI, 1968), p. 1.

[537]Gustavo Gutiérrez, *A Theology of Liberation* (Maryknoll, NY: Orbis Books, 1973), p. 13.

[538]Gustavo Gutiérrez, *The Power of the Poor in History* (Maryknoll, NY: Orbis Books, 1983), p. 60.

[539]Ibid., pp. vii-viii. For a clear exposition on metholological questions on the theology of liberation, see: Juan Luís Segundo, S.J., *The Liberation of Theology*; Hugo Assmann, *Theology for a Nomad Church*; Raul Vidales, *Cuestiones en turno al método en la teología de la liberación* (Lima: MIEC-

meant that in liberation theology the principal locus of the theological enterprise shifted from academe to the church community itself, with a special emphasis upon the poor as the privileged subject of theology. In his famous essay, "Theology from the Underside of History," Gutiérrez further asserted:

> From the beginning, the theology of liberation posited that the first act is involvement in the liberation process, and that theology comes afterward, as a second act... [that seeks] to work from the viewpoint of the poor – the exploited classes, marginalized ethnic groups, and scorned cultures. This led it to take up the great theme of poverty and the poor in the Bible. As a result the poor appear within this theology as the key to an understanding of the meaning of liberation and the meaning of the revelation of a liberating God.[540]

Raul Vidales extended further upon this concept:

> The hermeneutic principle is not so much a datum as a person: Jesus Christ. More specifically here, it is Christ in the person of our lowliest fellow human beings... Faith is positive only insofar as it is a human act. Only when it is a human act, only when it is accepted and understood by a human being, is it a font and wellspring of theology. The "faith" and "reason" of theological tradition in its purest form find their dialectical unity in this love-inspired praxis of liberation. Hence this praxis constitutes an essential element of the hermeneutical process itself when viewed from the perspective of liberation.[541]

In *The Liberation of Theology*, Juan Luís Segundo noted that the most significant contribution of liberation theology is not a new content to Christian faith,

---

JECI, 1974); along with the entire issue of *Estudios Centroamericanos* (August-September, 1975).
[540]Gustavo Gutiérrez, "Theology From the Underside of History," in *The Power of the Poor in History*, p. 200.
[541]Raul Vidales, "Methodological Issues in Liberation Theology," in Rosino Gibellini (ed.), *Frontiers of Theology in Latin America* (Maryknoll, NY: Orbis Books, 1979), p. 50.

but a method to understanding it: "The one and only thing that can maintain the liberative character of any theology is not its content, but its methodology. It is the latter that guarantees the continuing bite of theology, whatever terminology may be used and however much the system tries to reabsorb itself."[542] Gutiérrez echoed this notion, and stressed that the theology of liberation does not involve a new content, but "a new way to do theology,"[543] through which the individual Christian and the community of faith are called to a praxis that entails "real charity, action, and commitment to the service of men and women."[544] In this sense, as Leonardo and Clodovis Boff pointed out:

> Liberation theology is not a *theological movement*, but *theology in movement*. Latin American theology is therefore not so much a source or a focal point of liberation theology as, more modestly, a humble catalyst and relatively dynamic element in this universal current. But until its central inspiration has been incorporated into theology as a whole, liberation theology has to appear as a particular current, devoted to what its name implies, distinct from other currents and programmatic in character. But even at this stage it is open to all theology and conscious of the fact that its final destiny is to disappear as a particular theology and become simply theology.[545]

In his pivotal work, *The Liberation of Theology*, Juan Luís Segundo utilized the technique of the "hermeneutic circle," in order to force an ongoing interaction between the text of the Scriptures and its interpretation in various contexts.[546] He

---

[542]Juan Luís Segundo, S.J., *The Liberation of Theology* (Maryknoll, New York: Orbis Books, 1976), pp. 39-40.
[543]Gustavo Gutiérrez, *A Theology of Liberation*, p. 15.
[544]Gustavo Gutiérrez, *A Theology of Liberation*, p. 19.
[545]Leonardo Boff and Clodovis Boff, *Introducing Liberation Theology* (Maryknoll, NY: Orbis Books, 1987), p. 83.
[546]On this overall method, see Norman Gottwald (ed.), *The Bible and Liberation: Political and Social Hermeneutics* (Maryknoll, NY: Orbis Books, 1983), and Xosé Miguelez, *La Teología de la liberación y su método* (Barcelona: Editorial Herder, 1976).

indicated that the method "involves the continuous change in the interpretation of the Bible, which is dictated by the continuing changes in our present-day reality, both individual and societal."[547] The fundamental hermeneutic circle moves from people to God and from God to people; from history to faith and from faith to history; from human word to the Word of God, and from the Word of God to human word; from human justice to the righteousness of God, and from God's righteousness to human justice; from the poor to God, and from God to the poor. Segundo posited: "The hermeneutical circle... summons us to a task in which we cannot prescind from sociology, that is, the study of the human attitudes that are bound up with social structures."[548] By scrutinizing present reality, this approach raises questions for the theologian that are "rich enough, general enough, and basic enough to force us to change our customary perceptions of life, death, knowledge, society, politics, and the world in general."[549] When such new and probing questions are applied to the scriptural texts, traditional interpretations of these texts must also change, or else the responses would stand to be hollow or void.

For Juan Luís Segundo, the hermeneutic circle always involved the engagement of a specific problem and a desire or commitment to find a solution to the problem. On the most basic level, Segundo's method involved "the continuous change in our interpretation of the Bible, in function of the continuous changes in our present reality, both individual and social."[550] As Segundo asserted: "A hermeneutic circle always supposes a profound human commitment, that is, a consciously accepted partiality, based certainly not on theological criteria but on human ones."[551]

---

[547]Juan Luís Segundo, S.J., *The Liberation of Theology* (Maryknoll, NY: Orbis Books, 1976), p. 7.
[548]Ibid., p. 47.
[549]Ibid., p. 8.
[550]Juan Luís Segundo, S.J., *Masas y minorías en dialectica de la liberación* (Buenos Aires: La Aurora, 1973), p. 102.
[551]Ibid., pp. 108-109.

Segundo posited that "the one key to open up for us the message of God would be... a revolutionary commitment in favor of the oppressed... a sensibility of heart toward the poor."[552] He envisioned this shift as a profound orientation towards action and commitment, that "propels me in an open, receptive way toward Jesus himself... which grounds my faith in *him* and no longer in any other person, no matter how trustworthy or attractive, [and] appears on the level of political commitment and of revolutionary political commitment on behalf of the oppressed."[553] Segundo held that this process became "a specific Christian contribution, a revolutionary commitment, and a new understanding of the Gospel [which] constitute a hermeneutic circle."[554] Within the hermeneutic circle, Segundo distinguished four essential steps:

> *First*, there is our way of experiencing reality, which leads us to ideological suspicion. *Secondly*, there is the application of our ideological suspicion to the whole ideological superstructure in general and to theology in particular. *Thirdly*, there comes a new way of experiencing theological reality that leads us to exegetical suspicion – that is, to the suspicion that the prevailing interpretation of the Bible has not taken important pieces of data into account. *Fourthly*, we have our new hermeneutic – that is, our new way of interpreting the fountainhead of our faith (i.e., Scripture) with the new elements at our disposal.[555]

In light of this hermeneutic, the definition of liberation theology was framed with a more refined Christological thrust by Leonardo Boff: "The theology of liberation means critical reflection on human praxis (of human beings generally and of Christians in particular) in the light of the praxis of Jesus and the demands of

---

[552]Ibid., pp. 92-93.
[553]Ibid., p. 102.
[554]Ibid., p. 94.
[555]Juan Luís Segundo, S.J., *The Liberation of Theology*, p. 19.

faith."[556] In that sense, liberation theology is not a theology of the poor taken as a new theme, or a theology for the poor, addressed in a paternalistic fashion, but seeks to set in motion from a point of departure in the poor, the poor themselves as artisans of their own destiny, and as historical subjects.[557]

The novelty of liberation theology offered a different historical, social, and political consciousness among the poor. As Gutiérrez pointed out, the option for the poor proved to be so controversial in Latin America and throughout the rest of the world because the question is not merely "about having social sensitivity, but about the poor being the subject of their own history... They have the capacity to evangelize: they are not only the objects of our evangelization, rather they are taking the announcement of the Gospel into their own hands."[558]

Gutiérrez positioned himself in the vanguard of the theologians of liberation, when he noted that Latin Americans tended to talk about liberation from oppression, while inhabitants of the Northern Hemisphere more often spoke about rights and freedoms (commonly secured by encroachments upon the freedoms of others).[559] In *A Theology of Liberation*, Gutiérrez argued that biblical injunctions overrode any natural law mandates. He stressed the primacy of Scripture in the formulation of a social ethic.[560] Segundo echoed this premise: "What are called 'human rights' are certain freedoms particularly useful to the middle classes. And they have been

---

[556]Leonardo Boff, "*Eine kreative Rezeption des II. Vatikanums aus ser Sicht der Armen: Die Theologie der Beifreiung," in Orientierung* 46 (1979), p. 640. Boff repeated this definition, almost verbatim, in *When Theology Listens to the Poor* (San Francisco: Harper & Row, 1988), p. 14.
[557]See Raul Vidales, "*Sujeto histórico de la teología de la liberación,*" in Jorge Pixley and Jean-Pierre Bastian (eds.), *Praxis cristiana y producción teológica* (Salamanca: Sigueme, 1979), pp. 17-30, as well as Jon Sobrino, S.J., "The Church of the Poor: Resurrection of the True Church," in *The True Church and the Poor*, pp. 84-124.
[558]Gustavo Gutiérrez, "Church of the Poor," pp. 21-22.
[559]In his critique of Gutiérrez's *A Theology of Liberation*, North American Jesuit social ethicist David Hollenbach expressed surprise at the lack of any entry on "human rights" or "human dignity." See David Hollenbach, S.J., *Claims in Conflict*, p. 204.
[560]Gustavo Gutiérrez, *A Theology of Liberation*, pp. 33-35.

defended by the very people who have generated poverty and misery in the past and the present."[561] As Jon Sobrino noted:

> It is from the poor that theology receives its new eyes to see the Gospel and historical reality more correctly, and thus to seize the real theological problems and orientate its response in the proper direction. In a word, the poor, with a radicality and authenticity hardly attainable elsewhere, render present the *res theologica.*[562]

Within the theology of liberation, the notion of "praxis" served not merely the goal, but also the criterion of theological method. Johannes Baptist Metz defined "praxis" as integral to faith:

> Christianity is in its very being, as messianic praxis of discipleship, political. It is mystical and political at the same time, and it leads us into a responsibility, not only for what we do or fail to do but also for what we allow to happen to others in our presence, before our eyes... It is of the very essence of the Christian faith that it is never just believed, but rather...enacted.[563]

Liberation theologians utilized the term praxis to indicate that the liberation they seek is more than a technocratic or economic development – but rather, has religious, social, political, and personal dimensions.[564] In his early address that gave birth to the theology of liberation, at Chimbote, Peru in July, 1968, Gustavo Gutiérrez announced, "One cannot be a Christian in these times without a commitment to

---

[561]Juan Luís Segundo, S.J., *Faith and Ideologies*, p. 303, n.13.

[562]Jon Sobrino, S.J., "Foreword," in Pablo Galdámez, *Faith of a People: The Story of a Christian Community in El Salvador, 1970-1980* (Maryknoll, NY: Orbis Books, 1986), p. xvi.

[563]Johannes Baptist Metz, *The Emergent Church: The Future of Christianity in a Postbourgeois World* (NY: Crossroad, 1981), p. 27.

[564]See Clodovis Boff, *Theology and Praxis* (Maryknoll, NY: Orbis Books, 1987), Rebecca Chopp, *The Praxis of Suffering* (Maryknoll, NY: Orbis Books, 1986), and Charles Davis, "Theology and Praxis," in *Cross Currents* (Summer, 1973), pp. 154-168.

liberation. To be a Christian in our epoch, it is necessary to commit oneself in one way or another in the process of human emancipation."[565] After the initial act of commitment, liberation theology charged each believer to verify in action his or her faith witness. In Gutiérrez's words, "Solidarity with the poor implies... a liberating social praxis: that is, a transforming activity directed towards the creation of a just, free society."[566] In *A Theology of Liberation*, Gutiérrez reflected: "In Latin America, we are in the midst of a full-blown process of revolutionary ferment."[567] In response to this perception, in an essay first published in 1973 on "Liberation Praxis and Christian Faith," Gutiérrez made use of the notion of "class struggle" as an interpretive key to liberation theology.

> An option for the poor is an option for one class against another. An option for the poor means a new awareness of class confrontation. It means taking sides with the dispossessed. It means entering the world of the exploited social class, with its values, its cultural categories. It means entering into solidarity with its interests and its struggles.[568]

Even at this juncture, Gutiérrez did not call for violent "class struggle." Nor did he lionize it as the "driving force in history." He merely affirmed that the Church should acknowledge the fact of class struggle and situate itself on the side of the poor.[569] At this point in his career, Gutiérrez dabbled in Marxist-socialist analysis,[570]

---

[565]Gustavo Gutiérrez, "Toward a Theology of Liberation," p. 75.
[566]Gustavo Gutiérrez, "Liberation, Theology, and Proclamation," p. 60.
[567]Gustavo Gutiérrez, *A Theology of Liberation*, p. 89.
[568]Printed in English as "Liberation Praxis and Christian Faith," in Gustavo Gutiérrez, *The Power of the Poor in History*, p. 45. For a similar perspective, see also Leonardo Boff and Clodovis Boff, *Liberation Theology: From Dialogue to Confrontation*, p. 60.
[569]See Gustavo Gutiérrez, *A Theology of Liberation*, pp. 272-279.
[570]For a useful discussion of Marxist analysis in liberation theology, see Joseph Laishley, "Theological Trends: The Theology of Liberation I and II," in *The Way* 17 (July, 1977), pp. 217-218 and (October, 1977), pp. 301-311, as well as Segundo Galilea, "The Theology of Liberation," in *Lumen Vitae* 33 (1978), p. 342.

as evidenced in his presentation at the conference at Santiago, Chile in 1972, sponsored by "Christians for Socialism."[571] Its final document, drafted by Hugo Assmann, Gutiérrez, and Giulio Girardi, argued that "the task of fashioning socialism is the only way to combat imperialism and break away from our situation of dependence."[572] The document held out the possibility of a "middle way" between liberal capitalism and socialism, and urged Christians to take "a definite stand on the side of the exploited in order to break the alliance" between Christianity and the ruling classes.[573] In his earlier writings, Gutiérrez also spoke of the need to transform society by means of "a radical change in the foundation of society, that is, the private ownership of the means of production."[574]

In a like vein, in late 1970, Cardinal Raul Silva of Chile told a Cuban journalist:

> I believe that socialism contains important Christian values, and in many respects is very superior to capitalism – the value it places on work, and the primacy of the person against capital. I think that other extraordinary values of socialism are its break with the necessity and tyranny of the pursuit of profit and its ability to coordinate all levels of production. I believe that these ideals which it espouses are very close to the Church's preferred goals in the organization of society.[575]

---

[571]See Robert McAfee Brown, *Theology in a New Key* (Philadelphia: Westminster, 1978), pp. 55-56, as well as Arthur McGovern, S.J., *Liberation Theology and Its Critics: Toward an Assessment* (Maryknoll, NY: Orbis Books, 1989), pp. 140-141.

[572]Cited in John Eagleson (ed.), *Christians and Socialism* (Maryknoll, NY: Orbis Books, 1980), p. 163. For the complete text, see Carlos Oviedo Camus (ed.), *Documentos del Episcopado de Chile, 1970-1973* (Santiago de Chile: Ediciones Mundo, 1974), pp. 58-100.

[573]Cited in John Eagleson (ed.), *Christians and Socialism* (Maryknoll, NY: Orbis Books, 1980), p. 173.

[574]Gustavo Gutiérrez, *A Theology of Liberation*, p. 202.

[575]*Ultíma Hora*, November 12, 1970, p. 2.

In April, 1971, under the leadership of the Jesuit theologian Gonzalo Arroyo, the "Group of Eighty" Chilean social activist priests issued its "Declaration of the Eighty," wherein they stated:

> As Christians, we do not see any incompatibility between Christianity and socialism. Quite the contrary is true. As the Cardinal [Raul Silva] of Santiago said last November, "There are more gospel values in socialism than there are in capitalism." The fact is that socialism offers new hope that humanity can be more complete, and hence more evangelical – that is, more conformed to Jesus Christ, who came to liberate us from any and every form or bondage.[576]

Even so consistent a critic of liberation theology as Alfonso Lopez Trujillo partially concurred: "We are convinced that capitalism is a human failure."[577]

Juan Luís Segundo argued that a choice between socialism and capitalism can and ought to be made. He defined socialism as "a political regime in which ownership of the means of production is taken away from individuals and handed over to higher institutions whose main concern is the common good."[578] Appealing to the example of Jesus and of the Hebrew Prophets, Segundo asserted that they made bold political decisions not through the application of theological criteria, but by a compassionate, direct response based on evaluations of present day realities. He argued that Christian theology must do the same by confronting a decision for socialism.[579] The same point was forcefully made in the "Final Document of the

---

[576]Declaration of the Eighty," cited in Alfred T. Hennelly, S.J., *Liberation Theology: A Documentary History*, p. 143. See also Pablo Richard, *Origen y desarrollo del Movimiento Cristianos por el Socialismo, Chile, 1970-1973* (Paris: Centre Lebret, 1975).

[577]Alfonso Lopez Trujillo, *Liberation or Revolution?: An Examination of the Priest's Role in the Socio-Economic Class Struggle in Latin America* (Huntington, IN: Our Sunday Visitor, 1977), p. 101.

[578]Juan Luís Segundo, S.J., "Capitalism Versus Socialism: *Crux Theologica*," in Rosino Gibellini (ed.), *Frontiers of Theology in Latin America*, p. 249.

[579]Juan Luís Segundo, S.J., "Liberation, Theology and Proclamation," in Rosino Gibellini (ed.), *Frontiers of Theology in Latin America*, pp. 253-256.

Convention" of "Christians for Socialism," in their statement of April 30, 1972.[580] In April, 1972, at the height of the Chilean socialist regime of Salvador Allende, a group of four hundred priests and lay people attended the founding congress of the movement "Christians for Socialism."[581] Estimates placed over ten percent of the Chilean Catholic clergy of the early 1970's as actively involved with "Christians for Socialism," along with many religious, laity, and Protestant pastors.[582]

Writing in the early 1970's in *A Theology of Liberation*, Gustavo Gutiérrez advocated that theology should engage in "direct and fruitful confrontation with Marxism... in reflecting on the meaning of the transformation of this world and of the action of man in history."[583] He identified Marxist analytical tools as "perhaps the most fruitful and far-reaching approach" for achieving the goals of integral liberation, which "can even mean taking the path of socialism."[584] Gutiérrez called for the creation of an entirely new social order, and identified socialism as the most fruitful and far-reaching approach to liberation. But he was far more cautious in speaking of socialism than Segundo. Gutiérrez contended that while no monolithic orientation exists within the liberation movement, it can permit following the path of socialism, although the inherent ambiguities of the term require careful distinctions.[585] However, in a 1974 essay he revised his thinking on this matter to argue that

---

[580]John Eagleson (ed.), *Christians and Socialism*, pp. 160-175.

[581]See "*Evangelio, Politica, y Socialismo*," in Carlos Oviedo Camus (ed.), *Documentos del Episcopado de Chile, 1970-1973* (Santiago de Chile: Ediciones Mundo, 1974); Roger Vekemans, S.J., *Teología de la Liberación y Cristianos por el Socialismo* (Bogotá: CEDIAL, 1976); and, Pablo Richard, *Origen y desarrollo del Movimiento Cristianos por el Socialismo, Chile, 1970-1973* (Paris: Centre Lebret, 1975).

[582]See Franz Vanderschueren and Jaime Rojas, "The Catholic Church of Chile: From 'Social Christiantity' to 'Christians for Socialism,'" in *LARU Studies 1* (February, 1977), pp. 58-59; Bartolomeo Sorge, "*El movimiento de los 'Cristianos por el Socialismo*,'" in *Criterio*, September 12, 1974, pp. 488-497; and, Brian H. Smith, *The Church and Politics in Chile: Challenges to Modern Catholicism* (Princeton, NJ: Princeton University Press, 1982).

[583]Gustavo Gutiérrez, *A Theology of Liberation*, p. 9.

[584]Ibid., pp. 90, 111.

[585]See Gustavo Gutiérrez, "Liberation, Theology, and Proclamation," p. 129.

authentic liberation "is not identified with any social form, however just it may appear at the time."[586]

Paul Sigmund posited two distinct and variant stages in the development of liberation theology: an earlier, Marxist phase and one that later focused its attention on the CEB phenomenon.[587] This shift in posture indicated that by the late 1970s and early 1980s, the central thrust of liberation theology became less enamored of Marxist methodology, and in the words of José Comblin, "increasingly less socio-political and more religious and ecclesial."[588] In its early stages, some liberation theologians like Pablo Richard,[589] Hugo Assmann,[590] Juan Luís Segundo,[591] and Gustavo Gutiérrez did not hesitate to use Marxist-socialist instruments as a tool of analysis for understanding the present-day reality in Latin America. Marxist ideas and terminology such as "praxis," "ideology," and "structural change" were borrowed and recast in the idiom of the theology of liberation. Assmann admitted, at this time of writing, "for most of those who use this language, this implies the use of a sociological analysis derived from Marxism."[592] Gutiérrez cited the Peruvian Marxist sociologist José Carlos Mariátegui as his model for adapting Marxism as a flexible method for interpreting society.[593] In his own formulation of the theology of

---

[586]Cited in Gustavo Gutiérrez, "Liberation, Theology, and Proclamation," p. 74. British Marxist theorist Alistair Kee took the leftist-leaning pioneering liberation theologians to task for not being sufficiently Marxist in their analysis. See his *Marx and the Failure of Liberation Theology* (London: SCM, 1990).

[587]See Paul Sigmund, "Whither Liberation Theology?," in *Crisis* (January, 1987), pp. 5-14, along with *Liberation Theology at the Crossroads* (NY: Oxford University Press, 1990), pp. 157-159, 177.

[588]José Comblin, "The Church and the Defense of Human Rights," in Enrique Dussel (ed.), *The Church in Latin America: 1492-1992*, p. 448.

[589]Pablo Richard, *Death of Christendoms, Birth of the Church* (Maryknoll, NY: Orbis Books, 1987).

[590]Hugo Assmann, *Theology for a Nomad Church* (Maryknoll, NY: Orbis Books, 1976).

[591]Juan Luís Segundo, S.J., "Capitalism Versus Socialism: *Crux Theologica*," in Rosino Gibellini (ed.), *Frontiers of Theology in Latin America* (Maryknoll, NY: Orbis Books, 1979), pp. 240-259.

[592]Hugo Assmann, *Theology for a Nomad Church*, p. 16.

[593]Gustavo Gutiérrez, *A Theology of Liberation*, pp. 90, 220. See also Arthur McGovern, *Liberation Theology and Its Critics*, p. 140, and Robert McAfee Brown, *Gustavo Gutiérrez*, pp. 26-27.

liberation, Gutiérrez was deeply influenced by three Peruvian theorists and writers: José Carlos Mariátegui, César Vallejo, and José María Arguedas.[594] Gutiérrez reflected on the elements that conspired to form this new perspective:

> I discovered three things. I discovered that poverty was a destructive thing, something to be fought against and destroyed, not merely something which was the object of our charity. Secondly, I discovered that poverty was not accidental. The fact that these people are poor and not rich is not just a matter of chance, but the result of a structure. It was a structural question. Thirdly, I discovered that poor people were a social class. When I discovered that poverty was something to be fought against... it became crystal clear that in order to serve the poor, one had to move into political action.[595]

As liberation theology evolved into its second decade, in the main, when Marxist theory or analysis were utilized at all, it was only as an instrument of clarification in order to expose mechanisms of oppression and to explode the false expectation that the poor are unable to encounter solutions to their plight within the boundaries of liberal capitalism. As the Leonardo and Clodovis Boff later commented:

---

[594]On the influence of these three Peruvian figures upon Gutiérrez, see the following essays in the *feschrift* honoring him on his sixtieth birthday, *Expanding the View: Essays in Honor of Gustavo Gutiérrez*: Gustavo Gutiérrez, "Expanding the View," p. 22; Frei Betto, "Gustavo Gutiérrez: A Friendly Profile," p. 36; Stephen Judd, M.M., "Gustavo Gutiérrez and the Originality of the Peruvian Experience," pp. 68-69; as well as Robert McAfee Brown, *Gustavo Gutiérrez: An Introduction to Liberation Theology*, pp. 27-31. Frei Betto quite correctly asserted: "Nonetheless there is no denying the European roots [of Gutiérrez's thought] springing from [Jacques] Maritain's integral humanism, [Emmanuel] Mounier's committed personalism, [Pierre] Teilhard de Chardin's progressive evolutionism, [Henri] de Lubac's social dogmatics, [Yves] Congar's theology of the laity, [Louis] Lebret's theology of development, [José] Comblin's theology of revolution, or [Johannes Baptist] Metz's political theology," in *Expanding the View*, p. 32.

[595]Recounted from the notes of Gutiérrez's talk at El Escorial by José Míguez Bonino, in Bonino's chapter contained in Sergio Torres and John Eagleson (eds.), *Theology in the Americas* For the relevant excerpts of Gutiérrez's address in English, see Gerald Anderson and Thomas F. Stransky, C.S.P. (eds.), *Mission Trends No. 3* (NY: Paulist Press, 1976), pp. 64-69.

> Marxism is a secondary, peripheral issue. When Marxism is used at all, it is used only *partially* and *instrumentally*. The popes themselves, the bishops, and many non-Marxist social scientists do the same thing. It is the faith that assimilates and subsumes elements of Marxism, then, and not the other way around... We confess: The difficult subsumption of Marxist elements has not always been effected with adequate lucidity, perspicacity, and maturity. But we are improving along the way.[596]

José Míguez Bonino reflected the ongoing refinement of his view: "I have more and more come to think in terms of a long humanist-socialist tradition, with early Christian and Hellenic roots which have developed in the modern world, in which Marx has played an insistent – even decisive – part, but which he has neither created nor fulfilled."[597] Juan Luís Segundo observed further:

> There are problems connected with applying the label "Marxist" to a line of thought or a source of influence... Philosophic thought would never be the same after Aristotle as it was before him... After Marx, our way of conceiving and posing the problems of society will never be the same again... In that sense, Latin American theology is certainly Marxist. I know that my remark will be taken out of context, but one cannot go on trying to forestall every partisan or stupid misunderstanding forever.[598]

In 1974, Dom Helder Câmara defended his preference for utilizing Marxist analysis in a speech delivered at the University of Chicago: "As the University of Chicago chose to take upon herself the responsibility of celebrating St. Thomas's

---

[596]Leonardo Boff and Clodovis Boff, *Liberation Theology: From Confrontation to Dialogue*, pp. 22-23. Compare the statement of Ronaldo Muñoz that in Chile from 1967-1973, "The Christian-Marxist confrontation... was not always carried out with sufficient maturity and critical awareness," in "*Reacciones de los teologos latinamericanos a propósito de la 'Instrucción*,'" in *Revista Latinoamericana de teología* I (May-August, 1984), p. 239.
[597]José Míguez Bonino, "For Life Against Death: A Theology That Takes Sides," p. 125.
[598]Juan Luís Segundo, S.J., *The Liberation of Theology*, p. 35.

Seventh Centenary, we have the right to the best way to honor the centenary... [which] should be for the University of Chicago to try, today, to do with Karl Marx what St. Thomas, in his day, did with Aristotle."[599] Câmara further suggested that a new methodology be employed by theology to utilize analytical methods as a tool for evaluating social reality from the viewpoint of the poor. Even the careful, erudite American Jesuit theologian of the mid-Twentieth Century, John Courtney Murray, described the Christian-Marxist dialogue as "a very tricky but necessary thing," while he concluded, "We have to listen to the Marxist critique of religion. We can learn much [through it] about our faith."[600]

The vanguard of liberation theologians appropriated the tools of Marxist-socialist analysis in light of the Thomistic axiom that all truth, no matter who utters it, is from the Holy Spirit: "All truth, no matter who speaks it, derives from the Holy Spirit."[601] Liberation theology utilized Marxism as an instrument, in order to offer "methodological pointers" that challenge prevailing modes of liberal capitalism, – but not as the guide for theological reflection – a position reserved for Jesus Christ and the Word of Scripture.[602] In a work first published in 1986, the Boff brothers pointed out that liberation theology freely borrows from Marxism certain "methodological pointers" that have proved fruitful in understanding the world of the oppressed, such as: a). the importance of economic factors; b). attention to class

---

[599]Dom Helder Câmara, "Thomas Aquinas and Karl Marx: The Challenge to Christians," in *Church and the World* 10 (Chicago: University of Chicago Press, 1972). See also James V. Schall, S.J., *Liberation Theology In Latin America: With Selected Essays and Documents* (San Francisco: Ignatius Press, 1982), pp. 283-284, and Michael Novak, "Liberation Theology and the Pope," in Quentin L. *Quade, The Pope and Revolution: John Paul II Confronts Liberation Theology* (Washington, DC: Ethics and Public Policy Center, 1982), pp. 78-79.

[600]Cited in Donald Pelotte, S.S., *John Courtney Murray: Theologian in Conflict* (NY: Paulist Press, 1975), p. 102.

[601]From the scholastic dictum: "*Omne verum, a quocumque dictatur, a Spiritu Sancto est.*"

[602]On this point, see the remarks of Leonardo Boff and Clodovis Boff, *Introducing Liberation Theology*, p. 28.

struggle; and, c). the mystifying power of ideologies, including religious ones. As the Boffs ultimately concluded: "Liberation theology, therefore, maintains a decidedly critical stance in relation to Marxism... Marxist materialism and atheism do not even constitute a temptation for liberation theologians."[603] They noted additionally: "Marx is not the godfather of liberation theology. The tool of Marxist analysis is a mediation. It might be dangerous, but it is useful in order to understand social reality."[604]

This movement away from a more uncritical acceptance of Marxist-socialist thought among the pioneers of liberation theology was paralleled in the work of José Porfirio Miranda, who revised the lines of thought contained within his earlier works, such as *Marx and the Bible*[605] and *Marx Against the Marxists*.[606] In a subsequent essay, Miranda more fully rejected Marxism, and concluded that its analysis was based on a false reductionism.[607] Elsewhere, Mirando concluded: "...precisely when the human being is really at stake the Marxist foundations are inadequate..."[608] As an example of the shift in the utilization of Marxist categories, one notes that in the course of time Gutiérrez adopted a much more nuanced and critical stance toward Marxism and dependency analysis, and argued that theology's use of social science should be subject to continual evaluation and reassessment. He revamped the entire section in the original edition of *A Theology of Liberation* entitled "Christian

---

[603]Leonardo Boff and Clodovis Boff, *Introducing Liberation Theology*, p. 28.
[604]Leonardo Boff and Clodovis Boff, "The Cry of Poverty Coming From Faith," in *DIAL* (April 26, 1984), p. 931, published also in the London *Tablet* (September 8, 1984), p. 856.
[605]José Porfirio Miranda, *Marx and the Bible: A Critique of the Philosophy of Oppression* (Maryknoll, NY: Orbis Books, 1974).
[606]José Porfirio Miranda, *Marx Against the Marxists* (Maryknoll, NY: Orbis Books, 1980).
[607]José Porfirio Miranda, "Is Marxism Essentially Atheistic?," in *Journal of Ecumenical Studies* 22 (Summer, 1985). On this point, see also the famous letter of Father Pedro Arrupe, S.J., the general of the Jesuit Order, "Letter to the Provincials of Latin America on Marxist Analysis," *Acta Romana Societatis Iesu* 18:1 (1980).
[608]José Porfirio Miranda, *Being and the Messiah* (Maryknoll, NY: Orbis Books, 1980), p. 37.

Brotherhood and Class Struggle,"[609] and re-titled it "Faith and Social Conflict" in the revised version.[610] In a 1986 essay devoted to the issue of Marxist analysis, Gutiérrez insisted that there was never any specific proposal in liberation theology to synthesize Marxism and Christianity.[611] By 1988, Gutiérrez stated flatly in an interview, "Socialism is not an essential of liberation theology; one can support liberation theology or do liberation theology without espousing socialism."[612]

For several months prior to the beginning of the 1968 Medellín Conference, the bishops were presented with a series of well-crafted position papers called "*ponencias*" that developed the theme of the "signs of the times in Latin America" and their Christian interpretation. Medellín has been hailed "as a decisive watershed in the history of the Church in Latin America."[613] Throughout the course of the Second Vatican Council, the progressive leadership of Manuel Larrain, Helder Câmara and other bishops manifested itself through their tireless efforts to pull the leadership of the regional Church of Latin America together, and to propel its social justice agenda into the future. During this period when Larrain served as President of CELAM, the Latin American bishops gathered each year in Rome during the sessions of the Council, in order to advance its agenda. At the time, Larrain proposed a regional Latin American conference in order to apply the vision of Vatican II. Pope

---

[609]Gustavo Gutiérrez, *A Theology of Liberation* (Maryknoll, NY: Orbis Books, 1973), pp. 272-279.
[610]Ibid., pp. 156-161.
[611]Gustavo Gutiérrez, "The Truth Shall Make You Free," in *The Truth Shall Make You Free*, pp. 85-91.
[612]Gustavo Gutiérrez, interview with Arthur McGovern, S.J., in *Liberation Theology and Its Critics*, p. 148. Elsewhere in the same book, McGovern points out that in the 1975 Peruvian summer school course that Gutiérrez taught, there were 200 pages of reading material about Marxism, whereas in the 1988 session of the same summer school "Marxism was never even mentioned," p. 164. It is instructive to note that in Gutiérrez's later book, *We Drink From Our Own Wells* (Maryknoll, NY: Orbis Books, 1988), the Bible merits nearly 400 references, while Marxism receives none.
[613]Alfred T. Hennelly, S.J., "Courage With Primitive Weapons," in *Cross Currents* (Spring, 1978), p. 9.

Paul VI and the bishops of CELAM embraced the idea, and the second conference took place at Medellín, Colombia from August 2 until September 2, 1968.

In the main, Medellín reflected the concerns of the burgeoning progressive element of the Latin American Church. Archbishop Marcos McGrath of Panama and Bishop Helder Câmara of Brazil helped to manage the agenda of the conference. Gustavo Gutiérrez and Pierre Bigo composed the document on "Peace"; Gutiérrez authored the draft on "Poverty"; and, Helder Câmara, Renato Poblete, and Bishop Samuel Ruíz Garcia of Mexico wrote the draft on "Justice."[614] As Enrique Dussel asserted, "...the thought of that [Medellín] Conference stands somewhere in the transitional phase between 'developmentalism' and the 'theology of liberation.'"[615] Although the Medellín conference never used the term "liberation theology," nor did it employ the phrase "preferential option for the poor," liberation theology began to take firm root prior to the conference, and permeated its agenda, as reflected in its documents on "Justice," "Peace," and "Youth." In this vein, as Segundo Galilea asserted, "We can claim that the idea of liberation and the theology of liberation acquired ecclesial status at the Medellín conference."[616]

In an early commentary on the documents of Medellín, Gustavo Gutiérrez reflected:

> ...from a variety of sources inside the Latin American Church, the term "development" is gradually being replaced by the term "liberation." The word and the idea behind it express the desire to get rid of the condition of dependence, but even more than that they underline the desire for the oppressed people to seize the reins of their own destiny and shake free from the present servitude, as a symbol of

---

[614]See Christian Smith, *The Emergence of Liberation Theology*, p. 160.
[615]Enrique Dussel, *History and the Theology of Liberation*, p. 115.
[616]Segundo Galilea, *La teología de la liberación después de Puebla* (Santiago de Chile: Ediciones ISPLAG, 1979), p. 22, and "The Theology of Liberation: A General Survey," in *Lumen Vitae* XXIII (1179:3), p. 337.

> the freedom from sin promised by Christ. This liberation will only be achieved by a thorough change of structures.[617]

The Medellín documents strikingly condemned what they addressed as "structural injustice." The opening words of the "Document on Peace" emphasized this point:

> If "development is the new name for peace," Latin American underdevelopment, with its own characteristics in the different countries, is an unjust situation which promotes tensions that conspire against peace... This injustice nullifies the eventual positive effect of external aid and constitutes a permanent menace against peace, because our countries sense that "one hand takes away what the other hand gives" (nos. 1, 9).

In the "Document on Peace," the bishops denounced the extreme inequality that divided the social classes (no. 3). They decried international imperialism, and placed the principal guilt for the economic dependence of Latin American countries on foreign monopolistic powers (no. 9). They further denounced the use of violence, and observed that situations of injustice were so grave and rampant as to constitute "institutional violence" (nos. 16-19).

The expressed theme of the Medellín Conference was "the Church in the Current Transformation of Latin America in Light of the Council."[618] Since Latin America was a region that was both poor and Christian, at Medellín it seemed incumbent upon the Latin American bishops to take seriously the intuition of Pope John that the Church is and wants to be "the Church of the poor." Vatican II

---

[617]See the Gustavo Gutiérrez, "A Latin American Perception of a Theology of Liberation," in Louis Michael Colonese (ed.), *Conscientization for Liberation*, p. 67, as well as his comments on "The Theology of Liberation: A General Survey," in *Lumen Vitae* XXXIII (1978:3), p. 337.
[618]The standard English source for quotations from the Medellín documents cited is Louis Michael Colonnese (ed.), *The Church in the Present Day Transformation of Latin America in the Light of the Council: Vol. II, Conclusions* (Washington, DC: Secretariat for Latin America, National Conference of Catholic Bishops, 1979 edition).

produced a theological atmosphere marked by great freedom and creativity. This renewal offered Latin American theologians the impetus to reflect in their own idiom and categories about pastoral problems affecting their own countries.

Medellín attempted to answer the question of what is required of the Church if it is to be a universal sacrament of salvation in a world marred by poverty and injustice. At Medellín, the Latin American bishops analyzed their indigenous realities, and in so doing adopted a new terminology: of "structural injustice"; of participation"; of "conscientization"; of "institutional violence"; and, of "preference for the poor." The Medellín conclusions gave rise to a new tone and a new praxis within the Church of Latin America. The Medellín conference provided the impulse for the main lines along which the Church was to develop in the ensuing decades. As Gustavo Gutiérrez noted:

> This reversal, this expression of the maturity of the Latin American Christian community – and, above all, the expression of the misery, hope and commitment in which the peoples of Latin America live – gave Medellín its thrust and power... It is the viewpoint of the poor that gives Medellín its character and originality, whatever may have been its inevitable lacunae and shortcomings.[619]

The theme of liberation of the poor and oppressed resonated consistently as a major concern of the Medellín Conference.[620] By the time of Vatican II, the people of the developing nations constituted nearly eighty percent of humankind. For these masses, the turn in theological reflection and practice afforded new hope, and offered them a new voice. At Medellín, the Church in Latin America came to fuller stature,

---

[619]Gustavo Gutiérrez, "Theology from the Underside of History," in *The Power of the Poor in History*, p. 199.

[620]See Ricardo Antoncich, *El tema de la liberación en Medellín y el Sinodo de 1974* (Lima: *Comisión Episcopal de Acción Social*, 1975), and José Damart, *Irupción y caminar de la Iglesia de los pobres: presencia de Medellín* (Lima: Instituto Bartolomé de las Casas, 1989).

and received a new central thrust and dynamism. As Jon Sobrino observed, "The Medellín Conference – the most important symbol of the new magisterium – was possible not simply because of Vatican II. Vatican II was indeed a condition for Medellín, but the real efficient cause of that Conference is to be found in the poor."[621] While Vatican II created the conditions that made Medellín possible, much of the approach, language, and commitment of Medellín represented a major advance on the Council, as the Latin American bishops embraced a new approach, a new language, and a new option, in solidarity with the poor. They sought to "make the Church the humble servant of all our people" ("Document on Poverty," no. 8), and to give "preference to the poorest and most needy sectors" ("Document on Poverty," no. 9). The bishops at Medellín declared that "solidarity with the poor... means that we make ours their problems and struggles, that we know how to speak with them" ("Document on Poverty," no. 10).

After Medellín, in a concerted way, the Church began to ask, "How can the Gospel speak to the poor, to a marginalized people considered as non-persons in the modern world?" The interpretation of the Bible from the "underside," from the perspective of the poor, came to be seen as central to the task and method of this new theology.[622] In the previous era of church history, theologians like John Mackay of Princeton Theological Seminary suggested that in Latin American Christianity, the masses worshipped either a baby Jesus or a dead Christ, neither of whom had any power.[623] In the main, an air of resignation and fatalism pervaded the religious experience of the region, which the Church often perpetuated and reinforced with promises of rewards in heaven for the earthly sacrifices endured by the downtrodden

---

[621]Jon Sobrino, S.J., *The True Church and the Poor*, p. 113.
[622]See Gustavo Gutiérrez, "Theology From the Underside of History," in *The Power of the Poor in History*, pp. 169-221.
[623] John Mackay, *The Other Spanish Christ* (NY: Macmillan, 1932).

masses. As Helder Câmara noted: "We clergy are responsible for the fatalism always shown by the poor in the resignation with which they acknowledged their poverty and the backwardness of the underdeveloped nations. Here Marxists show their perception in seeing religion as an alienated and alienating force, as, – in other words, – the opium of the people."[624]

The Medellín documents called for "the liberation of the entire human being and all human beings" ("Document on Youth," no. 15). They emphasize that "Christ... focused his Mission around proclaiming the liberation of the poor... [who] place before the Church a challenge and a Mission that it cannot sidestep" ("Document on Poverty," no. 7). They continued in the same vein: "We wish the Latin American Church to be the evangelizer of the poor and one with them" (no. 8).[625] The bishops at Medellín called for the deliverance of "human beings from [their] cultural, economic, and political servitude" ("Document on Education," no. 7), and, in like manner, scored the existence of "unjust social, political, economic and social inequalities" that typify the Latin American experience ("Document on Peace," no. 14).

Influenced by *Gaudium et Spes* and *Populorum Progressio*, the Latin American bishops pondered the disturbing picture brought into focus by an analysis of the "signs of the times" within their region. As Segundo Galilea suggested, "Medellín's characteristic way (both creative and selective) of conceiving liberation is due both to its analysis of specific signs of the times and to *Populorum Progressio*, in which the Church renews its commitment to the integral promotion of the poorest

---

[624]Cited in Joséf Lukacs, "The Problem of Poverty and the Poor in Catholic Social Teaching: A Marxist Perspective," in Charles E. Curran and Richard A. McCormick, S.J. (eds.), *Readings in Moral Theology No. 5: Official Catholic Social Teaching*, p. 312 n.4.

[625]Jon Sobrino, S.J., suggests that the aforementioned points "give us a hermeneutical principle from which there is no turning back," in *The True Church and the Poor*, p. 257.

of peoples (a point that was inadequately made at the Council)."[626] As the Medellín documents stated conclusively: "We must sharpen the awareness of our duty of solidarity with the poor, which love imposes on us. This solidarity means that we make our own their problems and their struggles, that we know how to speak with them" ("Document on Poverty," no. 10). Instead of simply applying the teaching of the Second Vatican Council to the Latin American scene, the bishops at Medellín sought to enrich the conciliar teachings from a point of departure based in the reality of the poor and oppressed of the continent. As the beginning of the "Document on Justice" asserted: "The misery that besets large masses of human beings in all of our countries... as a collective fact, expresses itself as injustice that cries out to the heavens... evident in the unjust social structures which characterize the Latin American situation" (nos. 1, 2). The Medellín "Document on Peace" argued that justice and peace could prevail only "by means of dynamic action of awakening ("*concientización*") and by the organization of the popular sectors that are capable of pressing public officials who are often impotent in their social projects without popular support" (no. 2).

The bishops at Medellín redefined the Mission of the Church in concrete terms: "The Latin American Church has a message for all on this continent who hunger and thirst for justice" ("Document on Justice," no. 3). They asserted that "the misery that besets large masses of human beings in all of our countries... as a collective fact, is an injustice that cries to heaven," and called "for total emancipation – liberation, from all servitude" ("Document on Justice," no. 1). They scored the reality of structural injustice in the "Document on Justice": "... in many instances, Latin America finds itself faced with a situation of injustice that can be called

[626]Segundo Galilea, "Latin America in the Medellín and Puebla Conferences: An Example of Selective and Creative Reception of Vatican II," in Giuseppe Alberigo, *et al.* (eds.), *The Reception of Vatican II*, p. 64.

institutionalized violence" (no. 16). At Medellín, the Latin American Church made a conscious effort to seek to liberate and to humanize the situation of the oppressed peoples of their continent. The bishops renewed their commitment to the integral promotion of the poorest among them, and for the first time, made use of the word and theme of "liberation" in an official church document. The Medellín documents espoused an integral liberation aimed toward "authentic development – that is, deliverance for each and every one from less human to more human conditions of life" ("Introduction to Conclusions," no. 6). They advocated the attempt to free the downtrodden "from the slavery to which sin has subjected them – hunger, misery, oppression, and ignorance, in a word, injustice and hatred, which have their origins in human selfishness" ("Document on Justice," no. 3). Medellín gave impetus to the emergence of a "liberation perspective" and to the unfolding growth of the grassroots communities (*comunidades de base*). From this context a new theology developed, based on the aspirations and agonies of the poor of Latin America.

Without employing the precise phrase, Medellín lent credence to the notion that the Church must employ a "preferential option for the poor." This central thrust emerged as the first flowering of the theme of liberation that began to be refined systematically only after Medellín. The Medellín documents showed a new awareness by the Church of the reality of poverty. The Medellín "Document on Youth" stated: "The Church in Latin America should be manifested, in an increasingly clear manner, as truly poor, Missionary, and paschal, separate from all temporal power and courageously committed to the liberation of each and every person" (no. 15). As Gustavo Gutiérrez pointed out:

> The exact expression ["preferential option for the poor"] cannot be found in the Medellín documents – but the idea is clearly there. 'Preferential' and 'option' do appear in Medellín, and 'poor' is the

> central point. The full expression comes from the years immediately following Medellín and is explicitly found in Puebla.[627]

In the Medellín "Document on Poverty," under the heading of "Solidarity and Preference for the Poor," the bishops already spoke of the need to "give a preference to the poorest and neediest, and to those who are segregated for any reason. We must encourage and step up the studies and initiatives that are directed to this end" (no. 9). This renewed theological emphasis on the role of the Church *vis à vis* the poor was not intended to be exclusive. As Gustavo Gutiérrez pointed out in a subsequent essay:

> The very word "preference" denies all exclusiveness and seeks rather to call attention to those who are the first – though not the only ones – with whom we should be in solidarity... [F]rom the very beginning of liberation theology, as many of my writings show, I insisted that the great challenge was to maintain both the universality of God's love and God's predilection for those who are on the lowest rung of the ladder of history. To focus exclusively on the one or the other is to mutilate the Christian message. Therefore every attempt at such an exclusive emphasis must be rejected.[628]

At Puebla, in 1979, the explicit formula of the "preferential option for the poor" emerged in a formal church document and gained currency, but the phrase began to take root in Latin America following the Medellín Conference. As Gustavo Gutiérrez recounted in a 1993 interview:

> The first use of the term, "the preferential option for the poor," was by me in my 1973 article, "*Fe cristiana y praxis de liberación*," which appeared in *Signos de liberación*. At least that is the first use of the term of which I am aware. I do not know of anyone else using

---

[627]Gustavo Gutiérrez, "Church of the Poor," *Born of the Poor*, p. 15.
[628]Gustavo Gutiérrez, "Expanding the View," p. 12.

> it beforehand. Medellín used various aspects of the expression, but as far as I know, this [essay] was the first time that this actual expression was utilized.[629]

Gutiérrez expounded upon this point greatly in an interview conducted in 2003:

> I do believe that the option for the poor has become a part of the Catholic social teaching. The phrase comes from the experience of the Latin American Church. The precise term was born somewhere between the Latin American bishops' conferences in Medellín (1968) and Puebla (1979). In Medellín, the three words (option, preferential, poor) are all present, but it was only in the years immediately following Medellín that we brought these words into a complete phrase. It would be accurate to say that the term 'preferential option for the poor' comes from the Latin American church, but the content, the underlying intuition, is entirely biblical. Liberation theology tries to deepen our understanding of this core biblical tradition. The preferential option for the poor has gradually become a central tenet of the church's teaching.[630]

The bishops at Medellín sought to move the Church away from its alliance with the rich and powerful: "The poverty of the Church and her members in Latin America should be a sign and a commitment: a sign of the inestimable value of poverty in God's eyes, and a commitment to solidarity with those who are suffering" ("Document on Poverty," no. 7). The bishops identified a renewed role for themselves:

> To us, the pastors of the Church, belong the duty to educate the Christian conscience, to inspire, stimulate and help orient all the initiatives that contribute to the human formation. It is also up to us to denounce everything which, opposing justice, destroys peace... [to

---

[629]Interview conducted by me with Father Gustavo Gutiérrez at Boston College, Chestnut Hill, Massachusetts, arranged courtesy of Father Robert Imbelli, M.M., July 9, 1993.

[630]Daniel Hartnett, "Remembering the Poor: An Interview with Gustavo Gutiérrez," in *America* (February 3, 2003), p. 14.

> seek] to defend the rights of the poor and oppressed according to the gospel commandment, urging our government and upper classes to eliminate anything that might destroy social peace ("Document on Peace," nos. 20, 22).

In the "Document on Justice," the bishops affirmed: "The Church – the People of God – will lend its support to the downtrodden of every social class so that they might come to know their rights and make use of them" (no. 1). Finally, the bishops at Medellín called for a shift on the part of the Church to become what John XXIII dubbed the "Church of the Poor," in order to denounce the unequal distribution of the world's goods and the social sin that sustains it, and to embrace a simpler lifestyle of evangelical poverty, voluntarily assumed, in line with a tradition taken by the bishops to be "a constant factor in the history of salvation" ("Document on Poverty," [no. 5]).

Medellín served as a watershed event for the Church in Latin America and beyond. At the conclusion of the conference, Paul VI confided to Bishop Eduardo Pironio, then General-Secretary of CELAM: "The Latin American Church had arrived at a degree of maturity and an extraordinary equilibrium that made it capable of assuming fully its own responsibility.[631] As Donal Dorr observed:

> Medellín was to be a turning point in the life of the Latin American Church – and indeed of the Catholic Church as a whole... [It] became the charter for those who were working for a radical renewal of the Church in Latin America. But the influence did not stop there. Medellín gave inspiration to committed Christians all over the world... The major documents concerned with social justice issued by Rome in the following decade have to be understood as being at least partly a reaction to all that is represented by Medellín...[632]

---

[631]In *Boletín CELAM* nos. 15/16 (1968), cited in Edward Cleary, O.P., *Crisis and Change: The Church in Latin America Today*, p. 43.
[632]Donal Dorr, *Option for the Poor*, p. 158.

The meaning of Medellín was to call the Church to pay deeper heed to social issues, but it also possessed a more radical charge. As Gustavo Gutiérrez noted, this new direction sought "to change the focus of the Church – the center of its life and work – and to be present, *really* present, in the world of the poor – to commit the Church to living in the world of the poor."[633] From a North American perspective, Alfred Hennelly concluded that the primary impact of the Medellín Conference was:

> ...to institutionalize in its decrees the experience and practice of a significant number of Catholics in every stratum of the Church from peasants to archbishops. It thus provided legitimization, inspiration, and pastoral plans for a continent-wide preferential option for the poor, encouraging those who were already engaged in the struggle and exhorting the entire Church, both rich and poor, to become involved.[634]

The Medellín Conference decisively plunged the Latin American Church in the direction of the option for the poor, and plotted the world Church on a decisive course of social activism. As Bishop Pedro Casadáliga of Brazil wrote: "The Spirit has decided to administer the eighth sacrament: the voice of the people!"[635] In the wake of the commitments made at Medellín, Leonardo Boff asserted, "For the moment [the Church] is moving outward and plunging deeper... its orientation to the liberation of the poor enjoys a far broader support base now and a great deal more official recognition... Medellín was the baptism of the Latin American Church..."[636] As the following chapter shall indicate, "Puebla was its confirmation,"[637] though not without much intervening struggle and pain.

---

[633]Gustavo Gutiérrez, "Church of the Poor," p. 18.
[634]Alfred T. Hennelly, S.J., *Liberation Theology: A Documentary History*, p. 89.
[635]Pedro Casadáliga, *Cantares de la entere libertad* (Managua, Nicaragua: SEBO, 1984), p 73.
[636]Leonardo Boff, *Faith on the Edge: Religion and Marginalized Existence*, p. 28.
[637]Ibid.

Chapter Four

The Breakthrough at Puebla and Beyond

In a famous letter to O'Neill Daunt, Cardinal John Henry Newman, the giant of Nineteenth Century English Catholicism wrote: "We must recollect, there has seldom been a Council without great confusion after it..."[638] Vatican II was frequently dubbed "Newman's Council," since he anticipated so many of its directions and reforms in the prior century.[639] As Newman scholar C. S. Dessain remarked:

> At the Second Vatican Council... the things Newman fought for were brought forward – freedom, the supremacy of conscience, the Church as communion, a return to Scripture and the Fathers, the rightful place of the laity, work for unity, and all the efforts to meet the needs of the age, and for the Church to take its place in the modern world.[640]

Newman's words proved to be a prophetic utterance a hundred years later, in the wake of Vatican II. He frequently opposed the dualism that marked the Catholicism of his age: "It would be a great mistake for us to suppose that we need quit our temporal calling, and go into retirement, in order to serve God acceptably. Christianity is a religion for the world, for the busy and influential, as well as for the

---

[638]John Henry Newman, Letter to Mr. O'Neill Daunt (August 7, 1870), cited in Wilfred Ward, *The Life of John Henry Cardinal Newman/ Based on His Private Journals and Correspondence*, Volume II (London: Longmans, Green, & Co., 1912), p. 310.
[639]See C. S. Dessain, *Newman's Spiritual Themes* (Dublin: Veritas Publications, 1977), p. 116.
[640]Ibid., p. 30.

poor."[641] In a sermon entitled, "Doing Glory to God in Pursuits of the World," Newman expounded upon this theme:

> It should be recollected that the employments of this world though not themselves heavenly, are after all the way to heaven... The Christian will feel that the true contemplation of his Saviour lies *in* his worldly business; that as Christ is seen in the poor, and in the persecuted, and in children, so is he seen in the employments he puts upon his chosen, whatever they be; that in attending to his own calling he will be meeting Christ; that if he neglect it, he will not on that account enjoy his presence at all the more, but that while performing it, he will see Christ revealed to his soul amid the ordinary actions of the day, as by a sort of sacrament.[642]

In his classic "Essay on the Development of Christian Doctrine," Newman wrote of the character of "the development of Christianity, both as a policy and a doctrine":

> In time, it enters upon strange territory; points of controversy alter [its] bearing; parties rise and fall about it; dangers and hopes appear in new relations, and old principles appear under new forms; it changes with them in order to remain the same. In a higher world it is otherwise; but here below to live is to change, and to be perfect is to have changed often.[643]

---

[641]John Henry Newman, *Historical Sketches* (London: Longmans, Green, & Co., 1881 edition), p. 94.
[642]John Henry Newman, "Doing Glory to God in Pursuits of the World," in *Parochial and Plain Sermons* Volume VIII (London: Longmans, Green, & Co., 1881 edition), pp. 154, 165. Note the parallel to this thinking of Newman in the address to *campesinos* of Pope Paul VI in Mosquera, Colombia on August 23, 1968: "You are a sign, an image, a mystery of the presence of Christ.... And all the Church's tradition recognizes in the poor the sacrament of Christ – not indeed identical with the reality of the Eucharist, but in perfect analogical and mystical correspondence with it. Besides, Jesus himself has told us so in a solemn page of his Gospel, where he proclaims that every person who suffers, everyone who is hungry, sick, unfortunate, in need of compassion and assistance, is himself, as if he himself were that unlucky person, in accordance with the mysterious and potent evangelical sociology, in accordance with the humanism of Christ." Cited in *Osservatore Romano* (August 24, 1968), p. 1.
[643]John Henry Newman, *An Essay on the Development of Christian Doctrine* (London: Longmans, Green, & Co., 1881 edition), p. 40.

Elsewhere in the same essay, Newman insisted:

> If Christianity is to be a universal religion, suited not to one locality or period, but to all times and places, it cannot but vary in its relations and dealings towards the world around it, that is, it will develop. Principles require a very various application according to persons and circumstances, and must be thrown into new shapes according to the form of society which they are to influence.[644]

The new theology that emerged in Catholicism during the late 1960's reflected the dramatic shift in emphasis that Newman portended. Johannes Baptist Metz reflected upon this trend:

> Properly speaking, the so-called hermeneutic problem of theology is not the problem of how systematic theology stands in relation to historical theology, how dogma stands in relation to history, but what is the relation between theory and practice, between understanding the faith and social practice.[645]

Nowhere was this development experienced more keenly than in Latin America, where radical changes were in the offing for the Roman Catholic Church. Concerning the application of the sociological theory of dependence, Gustavo Gutiérrez noted:

> There is probably no more obvious example of a committed science anywhere today than sociology in Latin America, which has taken the decisive step of making "dependence" the central theme of its investigations into the real situation in Latin America. This situation of dependence is the basic starting-point for the process of liberation.

---

[644]Ibid., p. 58.
[645]Johannes B. Metz, *Theology of the World* (NY: Herder & Herder, 1969), p. 112.

> On the theological level an analysis of dependence has produced the language of the theology of liberation.[646]

When Pope John XXIII opened the windows of the Church to a "New Pentecost," the winds of change began to transform a rarefied approach to the reality of structural poverty that long held sway in Roman Catholicism.

Even so progressive a church leader as Pope John XXIII was slow to arrive at this realization. In an address to the bishops of Latin America in November, 1958 he made no mention of poverty.[647] Although Pope John's successor, Pope Paul VI, addressed the subject of poverty more than any of his predecessors, he also composed an allocution on the purposes and method of theology early in his pontificate without ever adverting to the subject of poverty.[648] But by 1970, when the "Pilgrim Pope" visited the shanty town of Tondo in the Philippines, Paul VI responded to a peasant's question concerning what it means to say that the Church loved the poor:

> It means that the Church recognizes your dignity as human persons and children of God; your equality with all other people; the preference that is due to you because you have many needs, so that you may have fulfilled lives and well-being, material as well as spiritual. I feel I must proclaim, here more than anywhere else, "the rights of the human person," for you and for all the poor people of the world.[649]

---

[646]Gustavo Gutiérrez, *The Power of the Poor in History*, pp. 101-102. On this point, see also Ismael Garcia, *Justice in Latin American Theology of Liberation* (Atlanta: John Knox Press, 1987), pp. 32-37.

[647]Pope John XXIII, "*Ringrazia di vero*," (November 15, 1958) *A.A.S.* 50 (1958), pp. 997-1005. Apropos of this point, Christine Gudorf remarked: "There was nothing in that address which in any way distinguished it from an address on the Church in any other part of the world," in *Catholic Social Teaching on Liberation Themes* (Washington, DC: University Press of America, 1981), p. 71.

[648]Pope Paul VI, "*Libentissimo sane animo*" (October 1, 1966), cited in *Osservatore Romano* (October 2, 1966), p. 1.

[649]Pope Paul VI, spontaneous remarks made at Tondo in Italian and translated into Tagalog, reported in Pope Paul VI, *Insegnamenti di Paulo VI* Volume VI (1970) (Vatican City: Libreria Editrice Vaticana, 1977), p. 1263. Of this statement, Peter Hebblethwaite said, "Brief and no doubt superficial

As the present study already demonstrated, the decade of the 1970s began with an increased awareness of underdevelopment and the injustices that flowed from it. By the middle of that decade the first symptoms appeared of a far deeper worldwide crisis produced by the widening gaps between the rich, industrial nations of the north and the debtor nations of the south, spurred by the international monetary and economic systems that were so linked to the skyrocketing prices of petroleum products that ensured in the wake of 1973 Arab – Israeli "Yom Kippur War."[650] As a 1988 Vatican document suggested:

> In this situation, before the whole of the Western developed countries and those of the Eastern collectivist bloc, the Third World demanded new monetary and trade structures in which the rights of poorer peoples would be respected, as well as justice in economic relations. While the Third World's malaise was growing, some countries, in echoing their suffering, demanded greater justice in the distribution of world income. The entire system of the international division of labor and the structure of the world economy entered into a deep crisis. Consequently, a radical revision was required of the very structures which had led so such an unequal economic development.[651]

As the 1970's progressed, the John F. Kennedy-inspired "Decade of Development" fizzled as a dismal failure, as the prosperity of the moneyed classes failed to trickle down to the poorest sectors. From the ruins of the theology of development emerged a new "theology of liberation," whose centerpiece was the

---

as it was, this encounter enabled him to set out a preferential option for the poor," in Peter Hebblethwaite, *Paul VI: The First Modern Pope*, p. 567.

[650]For the classic study of this phenomenon, see Barbara Ward, *The Rich Nations and the Poor Nations* (NY: W. W. Norton, 1962).

[651]Congregation for Catholic Education, *Guidelines for the Study and Teaching of the Church's Social Doctrine in the Formation of Priests*, p. 30.

"preferential option for the poor." In Latin America, this movement occupied center stage in the realm of theological discourse.

Even before the 1968 Medellín Conference, the pattern set by colonial era advocates for the poor like St. Peter Claver, Bartolomé de las Casas, and Antonio de Montesinos echoed in the works of progressive church leaders. In a 1967 pastoral letter on "The Bishop's Role Today," Bishop Rubén Restrepo of Colombia discussed the bishop's tasks as expressed in the documents of Vatican II, and the implications for his pastoral work:

> Christ's attitude of service is reflected first and foremost in attention to the poor and suffering, to those who particularly mirror the image of the poor and suffering Christ. If any preference or priority has place in my episcopal role, it will be shown to the poor and needy, for attention to them is a sign of God's Kingdom.[652] Medellín was the great turning point in the modern history of the Church in Latin America. At the Medellín conference, the language of "liberation" leapt to the fore, while the vapidly optimistic theology of "development' commensurately faltered and ceded ground. As the Medellín "Document on Poverty" stated The Lord's mandate is to preach the Gospel to the poor. We must therefore distribute our apostolic personnel and efforts so as to give preference to the poor and neediest, and to those who are segregated for any reason. We must encourage and step up the studies and initiatives that are directed to this end... We wish to heighten our awareness of the obligation to have solidarity with the poor... (nos. 9 – 10).

Panamanian Archbishop Marcos McGrath reflected on this reality: "The Medellín conclusions are remarkable; they produced – albeit gradually – a new image of the Latin American Church. Without Medellín, Puebla could not have occurred; nor could Medellín have been expected to achieve the maturity, balance, and unity of a

---

[652]Bishop Rubén Isaza Restrepo, "The Bishop's Role Today," in The Social Action Department of the Peruvian Catholic Bishops, *Between Honesty and Hope*, p. 117.

single text that Puebla did."[653] In 1969, SODEPAX, the joint venture between the Vatican Pontifical Commission *Iustitia et Pax* and the social justice department of the World Council of Churches produced a report entitled, *In Search of A Theology of Development*, which indicated that after the Medellín conclusions, "developmentalism" yielded viability, and was supplanted by the model of "liberation."[654] As Gustavo Gutiérrez suggested, "It was the texts of the Episcopal Conference of Medellín of 1968 that brought to public attention the theme of liberation as the pivot for apprehending faith."[655]

The SODEPAX conference held in Switzerland in November, 1969 was hailed by Peter Hebblethwaite as "the starting point for [Gutiérrez's] groundbreaking book, *Teologia de la liberación, perspectivas*."[656] Gutiérrez himself traced the beginnings of this movement to a collection of documents written between 1966 and 1968 entitled *Signos de renovación*.[657] He stated that, "It was then that we first started down the rocky road of the 'defense of the rights of the poor.'"[658] When Gutiérrez saw the original Spanish text of *A Theology of Liberation* published in Lima in 1971 (which he actually wrote in late 1970 and early 1971), it capped the development phase of the embryonic Latin American theology of liberation. In one of the early essays in this preliminary work, Gutiérrez viewed the neophyte school of liberation theology as the fruit of reflection on "an option made by the Latin

---

[653]Marcos McGrath, C.S.C., "The Conferences and the Latin American Church," in Edward L. Cleary, O.P. (ed.), *Born of the Poor*, pp. 78-79.
[654]SODEPAX, *In Search of A Theology of Development* (Cartigny, Switzerland: World Council of Churches, 1970).
[655]Gustavo Gutiérrez, "Liberation Movements and Theology," in Edward Schillebeeckx and Bas van Iersel (eds.), *Jesus Christ and Human Freedom* (NY: Herder & Herder, 1974), p. 139 n. 11.
[656]Peter Hebblethwaite, *Paul VI: The First Modern Pope*, p. 523 n. 1.
[657]*Signos de renovación* (Lima: CEP, 1968).
[658]Gustavo Gutiérrez, *Signos de lucha y esperanza: testimonios de la Iglesia en América Latina: 1973-1978* (Lima: CEP, 1978), p. 1.

American Church."[659] Gutiérrez argued in the text that "the authentic unity of the Church necessarily implies the option for the oppressed and exploited of this world."[660] The May, 1971 "working paper" of the Chilean bishops on "The Gospel, Politics, and Socialisms" described the Church's social policies as involving:

> ...a very special preference for the poor... Christians must take as their own the overall option that was affirmed by the Latin American episcopate at Medellín. This option should be the basic criterion for their outlook and activities. According to this option asserted at Medellín, fidelity to the Gospel of Jesus Christ today requires Christians to commit themselves to thoroughgoing and urgently needed social transformations.[661]

The Chilean bishops aptly left the choice of a specific economic system to the conscience of the individual believer.

Paul VI's next major statement on social questions, issued in May, 1971, was the apostolic letter *Octogesima Adveniens*, written to commemorate the 80th anniversary of *Rerum Novarum.* While *Populorum Progressio* was then only four years old, many new issues circumscribing the social question already arose. In the wake of the post-*Humanae vitae* controversy engendered by the so-called "birth control encyclical," Paul VI never published another encyclical.[662] Although he

---

[659]Gustavo Gutiérrez, "The Option Before the Latin American Church," Part 3 of *A Theology of Liberation* (Maryknoll, NY: Orbis Books, 1973), pp. 49-78. On this point, see Enrique Dussel, "Recent Latin American Theology," in Enrique Dussel (ed.), *The Church in Latin America: 1492-1992*, pp. 393-394.

[660]Gustavo Gutiérrez, "The Church: Sacrament of History," in *A Theology of Liberation*, p. 277.

[661]"Declaration of the Bishops of Chile," in Alfred T. Hennelly, S.J., (ed.), *Liberation Theology: A Documentary History*, p. 144. See also Paul Sigmund, "Revolution and Counterrevolution in Chile," in *Liberation Theology and the Church*, pp. 40-41, as well as Pablo Richard, *Origen y desarrollo del Movimiento Cristianos por el Socialismo, Chile, 1970-1973* (Paris: Centre Lebret, 1975).

[662]Don Pasquale Macchi noted that Paul VI did not want to issue another encyclical so as not to denature the papal teaching office following the post-*Humanae vitae* uproar: "He did not want an encyclical, a solemn form of the teaching magisterium, to be treated as though it were merely a matter of opinion even by the bishops." See Carlo Cremona, *Paolo VI* (Milan: Rusconi, 1991), p. 230. In

addressed the letter to Cardinal Maurice Roy, president of the Pontifical Commission (now Council) *Iustitia et Pax*, he clearly intended its thrust to address the entire Catholic world. Whereas previously John XXIII and Paul VI echoed the language of development, Medellín reflected the language of liberation, and augured an important shift in emphasis from economics to politics: "Politics is the best way – if not the only way – of living out one's Christian commitment, in service to others" (no. 46). Commentators such as Paul Surlis perceived it to be "unintelligible unless it is seen as a response to the Medellín declarations of 1968."[663] Elsewhere, Surlis suggested that "the meaning and intent of the phrase, 'option for the poor' is found in *Octogesima Adveniens*,"[664] whereby it stated: "In teaching us charity, the Gospel instructs us in the preferential respect due to the poor and the special situation they have in society: the more fortunate should renounce some of their rights so as to place their goods more generously at the service of others" (no. 23; cf. no. 42). Without explicitly naming it, Paul VI endorsed the methodology of liberation theology:

> In the face of such widely varying situations it is difficult for us to utter a unified message and to put forward a solution which has universal validity. Such is not our ambition, nor is it our Mission. It is up to the Christian communities to analyze with objectivity the situation which is proper to their own country, to shed on it the light of the Gospel's unalterable words and to draw principles of reflection, norms of judgment and directives of action for the social teaching of the Church (no. 4).

---

the ranking of papal documents, encyclicals receive pride of place, whereas the *epistulae apostolicae* (the classification of *O.A.*) rank third, behind *litterae encyclicae*, and *epistulae encyclicae*. The ranking of such official papal documents is detailed in Thomas Harte, *Papal Social Principles* (Gloucester, MA: Peter Smith Publishers, 1960), p. 7.

[663]Paul Surlis, "The Relation Between Social Justice and Inculturation in the Papal Magisterium," in *Irish Theological Quarterly* 52 (1986), p. 255.

[664]Paul Surlis, "Option for the Poor," in *The New Catholic Encyclopedia* Volume 17 (NY: McGraw-Hill, 1990), p. 339.

Father J. Bryan Hehir hailed *Octogesima Adveniens* as "perhaps the most creative yet least known of the social teachings"[665] that reflected a radically new methodology that departed from the categories of natural law, and emphasized that "we are instructed by the Gospel" (no. 23) in the proper respect for the poor. As Peter Hebblethwaite concluded, "Paradoxically, *Octogesima Adveniens* gained authority by being less authoritative. It breathed a different spirit, and was like moving into another world, where a different set of values operated. They derived not from Europe but from Latin America. The visit [of Paul VI] to Medellín had not been in vain."[666]

The Second Synod of World Bishops held in Rome in the fall of 1971 served to institutionalize and universalize this vision in its final document on "Justice in the World," which viewed the Church's involvement in the issue of justice to rest not only within the framework of the natural law, but to be more centrally rooted in the core message of the Gospel itself. A staffer for the Pontifical Commission for Justice and Peace, Juan Alfaro, S.J. suggested that in the text of "Justice in the World" appeared for "the first time in a magisterial statement of the Church the biblical concept of liberation."[667] Paul Surlis lauded this synodal document as "to action on behalf of justice and peace in our time what Nicaea or Chalcedon were to Christology in theirs."[668] Donal Dorr classified it as "one of the most important statements on social justice ever issued by Rome."[669]

---

[665] J. Bryan Hehir, "John Paul II: Continuity and Change in the Social Teaching of the Church," p. 249.
[666] Peter Hebblethwaite, *Paul VI: The First Modern Pope*, p. 577.
[667] Juan Alfaro, S.J., *Theology of Justice in the World* (Rome: Pontifical Commission *Iustitia et Pax*, 1973), p. 11. Charles M. Murphy made the identical point in "Action for Justice as Constitutive of the Preaching of the Gospel: What Did the 1971 Synod Mean?," in Charles E. Curran and Richard A. McCormick, S.J. (eds.), *Readings in Moral Theology No. 5*, p. 150.
[668] Paul Surlis, "The Relation Between Social Justice and Enculturation in the Papal Magisterium," p. 258.
[669] Donal Dorr, *Option for the Poor*, p. 177.

In the oft-quoted line from the synodal document on "Justice in the World," its framers asserted that: "...action on behalf of justice and participation in the transformation of the world appear to us as a constitutive dimension of the preaching of the Gospel" (no. 6).[670] The Synod's "Final Document" critiqued the rampant structural injustice that pervaded the contemporary world:

> Serious injustices... are building around the world of human beings a network of domination, oppression and abuses which stifle freedom and which keep the greater part of humanity from sharing in the building up and enjoyment of a more just and fraternal world... These stifling oppressions constantly give rise to great numbers of "marginal" persons, ill-fed, inhumanly housed, illiterate and deprived of political power as well as of the suitable means of acquiring responsibility and moral dignity (nos. 3, 10).

According to "Justice in the World," the key to the structural injustices of the modern world flowed from a lack of participation by peoples in determining their own destiny. The action required is to be "directed above all at those people and nations which because of various forms of oppression and because of the present character of our society are silent, indeed voiceless victims of injustice" (no. 20). As Dorr suggested, this teaching went a step beyond "what Paul VI had said in *Octogesima Adveniens* about the need to move from economics to politics. For it applies this principle to the action of the Church itself in a way that is reminiscent of the commitment undertaken by the Latin American bishops at Medellín."[671]

---

[670]As Peter Hebblethwaite noted, "['Justice in the World'] was not therefore an optional extra or something you tacked on when you had put across the 'spiritual' message of the Gospel: the social teaching was essential to it. This was the 'launch pad' of liberation theology and much else besides." Cited in *Paul VI: The First Modern Pope*, p. 504.

[671]Donal Dorr, *Option for the Poor*, pp. 182-183. For a detailed survey that enumerates ten reasons why the social teaching of the 1971 Synod's "Final Document" advanced beyond *Gaudium et Spes*, *Populorum Progressio*, and *Octogesima Adveniens*, see John F. X. Harriott, S.J., "The Difficulty of Justice," in *The Month* (January, 1972), pp. 4-18.

The 1975 Apostolic Exhortation of Pope Paul VI, *Evangelii Nuntiandi*, moved beyond "Justice in the World" and sought to embrace even further the language of liberation. Paul devoted fifteen paragraphs of the text to the relationship between evangelization and liberation (nos. 25-39). Leonardo and Clodovis Boff hailed it as "one of the most profound, balanced, and theological expositions yet made of the longing of the oppressed for liberation."[672] Pope Paul sought "to remove the ambiguity which the word 'liberation' very often takes on in ideologies, political systems or groups," as the Church strove to "insert the Christian struggle for liberation into the universal plan of salvation that it proclaims" (no. 38). Pope Paul amplified this point:

> The Church, as the bishops repeated, has the duty to proclaim the liberation of millions of human beings, many of whom are its own children – the duty of assisting the birth of this liberation, of giving witness to it, of ensuring that it is complete. This thrust is not foreign to evangelization (no. 30).

In *Evangelii Nuntiandi*, Paul eloquently linked the message of the Gospel and social morality:

> Between evangelization and human promotion – development, liberation – there exist many strong bonds. Bonds of an anthropological order, because the person we evangelize is not an abstract being, but rather a being who is subject to economic and social problems. Bonds of a theological order, because one cannot disconnect God's creative act from God's plan for redemption which itself reaches to very concrete situations of injustice which must be combated and of justice which must be restored (no. 31).

[672]Leonardo Boff and Clodovis Boff, *Introducing Liberation Theology*, p. 76.

Pope Paul cautioned against the extreme tendency of the burgeoning theology of liberation to allow tools of social analysis to dominate theological reflection:

> Many, even generous Christians who are sensitive to the dramatic questions involved in the problem of liberation, in their wish to commit the Church to the liberation effort, are frequently tempted to reduce her Mission to the dimension of a merely temporal project. They would reduce her aims to a man-centered goal: the salvation of which it is the messenger reduced to material well-being... If this were so, the Church would lose her fundamental meaning. Its message of liberation would no longer have any originality and would be easily open to monopolization and manipulation by ideological systems and political parties (no. 32).

As Paul VI concluded: "The Church links human liberation and salvation in Christ, but it never identifies them, because it knows through revelation, historical experience and the reflection of faith that not every notion of liberation is necessarily consistent and compatible with an evangelical vision of the human person, things, and events" (no. 35).

In this light, Clodovis Boff commented:

> Medellín had already broached the liberation thematic. But it was just a beginning. No further development was guaranteed – until the 1974 Synod of Bishops brought the same problematic under discussion with great vigor. Then the results of the synod were gathered together in *Evangelii Nuntiandi*, in 1975. Now the language of liberation flowed smooth and sure. The signal had been given. All that was left for Puebla to do was to *consecrate* the language of liberation, along the lines of *Evangelii Nuntiandi*. It didn't consecrate the so-called theology of liberation. And it would have had no business in doing so. But Puebla collected its most expressive

results, setting up some solid framework for further developing that theology.[673]

Although the pontificate of Paul VI appeared to move in the direction of embracing the concept of liberation as a centerpiece in Catholic social teaching, a conservative reaction erupted in the years between Medellín and Puebla. 1972 saw the election of Colombian Archbishop Alfonso Lopez Trujillo as secretary-general of CELAM, an event that can be viewed as something of a watershed.[674] At the time, Lopez Trujillo was convinced that two distinct forms of liberation theology existed: one of European extraction that stressed politics; and, one of Latin American origin, more related to socio-economic and spiritual themes. As Françios Houtart commented, a conservative reaction was brewing:

> It was then that the activities started in this field. The first step was, in 1973, a meeting in Bogotá about the theme of liberation... The review, *Tierra Nueva*, founded in Bogotá, specialized in refuting the theology of liberation... A working group was set up in cooperation with German theologians, the "Church and Liberation" study circle... [A]n important report on the "world propagation of the theology of liberation" described it as a "contagious virus" and denounced in rather violent terms the persons and institutions spreading it.[675]

During this time, beginning with the CELAM assembly held at Sucre, Bolivia in November, 1972, the first sustained opposition to liberation theology mounted. (At this meeting, Lopez Trujillo was elected General-Secretary of CELAM, a post

---

[673]Clodovis Boff, "Society and the Kingdom: A Dialogue Between a Theologian, A Christian Activist, and a Parish Priest," in Leonardo Boff and Clodovis Boff, *Salvation and Liberation: In Search of a Balance Between Faith and Politics* (Maryknoll, NY: Orbis Books, 1984), pp. 67-68.

[674]Lopez Trujillo experienced a meteoric rise in his ecclesiastical career: He was named Auxiliary Bishop of Bogotá in 1971; Ordinary of the Archdiocese of Medellín in 1979; and, Cardinal Archbishop of the same See in 1983, before being transferred to the Pontifical Council for the Family in the Vatican.

[675]François Houtart, "Theoretical and Institutional Bases of the Opposition to Liberation Theology," in Marc H. Ellis and Otto Maduro (eds.), *Expanding the View*, pp. 120-121.

he held until 1979, when he succeeded Cardinal Eduardo Pironio as its President). Prominent among the critics of liberation theology was the Brazilian Franciscan theologian Boãventura Kloppenburg, who at gatherings in Bogotá in November, 1973, detailed his principal objections to the main currents of the theology of liberation.[676] A further, crucial meeting was held in Lima, in September, 1975, from which all practitioners of liberation theology were banned.[677] During this same period, the Belgian Jesuit, Roger Vekemans, issued a blistering attack on "Liberation Theology and Christians for Socialism [the Chilean experiment]", that utilized the same type of arguments that later appeared in the "Instruction on Certain Aspects of Liberation Theology" issued by the Congregation for the Doctrine of the Faith in August, 1984.[678] In 1970, Vekemans settled in Colombia as an exiled Missionary from Chile, and founded a right wing religious think-tank called "CEDIAL" (The Center for the Study of Development and Integration in Latin America), in addition to founding the periodical, *Tierra Nueva*. During this period, the chief criticisms of the theology of liberation centered upon four key areas: the use of Marxist dialectic as a tool of social analysis; reflection on the nature and person of Jesus the Christ; forms and expressions of church life; and, social doctrine. Enrique Dussel asserted of Vekemans and Lopez Trujillo:

> [These] two men coordinated the fight against the theology of liberation, which began before the publication of the first books. In

---

[676]See Boãventura Kloppenburg, O.F.M., *Temptations for the Theology of Liberation* (Chicago: Franciscan Herald Press, 1975), and his *The Practical Church* (Chicago: Franciscan Herald Press, 1976) for a presentation of his concerns.

[677]See François Houtart, "*Le Counseil Episcopal d'Amèrique Latine Accentue son Changement*," in *Informations Catholiques Internationales* 481 (1975), pp. 10-24.

[678]See Roger Vekemans, S.J., *Teologia de la liberación y cristianos para el socialismo* (Bogotá: Indo-American Press Service, 1976). Of Vekemans' journal, Enrique Dussel remarked: "*Tierra Nueva* [was] designed exclusively to combat liberation theology. Everything which later appeared in Roman documents can already be found in *Tierra Nueva* ten years earlier." Cited in "The Church and Defence of Human Rights," p. 449.

> fact, the fight began a day after Medellín... [They] coordinated a powerful triangle, Bogotá-Frankfurt-Rome, bringing together the German and Colombian episcopates with certain circles in Rome. [Vekemans] opened congresses and an extensive campaign of defamation... After nearly fifteen years of denunciation [they] succeeded in getting the Roman authorities to act.[679]

The greatest concern voiced by Vekemans and Lopez Trujillo centered upon the application of means of Marxist analysis by liberation theologians. In Lopez Trujillo's opening speech at the eighteenth assembly of CELAM in 1981, he charged: "The problem is not that they speak loudly when talking about the poor, but that they make an ideological use of a Marxist instrument of analysis... and this is in contradiction with the magisterium of the Church."[680] Lopez Trujillo and his allies expressed the fear that the base communities [CEBs] might tend to divide the Church by creating an artificial cleavage between the institutional, hierarchical Church, and the "Church of the people" ("*Iglesia popular*"), or of the poor, founded on a network of base communities committed to the social justice agenda and the needs of the poor.[681] The overall direction embarked upon by CELAM's new leadership appeared to be a total reversal from that marked out by its founding vision, framed by Dom Manuel Larrain and Dom Helder Câmara. As Alfred Hennelly noted, "I would have to emphasize that this is truly an astonishing spectacle. Within the brief space of four years, an organization that was speeding along the road of implementation of

---

[679]Enrique Dussel, "The Church and Defence of Human Rights," in *The Church in Latin America: 1492-1992*, p. 449.

[680]Cited in François Houtart, "Theoretical and Institutional of the Opposition to Liberation Theology," p. 116.

[681]On this theme, see Boãventura Kloppenburg, O.F.M., *The People's Church* (Chicago: Franciscan Herald Press, 1978), in which the author leaves fifty-three questions about liberation theology "unanswered," and concludes that it is more of an ideology than a theology. He addressed the same concerns in *Temptations for a Theology of Liberation* (Chicago: Franciscan Herald Press, 1974).

Medellín was suddenly thrown into reverse gear, with a great shock to all involved."[682]

During this period, Vatican policy toward Latin America was largely shaped by Cardinal Sebastiano Baggio, the President of the Pontifical Commission for Latin America. Baggio sought to marginalize the influence of progressive prelates such as Helder Câmara, Paulo Evaristo Arns, Oscar Romero, and Raul Silva. After the Medellín conference, Cardinal Antonio Samore, the Holy See's delegate at CELAM II and then-President of the Pontifical Commission for Latin America was likewise sacked. As Enrique Dussel observed: "[Cardinal Samore] was held responsible for the [alleged] excesses of Medellín; the Vatican immediately reacted against Medellín."[683] The conservative reaction presaged the so-called "Catholic Restoration" initiated in the early years of the pontificate of John Paul II.[684] Dussel noted further: "It can be said that almost all of the bishops who have taken strong stands against the abuses of the military dictatorships were fought in Rome, were subjected to apostolic visitations, and, once they were retired, were given successors with totally opposite views with the task of undoing all they had done."[685] The isolation and minimization of the influence of progressive prelates like Brazil's Dom Helder Câmara and Bishop Pedro Casaldáliga and Peru's Cardinal Juan Landázuri Ricketts by Rome afforded further evidence of this trend.

By the dawn of the decade of the 1980's, as theologians of liberation were silenced, removed from teaching posts, or exiled, Latin American theology began to extend out and take root in the rest of the developing and industrialized world, and

---

[682]Alfred T. Hennelly, S.J, "Progress and Opposition: (1968-1973)," in *Liberation Theology: A Documentary History,* p. 123.
[683]Enrique Dussel, "The Church and Defence of Human Rights," p. 441.
[684]See Jan Grootaers, *De Vatican II a Jean Paul II, Le Grand Tournant de l'Eglise* (Paris: Centurion, 1981); Paul Johnson, *Pope John Paul II and the Catholic Restoration* (NY: St. Martin's, 1981); and, Giancarlo Zizola, *Restaurazione di papa Wojtyla* (Rome: Garzanti, 1985).
[685]Enrique Dussel, "The Church and Defence of Human Rights," p. 441.

undertook a broad-based dialogue, without official sanction or control. Gustavo Gutiérrez and Leonardo Boff were the highest profile objects of this intense scrutiny, though the specifics of their investigations are beyond the scope of this study.[686] In spite of this hostile trend, the succession of meetings of the "Ecumenical Association of Third World Theologians" [EATWOT] took place first, in Dar es Salaam, Tanzania, in 1976; second, in Accra, Ghana, in 1977; third, in Wennappuwa, Sri Lanka, in 1979; fourth, in Sao Paulo, Brazil, in 1980; fifth, in New Delhi, in 1981; and finally, in Oaxtepec, Mexico, in 1986.[687] Clearly, at this stage of its development, the theology of liberation was beginning to expand, "from the margins to the center." In the 1970's, progressive hierarchies in Brazil and Peru continued to advance the liberation agenda.[688] At their forty-second assembly in January, 1973, the Peruvian bishops declared:

> The liberating Mission of the Church, which is the effective proclamation of the Gospel, means a hope-filled option for all people, in fraternal solidarity, but especially for those who suffer injustice, the poor and oppressed... it is clear that solidarity with the poor and oppressed also involves acting to change the unjust structures that maintain the situation of oppression.[689]

---

[686]The relevant details are readily accessible in the following sources: Robert McAfee Brown, *Gustavo Gutiérrez: An Introduction to Liberation Theology* (Maryknoll, NY: Orbis Books, 1990), especially pp. 131-156, and Harvey Cox, *The Silencing of Leonardo Boff: The Vatican and the Future of World Christianity* (Oak Park, IL: Meyer-Stone Books, 1988).

[687]The papers of these respective conferences were published in English by Orbis Books, the publishing arm of the Maryknoll order: Sergio Torres and Virginia Fabella, M.M. (eds.), *The Emergent Gospel: Theology From the Developing World* (Maryknoll, NY: Orbis Books, 1978); Kofi Appiah-Kubi and Sergio Torres (eds.), *African Theology En Route* (Maryknoll, NY: Orbis Books, 1979); Virginia Fabella, M.M. (ed.), *Asia's Struggle for Full Humanity* (Maryknoll, NY: Orbis Books, 1980); and Sergio Torres and John Eagleson (eds.), *The Challenge of Basic Christian Communities* (Maryknoll, NY: Orbis Books, 1981).

[688]See Enrique Dussel, "The Church From 1972 to 1992," in *The Church in Latin America*, pp. 171-172.

[689]Cited in *Praxis de los padres en América Latina* (Bogotá: CELAM, 1979), p. 496.

The Peruvian hierarchy, confronted by criticism from some conservative elements within the Church concerning the *aggiornamento* undertaken at Vatican II and Medellín, reaffirmed their position: "We are renewing this loyalty and fidelity, precisely now that the guidelines laid down at Medellín are in danger of being forgotten."[690] The bishops of Peru continued on this trajectory in November, 1971, when they issued a preparatory document on the forthcoming Synod (in whose drafting Gustavo Gutiérrez had a major hand):[691]

> For the Peruvian ecclesial community this implies opting for the poor and marginal peoples as a personal and communal commitment... opting for those who today experience the most violent forms of oppression is for us an efficacious way of also loving those who, possibly unconsciously, are oppressed themselves by their very situation of being oppressors.[692]

This trend gained major sanction at the 1979 CELAM III conference at Puebla, Mexico, where the Latin American bishops adopted and popularized the preferential option for the poor, which they "understood as solidarity with the poor and as a rejection of the situation in which most people on this continent live" (no. 1156).[693] In this respect, as Juan Carlos Scannone noted, "The relation between Medellín and Puebla is sometimes presented as analogous to the relation between

---

[690] *Praxis de los padres in América Latina*, p. 847.

[691] See Paul Sigmund, *Liberation Theology and the Church*, p. 44.

[692] Bishops of Peru, "Justice in the World" (1971)," in Alfred T. Hennelly, S.J. (ed.), *Liberation Theology: A Documentary History*, p. 128. See also Juan Carlos Scannone, *Teologia de la liberación y praxis popular* (Salamanca: Ediciones Sigueme, 1976), pp. 109-110.

[693] For overall assessments of Puebla, see: Philip Berryman, "What Happened at Puebla," in Daniel H. Levine, *The Church and Politics in Latin America*; Enrique Dussel, *De Medellín a Puebla* (Mexico City: Editorial Edicol, 1979), and his *History of the Church in Latin America: 1492-1992* (Grand Rapids, MI: Eerdmans, 1981), pp. 229-239; Alexander Wilde, "Ten Years of Change in the Church: Puebla and the Future," in Daniel H. Levine, *The Church and Politics in Latin America*; as well as the essays contained in Sergio Torres and John Eagleson (eds.), *Puebla and Beyond.*

baptism and confirmation..."[694] Leonardo Boff added, "If Medellín was the baptism of the Latin American Church, Puebla was its confirmation."[695]

The Puebla "Final Document" acknowledged the "disregard and even hostility" (no. 1134) with which some elements within the Church and outside of it regarded the conclusions of Medellín. Puebla advanced upon the Medellín documents to offer a developed Christology, linked to the explicit charism of the "option for the poor": "Service to the poor really calls for constant conversion and purification among all Christians. That must be done if we are to achieve fuller identification each day with the poor Christ and our own poor" (no. 1140). The "Final Document" echoed the words of Pope John Paul's opening address at the Puebla conference: "As the Pope told us, the evangelical commitment of the Church, like that of Christ, should be a commitment to those most in need. Hence the Church must look to Christ when it wants to find out what its evangelizing activity should be like" (no. 1141). In doing so, the Puebla "Final Document" adopted and extended upon the established method of liberation theology: seeing (analyzing social reality); judging (reflection in the light of faith); and acting (determining an appropriate pastoral response).

The presence of the new Pope, John Paul II, was strongly felt at Puebla. He stressed that the option for the poor ought to spring from the core evangelical message of the Christian scriptures, and not rest mainly on socio-economic or political motivations (for instance, as he noted in his "Address to Nuns)."[696] In his "Homily at the Basilica of Guadalupe," John Paul II introduced for the first time his

---

[694]Juan Carlos Scannone, "Interpretations of Puebla," in *Lumen Vitae* XXXIV (1979), p. 501. On this analogy, see Antonio Libanio Christo, "*Tendencias políticas en Puebla*," in *Revista Eclesiastica Brasileira* 39 (1979), pp. 98-99, and Juan Jimenez Limón, "*Cómo estaba Dios en Puebla?: Ensayo de interpretación*," in *Christus* 44 (1979), pp. 75-80.

[695]Leonardo Boff, *Faith on the Edge*, p. 28.

[696]See Ricardo Antonich, "The Church's Social Doctrine at Puebla," in *Lumen Vitae* XXXIV (1979), p. 575.

recurring concern and preoccupation that in order to be evangelical, the option for the poor should be inspired by a "preferential" but not exclusive love, a theme that the Latin American bishops appropriated in the "Final Document"(cf. nos. 15, 27, 205, 268, 270, 1141, 1165).

Juan Carlos Scannone viewed the "generative core of the (Puebla Final) Document... [to be] the preferential option for the poor,"[697] a term that appeared explicitly seven times in the Final Document.[698] In a seminal article in which he identified Puebla as a "serene affirmation of Medellín," Jon Sobrino identified the option for the poor as "the theoretical reference for the mission of the whole Church and an essential element of all those missions without exception."[699] One section of the Puebla document that merited special attention was the chapter entitled, "A Preferential Option for the Poor" (nos. 1134-1165). The bishops assembled at Puebla echoed this assessment: "With its preferential but not exclusive love for the poor, the Church present at Medellín was a summons to hope for more Christian and humane goals, as the Holy Father pointed out... This Third Episcopal Conference in Puebla wishes to keep this summons alive and to open up new horizons of hope" (no. 1165).

Although the Puebla documents did not attempt to give a systematic account of the meaning of the term, the "preferential option for the poor," they stressed "the need for conversion on the part of the whole Church to a preferential option for the poor, an option aimed at their integral liberation" (no. 1134). As the "Final Document" asserted: "Despite the distortions and interpretations of some, who vitiate the spirit of Medellín, and despite the disregard and even hostility of others, we affirm the need for conversion on the part of the whole Church to a preferential

---

[697]Juan Carlos Scannone, "Interpretations of Puebla," p. 502.

[698]See nos. 382, 707, 711, 733, 769, 1134, and 1217.

[699]Jon Sobrino, S.J., "*Puebla, serena afirmación de Medellín,*" in *Christus* 44 (1979), p. 50. On this point see also Leonardo Boff, "*Puebla: ganhos, avanços, questoes emergentes," in Revista Eclesiastica Brasileira* 39 (1979), p. 49.

option for the poor, an option aimed at their integral liberation" (no. 1134). The "Final Document" confronted the reality of structural injustice: "Analyzing this situation more deeply, we discover that this poverty is not a passing phase. Instead it is the product of economic, social, and political situations and structures, though there are also other causes for the state of misery. In many instances this state of poverty within our countries finds its origin and support in mechanisms which, because they are impregnated with materialism rather than any authentic humanism, create a situation on the international level where the rich get richer at the expense of the poorer, who get even poorer" (no. 30). This terminology suggested that the bishops at Puebla abandoned their optimistic expectation to be able to reform the prevailing economic systems. The language of liberation employed at Puebla implied the necessity of massive structural change, as reflected in the use of the following terminology: "structural changes" (nos. 134, 1055); the need for the "transformation of structures" (no. 438); the desire to reach the very bases of society (nos. 388, 438, 1055, 1196, 1250); and, the ongoing need to cry out for the formation of a new society (nos. 12, 642, 842, 1119, 1305).

Medellín warned against the "muted cry [that] wells up from millions of human beings, pleading with their pastors for a liberation that is nowhere to be found in their case" ("Poverty," no. 2). Puebla noted that this cry "might well have seemed muted back then," but that in 1979 was "loud and clear, increasing in volume and intensity, and at times full of menace" (no. 89). The Latin American bishops at Puebla reflected: "The vast majority of our sisters and brothers continue to live in a situation of poverty and misery which has gotten worse; they lack the most elementary of material goods, in contrast to the accumulation of wealth in the hands of a minority, often at the cost of the poverty of the many... In this category are mainly our Indians, peasants, workers, marginal people of the cities, and especially the women in these social sectors, on account of their doubly oppressed and marginalized condition" (no. 1135; cf. no. 29). In this respect, as Jon Sobrino commented, in the decade that ensued after Medellín, "We are in a different situation here in Latin America ten years later, so we have to do something else. Puebla is very conscious that... the situation is worse than at Medellín, there is more poverty, more political repression. Puebla stated and reaffirmed that."[700]

Progressive elements within the Latin American Church were largely bypassed or excluded at CELAM III, both as *periti* as well as in the work of the preparatory commissions. The various categories of representatives at Puebla were manipulated to reflect: the new direction taken by the Vatican's Commission on Latin America; the conservative elements within the Roman Curia; along with the prevailing ideology of the CELAM leadership, represented by then-Archbishop Alfonso Lopez Trujillo. As Robert McAfee Brown observed:

> ...those officially excluded from participation at Puebla represented a veritable *Who's Who in Latin American Liberation Theology*. In addition to Gustavo [Gutiérrez], the officially unwelcomed included people of the stature of Juan Luís Segundo, Hugo Assmann, Jon Sobrino, Ignacio Ellacuría, Raul Vidales, Enrique Dussel, Segundo Galilea, Pablo Richard, and José Comblin. Anybody who was somebody was not there.[701]

The Brazilian delegation was pared almost in half, to forty representatives. The twelve voting bishops nominated by the Holy See were markedly conservative in their ecclesiastical orientation. Representation of the Latin American Confederation of Religious (CLAR), which clung to the agenda of Medellín, was virtually excluded. A large number of curial representatives were named, which gave the appearance of a "stacked deck." All of the major figures of Latin American liberation theology

---

[700]Jon Sobrino, S.J., "*Puebla, serena afirmación de Medellín*," p. 53. See also B. Villegas, "*Ante la opción de Puebla por los pobres*," in *Mensaje* 28 (1979), pp. 530-535.
[701]Robert McAfee Brown, *Gustavo Gutiérrez: An Introduction to Liberation Theology*, p. 38 .

were excluded as *periti*. Among the invited, officially sanctioned theological advisors, only one, Lucio Gera of Argentina, had any links to the theology of liberation.[702] This systemic pattern of exclusion was widely dismissed by conference organizers as paranoia. However, it proved to be rooted in fact when the dictated audiocassette of a letter from Archbishop Alfonso Lopez Trujillo[703] to his compatriot, Bishop Luciano Duarte of Brazil, found its way into the press: ...get your bombers ready, then, and a little of your sweet 'poison,' because we will need you to be in top form both at Puebla and in the CELAM assembly. It is my belief that you ought to undergo training just as boxers do before stepping into the ring... May your blows be always in the spirit of the Gospel – and well aimed.[704]

For their part, the progressive element within the Latin American Church managed to hold serve. The worst consequences of the conservative assault were blunted. No proponent of liberation theology was condemned at Puebla, and the ideology and dynamic advances set in motion at Medellín failed to be reversed. In spite of the attempts to mute the thrust of Medellín, the denunciation of injustice and inequality that emerged from Puebla was stronger and more clearly framed than at Medellín. The structural causes of poverty were scored; CEB's were affirmed and promoted; a stronger emphasis upon the Church's option for the poor was registered; and, human rights were endorsed as integral to work of proclaiming the Gospel. On

---

[702]See Julian Filowski and Francis McDonough (eds.), *Reflections on Puebla* (London: Catholic Institute for International Relations, 1980), p. 14.

[703]For the works of Lopez Trujillo related to Puebla, see his: *De Medellín a Puebla* (Madrid: Biblioteca de Autores Cristianos, 1980); *Opciones e interpretaciones a la luz de Puebla* (Bogotá: n.d.); and, *Liberation or Revolution?: An Examination of the Priest's Role in the Socio-Economic Class Struggle in Latin America* (Hungtington, IN: Our Sunday Visitor Press, 1977).

[704]Cited in Julian Filowski and Francis McDonough (eds.), Reflections on Puebla, p. 15. See also: Penny Lernoux, *Cry of the People: United States Involvement in the Rise of Fascism, Torture and Murder, and the Persecution of the Catholic Church in Latin America* (NY: Doubleday, 1980), p. 435, and her essay, "The Long Path to Puebla," in John Eagleson and Philip Sharper (eds.), *Puebla and Beyond*, pp. 20-37.

a decidedly uneven playing field, as one pundit asserted, "The visiting team managed a tie."[705] As Donal Dorr concluded: "The major issue facing the Puebla Conference was not really whether it would say something strikingly new and radical. Rather, it was whether it would re-affirm the basic thrust of Medellín or whether it would allow the commitments of Medellín to die the death of a thousand qualifications."[706] In reality, Puebla was neither a beginning nor an end, but a dramatic stage along the trajectory of the unfolding embrace by the Church of the preferential option for the poor. This direction fueled and directed the larger agenda of the social Mission of the Universal Church.[707]

A further development that fueled the mix occurred when Pope John Paul II named Cardinal Josef Ratzinger as Prefect of the Congregation of the Doctrine of the Faith (the former "Holy Office") in January, 1982. Cardinal Ratzinger sought proactively to curb what he perceived to be the theological excesses perpetrated in the wake of Vatican II. Pope John Paul afforded Ratzinger a wide berth to impose his agenda. He fired an opening salvo in an interview published in the conservative Italian monthly, 30 *Giorni* that featured a set of "Preliminary Notes" that Ratzinger penned on liberation theology. Ratzinger claimed to critique only those positions that "have embraced the Marxist fundamental option," and concluded that the "phenomenon of liberation theology [is] a fundamental threat to the Faith of the

---

[705]"*Empate en cancha ajena,*" in the Spanish original. Cited in Philip Berryman, "What Happened at Puebla," in Daniel Levine (ed.), *The Church and Political Conflict in Latin America* (Chapel Hill, NC: University of North Carolina Press, 1986), p. 78.

[706]Donal Dorr, *Option for the Poor*, p. 261.

[707]For an interesting ecumenical counterpart, see the "Final Document" of the International Ecumenical Congress of Theology that took place in São Paulo in 1980: "The promotion of total liberation, the common suffering, and the sharing of the hopes and joys of the poor have put in clear relief all that we Christians hold in common. In this option for the poor and in the practice of justice, we have deepened the roots of our faith in the one Lord, the one Church, and the one God and Father... In our ecclesial commitment we confess the Church of Jesus Christ as his body in history and as sacrament of liberation," cited in Sergio Torres and John Eagleson (eds.), *The Challenge of Basic Christian Communities* (Maryknoll, NY: Orbis Books, 1981), pp. 243-244.

Church." He cautioned against his perception of the danger that some proponents of liberation theology sought to turn the post-conciliar image of the "People of God" into a Marxist myth, thereby perverting it into the catalyst of a "process of progressive liberation... and the real interpreter of the Bible."[708] Cardinal Ratzinger launched a frontal assault on the theology of Gustavo Gutiérrez in 1984[709] that followed the February, 1983 letter from the C.D.F. to the Peruvian Episcopal Conference which demanded a critical examination of Gutiérrez's doctrinal orthodoxy.[710] A similar probe was launched into the work of Leonardo Boff. In May, 1984, Ratzinger wrote to Boff, and attacked his alleged "ecclesiological relativism" as well as his "sociological" analysis that criticized the Church for being a tool of capitalistic consumption.[711] In March, 1984, Cardinal Ratzinger called the doctrinal commissions of the national conferences of Latin America to a summit meeting in Bogotá, at which he denounced the "Marxist affinities" of liberation theology.[712]

On the opposite side of the controversy, perhaps the clearest, early systematic articulation of the preferential option for the poor appeared in the acceptance speech

---

[708]For the English version of this material, see Joseph Ratzinger, *The Ratzinger Report* (San Francisco: Ignatius Press, 1985), pp. 174-186.

[709]For the text of Ratzinger's ten observations on Gutiérrez's theological output, see *Tierra Nueva* 51 (October, 1984), pp. 94-96.

[710]See Sergio Torres, "Gustavo Gutiérrez: An Historical Sketch," in Marc H. Ellis and Otto Maduro (eds.), *The Future of Liberation Theology* (Maryknoll, NY: Orbis Books, 1989), p. 98. Interestingly, a month before his death, Karl Rahner, S.J. wrote to Gutiérrez: "I have read all through your works and can find nothing in them that is against orthodoxy," cited in *The National Catholic Reporter* (April 20, 1984), p. 1.

[711]See "*Respuesta de Leonardo Boff a la carta del Cardenal Joseph Ratzinger,*" in *Revista Latinoamericana de Teologia* I (September – December, 1984), pp. 340-371, as well as Leonardo Boff and Clodovis Boff, *Liberation Theology: From Dialogue to Confrontation*, pp. 73-100.

[712]See *Misión Abierta* 1 (February, 1985), pp. 9-13. It is important to note that from the first appearance of these charges, respected church leaders like Cardinal Pãolo Evaristo Arns of Brazil challenged such blanket assertions: "The option for the poor is not a class option in the Marxist sense... The Marxist perception is quite different from the Christian option for the poor." Cited in Gregory Baum, "Liberation Theology and the Supernatural," in *The Ecumenist* 19 (1981), p. 84.

of Archbishop Oscar Arnulfo Romero, who received an honorary doctorate from the Catholic University of Louvain, *honoris causa*, on February 2, 1980.[713] As Romero suggested in his acceptance speech at Louvain:

> In a word, the Church has not only turned toward the poor, it has made of the poor the special beneficiaries of its Mission because, as Puebla says, "God takes on their defense and loves them. The Church has not only incarnated itself in the world of the poor, giving them help; it has also firmly committed itself to their defense."[714]

Romero viewed this task as integral to the Mission enjoined by the Gospel:

> ... in keeping with the Gospel, I am talking about an authentic option for the poor, of becoming incarnate in their world, of proclaiming the good news to them, of giving them hope, of encouraging them to engage in a liberating praxis, of defending their cause and sharing their fate. The Church's option for the poor explains the political dimension of the faith in its fundamentals and in its basic outline. Because the Church has opted for the truly poor, not for the fictitiously poor, because it has opted for those who are really oppressed and repressed, the Church lives in a political world, and it

---

[713]The Belgian Church enjoyed a close, reciprocal relationship with the Church of El Salvador and supplied many missionaries to the local Church there. For background on this event, see James Brockman, S.J., *Romero: A Life* (Maryknoll, NY: Orbis Books, 1991), pp. 224-226. For the complete text of the address, "The Political Dimension of the Faith from the Perspective of the Preferential Option for the Poor," see Alfred T. Hennelly, S.J., *Liberation Theology: A Documentary History*, pp. 292-303, as well as Jon Sobrino, S.J., *et al.* (eds.), *Archbishop Romero/ Voice of the Voiceless: The Four Pastoral Letters and Other Statements* (Maryknoll, NY: Orbis Books, 1985), pp. 177-187. Brockman noted the influence of Sobrino on this document: "As he had done with the second pastoral letter, Romero had asked Jon Sobrino to prepare a draft of the speech. But, instead of rewriting it, this time he simply added an introduction and lightly touched up Sobrino's text. He also noted in his diary that other priests had helped him 'express better the pastoral sentiments in the speech.' Its language was more theological than that of his homilies, but the thought was the same." Cited in James R. Brockman, S.J., *Romero: A Life*, p. 226.

[714]Oscar Romero, "The Political Dimension of the Faith," cited in Alfred Hennelly, S.J. (ed.), *Liberation Theology: A Documentary History*, p. 296.

> fulfills itself through politics. It cannot be otherwise if the Church, like Jesus, is to turn itself toward the poor.[715]

The previous day, in a homily, Romero proclaimed:

> Awakening to these realities and feeling their impact, far from leading us away from our faith, has sent us back to the world of the poor as our rightful place – has moved us, as a first, basic step, to take flesh in the world of the poor. This is where we have found the actual faces of the poor that we hear about in Puebla.[716]

In his Louvain acceptance speech, Romero insisted that the Church must enter into "the real world of the poor":

> ...this is not what some call "reducing" Christian hope to the temporal, the "human"... The nearness to the world of the poor, as we see, will be both an incarnation and a conversion. Changes have been needed in the Church – in our pastoral activity, in our education, in our religious and priestly life, and in our lay movements. We have not managed to make these changes, because our eyes have been riveted on the Church alone. We have been turned inward. Now we shall be able to make these changes, because we have turned outward – turned to the world of the poor.[717]

As Gutiérrez asserted in *The Power of the Poor in History*,[718] the Louvain address of Romero insisted that the rest of the Church must learn from the materially poor:

> The world of the poor, with its very concrete social and political characteristics, teaches us where the Church can incarnate itself in such a way that will avoid the false universalism that inclines the

---

[715]Oscar Romero, "The Political Dimension of the Faith," p. 298.
[716]Cited in Pablo Galdámez, *Faith of a People: The Life of a Basic Christian Community in El Salvador*, p. 21.
[717]Oscar Romero, "The Political Dimension of the Faith," pp. 298.
[718]Gustavo Gutiérrez, *The Power of the Poor in History*, p. 105.

> Church to associate itself with the powerful. The world of the poor teaches us what the nature of Christian love is... a love that should be freely offered, but that seeks to be effective in history. The world of the poor teaches us that the sublimity of Christian love needs to be mediated through the overriding necessity of justice for the majority. It ought not to turn away from honorable conflict. The world of the poor teaches us that liberation will arrive only when the poor are not simply on the receiving end of handouts from governments or from the Church, but when they themselves are the masters of, and protagonists in, their own struggle and liberation, thereby unmasking the root of false paternalism, including ecclesiastical paternalism.[719]

With characteristic humility, Romero summarized his contribution to furthering the dialogue on the place of the preferential option for the poor in the life of the Church:

> You all know the words of Scripture [relating to the option for the poor], given prominence by Vatican II. During the 1960's, several of your [Belgian] bishops and theologians helped to throw light on the essence and the Mission of the Church understood in these terms. My contribution will be to flesh out those beautiful declarations from the standpoint of my own situation, that of a small Latin American country, typical of what today is called the Third World. To put it in one word – in a word that sums it all up and makes it concrete – the world that the Church ought to serve is the world of the poor.[720]

In his role as a bishop, Archbishop Romero frequently imparted his teaching from the pulpit. Even after the repeated bombing of his diocesan radio station, YSAX, copies of his homilies were mass produced and distributed by audio-cassette throughout the country. They formed a privileged locus for his theological reflection

---

[719]Oscar Romero, "The Political Dimension of the Faith," pp. 299-300.

[720]Ibid., p. 294. On this point, see also Stephen J. Pope, "Partiality and the Preferential Option," pp. 250-251.

on the "option for the poor," at the "common sense" level of theological communication, to borrow the phrase of Bernard Lonergan's *Method in Theology*.[721] Aware of the charge that socially active lay leaders, religious, and were frequently derided as "Marxists marching under the banner of Christ," Romero offered the following rejoinder: "When we speak of the Church of the poor, we are not using a Marxist dialectic, as though there were another Church of the rich. What we are saying is that Christ, inspired by the Spirit of God, declared, 'The Lord has sent me to bring good news to the poor' [LK 4:18] – words of the Bible – so that to hear Him one must become poor."[722]

When Romero met in a private audience with Pope John Paul II, on January 30, 1980, he told the Pope: "Holy Father, in my country it is very dangerous to speak of anti-communism, because anti-communism is what the right proclaims, not out of love for Christian sentiments, but out of a selfish concern to preserve its own interests... We must always defend and preserve the spiritual and Christian values of our people."[723] In his preaching, Romero consistently insisted: "Let not the Church's Mission of evangelizing and working for justice be confused with subversive activities. It is very different – unless the Gospel is to be called subversive, because it does indeed touch the foundations of an order that should not exist, because it is unjust."[724] Romero recognized that being the "voice of the voiceless" would not meet with universal acceptance or praise: "These homilies try to be this people's voice. They try to be the voice of those who have no voice. And

---

[721]See Bernard Lonergan, S.J., *Method in Theology (*NY: Seabury Press, 1972).

[722]Oscar Romero, sermon of December 3, 1978, cited in James Brockman, S.J. (ed.), *The Violence of Love*, p. 124.

[723]Cited in James Brockman, S.J., *Romero: A Life*, p. 224.

[724]Oscar Romero, sermon of August 6, 1979, cited in James Brockman, S.J. (ed.), *The Violence of Love*, p. 183.

so, without doubt, they displease those who have too much voice."[725] In one of his most famous homilies, Archbishop Romero proclaimed:

> Christ invites us not to be afraid of persecution because, believe me, sisters and brothers, anyone who commits themselves to the poor must suffer the same fate as the poor. And in El Salvador we all know what the fate of the poor is: to be disappeared, tortured, arrested, appear as corpses... I am glad, brothers and sisters, that our Church is persecuted, precisely because of its preferential option for the poor... They are witnesses to a Church incarnate in the problems of the poor.[726]

For Romero, in order for the Church of Rome to become the "Church of the poor,"[727] to borrow the salubrious phrase of John XXIII, repeated in John Paul II's 1981 encyclical, *Laborem excercens* (no. 8), the Church stands in need of continuous conversion:

> ...if we really want to know the meaning of conversion and faith and confidence in another, all of us must become poor, or at least make the cause of the poor our inner motivation. That is when one begins to experience faith and conversion; when one has the heart of the poor, when one knows that financial capital, political influence, and power are worthless, and that without God we are nothing.[728]

---

[725]Oscar Romero, sermon of July 29, 1979, cited ibid., p. 183.
[726]Cited in Jon Sobrino, S.J., "Suffering, Death, Cross, and Martyrdom," in Ignacio Ellacuría and Jon Sobrino (eds.), *Mysterium Liberationis*, p. 715.
[727]As Bishop Pedro Casaldáliga noted in his journal: "On the way out of Managua a large billboard – out of sheer religious concern – proclaims- 'There is only one God.' Underneath it someone from the people has added in a very gospel manner, 'The God of the poor.'" See Pedro Casaldáliga, *Prophets in Combat: The Nicaraguan Journal of Bishop Pedro Casaldáliga* (London: Catholic Institute for International Relations, 1987), p. 42.
[728]Oscar Romero, sermon of February 18, 1979, cited in James Brockman, S.J. (ed.), *The Violence of Love*, p. 147.

Elsewhere, Romero stressed: "The Church's good name is not a matter of being on good terms with the powerful. The Church's good name is a matter of knowing that the poor regard the Church as their own, of knowing that the Church's life on earth is a call on all, on the rich as well, to be converted and be saved along with the poor, for they are the only ones called blessed."[729]

In more dramatic fashion, later that year Romero preached:

> I am glad, sisters and brothers, that our Church is persecuted precisely for its preferential option for the poor and for trying to become incarnate in the interest of the poor and for saying to all the people, to rulers, to the rich and powerful: if you do not become poor, if you do not concern yourself for the poverty of our people as though they were your own family, you will not be able to save society.[730]

Beyond that, in Romero's mind, "The Christian who does not want to live this commitment of solidarity with the poor is not worthy to be called Christian."[731]

Archbishop Romero and his pastoral collaborators paid dearly for the witness embodied by this stance:

> Each priest killed [within El Salvador by the death squads] is for me a new concelebrant in the Eucharist of our archdiocese. I know that they are here giving us encouragement by having to know how to die without fear, because each one's conscience was committed to this law of the Lord: *the preferential option for the poor.*[732]

---

[729]Oscar Romero, sermon of February 17, 1980, cited ibid., p. 227.

[730]Oscar Romero, sermon of July 15, 1979, cited ibid., p. 177. Note the similarity between this sermon and the one given at Yankee Stadium in New York City by Pope John Paul II on October 2, 1979, cited in *Pilgrimage of Peace: The Collected Speeches of John Paul II in Ireland and the United States* (NY: Farrar, Straus & Giroux, 1980), pp. 87-90.

[731]Oscar Romero, sermon of February 17, 1980, cited in James Brockman, S.J. (ed.), *The Violence of Love*, p. 227.

[732]Oscar Romero, sermon of September 2, 1979, cited ibid., p. 195. On the dramatic rise of martrydom in Latin America, see Bishop Pedro Casaldáliga, "Martyrdom," in *In Pursuit of the Kingdom: Writings 1968-1988* (Maryknoll, NY: Orbis Books, 1990), pp. 187-199; Instituto de Estudios Centroamericanos, *The Jesuit Assassinations: The Writings of Ellacuría, Martín Baró, and Segundo Montes, with a Chronology of the Investigation* (Kansas City, MO: Sheed & Ward, 1990);

In another place, he reflected upon the same point:

> The Church suffers the fate of the poor, which is persecution. Our Church lories that it has mingled the blood of its priests, its catechists, and its communities with that of the massacred people and has continually borne the mark of persecution. Because it disquiets, it is slandered, and its voice crying against injustice is disregarded.[733]

As Romero further persisted: "Christ invites us not to fear persecution. Believe me, sisters and brothers, anyone committed to the poor must suffer the same fate as the poor. And in El Salvador we know the fate of the poor: to be taken away, to be tortured, to be jailed, to be found dead."[734] He offered further clarification of the true significance of the preferential option for the poor: When we say, "for the poor," we do not take sides with one social class, please note. What we do, according to Puebla, is invite all social classes, rich and poor without distinction, saying to everyone: Let us take seriously the cause of the poor as though it were our own – indeed as what it really is, the cause of Jesus Christ, who on the final judgment day will call salvation to those who treated the poor with faith in him: "Whatever you did to one of these poor ones – the neglected, blind, lame, deaf, mute – you did to me [MT 25:40]."[735]

Nowhere was Romero more clear in his proclamation of this theme than in a Sunday sermon delivered on February 17, 1980, shortly after his return to San Salvador from Louvain:

William J. O'Malley, S.J., *The Voice of Blood: Five Christian Martyrs of Our Time* (Maryknoll, NY: Orbis Books, 1980); Jon Sobrino, Ignacio Ellacuría, *et al.*, *Companions of Jesus: The Jesuit Martyrs of El Salvador*; Jon Sobrino, S.J., "The Subjective Testimony of the Church in Persecution and Martyrdom," in *The True Church and the Poor*, pp. 171-184; and, Martin Lange and Reinhold Iblacker, *Witnesses of Hope: The Persecution of Christians in Latin America* (Maryknoll, NY: Orbis Books, 1981).

[733]Oscar Romero, sermon of February 17, 1980, cited in James Brockman, S.J. (ed.), *The Violence of Love*, p. 226.

[734]Oscar Romero, sermon of February 17, 1980, ibid., p. 228.

[735]Oscar Romero, sermon of September 9, 1979, ibid, p. 196.

> The poor have shown the Church the true way to go. A Church that does not join the poor in order to speak out from the side of the poor against the injustices committed against them is not the true Church of Jesus Christ... The world of the poor is the key to understand the Christian faith, the Church's activity, and the political dimension of the faith and the Church's activity. The poor are the ones who tell us what the world is and what service the Church must offer to the world.[736]

Archbishop Romero understood this stance to be more God-centered than anthropocentric, an option enjoined upon believers by their God: "We know that every effort to better society, especially when injustice and sin are so engrained, is an effort that God blesses, that God wants, that God demands of us."[737] Shortly after he uttered these words, a high caliber shell from an assassin's rifle penetrated Romero's heart. His last spoken words framed his legacy, and his judgment, upon the contemporary Christian community.

The Brazilian Missionary bishop, Pedro Casaldáliga composed an elegy entitled, "Saint Romero of the Americas, Pastor and Martyr"

> You knew how to drink
> the double chalice
> of altar and people
> With a single hand anointed to serve.
> Saint Romero of the Americas, our pastor and martyr,
> No one
> will silence
> your final sermon![738]

---

[736]Oscar Romero, sermon of February 17, 1979, ibid., pp. 224-225.

[737]Oscar Romero, sermon of March 24, 1980, ibid., p. 242.

[738]Pedro Casaldáliga, *Prophets in Combat*, p. 109. Officially, nearly two decades after his assassination while celebrating Mass in the chapel of the Divine Providence Hospital outside San Salvador on Palm Sunday, 1980, Romero was declared "Venerable" by Pope John Paul II, the first of the tri-fold steps (prior to beatification and canonization) toward official recognition of sanctity in the Roman Catholic faith tradition. At the grassroots, by acclamation, his personal holiness and excellence of orthodoxy were already long recognized and revered throughout Latin America and beyond.

Romero could only begin to fathom the contest brewing in Rome over the "preferential option for the poor" as an integral theme of Catholic social teaching.

Chapter Five

John Paul II and the "New Evangelization"

Among the various pontiffs who occupied the See of Peter during the course of the twentieth century, the one who unquestionably exerted the greatest impact on a global scale was Pope John Paul II. By the time of his silver jubilee in October, 2003, he completed more than one hundred major overseas pilgrimages to countries on every inhabited continent and inched forward towards becoming the second longest serving Pope in history. During his flight to Brazil prior to his pastoral visit in 1980, he told a member of his press entourage: "My job is to teach, but I teach learning and I learn teaching."[739]

At times, various partisans ascribed to John Paul the desire to turn back the clock on Catholic social teaching in an attempt to restore it to a more "traditionalist" posture. Such claims proved unfounded and failed to take into account the complexity of John Paul as a thinker and the many facets of the agenda that he embraced and sought to advance when he ascended to the papacy. Along the lines of this perspective, Irish social ethicist Donal Dorr asserted:

> As regards the content of his social teaching there is no "backtracking" from the position of Paul VI or John XXIII. Indeed, he has taken much stronger stands against injustice and in defense of human rights than were ever taken by his predecessors. On the two

---

[739]David Willey, *God's Politician: Pope John Paul II, The Catholic Church, and the New World Order* (NY: St. Martin's Press, 1992), p. 120. For a comprehensive theological assessment of John Paul II's mature pontificate, see Avery Cardinal Dulles, S.J., *The Splendor of Truth* (NY: Herder & Herder, 2003 revision).

> key issues of liberation and the "option for the poor," his teaching has moved forward further than Paul VI rather than backward to an older line.[740]

No less seasoned an observer than former Soviet Premiere Mikhail Gorbachev testified to the pivotal role that John Paul played in the restructuring of the new world order: "Everything that happened in Eastern Europe during the last few years would not have been possible without the presence of this Pope, without the leading role – the political role – that he was able to play on the world stage."[741] On certain levels, John Paul eschewed political involvement by clergy. As he told a group of seventy-four priests whom he ordained in Brazil in 1980: "You are not doctors or social workers, you are not politicians or trade unionists."[742] Earlier the same year, on his first pastoral visit to Africa, John Paul exhorted a group of priests in Zaire to "Be pastors, not politicians."[743] Yet in contrast, in an interview published in *La Stampa* in 1992 John Paul clarified in a nuanced way his own acceptance of Gorbachev's claim that he exerted pivotal political impact on Eastern Europe:

> I do not believe that one can talk about a political role in the strict sense, because the Pope has his mission to preach the Gospel. But in the Gospel there is the human person, respect for the human person, and, therefore, human rights, freedom of conscience and everything that pertains to humans. If this has political significance, then, yes, it applies also to the Pope.[744]

---

[740]Donal Dorr, *Option for the Poor* (1992 revision), p. 361.

[741]Mikhail Gorbachev, cited in *The Irish Times* (March 4, 1992), p. 9. See also David Willey, *God's Politician: Pope John Paul II, The Catholic Church, and The New World Order*, p. xii.

[742]Cited in Paul Johnson, *Pope John Paul II and the Catholic Restoration* (NY: St. Martin's Press, 1981), p. 102. Several years later, he echoed these sentiments almost verbatim in an address to newly ordained Salvadoran priests. See John Paul II, "Address to Priests, San Salvador," in *Osservatore Romano* (October 7-8, 1983), p. 4.

[743]John Paul II, "'Be Pastors, Not Politicians': Address to Priests," Kinshasa, Zaire, May 4, 1980, in *Origins* (May 22, 1980), p. 101.

[744]See Donal Dorr, *Option for the Poor* (1992 revision), p. 361.

For John Paul II, the Church's political role was intimately connected to its mission to preach the Gospel. In a 1983 talk to the Latin American bishops' conference, he announced that the theme for the CELAM IV meeting slated to be held in Santo Domingo in observance of the Columbus quincentennial in 1992 would be "The New Evangelization." He defined the task of the gathering in the Dominican Republic to be "a commitment not to re-evangelization but to a new evangelization, new in ardor, methods, and expression."[745] The theme of "the New Evangelization" served as a constant determinant of John Paul's social doctrine, since he believed that authentic human development must be grounded in an ever deepening proclamation of the message of salvation in Jesus Christ.[746] Speaking to the bishops of Colombia during their 1984 *ad limina* visit (and citing the Puebla "Final Document"), John Paul asserted: "The greatest service that we can render to another is evangelization, which prepares them to fulfill themselves as children of God, liberates them from injustice, and leads them to fuller life."[747] John Paul viewed evangelization as directed to all humanity, not just the materially poor: "Evangelization must uplift humanity, giving them above all faith, salvation in Christ, the means and instruction to obtain these. For truly poor are those who lack material necessities, but even poorer are those who are ignorant of the path that God points out to them."[748]

In his 1979 opening address at Puebla, John Paul emphasized the linkage in evangelization between "the truth about Jesus Christ... about the Church's mission...

---

[745]"Pope John Paul to CELAM: The Task of the Latin American Bishop," in *Origins* 12 (March 24, 1983), p. 661. For an excellent overview of this theme from a North American perspective, see Avery Dulles, S.J., "John Paul II and the New Evangelization," in *America* (February 1, 1992), pp. 52-69.
[746]On these points, see the following encyclicals of John Paul II: *Centesimus Annus* (no. 54), *Sollicitudo Rei Socialis* (no. 41), and *Redemptoris Mater* (no. 58).
[747]Insegnamenti II/2 (1984), p. 999.
[748]John Paul II, "Address to the Latin American Bishops Conference in Santo Domingo," *Osservatore Romano* (October 14, 1984), p. 1.

[and] about human beings" (1:2 – 1:9). In a more explicit vein, he connected these three strands in 1992 at CELAM IV in Santo Domingo. He called upon the assembled bishops to direct their focus towards: "three doctrinal and pastoral elements... three axes of the new evangelization... a deep and solid Christology... a healthy anthropology, and... a clear and correct ecclesiological vision."[749] John Paul's theology did not represent a retreat or retrenchment from the advances of the Second Vatican Council, which he reiterated was the constant reference point of his ministry and the great, defining religious event of the twentieth century, but it continued to form a part of the sweep of the trajectory begun by John XXIII and Vatican II. As John Paul II's opening address at Puebla stressed:

> This is very much in line with the view of Vatican II: i.e., that to achieve a life worthy of a human being, one cannot limit oneself to *having more*, one must strive to *be more* (G.S., no. 35). So drink at these authentic fonts, Brothers. Speak in the idiom of Vatican II, John XXIII and Paul VI. For that is the idiom that embodies the experience, the suffering, and the hope of contemporary humanity (III, 4).

In this same vein, the 1992 CELAM IV Final Document asserted: "New evangelization demands that the Church undergo a pastoral conversion. Such a conversion must be in keeping with the [spirit of the Second Vatican] Council" (no. 30).

John Paul regularly insisted that the Church's social Mission must include the truth about human beings, a clear and correct anthropology. The human person had long emerged as the centerpiece of Catholic social thought,[750] but John Paul's legacy sharpened and refined Catholic social teaching on the dignity of the human person.

---

[749]John Paul II, "Opening Address of the Holy Father," in Secretariat for Latin America, *Santo Domingo/ Fourth General Conference of Latin American Bishops*, p. 6.
[750]See J. Bryan Hehir, "Continuity and Change in Social Teaching," p. 253.

He stressed in the "Opening Address" at Puebla that the Church "opts solely for the human being" (III, 3), that "the Church's concern is for the whole human being" (III, 4). This anthropology can never be separated from a "deep and solid Christology," which reveals the truth about Jesus Christ. As he addressed the poor in the Barrio Santa Cecilia, in Guadalajara, Mexico, on February 1, 1979:

> The Pope loves you because you are the beloved of God. When he established his family, the Church, he had present before him the poor and needy human race, and to redeem that race he sent his very own son, who was born a poor man and lived among the poor in order to enrich us through his poverty... the figure of Christ, hanging on the Cross as the price for the redemption of the human race, is a penetrating call to spend our lives in the service of the needy, in accordance with the movement of a love that... sides not with injustice but with the truth.[751]

In the assessment of one of his biographers, George Williams: "In the perspective of generations of Christian scholarship it will come to be noted that the evolving papal stress on the dignity of man received its most notable and swift expansion in the pre-papal and papal pronouncements of Pope John Paul II."[752] John Paul believed that the transcendence of the human being was the constitutive dimension of every human being. As he indicated in the first encyclical of his pontificate, *Redemptor Hominis*:

> Man is the full truth of his existence, of his personal being and also of his community and social being... this man is the primary route that the Church must travel in fulfilling her mission: man is the primary and fundamental way for the Church, the way traced out by Christ

---

[751]Cited in Donal Dorr, *Option for the Poor* (1992 revision), pp. 76-77.
[752]George H. Williams, *The Mind of John Paul II: Origins of His Thought and Action* (NY: Seabury Press, 1981), p. 264.

> himself, the way that leads invariably through the mystery of the Incarnation and the Redemption (no. 1).[753]

John Paul echoed the line of reasoning of *Redemptor Hominis* (no. 14) in an address delivered during his 1980 pastoral visit to Brazil: "It is the mission of the Church to travel the human path because the human person – without any exception whatsoever – has been redeemed by Christ, and because with the human – with each human being, without any exception whatsoever – Christ is in a way united even when that person is unaware of it."[754]

J. Bryan Hehir suggested that "the principal way in which John Paul II addresses the social questions is through human rights categories."[755] John Paul not only applied the human rights teaching of his immediate predecessors, but he proceeded to develop his own distinctive interpretation of human rights in the direction of political-civil and social-cultural-economic rights. As he noted in a 1981 allocution: "The Church would not be faithful to the Gospel if she were not close to the poor and if she did not defend their rights."[756] John Paul stridently argued that the reason for the Church's sustained defense of the rights of the poor is the unjust distribution of wealth and engrained, structural injustice.

The Puebla "Final Document" contained a text from his opening address at the conference: "...there arises a grave structural conflict: 'The growing affluence of a few people parallels the growing poverty of the masses'" (no. 1209). In the preceding paragraph of this same opening address, John Paul stated more directly:

---

[753]John Paul II, *Redemptor Hominis* (Washington, DC: United States Catholic Conference, 1979).
[754]John Paul II, "The Eucharist is Love and Charity from Which Brotherly Sharing Springs," Brazil, July 9, 1980, in *John Paul II/ Brazil: Journey in Light of the Eucharist* (Boston: St. Paul Editions, 1980), p. 329.
[755]J. Bryan Hehir, "Continuity and Change in Social Teaching," p. 137. For a fuller treatment of this issue, see David Hollenbach, S.J., *Claims in Conflict: Retrieving and Renewing the Catholic Human Rights Tradition* (NY: Paulist Press, 1979).
[756]John Paul II, "The Church in the World of the 80's," in *Origins* 10 (1981), p. 496.

"...this poverty is not a passing phase. Instead it is the product of economic, social, and political situations and structures... [that] create a situation on the international level where the rich get richer at the expense of the poor, who get even poorer" (III, 3). In his homily at Yankee Stadium delivered on October 2, 1979, he expanded upon this theme: "...you will also want to seek out the structural reasons which foster or cause the different forms of poverty in the world and in your own country, so that you can apply the proper remedies."[757] He reiterated this point in his address to the shanty dwellers in the Tondo area outside Manila, during his February, 1981 pastoral visit to the Philippines: "You [people of means] must give a lot. And you must think about how to give – how to organize socio-economic life... in such a way that will tend to bring about equality between people, rather than putting a yawning gap between them" (no. 4).[758] In this same vein, he concluded:

> Do all that you can, especially you who have decision-making powers, you upon whom the situation of the world depends, do everything to make the life of every person in your country more human, more worthy of the human person. Do all you can to ensure the disappearance, albeit gradually, of that yawning gap that divides the few "excessively rich" from the great masses of the poor, the people who are subjugated in grinding poverty (no. 5).[759]

Although Mikhail Gorbachev's published remarks underscored John Paul's preoccupation with "East-West" issues, in time the Pope's concerns and purview shifted more heavily upon the "North-South" conflict that stemmed from the problems of debt and underdevelopment, and drove the nations south of the Tropic of Cancer into deeper financial distress and economic misery. John Paul indicated

---

[757]John Paul II, "Homily," Yankee Stadium, in *Pilgrimage of Peace: The Collected Speeches of John Paul II in Ireland and the United States* (NY: Farrar, Straus & Giroux, 1980), p. 88.
[758]John Paul II, "Address to the Poor of Tondo," in *A.A.S.* (1981), pp. 855-856.
[759]Ibid., p. 856.

this new direction in the text of his 1981 social encyclical *Laborem Exercens* that commemorated the eightieth anniversary of *Rerum Novarum,* in which he discussed "the tensions making themselves felt in the world not only between East and West, but also between North and South" (no. 7).

From his 1979 address at the U.N.[760] to the array of social encyclicals that continued to mark his mature pontificate, Pope John Paul urged the development of a new order for world politics. Underlying his concern was his highly developed anthropology that offered a criterion by which to judge both economic and social systems. In a striking address delivered at Edmonton, Canada in September, 1984, he spoke of the global situation in terms of the exploitation of poor southern nations by rich northern ones:

> ..the South becoming always poorer... and the rich becoming always richer... This poor South will judge the rich North. And the poor people and poor nations – poor in different ways, not only lacking food, but also deprived of freedom and other human rights – will judge those people who take those goods away from them, amassing them to themselves the imperialistic monopoly of economic and political supremacy at the expense of others.[761]

The North-South conflict received fuller attention in his 1988 social encyclical, *Sollicitudo Rei Socialis*, wherein John Paul II discoursed against the struggle against material poverty and underdevelopment in the South, and the moral and spiritual

---

[760] John Paul II, "Address at the General Assembly of the United Nations" (October 2, 1979), in *Pilgrimage of Peace*, pp. 68-78.

[761] John Paul II, "Development: The Progress of All the Disadvantaged," in *Origins* 14 (October 4, 1984), p. 247. Interestingly, part of this quotation incorporates verbatim the text of the *Canadian* Catholic Bishops' pastoral letter on the economy, "Ethical Reflections on the Economic Crisis" (Ottawa, Ontario: Canadian Conference of Catholic Bishops' Episcopal Committee on Social Affairs, 1983). See the relevant excerpt in *The [Toronto] Globe and Mail* (January 1, 1983), p. T-15.

poverty caused by "overdevelopment" in the North (cf. no. 28). Likewise, in his 1991 encyclical, *Redemptoris Missio*, John Paul extended upon this line of thought:

> ..a soul-less development cannot suffice for human beings, and an excess of ffluence is as harmful as excess poverty. This is a "development model" which the North has constructed and is now spreading to the South, where a sense of religion as well as human values is in danger of being overwhelmed by a wave of consumerism (no. 59).[762]

Although certain Vatican insiders believed that in the early years of John Paul II's pontificate "the word *liberation* [was] not part of the Pope's ordinary vocabulary,"[763] he later adopted a nuanced usage of the term. In a general audience of February 21, 1979, shortly after returning from his first trip to Latin America, he noted:

> Liberation, then, is certainly a reality of faith, one of the fundamental biblical themes, which are a deep part of Christ's salvific Mission. This topic [of liberation] has never ceased to constitute the content of the spiritual life of Christians. The Conference of Latin American Bishops bears witness that this subject returns in a new historical context; therefore it must be taken up again in the teaching of the Church, in theology, and in the apostolate.[764]

During the same Wednesday audience, John Paul concluded:

> the "theology of liberation" is often connected (sometimes too exclusively) with Latin America. But it must be admitted that one of the great contemporary theologians, Hans Urs von Balthasar, is right

---

[762]John Paul II, "*Redemptoris Missio*/Encyclical on Missionary Activity," in *Origins* 20 (January 31, 1991), p. 558.

[763]Roger Heckel, S.J. (ed.), *The Theme of Liberation/Texts of John Paul II* (October, 1978- November, 1979) (Vatican City: Pontifical Council *Iustitia et Pax*, 1980), p. 2.

[764]John Paul II, "Liberation Theology Involves 'That Truth Which Made Us Free'" (February 21, 1979), in *Osservatore Romano* (February 26, 1979), p. 1.

> when he demands a theology of liberation on a universal scale... The task of theology is to discover its authentic meaning in its various concrete, historical, and contemporary contexts.[765]

In 1980, during an address to the bishops of CELAM during his first Brazilian trip, John Paul returned to this theme, in a manner that was critical of some of the fledgling currents of the theology of liberation:

> An important theme at the Puebla conference was liberation... It is indispensable to distinguish, in the variety of treatments and currents of liberation, between what implies "a right Christian concept of liberation" [Opening Address at Puebla, III, 5], "in its integral and deep meaning as stated by Jesus" [III, 6], and other forms of liberation that are different and are even at odds with Christian commitment. The criteria offered by the Church must be faithfully applied.[766]

In the ensuing paragraph of the same address, John Paul cited the Puebla "Final Document," and dismissed the dialectic of the class struggle (no. 486), the "risk of ideologization," and projected dire the consequences to flow from recourse to Marxist analysis (no. 545).[767] This caution was evidenced by John Paul II on the plane ride to Puebla the previous year. He told a *New York Times* reporter: "Liberation theology is a genuine theology. But it can perhaps be a false theology. If theology begins to be politicized, if it starts to apply doctrines of political systems, ways of analysis which are not Christian, then this is no longer theology. Liberation theology, surely, but which one?"[768]

---

[765]Ibid., p. 12.

[766]John Paul II, "Address to the Bishops of CELAM," (Rio de Janiero, July 2, 1980), in *John Paul II, Addresses and Homilies Given in Brazil* (Washington, DC: National Catholic News Service, 1980), p. 17.

[767]Ibid., no.8, p. 17.

[768]Interviewed in the *New York Times* (January 31, 1979), p. 1.

In the course of time John Paul came to embrace a broader understanding of the tenets of liberation theology. Following the line of both the Medellín and Puebla documents, in his letter to the Brazilian bishops of April, 1986, he noted: "The poor of this country, whose pastors you are, and the poor of this continent are the first to feel the urgent need of this Gospel of radical and integral liberation. To deny them would be to defraud and disillusion them" (no. 6).[769] Elsewhere in the same document he concluded:

> ...the theology of liberation is not only timely but useful and necessary. It should constitute a new stage – in close connection with the former ones – of the theological reflection initiated with the apostolic tradition and continued by the great Fathers and Doctors, by the ordinary and extraordinary magisterium, and in more recent years by the rich patrimony of the Church's social doctrine... May God help you to be unceasingly watchful so that a correct and necessary theology of liberation can develop in Brazil and in Latin America in a homogenous and not heterogeneous fashion with relation to the theology of all times, in full fidelity to church doctrine, attentive to a preferential but not excluding or exclusive love for the poor (no. 5).[770]

In his 1988 encyclical, *Sollicitudo Rei Socialis*, John Paul demonstrated more of a centrist tone, as he advocated new ways of confronting poverty and under-development in the Third World in the tradition of Pope Paul VI's encyclical, *Populorum Progressio*, which:

> ...makes liberation the fundamental category and the first principle of action. The positive values as well as the deviations and risks of deviations which are damaging to the faith and which are connected to this form of theological reflection and method have been appropriately pointed out... This is in fact the purpose of

---

[769]John Paul II, "Letter to Brazilian Episcopal Conference" (Vatican City, April 9, 1986), in Alfred T. Hennelly, S.J. (ed.), *Liberation Theology: A Documentary History*, p. 504.
[770]Ibid., pp. 503-504.

> development, or rather liberation and development, taking into account the intimate connection between the two (no. 46).[771]

In his address to the bishops of Latin America delivered at the beginning of the CELAM IV conference in Santo Domingo in October, 1992, John Paul devoted an entire section to the theme of "development" (cf. Part III).[772] The Santo Domingo "Final Document" reflected a decided tendency to favor the language of "development" over that of "liberation" (cf. nos. 15, 31, 39). The "four key words" cited within the text (cf. no. 47) to encapsulate the Church's "social and spiritual heritage" (i.e., "reconciliation," "solidarity," "integration," and "communion"),[773] conspicuously omitted any mention of the term "liberation." In reality, Cardinal Angelo Sodano, the Vatican Secretary of State, left the impression in a press interview that "the only option to be made in Santo Domingo is the option for Christ."[774] However, a principal theme of the theology of liberation, that of the "preferential option of the poor," weathered this diversion and remained encapsulated within the Santo Domingo final document, and in the pronouncements of Pope John Paul II at CELAM IV as well.

Regarding the appropriation of the specific term, the "preferential option for the poor," John Paul II displayed deliberate reticence in its use during the early years of his pontificate, most likely because he perceived it to be a potential source of potential divisiveness within the Church and society, and identified it too closely

---

[771]Leonardo Boff scored the tendency of *Sollicitudo Rei Socialis* (no. 46) to equate development with liberation, since "liberation seeks to be an alternative to development." See "The Originality of the Theology of Liberation," in Marc H. Ellis and Otto Maduro (eds.), *Expanding the View*, p. 56.
[772]John Paul II, "Address to the Bishops of Latin America," in *Osservatore Romano* (October 14, 1992), p. 6.
[773]"'Put Christ on the Lips and Into the Hearts of Everyone:' The Final Message of the Fourth General Conference of the Latin American Episcopate to the Peoples of Latin America and the Caribbean," in *Osservatore Romano* (October 14, 1992), p. 7.
[774]Cited in 30 *Giorni* (November 11, 1992), pp. 25 – 26.

with partisan interests and ideologies.[775] As Paul Sigmund indicated, fear of the development of a "parallel church" emanating from within the base communities fueled a concern within Vatican circles that "'the preferential option for the poor' had been interpreted in terms of a quasi-class alignment, with the poor against the rich. This led the Vatican to substitute the phrase, 'preferential love, or love of preference of the poor,'"[776] a predilection evidenced in the rhetoric of John Paul II during his early pontificate in his allocutions and early social encyclicals.

In his opening address at Puebla, John Paul assiduously avoided the use of the term,[777] although he found an alternative way to express the concept, when he indicated that the Church "opts solely for the human being... [and] is prompted by an authentically evangelical commitment which, like that of Christ, is primarily a commitment to those most in need" (III, 3). During his first pastoral visit abroad in 1979, while in Mexico, he expressed this idea in similar words. In a sermon delivered at the Basilica of Our Lady of Guadalupe outside Mexico City, he described the Medellín conference as a call of hope that showed "a preferential yet

---

[775]This is a theme that John Paul II forcefully reiterated during his 1980 pastoral visit to Brazil. See the "Address to CELAM" (II, no. 8), in *A.A.S.* 72 (1980), p. 865; "Address to the Shanty Dwellers of Vidigal" (no. 5), in *A.A.S.* 72 (1980), p. 856; "Address to the Brazilian Bishops" (no. 6), in *A.A.S.* 72 (1980), p. 957; and, the "Address to the Workers in Morumbi Stadium, São Paulo" (no. 4), in *A.A.S.* 72 (1980), pp. 890-891.

[776]Paul Sigmund, *Liberation Theology at the Crossroads*, p. 188.

[777]This omission is all the more striking, in light of Cardinal Aloisio Lorscheider's observation that upon reading the Puebla Final Document, "one notes that the prophetic option, preferential and in solidarity with the poor, appears something like 646 times. Considering that the Puebla document has 1310 numbered paragraphs, it is evident even from the statistics that this option had a central position at Puebla." Cited in Rosino Gibillini, *The Liberation Theology Debate*, p. 49. Even with its due cautions, the introduction to the first Vatican Instruction on liberation theology, "Instruction on Certain Aspects of the 'Theology of Liberation'" (Vatican City, August 6, 1984), issued under the aegis of the Congregation for the Doctrine of the Faith, noted: "This warning should in no way be interpreted as a disavowal of all those who want to respond generously and with an authentic evangelical spirit to the 'preferential option for the poor.'" Later, the same document asserted: "The different theologies of liberation are situated between the preferential options for the poor forcefully reaffirmed without ambiguity after Medellín at the conference of Puebla..." (VI, 5). Cited in Alfred T. Hennelly, S.J. (ed.), *Liberation Theology: A Documentary History*, p. 394.

not exclusive love for the poor."[778] In the famous address to the poor of Guadalajara, on January 29, 1979 John Paul said: "I feel solidarity with you because, being poor, you are entitled to my particular concern. I tell you the reason at once: The Pope loves you because you are God's favorites."[779] In his remarks to peasants and Indians at Cuilapan later on the same day, he was even more forceful, standing in the tradition of his predecessor, Pope Paul VI:

> With him I would like to reiterate – with an even stronger emphasis in my voice, if that were possible – that the present Pope wishes to be "in solidarity with your cause, which is the cause of the humble people, the poor people" [Paul VI, "Address to Peasants," August 23, 1968]. I wish to reiterate that the Pope is with the masses of people who are "almost always left behind in an ignoble standard of living and sometimes treated harshly and exploited" [ibid.]. I adopt the view of my predecessors, John XXIII and Paul VI, and of Vatican II [see *Mater et Magistra*; *Populorum Progressio*; *Gaudium et Spes* nos. 9, 71, etc.]. Seeing a situation that remains alarming, that is seldom better and sometimes even worse, the Pope chooses to be your voice, the conscience of consciences, an invitation to action, to make up for lost time, which has frequently been a time of prolonged sufferings and unsatisfied hopes.[780]

Later in the same address John Paul continued in the line on which Paul VI embarked in *Populorum Progressio*, when he noted that for the sake of oppressed workers:

> ...we must act promptly and thoroughly. We must implement bold and horoughly innovative transformations. Without further delay, we must undertake the urgently required reforms [*Populorum Progressio* no. 32]. It should not be forgotten that the measures taken have to be

---

[778]John Paul II, "Homily at the Basilica of Guadalupe," in John Eagelson and Philip Sharper (eds.), *Puebla and Beyond*, p. 74.

[779]John Paul II, "Address in the Santa Cecilia District," in *A.A.S.* 71 (1979), p. 220. He paraphrased this remark in the "Address at Monterey," in *A.A.S.* 71 (1979), p. 243.

[780]John Paul II, "Address to the Indians of Oaxaca and Chiapas," in John Eagleson and Philip Sharper (eds.), *Puebla and Beyond*, p. 82.

> suitable. The Church defends the legitimate right to private property in itself; but it is no less clear in teaching that there is always a social mortgage on private property, so that goods must serve the general purpose that God has given them. And if the common good requires it, there is no need to hesitate at expropriation itself, done in the right way [cf. *Populorum Progressio*, no. 24].

While initially Pope John Paul II assiduously avoided the use of the specific term, the "preferential option for the poor," at the Puebla conference, his public addresses delivered there bore major import for the outcome of the meeting. One indicator of this reality was the frequency with which his words were woven into the text of the final document. One could readily agree with Donal Dorr's assessment of John Paul's role at Puebla: "Quotations from his addresses were used as the basis for reaching consensus on divisive issues, notably the questions of liberation, 'option for the poor,' and the Church's attitude towards ideologies [Puebla nos. 489, 1141, 538, 551-552]."[781] The Puebla "Final Document" was written proof that the Pope succeeded in achieving the main purpose of his visit – to contribute to the unity of the Latin American bishops and to help them find a direction by which they could go forward together. Consequently, in the wake of Puebla, since it appeared to John Paul and his curial advisors to sound a partisan note with Marxist overtones, the phrase the "preferential option for the poor" tended to be shunned within the lexicon of official Catholic social teaching. For instance, the term never once appeared in the Vatican Congregation for Catholic Education's otherwise excellent 1988 *Guidelines for the Study and Teaching of the Church's Social Doctrine in the Formation of Priests*,[782] and was conspicuously absent from the major social encyclical issued the

---

[781]The Puebla "Final Document" strongly condemned three ideologies: liberal capitalism; Marxist collectivism; and, the so-called doctrine of "national security."

[782]Congregation for Catholic Education, *Guidelines for the Study and Teaching of the Church's Social Doctrine in the Formation of Priests* (Washington, DC: United States Catholic Conference, 1988).

same year, *Sollicitudo Rei Socialis*, in which John Paul continued to prefer to use the term, "love of preference for the poor" (cf. no. 42).

While Pope Paul VI earned the sobriquet, "the Pilgrim Pope," he was dwarfed by comparison with the rigorous travel schedule undertaken by John Paul II.[783] One might readily concur with Donal Dorr that:

> Of the various "pastoral visits" made by John Paul II to different parts of the world, by far the most significant, from the point of view of an "option for the poor," was his first trip to Brazil. It lasted twelve days – from 30 June to 11 July 1980. ...[T]he overall impression the Pope gave, was that of being broadly in solidarity with the main body of Brazilian bishops in their commitment to putting the Church on the side of the poor and oppressed.[784]

Among the major addresses delivered by John Paul were the talks given to one hundred and fifty assembled members of CELAM at Rio, and his speech to the episcopate of Brazil at Fortaleza. In John Paul's speech to the assembled representatives of CELAM, he noted: "You rightly called for a preferential option for the poor, neither an exclusive nor excluding one" (III, 7).[785] In his address to the Brazilian bishops on July 10, 1980, John Paul elucidated his understanding of the concept of the "preferential option for the poor":

---

[783]In an interview on National Public Radio's "The Morning Edition" on July 15, 2004, *The National Catholic Reporter* Vatican correspondent, John A. Allen, Jr. reported that while Pope Paul VI was lauded for making a total of seven trips outside of Italy, John Paul II would complete 104 international in more than twenty-five years as Pope when he journeyed to Lourdes to celebrate the Feast of the Assumption of the Blessed Virgin Mary on August 15, 2004.

[784]Donal Dorr, *Option for the Poor* (1992 revision), pp. 276-277. Interestingly, the addresses delivered during John Paul's second pastoral visit to Brazil in 1991 displayed considerably more reserve on issues of social justice. See his address in the shanty town of Vitoria in *Osservatore Romano* (November 4, 1991), p. 4, along with the address to Amazonian Indians in *Osservatore Romano* (October 28, 1991), p. 10 as a point of comparison.

[785]John Paul II, "Address to the Bishops of CELAM," Rio de Janiero, July 2, 1980, in *John Paul II: Addresses and Homilies Given in Brazil* (Washington, DC: United States Catholic Conference, 1980), p. 15.

> You know that the preferential option for the poor, forcefully proclaimed at Puebla, is not an invitation to exclusivism... But it is a call to special solidarity with the humble and the weak, with those who are suffering and weeping, who are humiliated and left on the fringes of life and society, in order to have them realize more fully their own dignity as human persons and children of God.[786]

The Pope expounded further upon this point during his visit to the Vidigal *favela* of Rio de Janiero on the same date:

> The Church of the poor speaks first and foremost of every person... It is not the Church of a class or social caste... The Church of the poor has not wished to serve political ends or power struggles. Indeed, it strives most assiduously to keep its words and actions from being utilized for a like end – from being manipulated (no. 5).[787]

During this visit, he symbolically removed his gold fisherman's ring, and gave it to be sold to help the poor.[788] As John Paul stressed in his address to the Brazilian workers at Morumbi Stadium: "The option for the poor is a Christian option; it is also the option of a society that is concerned with the true common good" (no. 4).[789]

John Paul continued to show an increased predilection to use the term the "preferential option for the poor" following his first visit to Brazil, though he often qualified it by adding the phrase, "but not exclusive." During a visit to the Philippines in 1981, he stated that the defense of the dignity of the poor is not a luxury item for the poor: "...the preference for the poor is a Christian preference! It is a preference that expresses the concern of Christ, who came to proclaim a message

---

[786]John Paul II, "Address to the Bishops of Brazil," in *A.A.S.* 72 (1980), p. 956.

[787]John Paul II, "Address to the Shanty Dwellers at Vidigal," in *A.A.S.* 72 (1980), p. 856. John Paul returned to this point in his 1981 social encyclical that commemorated the 80th anniversary of *Rerum Novarum, Laborem Exercens* (no. 20).

[788]For additional details relating to this event, see David Willey, *God's Politician: Pope John Paul II, The Catholic Church, and The New World Order*, p. 220.

[789]John Paul II, "Address to the Workers of Brazil at Morumbi Stadium," in *A.A.S.* 72 (1980), p. 891.

of salvation to the poor, for the poor are indeed loved by God, and God it is who guarantees their rights."[790] John Paul built upon the well-known expression of the Second Vatican Council that the Church is, and desires to be, the "Church of the poor" in his 1981 social encyclical, *Laborem Exercens* (no. 8), as well as in the addresses given during his 1980 visit to Brazil. John Paul's extensive travels and contacts within the developing nations yielded a gradual transformation in his perspective on the option for the poor reflected in his later social teachings.[791] One Peruvian observer suggested that much of the tenor of *Laborem Exercens* was specifically tailored to Latin America. Alberto Maguina Lorco[792] argued that an address of the Pope's announcing the encyclical and slated to be delivered two days before the original publication date (though subsequently postponed on account of the near-fatal assassination attempt on John Paul's life in May, 1981) plainly stressed its Latin American roots.[793] The address was interspersed with quotations from the Puebla conference, as well as public pronouncements from his visit to Brazil in 1980. As Gustavo Gutiérrez noted in his commentary on the encyclical: "The first social encyclicals were situated above all in a European context. *Populorum Progressio* then clearly intended to take a different tack. The present encyclical [*Laborem Exercens*] reinforces this latter point of view. Therefore, it should not seem strange

---

[790]John Paul II, "Justice and the Land," Bacolod, Philippines, in *Origins* 10 (February 19, 1981), p. 617.

[791]See, for instance, the assessment of Ernest Bartell, C.S.C., "*Laborem Exercens*: A Third World Perspective," in John W. Houck and Oliver F. Williams, C.S.C. (eds.), *Co-Creation and Capitalism: John Paul II's Laborem Exercens* (Washington, DC: University Press of America, 1983), pp. 174-198.

[792]Alberto Maguina Larco, "*Encíclica Laborem Exercens: Radicál Novedad*," in *Qué Hacer* (Lima) (November, 1981), pp. 66-99.

[793]The text of the address was subsequently published in *Osservatore Romano* (May 17, 1981), p. 20, but was never formally delivered, owing to the assassination attempt on the Pope's life by Mohammed Ali Aghet on the Feast of Our Lady of Fatima, May 13, 1981.

that *Laborem Exercens* has been less well received in Europe than in the Third World."[794]

In his "Apostolic Exhortation on the Family," *Familiaris Consortio* (November 22, 1981), John Paul II used the term "preferential option for the poor" in a passing reference for the first time in an official Vatican document: "The Christian family is thus called upon to offer everyone a witness of generous and disinterested dedication to social matters through a 'preferential option' for the poor and disadvantaged..." (no. 47).[795] In spite of this fact, Pope John Paul continued to display a pronounced reticence and discomfort with the unqualified use of the term. He clarified his thought on this matter while speaking at the opening of the CELAM meeting in Port-au-Prince, Haiti on March 9, 1983, whereby he lamented "the bitterness of those who, because of an erroneous option for the poor, feel that they are abandoned and forgotten in their aspirations and religious needs."[796] Later in the same address to the delegates of CELAM he again warned against the divisiveness of class struggle within the Church:

> The very poorest must find a preference in your fatherly hearts and your pastoral solicitude. Therefore you know and proclaim that a like option would be neither pastoral nor Christian were it to be inspired in mere political or ideological criteria, were it to be exclusive or excluding, or if it were to foment feelings of hatred, or a struggle among sisters or brothers.[797]

---

[794]Gustavo Gutiérrez, "*Commentario sobre Laborem Exercens*," in *Sobre El Trabajo Humano* (Lima: CEP, 1982), p. 19.

[795]John Paul II, "The Apostolic Exhortation on the Family," in *Origins* 11 (1981), p. 453.

[796]John Paul II, "Opening Address at CELAM Meeting, Port-au-Prince, Haiti, March 9, 1983," in *A.A.S.* 75 (1983), p. 772.

[797]John Paul II, "Opening Address at CELAM Meeting, Port-Au-Prince, Haiti, March 9, 1983," p. 773.

At this juncture in his pontificate, John Paul was very concerned with his perception of distortions in Catholic social teaching that emanated from Latin America, which he confronted in the third section of this address: "...it is necessary to spread and... to recover the *wholeness* of the message of Puebla, without deformed interpretations or deformed reductions, and without unwarranted applications of some parts and the eclipse of others."[798]

During the month of March, 1983, John Paul paid a pastoral visit to Central America that was marred with much controversy, especially the confrontations with the Sandinistas during his reception and celebration of an outdoor Mass in Nicaragua. In Managua, he warned against the possibility of "instrumentalization of the Gospel," and its subjugation to ideologies such as Marxism.[799] Some leftist and progressive elements complained in the Latin American press that John Paul "conspicuously made no reference to the 'preferential option for the poor,' preached by the Latin American Church since Medellín and confirmed as a principle for the whole Church by the Pope himself in the encyclical *Laborem Exercens*."[800] On February 2, 1984, when the President of CELAM and Archbishop of Medellín, Monseñor Alfonso Lopez Trujillo, was named a Cardinal, supporters of the developing theology of liberation were distraught to learn of the Pope's high measure of praise for the Colombian prelate: "His contribution to the study and clarification of theology, particularly of the so-called theology of liberation, has been and remains an eminent service to the Church."[801]

---

[798]John Paul II, cited ibid., 775-776.
[799]John Paul II, "Address in Managua, Nicaragua," in *A.A.S.* 75 (1983), pp. 720-722.
[800]"Central Americans Respond to Papal Visit," in *Latinamerica Press* (May 24, 1983), cited in Alfred T. Hennelly, S.J., *Liberation Theology: A Documentary History*, pp. 339-340.
[801]John Paul's affirmation of Lopez Trujillo was cited in *CELAM Bulletin* 181 (March-April, 1983), p. 1.

Evidence of a further chilling effect surfaced with the publication of the Congregation for the Doctrine of the Faith's "Instruction on Certain Aspects of the Theology of Liberation," on September 3, 1984.[802] This instruction was preceded by the publication by the Congregation for the Doctrine of the Faith of "Ten Observations on the Theology of Gustavo Gutiérrez," in March, 1983,[803] along with Ratzinger's own essay on "Liberation Theology" published afterwards.[804] Following the issuance of the instruction, Leonardo Boff received a letter of admonition from Cardinal Joseph Ratzinger,[805] prefect of the Congregation for the Doctrine of the Faith, and was summoned to Rome to respond to criticisms of his book, *Church: Charism and Power*.[806] The Vatican instruction on liberation theology admitted that many different varieties of liberation theology existed, and claimed to be speaking only of those that proposed:

> ...a novel interpretation of the content of faith and Christian existence [based on] concepts uncritically borrowed from Marxist ideology and recourse to a biblical hermeneutic marked by rationalism [that led to

---

[802]The English translation of this text is contained in Alfred T. Hennelly, S.J. (ed.), *Liberation Theology: A Documentary History*, pp. 393-414.

[803]Congregation for the Doctrine of the Faith, "Ten Observations on the Theology of Gustavo Gutiérrez (March 22, 1983)," in Alfred T. Hennelly, S.J. (ed.), *Liberation Theology: A Documentary History*, pp. 348-350.

[804]Joseph Cardinal Ratzinger, "Liberation Theology (March, 1984)," in Alfred T. Hennelly, S.J. (ed.), *Liberation Theology: A Documentary History*, pp. 367-374.

[805]For the text of Ratzinger's letter, see *Misión Abierta* (Madrid) No. 1 (February, 1985), pp. 9-13.

[806]Leonardo Boff, O.F.M., *Church: Charism and Power* (NY: Crossroad, 1985). On this occasion, Boff acceded to a year of silencing, and stated: "Of one thing I am sure: I prefer to walk with the Church than to go it alone with my theology. The Church is a reality of Faith that I assume. Theology is a product of reason that I discuss." Cited in "*Respuesta de Leonardo Boff a la carta del Cardenal Joseph Ratzinger*," in *Revista Latinoamericana de teologia* Vol. I, No. 3 (September – December, 1984), pp. 340-341. For fuller documentation of these events, see: Congregation of the Doctrine of the Faith, "Notification Sent to Father Leonardo Boff Regarding Errors in His Book, *Church, Charism and Power* (March 11, 1985)," in Alfred T. Hennelly, S.J. (ed.), *Liberation Theology: A Documentary History*, pp. 424-430; and, Leonardo Boff, "Defense of his Book, *Church, Charism and Power* (September 7, 1984)," in Alfred T. Hennelly, S.J. (ed.), *Liberation Theology: A Documentary History*, pp. 431-434.

> a] new interpretation which is corrupting whatever was authentic in the generous original commitment on behalf of the poor (VI, 9-10).[807]

The introduction to the instruction on liberation theology warned against tools of Marxist analysis used "in an insufficiently critical manner," but concluded: "This warning should in no way be interpreted as a disavowal of all those who want to respond generously and with an authentic evangelical spirit to the 'preferential option for the poor.'" It conceded that "the powerful and almost irresistible aspiration that people have for liberation constitutes one of the principal 'signs of the times' which the Church has to examine and interpret in the light of the Gospel" (I, 1). The instruction cautioned that:

> The different theologies of liberation are situated between the preferential option for the poor forcefully reaffirmed without ambiguity after Medellín at the conference of Puebla on the one hand, [while there exists] the temptation to reduce the Gospel to an earthly gospel on the other. We should recall that the preferential option described at Puebla is twofold: for the poor and for the young. It is significant that the option for the young has in general been passed over in total silence (VI, 5-6).

Finally, the instruction warned against the adoption of the theory of class struggle as an undergirding principle of the theology of liberation, which it charged went:

> ...so far as to identify God with history and to define faith as "fidelity to history," which means adhering to a political policy suited to the growth of humanity, conceived of as purely temporal messianism. As

---

[807]In his critique of the instruction, Juan Luís Segundo argued: "Even if Marxism did not exist – and today many of the most famous theologians in Latin America have nothing more than a polite relationship with Marxism – liberation theology would be condemned as a humanistic, earthly, and secular reduction of the Gospel of salvation," in *Theology and the Church: A Response to Cardinal Ratzinger and a Warning to the Whole Church* (San Francisco, CA: Harper & Row, 1987 revision), p. 91.

> a consequence, faith, hope, and charity are given a new content: they become "fidelity to history," "confidence in the future," and "option for the poor." This is tantamount to saying that they have been emptied of their theological reality (IX, 4-5).

Yet after the promulgation of the instruction, even Cardinal Josef Ratzinger, in a press conference announcing its publication, acknowledged that Marxism "contains certain valid, useful elements, but a much greater degree of vigilance, and a much more conscious criticism, are in order" than he encountered in the work of the theologians of liberation.[808]

Properly speaking, the first Vatican instruction on liberation theology issued in 1984 was not a condemnation of liberation theology, but served as a strong warning about its possible deviations. The tenor of its contents and the methodology employed in the preparation of the document subjected it to some well-deserved criticism. Some of the most sustained, systematic critique emanated from Juan Luís Segundo:

> In my view, and after the most careful analysis of which I am capable, the document emanating from it (the C.D.F.) has not yet presented proof that liberation theology, in its basic and universally known features, is a "grave deviation from Christian faith," still less that it is "a negation in practice" of that faith.[809]

Cardinal Paulo Evaristo Arns of Brazil, for instance, complained directly to Cardinal Joseph Ratzinger, the Prefect of the Congregation of the Doctrine of the Faith, that no input had been solicited from practitioners of the theology of liberation, and that no bishops with direct pastoral experience with oppressed peoples had actually been

---

[808]Cited in *Osservatore Romano* (December 3-4, 1984), p. 4.

[809]Juan Luís Segundo, *Theology and the Church: A Response to Cardinal Ratzinger and a Warning to the Whole Church,* p. 95.

consulted in the framing of the document, in contravention of the spirit of dialogue and collegiality.[810] The instruction and its preparatory documents were broadly regarded as an attack on liberation theology and its key proponents, especially by a circle of conservative theologians and prelates in Rome, Germany, and Latin America.

In anticipation of some negative impact from the instruction, a pre-emptive show of support for liberation theology issued from the editorial board of the prestigious international review of theology, *Concilium*, which published a "Statement of Solidarity with Liberation Theologians."[811] After the instruction was published, the highly respected Cardinal Archbishop of Milan, Jesuit scripture scholar Carlo Maria Martini, called for a special restraint in the criticism of this evolving expression of theology. In a statement carried on Vatican Radio, he stated that "the theology of liberation means encouragement for the oppressed," and pleaded that its exponents ought not to be "discouraged, but enlightened and encouraged, especially those who, in Latin America, bring it to genuine expression, often with a deep spirit of sacrifice."[812] In a like vein, the primate of Belgium, Cardinal Godfried Daneels, expressed concern about what the downstream effects of the instruction might be:

---

[810]For a fuller discussion of this matter, see: Ronaldo Muñoz, "*Reacciones de los teologos latinamericanos a propósito de la 'Instrucción,'*" in *Revista Latinoamericana de Teologia* Vol. I, No. 2 (May-August, 1984), p. 239; Harvey Cox, *The Silencing of Leonardo Boff: The Vatican and the Future of World Christianty* (Chicago: Meyer Stone Books, 1988), pp.100-101; 124-127; Juan Luís Segundo, *Theology and the Church: A Response to Cardinal Ratzinger and a Warning to the Whole Church* (SF: Harper & Row, 1987 revision); Leonardo Boff, "Vatican Instruction Reflects European Mindset (August 31, 1984)," in Alfred T. Hennelly, S.J. (ed.), *Liberation Theology: A Documentary History*, pp. 415-418; and, Gustavo Gutiérrez, "Criticism Will Deepen, Clarify Liberation Theology (September 14, 1984)," in Alfred T. Hennelly, S.J. (ed.), *Liberation Theology: A Documentary History*, pp. 419-424.

[811]Editorial Board of *Concilium*, "Statement of Solidarity with Liberation Theologians," in Alfred T. Hennelly, S.J. (ed.), *Liberation Theology: A Documentary History*, pp. 390-392.

[812]Cited in *La Repubblica* (September 9-10, 1984), p. 5.

> It is painful to see theologians blacklisted and their credibility harmed. The grassroots pastoral ministry suffers. Bishops ought to be encouraging to those who work in this ministry. There is something tragic in all this, after so much effort, with such encouraging initial results... Suffering can be salutary, but we should not aggravate it... We ought to be showing our support for the poor and for their theologians.[813]

Shortly before his death, the renowned Jesuit theologian Karl Rahner wrote to the Archbishop of Lima, Cardinal Juan Landázuri Ricketts, with the offer of his assurance that: "Liberation theology... is thoroughly orthodox, and is aware of its limits within the whole context of Catholic theology. Moreover, it is deeply convinced (correctly, in my opinion) that the voice of the poor must be listened to in the context of the Latin American Church."[814] In the midst of unrelenting scrutiny, the liberation theologians managed to marshal ample support for their ideas.

The initial criticism and subsequent dialogue precipitated by the first Vatican instruction on liberation theology succeeded in bearing fruit on a variety of levels. Pope John Paul II himself asked that the first instruction be modified with five new introductory sections. He appeared to distance himself personally from the instruction, as evidenced in his comment to the press: "It is Cardinal Ratzinger's."[815] One of the more balanced assessments of the impact of the first instruction came in a Peruvian newspaper interview with Gustavo Gutiérrez entitled, "Criticism Will Deepen, Clarify Liberation Theology." In it, Gutiérrez defended the use of Marxist analysis as a "methodological pointer":

---

[813]Cited in *De Standaard* (September 12, 1984), p. 2.
[814]Karl Rahner, S.J., "Letter to Cardinal Juan Landázuri Ricketts of Lima, Peru (March 16, 1984)," in Alfred T. Hennelly, S.J., *Liberation Theology: A Documentary History*, pp. 351-352.
[815]For a discussion of this turn events, see Bishop Pedro Casaldáliga, "On the *Ad Limina* Visit," in *In Pursuit of the Kingdom/Writings 1968-1988* (Maryknoll, NY: Orbis Books, 1990), p. 231.

> It is necessary to be very clear on this point: to deal with the poverty – the inhuman poverty, as Puebla said – lived by the great majority of the inhabitants of our country, and to shed the light of the Gospel on it, we must attain the most exact understanding available of the causes of this situation of poverty. It is necessary to make use of whatever tools human thought offers to help us understand our social reality.[816]

Even one of the more respected theologians of liberation, Ronaldo Muñoz, was forced to concede that "the Christian-Marxist confrontation... was not always carried out with sufficient maturity and critical awareness."[817]

By 1984, liberation theology and one of its centerpieces, the "preferential option for the poor," appeared poised to enter into a new stage. Chastened during the papal visits to Mexico and to Central America and rebuked by the tenor of the first instruction of the Congregation for the Doctrine of the Faith, liberation theologians began to move away from their earlier, more heavily Marxist-oriented phase with its accompanying, revolutionary rhetoric to direct their focus to more biblical and ecclesial themes, located more explicitly within the mainstream of official Catholic social teaching. They set out to place greater emphasis on the importance on remaining in communion with the institutional, hierarchical Church, especially from the perspective of the grassroots communities. This evolving, more conciliatory trend was reciprocated from the perspective of the institutional Church as well, as the public pronouncements of Pope John Paul, the final document of the 1985 Synod, and the 1986 instruction of the C.D.F. on liberation theology all served to indicate. John Paul's vast travels and first-hand interaction with the poor of the underdeveloped nations contributed greatly to his own ongoing refinement of his

---

[816]Gustavo Gutiérrez, "Criticism Will Deepen, Clarify Liberation Theology (September 14, 1984)," in Alfred T. Hennelly, S.J. (ed.), *Liberation Theology: A Documentary History*, p. 421.
[817]Ronaldo Muñoz, "*Reacciones de los teologos latinamericanos a propósito de la 'Instrucción,'*" p. 239.

views on the option for the poor as an option of the Universal Church.[818] While he did not use the term the "preferential option for the poor" in his address at Toronto, Canada on September 14, 1984, John Paul affirmed many of the central facets of Latin American liberation theology therein:

> The needs of the poor must take priority over the desires of the rich, the rights of workers over the maximization of profits, the preservation of the environment over uncontrolled industrial expansion, production to meet social needs over production for military purposes... The poor people and poor nations...will judge those people who take these goods away from them, amassing to themselves the imperialistic monopoly of economic and political supremacy at the expense of others.[819]

As Jean-Yves Calvez suggested, over the course of this period there occurred "something less known, not sufficiently known, namely, that the Pope, in a whole series of addresses in 1984-1985, was rather chagrined that he could have given the impression of not believing in the preferential option for the poor, of not believing in it strongly."[820] John Paul confronted this issue directly to a group of cardinals and bishops of the Roman Curia assembled at the Vatican on December 21, 1984:

> The option which is emphasized today with particular force by the episcopacy of Latin America, I have confirmed repeatedly... I gladly seize this occasion to repeat that engagement with the poor constitutes a dominant motif of my pastoral activity, a concern which

---

[818]His early trips to Latin America and the Caribbean Basin were particularly significant in this regard: to Mexico (1979); Brazil (1980); Haiti (1983); Peru and Ecuador (1985), and Colombia (1986).

[819]John Paul II, "Address on Christian Unity in a Technological Age," in *Origins* 14 (1984), p. 248. In fact, he directly cited material in this quotation from the Canadian Conference of Catholic Bishops' pastoral letter on the economy. For a concise assessment of the impact of the option for the poor on the developed countries of the West, see: Edward van Merrienboer, O.P., "The Poor as a Pastoral Option for Western Europe," in *New Blackfriars* 69 (February, 1988), pp. 56-61.

[820]Jean-Yves Calvez, S.J., "The Preferential Option for the Poor: Where Does It Come From For Us?," in John W. Padberg, S.J. (ed.), *The Disturbing Subject: The Option for the Poor* (St. Louis, MO: Studies in the Spirituality of the Jesuits, 1989), p. 23.

> is daily and ceaselessly part of my service of the People of God. I have made and I do make this option. I identify myself with it. I feel it could not be otherwise, since it is the eternal message of the Gospel. That is the option Christ made, the option made by the Apostles, the option of the Church throughout its two thousand years of history.[821]

On October 4, 1984, the feast of St. Francis of Assisi, John Paul told a group of Peruvian bishops assembled for an extraordinary convocation with Vatican officials and him in Rome:

> Reassure fully the members of your dioceses who work for the poor in an ecclesial and evangelical spirit, that the Church intends to maintain its preferential option for the poor and encourages the engagement of those who, faithful to the directives of the hierarchy, devote themselves selflessly to those most in need. That is an integral part of their mission.[822]

A few weeks previously, he told a group of Paraguayan bishops on their *ad limina* visit: "It is true that the precept to love all men and women admits no exclusion, but it does admit a privileged engagement in favor of the poorest."[823] Similarly, in his Christmas message of 1984, John Paul stated: "We affirm our solidarity with *all* the poor of the world."[824]

In July, 1986, as John Paul addressed an assembly of Colombian priests, he said:

---

[821]John Paul II, "Discourse to the Cardinals and Prelates of the Roman Curia," in *Osservatore Romano* (January 21, 1985), p. 9.
[822]John Paul II, "To the Peruvian Bishops, on the *Ad limina* Visit to Rome," in *Osservatore Romano* (October 5, 1984), p. 1.
[823]John Paul II, "The Paraguayan Bishops on their *Ad limina* Visit to Rome," in *La Documentation Catholique* 81 (1984), p. 1159.
[824]John Paul II, "Christmas Message," in *Origins* 14 (1985), p. 498.

> ...the options and the illumination Christians need in the area of human promotion and liberation, especially that of the very neediest, can only be made according to the example of Jesus and obtained in the light of the Gospel, which forbids recourse of methods of hatred and violence. Love, and a preferential option for the poor, must not be exclusive or excluding. Love for the poor does not mean regarding the poor as a class, let alone as a class caught up in a struggle, or as a Church separated from communion with and obedience to the shepherds appointed for them by Christ. Love, and the preferential option for the poor, must be implemented in the context of a conceptualization of the human being in his or her earthly and eternal calling.[825]

In December, 1986, John Paul addressed a famous Italian apostolic lay movement, the "*Communità di Sant' Egidio*" dedicated to the social apostolate, at Castelgondolfo, in words that once again explicitly affirmed the "preferential option for the poor":

> Today this option is discussed above all in Latin America. But it is also discussed with regard to the Universal Church, as the last [1985] Synod of Bishops confirmed. But today this option is discussed and reaffirmed in a new context. The option for the poor is the choice of the Gospel: it is the option of Christ and for Christ. His own choice was exactly that: an option for the poor. And the option for the poor is at the same time an option for Christ, in whatever century, in whatever situation, in whatever country it is made. This we know well..."[826]

John Paul convoked an extraordinary session of the Synod of Bishops to meet from November 25 – December 8, 1985, on the occasion of the twentieth anniversary of the closing of the Second Vatican Council, to reflect upon its meaning,

---

[825]John Paul II, "Address to Priests of Colombia at Medellín," in *A.A.S.* 78 (1986), p. 859.
[826]John Paul II, "Address to the *Comunità di S. Egidio*," in *Osservatore Romano* (December 14, 1986), pp. 6-8.

implementation, and effects. To alleviate fears that he might be inclined to turn back the clock on the reforms of the Council, as he convoked the Synod, he declared that Vatican II "remains the fundamental event in the life of the contemporary Church," and for him personally served as "the constant reference point of every pastoral action."[827] The perception that the theme of "restoration"[828] would dominate the agenda of the synod was widely shared, especially when the pope delegated much of the task of shaping its agenda to Cardinal Ratzinger and in light of a perceived shift in the appointment of conservative prelates and a crackdown on seminary faculties.[829] Josef Cardinal Ratzinger, the renowned German theologian, was appointed Prefect of the Congregation of the Doctrine of the Faith by John Paul in January, 1982.[830] Ratzinger was well known for his criticisms of liberation theology and of the supposed excesses that ensued in the wake of Vatican II described in magazine interviews in *30 Days* and later published in book form as *The Ratzinger Report*.[831] The task was laid to him to orchestrate the 1985 Synod. When one of the primary Synod co-presidents, the Belgian Primate, Cardinal Godfried Daneels, was asked at a press conference as to whether a process of "restoration" was transpiring, he replied: "The word 'restoration' appears nowhere in the preparatory documents of the Synod. It comes from elsewhere. We are here to have a Synod on the Council, not on somebody's book."[832] However, when he returned from a pastoral visit to

---

[827]Cited in Avery Dulles, S.J., *Vatican II and the Extraordinary Synod: An Overview* (Collegeville, MN: The Liturgical Press, 1986), p. 5.

[828]See, for instance, Paul Johnson, *John Paul II and the Catholic Restoration*, and Giancarlo Zizola, *La Restaurazione di Papa Wojtyla,* for a conservative and liberal perspective, respectively.

[829]See David Willey, *God's Politician: Pope John Paul II, The Catholic Church, and The New World* Order, pp. 120, 122.

[830]In 2003, John Paul II also appointed Ratzinger "Dean of the College of Cardinals," a largely honorific title with responsibilities incumbent upon the role following the death of the Pope and the election of his successor.

[831]Joseph Ratzinger, *The Ratzinger Report* (San Francisco, CA: Ignatius Press, 1986).

[832]Cited in Peter Hebblethwaite, *Synod Extraordinary: The Inside Story of the Rome Synod,* November/December 1985, p. 110.

Belgium in May, 1985, Pope John Paul responded to a reporter's question about what would be the agenda of the Synod with the aside: "Oh, I leave that sort of thing to Cardinal Ratzinger."[833] Apparently, the Pope considered the negative reactions to Ratzinger's book to be sufficient enough that he effected some distance between the cardinal prefect of the C.D.F. and himself in a conversation with an American reporter, while flying back from Africa on August 19, 1985: "What Cardinal Ratzinger says is his own opinion. He is free to express his own opinion. His opinion corresponds to many events, but it cannot be understood in this [context] that the Council, Vatican II, was a negative meaning for the Church. No, on the contrary."[834] Some of the then-surviving guiding lights of the Council, like Cardinal Leon-Josef Suenens, were quick to advance the opinion that a return to the *status quo ante* would be ill-advised and disastrous for the Church: "We must firmly reject the word 'restoration' that would signify a rejection of the Council and delight both the acknowledged and the secret ultraconservatives."[835]

One manifestation of this ideological battleground showed itself in the discussion over the incorporation of the term the "preferential option for the poor" within the text of the Synod's "Final Report." Two Brazilian prelates, Bishop José Ivo Lorscheiter, President of the CNBB, and his cousin, Cardinal Aloisio Lorscheider,[836] were permitted to lodge written interventions with the secretariat of the Synod that defended liberation theology. Their position was attacked at a press conference on November 30, 1985, by Bishop Dario Castrillon Hoyos, the Colombian General-Secretary of CELAM (and a lieutenant of Cardinal Alfonso

---

[833]Cited in Peter Hebblethwaite, *Synod Extraordinary*, p. 49.

[834]John Paul II, conversation, in English, to Bill Pritchard of the Catholic News Service, cited in Peter Hebblethwaite, *Synod Extraordinary*, p. 52. John Paul often cited the Council as the defining event in his papacy.

[835]Cited in the London *Tablet* (October 12, 1985), p. 1064.

[836]Despite the variant spellings of their surnames, they were blood relatives as first cousins.

Lopez Trujillo, CELAM's President). The content of the written interventions was further undermined during the Synod by Cardinal Eugenio de Araujo Sales of Rio de Janeiro. Cardinal Daneels was entrusted with brokering the final form of the sixteen page Latin document that became the "Final Report" of the Synod. In its working draft, as a summary of the positive achievements of the "Pastoral Constitution on the Church in the Modern World," he succeeded in retaining a reference to the "preferential option for the poor":

> A more profound perception of the relationship between the Church and the modern world. More radical testimony on the part of the Church in the area of human rights, justice, peace and freedom. Greater sensitivity to social problems. The preferential option for the poor, the oppressed, the outcast has entered into the Church's thought and practice.[837]

As Peter Hebblethwaite noted:

> The most remarkable statement is the comment on the "preferential option for the poor"; for there had been a determined attempt to whittle away this phrase of Medellín and Puebla... it was emasculated still further [in the 1984 C.D.F. instruction on liberation theology] as "a *concern* for the poor and the young" – a paternalistic approach which travestied the main point of this language, which was that one should be *with* the poor, not lecturing at them from an immense height.[838]

In light of the intramural squabbling within the "Final Report" promulgated by the Synod, it seemed surprising to find an entire section of the document entitled, "Preferential Option for the Poor." In part, it stated:

> After Vatican II, the Church became more aware of her Mission for service of the poor, the oppressed, and the marginalized. In this

[837]Cited in Peter Hebblethwaite, *Synod Extraordinary*, p. 112.
[838]Ibid., p. 113.

> preferential option, which is not to be understood as exclusive, the true spirit of the Gospel shines out... The Church must in prophetic fashion denounce every form of poverty and oppression and defend and support everywhere the fundamental and inalienable rights of the human person (D, 6).[839]

The concluding section of the Synod's "Final Report," entitled "Suggestions," stated: "[W]e should again examine what are the following aims, and how may they be put into practice: ... c). What is a preferential option for the poor?" (D, 7).[840] As the American Jesuit theologian Avery Dulles pointed out in his commentary on the Synod, under the rubric of the major theme of "Church and World":

> ...the Final Report accepts the "preferential option for the poor" enshrined in the Puebla Conference of 1979 and in many statements of John Paul II. It points out, as do those documents, that this option must not be interpreted as exclusive, as though it were a restriction on the universalism of Christian love. In its efforts to improve the lot of the poor, moreover, the Church must never lose sight of its preeminently spiritual Mission.[841]

Pope John Paul readily embraced this direction, and declared during the homily at the Synod's closing Mass on December 8, 1985: "The Synod has accomplished the purpose for which it was convoked: to celebrate, re-affirm, and promote the Council."[842] Pope John XXIII's longed-for vision of the "Church of the Poor" was revived as a distinct priority for the Universal Church in the acts of the 1985 Roman Synod.

---

[839]Ciited as "Appendix II: 'The Final Report,'" in Xavier Rynne, *John Paul II's Extraordinary Synod: A Collegial Achievement* (Wilmington, DE: Michael Glazier, 1986), p. 130.
[840]"The Final Report," cited in Xavier Rynne, *John Paul's Extraordinary Synod*, p. 131.
[841]Avery Dulles, S.J., *Vatican II and the Extraordinary Synod: An Overview*, p. 27.
[842]Cited in Peter Hebblethwaite, *Synod Extraordinary*, p. 140. These three phrases also appear in the "Introduction" (I, 2) of the "Final Report."

The eagerly awaited second, or more "positive" treatment of the Congregation for the Doctrine of the Faith concerning the theology of liberation, the "Instruction on Christian Freedom and Liberation," was delayed for publication until the spring of 1986. Over the course of the previous year, John Paul entered into extensive dialogue with representatives of the Brazilian Church,[843] among others, concerning the theology of liberation. He became increasingly sensitized to their concerns through the process of listening/awareness/dialogue that marked the discussions between the steering committee of the doctrinal commission of the Brazilian national bishops' conference [CNBB] and the representatives of the C.D.F. that met for several days in July, 1985. These colloquia were followed by the March, 1986 meeting that John Paul convened personally with the five Brazilian cardinals, the officers of the CNBB and the chairs of its regional secretariats in order to discuss the following items: liberation theology; the Boff case; and, the forthcoming [second] instruction of the Congregation for the Doctrine of the Faith on liberation theology. Cardinal Ratzinger submitted a draft of the second instruction to Pope John Paul for his approval, but the Pope was critical of its style and contents.[844] John Paul considered Ratzinger's final draft to be too ethereal and abstract, that the use of Scripture in the text seemed shallow and inadequate, and that it needed to deal more positively with the existence of Christian base communities [CEB's]. In this respect, the Pope put his stamp on this document and differentiated himself from Cardinal Ratzinger's viewpoints.[845] While the 1986 version stressed its continuity with its 1984 predecessor, the tenor of the new instruction in fact was markedly different. Its

---

[843]See Harvey Cox, *The Silencing of Leonardo Boff*, p. 114.

[844]For the relevant details, see Harvey Cox, *The Silencing of Leonardo Boff*, pp. 114-115.

[845]For a lengthy analysis of John Paul's approach to this document, see Peter Hebblethwaite, "Spiritual Points in Liberation Themes Basic to the Document: An Analysis," in *Liberation Theology and the Vatican Document: Perspectives From the Third World* (Quezon City, Philippines: Claretian Publications, 1987), pp. 85-95.

treatment of liberation theology was largely free from the harsh warnings and judgments of the preceding document. John Paul returned it to the C.D.F. for revisions and overhaul.

The second instruction on liberation theology was revised by the C.D.F. and released on April 5, 1986. It was widely taken to be recognition by Rome that the main tenets of the theology of liberation were authentically Christian and acceptably orthodox. The instruction committed the Roman Catholic Church to the concept of a "love of preference of the poor," and thereby sought to avoid the perceived exclusive overtones of the term that it perceived to be charged with problematic overtones of Marxist analysis, the "preferential option for the poor." In its fourth chapter, it noted: "The special option for the poor, far from being a sign of particularism or sectarianism, manifests the universality of the Church's being and Mission. This option excludes no one" (no. 68). Many commentators took this nuanced wording to be of great significance. In a conservative U.S. Catholic newspaper with close ties to the Vatican, *The National Catholic Register*, Robert Moynihan suggested:

> Even small changes in the phrasing of historic church documents can have a great significance. This document is no exception... The change from an *option* for the poor to the *love of preference* for the poor is an intentional effort on the part of the author, Joseph Ratzinger, to move away from a word with political and sociological connotations, toward a concept with a more traditional religious content.[846]

Other observers took a different view. As Alfred Hennelly suggested:

---

[846]Robert Moynihan, "New Vatican Document to Stress a Preferential Love For Poor, But Will Also Urge Reconciliation," in *The National Catholic Register* (March 23, 1986), p. 1.

> With respect to this [terminology]... a certain controversy has arisen in press eports concerning the phrase "a love of preference for the poor"; some accounts held that this was replacing the phrase "preferential option for the poor" which had come into common usage throughout the Latin American Bishops' Conference. Supposedly this was done to avoid the potentially divisive effects implied in a "preferential option." However, the phrase "special option for the poor" is used no less than three times in the pertinent section (no. 68), which clearly refutes the charge that it was being deliberately jettisoned. One may only speculate that the "love of preference" was also used in order to emphasize the Christian motivation of the option.[847]

With the appearance of the "Instruction on Christian Freedom and Liberation," a development that began during the 1970's and gained headway during the 1980's became even more apparent: liberation theology became increasingly less socio-political and increasingly ecclesial and religious in its primary orientation.[848] Leonardo Boff himself conceded that the instruction gave "a newly universal dimension [to] values that were initially only those of the Third World... After this, liberation theology will gain a new dimension."[849] In spite of the instruction's aversion to utilize the precise terminology of the "preferential option for the poor," the 1986 instruction served as something of a watershed document concerning the themes of liberation theology for the whole Church. As Alfred Hennelly noted:

> The document was well worth waiting for. Despite a loud chorus of criticism from various sources, it eminently succeeds in providing an excellent brief synthesis of the major themes of liberation theology. Thus we now have a formal Vatican endorsement (with all the

---

[847]Alfred T. Hennelly, S.J., "The Red-Hot Issue: Liberation Theology," in *America* (May 24, 1986), p. 427.
[848]See José Comblin, "The Theology of Liberation," in Enrique Dussel (ed.), *The Church in Latin America: 1492-1992*, p. 448.
[849]Cited in Harvey Cox, *The Silencing of Leonardo Boff*, p. 115.

> necessary caveats and provisos) of the liberation approach, not merely for Latin America or other parts of the Third World, but for the Universal Church.[850]

The 1986 C.D.F. instruction demonstrated a remarkable realignment of the Vatican's position on the theology of liberation, a veritable "about face" from the hard line adopted by Cardinal Ratzinger only two years previously. For their own part, the liberation theologians moderated their rhetoric and distanced themselves more and more from the tools of Marxist analysis. The tensions that brewed between the progressive wing of the Latin American Church and the Vatican more markedly eased with the appearance of a letter from Pope John Paul II addressed to the bishops of Brazil[851] in which he charged the CNBB with a special Mission to help guide the development of liberation theology, not only in Brazil, but throughout Latin America. Cardinal Bernadin Gantin of Benin personally presented and read the letter to the Brazilian bishops at the Pope's behest on April 12, 1986, the week after the publication of the second instruction. The Pope himself situated the thrust of this letter within the context of the two instructions of the C.D.F.:

> An expression and proof of the attention with which the Holy See participates in those efforts [in the service of the poor] are the numerous documents recently published, among them the two Instructions provided by the Congregation for the Doctrine of the Faith, with my explicit approval: one, regarding certain aspects of the theology of liberation (*Libertatis Nuntius* of August 6, 1984); the other, on Christian freedom and liberation (*Libertatis Conscientia* of March 22, 1986). These latter two, addressed to the Universal Church, have an undeniable pastoral relevancy for Brazil (no. 5).

---

[850]Alfred T. Hennelly, S.J., "The Red Hot Issue: Liberation Theology," p. 425.

[851]John Paul II, "Letter to Brazilian Episcopal Conference (Vatican City, April 9, 1986)," in Alfred T. Hennelly, S.J. (ed.), *Liberation Theology: A Documentary History*, pp. 498-506.

Earlier in the text of the letter, the Pope adverted to a special role for the Brazilian episcopacy:

> ...in this area also the Church, led by you, the bishops of Brazil, gives signs of being identified with the people, especially the poor, the suffering, those without influence, resources, and assistance. The Church consecrates itself to these with a love that is neither exclusive nor excluding but rather preferential (no. 3).

He emphasized the same point later in the text:

> May God help you to be unceasingly watchful so that a correct and necessary theology of liberation can develop in Brazil and in Latin America in a homogenous and not heterogeneous fashion with relation to the theology of all times, in full fidelity to church doctrine, attentive to a preferential but not excluding or exclusive love for the poor (no. 5).

Perhaps the most striking element contained in John Paul's letter appeared in the following portion of the text:

> ...we are convinced, we and you, that the theology of liberation is not only timely but useful and necessary. It should constitute a new state, – in close connection with former ones – of the theological reflection initiated with the apostolic tradition and continued by the great fathers and doctors, by the ordinary and extraordinary magisterium and, in more recent years, by the rich patrimony of the Church's social doctrine, expressed in documents from *Rerum Novarum* to *Laborem Exercens* (no. 5).

In light of the contentious atmosphere that marked the prior half decade, in an understandable collective gesture of relief the assembled Brazilian bishops burst into a spontaneous, sustained chorus of "Alleluias" the moment Cardinal Gantin concluded the papal letter as they realized the harmonious tack and the strong affirmation of the central tenets of the theology of liberation that John Paul II conveyed to the members of the Brazilian hierarchy.

In his sixth encyclical, dated March 25, 1987, *Redemptoris Mater*, John Paul again displayed his tendency to avoid the term the "preferential option for the poor" in an official document. He substituted instead the phrases, "love of preference for the poor"; "love of preference for the poor and humble"; and, "the 'option in favor of the poor'" (no. 37, nos. 3, 4 and 5).[852] In this letter crafted to mark a special Marian "Holy Year," the Pope wrote: "[W]e must also carefully safeguard the importance that 'the poor' have in the Word of the living God. These are themes and problems organically related with the Christian meaning of freedom and liberation" (no. 37). He maintained this tack in the body of his second social encyclical, *Sollicitudo Rei Socialis*, dated December 30, 1987 (to commemorate the twentieth anniversary of *Populorum Progressio*).[853] John Paul indicated as the purpose of the letter to meet the need for "a fuller and more nuanced concept of development" (no. 4). Along the lines of *Populorum Progressio*, John Paul linked "development" and "liberation" together in the body of the text, and asserted that "the process of development and liberation takes concrete shape in the exercise of solidarity" (no. 46). The Pope denounced the practice of both "Marxist collectivism" and "liberal capitalism" of increasing impoverishment of the poor nations, especially in the Southern Hemisphere, in their lust for power and profits (nos. 20-21). He cautiously adverted to the phenomenon of liberation theology:

---

[852]John Paul II, "*Redemptoris Mater*," in *Origins* 16 (1987), p. 763.

[853]Peter Henriot suggested that John Paul's "choice of 'love' over 'option' softens the conflict inherent in choosing sides... [though] he may thereby weaken the Gospel force of the call here," in Peter J. Henriot, S.J., *Opting for the Poor: A Challenge for North Americans* (Washington, DC: Center of Concern, 1990), p. 22.

> ...a new way of confronting the problems of poverty and underdevelopment has spread in some areas of the world, especially in Latin America. This approach makes liberation the fundamental category and the first principle of action. The positive values, as well as the deviations and risks of deviations which are damaging to the faith and are connected with this form of theological reflection have been appropriately pointed out (no. 46).

In terms consonant with liberation theology, he presented the concept of social sin both in terms of theological and social analysis: "...hidden behind certain decisions, apparently inspired only by economics or politics, are real forms of idolatry: of money, ideology, class, technology" (no. 37). The notion of the "option for the poor" received treatment in two paragraphs of the encyclical. In line with "the worldwide dimension which the social question has assumed," he twice advocated "this love of preference for the poor" (nos. 42, 47). As Pope John Paul stated:

> This is an option or special form of primacy in the exercise of Christian charity to which the whole tradition of the Church bears witness. It affects the life of each Christian inasmuch as he or she seeks to imitate the life of Christ, but it applies equally to our social responsibilities and hence to our manner of living, and to the logical decisions to be made concerning the ownership and use of goods (no. 42).

In this respect, as Gustavo Gutiérrez notes, "Some have claimed that the magisterium would be happy to see the expression *preferential option* replaced with *preferential love*, which, we are told, would change the meaning. It seems to us that the matter has been settled by the latest encyclical [*Sollicitudo Rei Socialis*] of John Paul II."[854]

Rocco Buttiglione, an Italian political philosopher with close ties to the Vatican, stated of *Sollicitudo Rei Socialis*: "This encyclical offers a new liberation

---

[854]Gustavo Gutiérrez, "Option for the Poor," in Ellacuría and Sobrino (eds.), *Mysterium Liberationis*, p. 240.

theology. It is a new liberation theology that surpasses the limits of the old one that is so thoroughly grounded in the Latin American experience and it is a theology that knows Communists."[855] But even bellwether liberation theologians like Gustavo Gutiérrez hailed the encyclical as a confirmation of their long-established positions, such as its concern with unjust social structures, the call for liberation, and the embrace of a love of preference for the poor.[856] This linkage by Gutiérrez apparently disturbed John Paul sufficiently that during his brief pastoral visit to Peru a few weeks later, he restated his criticisms of certain aspects of liberation theology (without directly condemning any of its practitioners), and decried the fact that the warnings of the two C.D.F. instructions had little impact on the "persistent error" that led some to pretend that the application "were addressed to others."[857] John Paul was not quite ready to abandon a certain hermeneutic of suspicion that marked his perception of the excesses that purportedly existed among certain theologians of liberation, though he seemed ready and willing to embrace some of its central tenets.

On December 7, 1990, John Paul issued an important encyclical about missionary activity entitled *Redemptoris Missio*.[858] Near the conclusion of the text, he emphasized that the option for the poor included aspects of both evangelization and social ministry:

> It is not right to give an incomplete picture of missionary activity as if it consisted principally in helping the poor, contributing to the liberation of the oppressed, promoting human development, or defending human rights. The missionary Church is certainly involved

---

[855]Cited in Roberto Suro, "The Writing of an Encyclical," in Kenneth A. Myers (ed.), *Aspiring to Freedom: Commentaries on John Paul II's Encyclical "The Social Concerns of the Church"* (Grand Rapids, MI: Eerdmans, 1988), pp. 162-163.

[856]See the remarks of Gutiérrez in *Latinamerican Press* (May 5, 1988), p. 2.

[857]Cited in *Latinamerica Press* (May 26, 1988), p. 1.

[858]John Paul II, "*Redemptoris Missio*/Encyclical on Missionary Activity," in *Origins* 20 (1991), pp. 541-568.

> on these fronts, but her primary task lies elsewhere: the poor are hungry for God, not just for bread and freedom (no. 83).

This encyclical echoed the Pope's declaration in *Laborem Exercens* (no. 8) and during his first visit to Brazil[859] that the Church throughout the world "wishes to be the Church of the poor." It placed the weight of the Pope's teaching authority in line with the Puebla pronouncements that "the 'poor deserve preferential attention... God has become their defender and loves them. It follows that the poor are those to whom the mission is first addressed, and their evangelization is par excellence the sign and proof of the mission of Jesus'" (no. 60).[860] Earlier in the same document, John Paul echoed the same concern:

> It is true the 'option for the neediest' means that we should not overlook the most abandoned and isolated human groups, but it is also true that individuals or small groups cannot be evangelized if we neglect the centers where a new humanity, so to speak, is emerging, and where new models of development are taking shape" (no. 37). As he noted, the Church's "mission consists essentially in offering people an opportunity not to 'have more' but to 'be more' by awakening their consciences through the Gospel. 'Authentic human development must be rooted in an ever deeper evangelization'" (no. 58).[861] The encyclical indicated that the mission of the Church was not "to work directly on the economic, technical or political level" (no. 58), i.e., in effecting change on the structural, rather than the individual level, but rather aimed for a kind of human development that "leads to conversion of heart and of thinking, fosters the

---

[859]John Paul II, "Address to the Residents of Favela Vidigal in Rio de Janiero, July 2, 1980," in *A.A.S.* 72 (1980), p. 854.

[860]Citing the Puebla "Final Document" (no. 1142).

[861]Citing his "Address to Clergy and Religious, Jakarta, Indonesia, July 2, 1989," in *Osservatore Romano* (October 11, 1989), p. 1.

> recognition of each person's dignity, encourages solidarity... and service of one's neighbor" (no. 59).[862]

John Paul II finally used the term the "preferential option for the poor" in a definitive, unambiguous way in a major social encyclical issued in May, 1991, *Centesimus Annus* (his ninth encyclical, issued to coincide with the centenary of Pope Leo XIII's *Rerum Novarum*, which appeared on May 15, 1891 and launched one hundred years of modern Catholic social teaching). John Paul situated the corpus of the Church's "social doctrine" within the mainstream of the tradition of which it formed "an essential part of the Christian message" (no. 5). Specifically, he remarked upon:

> ...the Church's constant concern for and dedication to categories of people who are especially beloved to the Lord Jesus. The contents of the text [of *Rerum Novarum*] are an excellent testimony to the continuity within the Church of the so-called "preferential option for the poor," an option which I defined as "a special form of primacy in the exercise of Christian charity"[863] (no. 11).

Later in the text of the same encyclical, John Paul II echoed Paul VI in *Evangelii Nuntiandi*:

> ..the social message of the Gospel must not be considered a theory, but above all else a basis and a motivation for action... Today, more than ever, the Church is aware that her social message will gain credibility more immediately from the witness of actions than as the result of its internal logic and consistency. This awareness is also a source of her preferential option for the poor, which is never

---

[862]Certain critics scored this approach as giving the appearance that the Church is too privatistic and dualistic, and contrary to the teaching of Paul VI in *Evangelii Nuntiandi* (nos. 18-20) concerning the need for changes in the economic and social structures of the world, and about transforming culture. See, for instance, the comments of Donal Dorr in *Option for the Poor* (1992 revision), pp. 338-339.
[863]The footnote in the original text cites *Sollicitudo Rei Socialis* (no. 42).

> exclusive or discriminatory toward other groups. This option is not limited to material poverty, since it well known that there are many other forms of poverty, especially in modern society – not only economic, but cultural and spiritual poverty as well" (no. 57).

John Paul concluded: "Love for others, and in the first place, love for the poor, in whom the Church sees Christ himself, is made concrete in the promotion of justice" (no. 58). In *Centesimus Annus*, John Paul II operated in a new key as reflected in his appropriation of the term the "preferential option for the poor," the term which he specifically appropriated for the first time in paragraphs eleven and fifty-seven of the text of the encyclical.

The fourth major Latin American bishops' conference plenary meeting [CELAM IV] occurred at Santo Domingo, Dominican Republic from October 12-28, 1992.[864] Once again, Pope John Paul II attended this CELAM conference. His presence was keenly felt in both the preparatory phases and in the outcome of the "Final Document," where the notion of the "preferential option for the poor" received strong papal and episcopal endorsement. The overall impact of this CELAM IV meeting was judged to be mixed. As Alfred Hennelly observed, "[T]his meeting was certainly not a leap forward nor an elegant step forward. Rather, it could only be called a *shaky step* into the future... I believe the Final Document was led by the Spirit of God to employ the biblical parable of the wheat and the weeds, with both fruitful and worthless results..."[865] A lack of sufficient pre-conference consultation and an unfortunate degree of factionalism[866] displayed caused one group of Latin

---

[864]For the principal texts of the conference, see Secretariat, Bishops' Committee for the Church in Latin America, Santo Domingo: Conclusions (Washington, DC: United States Catholic Conference, 1993).

[865]Alfred T. Hennelly, S.J., "A Report From the Conference," in *Santo Domingo and Beyond*, p. 24.

[866]See the remarks of the North American journalist, Peter Steinfels, "CELAM and the Vatican: A Preferential Option for Dickering," in *Commonweal* (November 20, 1992), pp. 5-6, as well as Francis McDonagh, "Legacy of Santo Domingo," in the *Tablet* (November 21, 1992), pp. 1489-1490.

American theologians to posit: "Medellín turned out a text greater than its participants. The Puebla document was similar to the assembly that produced it; and, the Santo Domingo document turned out to be inferior to its authors and to the Church that they represent."[867]

In his "Opening Address to the Bishops of Latin America" at Santo Domingo, John Paul stated:

> In continuity with the conference of Medellín and Puebla, the Church reaffirms her *preferential option for the poor*. It is neither an exclusive nor an excluding option, since the message of salvation is meant for all. "An option, in addition, which is based essentially on the Word of God and not on criteria offered by human science or by opposing ideologies, which often reduce the poor to abstract socio-political or economic categories." (III, 16)[868]

A few moments later, the Pope reiterated the same point: "There is no authentic human advancement, true liberation, or preferential option for the poor unless they are based on the very foundations of the person and the environment in which that person is to develop according to the Creator's plan" (III, 18).

Part II of the CELAM IV Final Document was entitled, "Jesus Christ: Evangelizer Living in His Church." In its chapter on "Human Development," the Latin American Bishops wrote that the "new evangelization" served as:

---

[867]José Maríns, Teo Trevissan, and Carol Chanona, "The Ecclesial Process of Latin America: The Assembly and the Document of Santo Domingo" [unpublished paper, 1993], p. 5. Cited in Guillermo Cook, "Santo Domingo Through Protestant Eyes," in Alfred T. Hennelly, S.J. (ed.), *Santo Domingo and Beyond*, p. 187.

[868]The quotation is from Pope John Paul's own "Discourse to the Cardinals and Prelates of the Roman Curia, December 21, 1984," in *Osservatore Romano* (January 21, 1985), p. 1. For the full text of the present address, see John Paul II, "Address to the Bishops of Latin America, in *Osservatore Romano* (October 14, 1992), p. 6.

> ...the basis for our commitment to a gospel-based and preferential option for the poor, one that is firm and irrevocable but not exclusive or excluding, as was very solemnly affirmed at the Medellín and Puebla Conferences... "The poor Church wants to energize the evangelization of our communities with the evangelizing potential of the poor"[869] (no. 178).

The same thrust was reflected in the following paragraphs:

> The Church, which is called to be ever more faithful to its preferential option for the poor, has played a growing role in such efforts. For that we thank God, and we urge that the path already opened be widened, since there are many more who have yet to tread on it (no. 179).

The text adopted as a "Pastoral Guideline" the need to "assume with renewed decision the gospel-inspired and preferential option for the poor, following the example and the words of the Lord Jesus..." (no. 180). Finally, in the "Conclusions" section of the Final Document, under the heading of "Primary Pastoral Directions," the Latin American bishops stated:

> We make ours the cry of the poor. In continuity with Medellín and Puebla, we assume with renewed ardor the gospel preferential option for the poor. This option, which is neither exclusive nor excluding, will, in imitation of Christ, shed light on all our evangelization activity. With that light, we urge the development of a new economic, social, and political order in keeping with the dignity of each and every person, fostering justice and solidarity, and opening the horizons of eternity for all of them (no. 296).

Of this segment of the Santo Domingo "Final Document," Francis McDonagh commented: "The commitments of this section are expressed in one paragraph in

---

[869]Citing here the "Conclusions," of the Puebla "Final Document" (no. 1147).

terms which could stand with any from the previous conferences [*viz.*, Medellín and Puebla]."[870]

As the aforementioned texts indicated, the CELAM IV conference at Santo Domingo resoundingly affirmed the notion of the "preferential option for the poor," which John Paul described as "firm and irrevocable," and a yardstick of "the measure of our following Christ." In essence, the "option for the poor" was taken to be an interpretive focus and unifying principle for the Santo Domingo documents, in continuity with what was already decided at Medellín and Puebla. As Jon Sobrino suggested:

> The Latin American Church must go on living by the spirit of Medellín [i.e., committed to a preferential option for the poor], not out of choice, but because there is not yet anything better. This does not mean of course that the Church does not have any new agendas, but rather that it is very dangerous to emphasize the need for newness, when for the most part that newness has been a reality in the Church since Medellín.[871]

Sobrino's observation emphasized the inadvisability of any attempt to jettison or re-invent the "option for the poor," since the reality that it presents is so deeply embedded in Christian tradition, along with the fact that "there is not yet anything better"[872] to supplant it.

A further indication of the impact of concept of the "preferential option for the poor" in the evolving social thought of John Paul II appeared in his selection of the theme, "If you want peace, reach out to the poor," as the text for the Pope's "World Day of Peace Message" to "the City and to the World" (*Ad orb et urb*) for

---

[870]Francis McDonagh, "Legacy of Santo Domingo," p. 1489.
[871]Jon Sobrino, S.J., "The Winds in Santo Domingo and the Evangelization of Culture," in Alfred T. Hennelly, S.J. (ed.), *Santo Domingo and Beyond*, p. 181.
[872]Jon Sobrino, S.J., "The Winds in Santo Domingo and the Evangelization of Culture," p. 184.

January 1, 1993. As the chief shepherd of the city of Rome, John Paul was well aware that even the Eternal City increasingly came to resemble a Third World capital near the turn of the Twenty-First Century, with its burgeoning numbers of the homeless, unemployed migrants, and a swelling refugee population, particularly from equatorial Africa, Albania and the former Yugoslavia. He told Mayor Pietro Giubilo of the "Eternal City": "Rome is a city with two faces. Next to immense treasures of religious, cultural, and human wealth may be observed sectors of multiple moral ills; corners of the Third World; points of great wealth and pockets of great poverty. There are the few who possess much, and the many who possess little."[873]

In his 1993 World Day of Peace address, the Pope John Paul emphasized: "Evangelical poverty is something that transforms those who accept it. They cannot remain indifferent when faced with the suffering of the poor; indeed, they feel impelled to share actively with God his preferential love for them (cf. *Sollicitudo Rei Socialis* no. 42)."[874] Not insignificantly, John Paul II concluded this address with a variation on the familiar sobriquet of Pope Paul VI:[875] "If you want peace, reach out to the poor!" (no. 5).

The ongoing process of listening, awareness, and dialogue that marked the development of the concept of the "preferential option for the poor" achieved a depth of maturity and a degree of official acceptance during the pontificate of John Paul II that ensured it of a secure place within the corpus of official Catholic social doctrine. In the end, Pope John Paul II declared liberation theology "necessary" for the Church,[876] a concession even granted in the second "Instruction on Liberation

---

[873]Cited in David Willey, *God's Politician: John Paul II, The Catholic Church, and The New World Order*, pp. 201-202.

[874]John Paul II, "1993 World Day of Peace Message," in *Osservatore Romano* (December 16, 1992), pp. 1-2.

[875]Cf. Pope Paul VI, "If you want peace, work for justice," in *Populorum Progressio* (no. 76).

[876]See his "Exhortation to the Representatives of the Brazilian National Bishops' Conference," March 13, 1986, no. 6; "To the Brazilian Episcopate," April 9, 1986, no. 5.

Theology" issued under the auspices of Cardinal Josef Ratzinger's Congregation for the Doctrine of the Faith, "*Libertatis Conscientia* (no. 98): "A theology of freedom and liberation and liberation… constitutes a demand of our time."

Chapter Six

Towards the New Millennium

The loss of the working classes in Europe was a scandal that rocked Catholicism in the nineteenth and early twentieth century. The official Church's response to the poor in a systematic way lagged until the advent of Pope John XXIII, the Second Vatican Council, and the 1968 second plenary meeting of the Latin American Bishops Conference [CELAM] in Medellín, Colombia. As Pope John XXIII recognized, the time had arrived for the Church "… to recognize the signs of the times, to take advantage of the opportunities offered, and to look toward distant horizons… It is not that the Gospel has changed. It is only that we have begun to understand it better."[877] By scrutinizing the "signs of the times," exponents of late Twentieth Century Catholicism began to penetrate the meaning of ancient texts and teachings that pertained to the poor, whom St. Lawrence described in antiquity as "the treasure of the Church." Pope Paul VI echoed this dynamic thrust in 1971 in *Octogesima Adveniens*:

> It is up to these Christian communities, with the help of the Holy Spirit, in communion with the bishops who hold responsibility and in dialogue with other Christian brethren and all men of good will, to discern the options and commitments which are called for in order to bring about the social, political and economic changes seen in many cases to be urgently needed (no. 4).

---

[877]Pope John XXIII, "Opening Speech to the Council" (October 11, 1962), in Walter Abbott, S.J. (ed.), *The Documents of Vatican II* (NY: America Press, 1966), p. 715. See also Bernard R. Bonnot, *Pope John XIII: Model and Mentor for Leaders* (Staten Island, NY: St. Paul's Publications, 2003), p. 263.

John XXIII believed that the modern era was not a time for new definitions, but for redefinition of the Christian faith in faithfulness to the tradition: "The substance of the ancient doctrine of the deposit of faith is one thing, and its formulation is another. The latter must be taken into greater account. Patience is needed. Everything has to be measured in the forms and proportions appropriate for a chiefly pastoral teaching."[878]

As John XXIII commented: "The Church must keep in mind new situations, new forms of life that open up new ways... [and] dedicate ourselves to the work that needs to be done in this modern world of ours."[879] For too long, Catholicism tended to view the poor as "*une masse résignée*," relegated to consideration as objects of charitable attention. By the late Twentieth Century, a new interpretive approach emerged. The focus shifted to include the action of the poor themselves, who sought to transform the structures of society by their reappropriation of history and to become the artisans of their own destiny.[880]

Gustavo Gutiérrez described John XXIII's radio address of September 11, 1962 that heralded the Second Vatican Council as "an important and significant predecessor"[881] to the embracement of the term "the preferential option for the poor." In this sense, the Church came to view the poor in a new light: as a privileged locus of theology; as a key to understanding the Christian faith; as a spur to the Church's activity; as a window into the political dimension of the faith; and also as the

---

[878]In Alberto Melloni, "*Sinossi critica dell' allocuzione di aperture del Concilio Vaticano II, 'Gaudet Mater Ecclesia (ottobre, 1962)*," in *Fede, Tradizione, Profezia: Studi du Giovanni XXIII e sul Vaticano II* (Brescia: *ISR-Edizione*, 1984), pp. 267-269. See also Mario Benigni and Goffredo Zanchi, *John XXIII: The Official Biography* (Boston, MA: Daughters of St. Paul, 2001), p. 393.
[879]Pope John XXIII, "Opening Speech to the Council," p. 714.
[880]On this point, see Christian Duquoc, *Libération et Progréssisme: Un Dialogue Théologique entre l'Amèrique Latine et Europe* (Paris: Editions du Cerf, 1987), pp. 35-48 and David Boileau (ed.), *Roger Aubert: Catholic Social Teaching/An Historical Perspective* (Milwaukee, WI: Marquette University Press, 2003, pp. 241-283.
[881]Gustavo Gutiérrez, "Expanding the View," p. 13.

privileged object of the Church's response, in service to the world. In his famous radio allocution of September 11, 1962, John XXIII reflected: "Confronted with the underdeveloped countries, the Church presents herself as what she is, and wants to be, the Church of all, and particularly, as the Church of the poor... [in order to redress] the miseries of social life that cry out for vengeance in the sight of God."[882] By stating this objective, Pope John expressed the longing that the Council would restore in the Church the concept of the "sacrament" of poverty, the hidden presence of Christ in the guise of those who suffer.[883]

As Archbishop Oscar Arnulfo Romero expressed it: "To put it in one word – in a word that sums it all up and makes it concrete – the world that the Church ought to serve is, for us, the world of the poor."[884] This post-Vatican II movement constituted a dramatic shift in the Catholic tradition,[885] so much so that Cardinal Avery Dulles could comment in his *tour de force* on the theology of Pope John Paul II, "The Church's 'preferential option for the poor' must be understood in a global context."[886] The embrace of the option for the poor by the Catholic Church in the wake of the Second Vatican Council represented a movement by the Mystical Body of Christ to be truer to itself and to acquire a livelier awareness of its authentic nature. To appropriate a phrase of Marie-Dominique Chenu, "the very essence of the Church was in question."[887] This shift led to a new way of being a person and a believer, a new way of living and professing the faith, a new way of being "called together" into the *ecclesia*. This dynamic transformation also served to separate and

---

[882]Cited in Giuseppe and Angelina Alberigo, *Giovanni XXIII*, pp. 357-358.
[883]On this point, see Marcel Gérard, "Documentation," in *Lumen Vitae* XVII (December, 1963), p. 685.
[884]Oscar Romero, "The Political Dimension of the Faith," p. 294.
[885]See Avery Dulles, S.J., "John Paul II and the New Evangelization," in *America* (February 1, 1992), p. 70.
[886]Aery Cardinal Dulles, S.J., *The Splendor of Faith: The Theological Vision of Pope John Paul II* (NY: Crossroad, 2003 revision), p. 181.
[887]Marie-Dominique Chenu, O.P., "Vatican II and the Church of the Poor," p. 56.

divide the faith community into two experiences, two worldviews, and two very distinct modalities of Church, in a world increasingly marked by "overdeveloped means, and underdeveloped ends."[888] The evolving tradition of Catholic social teaching increasingly charged people of good will to work towards a fundamental reshaping of society, both at the grass roots and global levels.

In the latter third of the twentieth century, Catholicism achieved a fuller understanding of its role to stand with the poor and marginalized in their quest for justice. Vatican II became the agent of change most responsible for the transformation and renewal of the Roman Catholic Church in the modern world. It catalyzed the Church's self-reflection despite the limitations imposed by its own pilgrim nature (as incomplete, imperfect, and in need of ongoing renewal and reform). In the wake of the Council, the Church sought to encounter the modern world. As Juan Alfaro, then a key staffer at the then-Pontifical Commission for Justice and Peace wrote:

> The present world situation requires of the Christian a new vision and praxis of the message of Christ... a deep and keen consciousness of the tremendous injustices perpetrated today in the economic, social, political and international fields; a frank attitude in denouncing the structures of oppression; an effective act of commitment for the integral liberation of humanity; an honest acknowledgment of our silence, even of our identification with the socio-economic structures that oppress the poor and the marginalized.[889]

---

[888]See Gustavo Gutiérrez, "Freedom and Liberation," in Gustavo Gutiérrez and Richard Schaull, *Liberation and Change* (Atlanta: John Knox Press, 1977), p. 77. The latter phrase derives from Paul VI's "Address to the International Seminar of Catholic European Periodicals and the African Society of Culture" (October 2, 1969), in *Paths of Peace*, p. 114.

[889]Juan Alfaro, S.J., *Esperanza Cristiana y liberación del hombre* (Barcelona: B.A.C., 1972), p. 217. See also his *Theology of Justice in the World* (Rome: Pontifical Commission Justice and Peace, 1972), pp. 44-45.

The first fruits of this movement showed themselves at the Medellín conference in 1968. Medellín lent credence and legitimated the pastoral plans for a continent-wide implementation of the preferential option for the poor. The documents of Medellín sought to encourage those already engaged in the struggle, and to exhort all segments of the Church to become involved in the task. Medellín served as an occasion of definition and a point of departure for this new emerging model of Church. The Church began to embrace the "preferential option for the poor" as a clear and effective means of articulating this agenda, in spite of whatever misunderstandings were accorded it, or the limitations that it appeared to retain.[890]

By the mid-1980's, an editorial that appeared in the prestigious international theological journal *Concilium* concluded: "The preferential option for the poor is the trademark of the Latin American Church. Today, however, it is becoming an option of the Universal Church... The preferential option for solidarity with the poor is nothing short of a Copernican revolution for the Church."[891] Aware of this development, Pope John Paul II told the assembled Latin American bishops who gathered at CELAM III in Puebla de Los Angeles, Mexico in 1979: "... drink at these authentic fonts, brothers. Speak in the idiom of Vatican II, John XXIII, and Paul VI. For that is the idiom that embodies the experience, the suffering, and the hope of contemporary humanity" ("Opening Address at Puebla," III, 4). When confronted with concrete situations, the Church began to re-read the texts and study the message anew, as John Paul II later noted, "with the desire of finding a *new application* of it."[892] The key to this new awareness was a commitment in favor of the oppressed

---

[890]See Gustavo Gutiérrez, "Expanding the View," p. 12.
[891]"Editorial: Theology from the Viewpoint of the Poor," in Leonardo Boff and Virgil Elizondo (eds.), *Option for The Poor: Challenge to the Rich Countries* (Edinburgh: T. & T. Clark, Ltd., 1986), p. ix. See also Thomas Massaro, S.J., *Living Justice: Catholic Social Teaching in Action* (NY: Sheed & Ward, 2000), p. 254.
[892]John Paul II, "Homily in Salvador Bahia" (July 1, 1980), in *Pronunçiamentos do Papa no Brasil* (Sao Paulo: Loyola, 1980), p. 192.

of the world, a marked desire to make the needs of the poor an object of preferential concern. In a 1981 allocution, John Paul II remarked: "The Church would not be faithful to the Gospel if she were not close to the poor and if she did not defend their rights."[893] John Paul II reflected this stance in his 1991 social encyclical, *Centesimus Annus*:

> ...the social message of the Gospel must not be considered a theory, but above all else a basis and a motivation for action... Today, more than ever, the Church is aware that her social message will gain credibility more immediately from the witness of actions than as a result of its internal logic and consistency. This awareness is also the source of her preferential option for the poor... (no. 57).[894]

In this respect, Pope John Paul II enunciated a maxim of liberation theology that theological reflection forms the "second act," whose first measure derives from involvement in concrete liberation praxis and the proclamation of the Word in order to alleviate the oppression of the materially poor.[895] The foremost exponent of the theology of liberation, Gustavo Gutiérrez, identified the "preferential option for the poor" as "the ultimate and most important reason for liberation theology."[896]

---

[893]John Paul II, "The Church in the World of the 1980's," in *Origins* 10 (1981), p. 490.
[894]Note the interesting comment of Donal Dorr: "The new emphasis on option for the poor calls into question this whole model of church influence and the corresponding status of the institutional Church and church leaders and theologians in society... It is quite evident that the outcome of all this has been a rather obvious disparity between the official teaching and the practical action of the Roman authorities. I have said that there are references to a preferential option for the poor in some of the Pope's [John Paul II] Latin American addresses. But they are hedged around with provisos and warnings. And, whatever may be thought about the addresses of the Pope, it is quite clear that there is little or no practical support from the Vatican for any really radical option... Concern for the poor, yes; 'option' for the poor, not yet, and perhaps not at all," in Jonathan Boswell, Francis McHugh and Johan Verstraeten (eds.), *Catholic Social Thought: Twilight or Renaissance?* (Leuven: Leuven University Press, 2000), pp. 254, 235.
[895]See Gustavo Gutiérrez, "The Historical Power of the Poor," in *The Power of the Poor in History*, p. 103.
[896]Gustavo Gutiérrez, "We Cannot Do Theology in a Dead Corner of History," p. 87.

The adoption by the Church of the "preferential option for the poor" marked a defining movement in the unfolding social role of the Roman Catholic Church as it struggled to interact with the modern world. The notion of the option for the poor found an echo in official church teaching, since it expressed two vital aspects of the Church's life that are challenging and interrelated: its universality and its concern for the poor and the vulnerable. The maturing theology that the option for the poor represented could no longer be easily denied, undercut, or dismissed as a mere fad. The 1986 Vatican Congregation for the Doctrine of Faith's "Instruction on Christian Freedom and Liberation" concluded that "the special option for the poor... manifests the universality of the Church's being and Mission... and is now an essential element in the understanding that the Church as a whole has of its task in the present world" (no. 68). In *Sollicitudo Rei Socialis*, issued in March, 1988, Pope John Paul II indicated that the option for the poor served as one of the "characteristic themes and guidelines of the magisterium" (no. 42). He situated the option for the poor within the "not only timely, but useful and necessary" context of liberation theology, subsequently expressed in his letter to the Brazilian bishops of April, 1986.[897]

As a new social locus of the Church emerged, Karl Rahner envisioned the shape of the shape of the Church to come to be poor, fewer in number, and scattered in the *diaspora*:

> The person of the future will encounter the Church of the future only when he or she sees the presence of Christ realized in the legitimate proclamation of the Gospel and in the remembrance of Christ's death and resurrection in the Eucharist. This is where the Christian of tomorrow will apprehend the actual nature of the Church, for this is

---

[897]John Paul II, "Letter to Brazilian Episcopal Conference," in Alfred T. Hennelly, S.J. (ed.), *Liberation Theology: A Documentary History*, p. 503.

> where the most original religious and theological experience will take place: in the community.[898]

In Latin America, this vision played out dramatically in the post-conciliar era, as a new catalyst emerged with the proliferation of basic Christian communities [CEB's] that sparked theological reflection in the Church, and from which "liberation theology draws its power and its future."[899] In this manner, the Church began to rethink and re-image itself "from below," from the perspective of the poor and marginalized. Increasingly, the Church realized that it was not enough to be *for* the poor, but that it needed to commit itself more tangibly to stand *with* the poor. As Gustavo Gutiérrez noted, this movement sought to "change the focus of the Church – the center of its life and work – and to be present, *really* present, in the world of the poor – to commit the Church to living in the world of the poor."[900]

The development of the theology of liberation in Latin America helped to catalyze the transition that moved Catholicism away from its Eurocentric roots "to a fully world religion... in which the sphere of the Church's life is in fact the entire world."[901] Marie-Dominique Chenu heralded the "new birth" of the theology and theologians of the developing nations as the onset of a "new paradigm"[902] that marked a new phase of the history of Christianity. Likewise, as Johannes Baptist

---

[898]Karl Rahner, S.J., *The Church After the Council*, p. 49.

[899]Pablo Richard, "Liberation Theology: A Difficult But Possible Future," in Marc H. Ellis and Otto Maduro (eds.), *Expanding the View*, p. 211.

[900]Gustavo Gutiérrez, "Church of the Poor," p. 18.

[901]Karl Rahner, S.J., "Towards a Fundamental Theological Understanding of Vatican II," in *Theological Studies* 40 (December, 1979), pp. 722, 719. Note Rahner's salient comment: "When one realizes what pre-conceptions many people had in those days – especially in Roman circles – of the course of the Council, one could see that it would have been naïve to assume a smooth course. Some participants, for example, believed beforehand that the Council had as its task merely to codify a little more solemnly than before old dogmatic assumptions, and that the real job had been effect finished before the opening of the Council. However, it happened otherwise," in *The Church After the Council* (NY: Herder & Herder, 1966), pp. 16-17.

[902]M.-D. Chenu, "A New Birth: Theologians of the Third World," in *Concilium* 144 (1981), p. 18.

Metz noted, much of the impetus for this change came from Latin America: "The Latin American churches are showing us a transformation process of unheard-of proportions – one which, in my view, is endowed with a providential importance for the whole Church, and in which, in one manner or another, we are all involved."[903] The Salvadoran Jesuit sociologist Ignacio Ellacuría articulated this viewpoint with greater clarity:

> In Latin America "the poor" are not a fringe group; they are the majority. In a real sense, they define what Latin America is: poor in health, poor in education, poor in living standards, poor in having a say in their own destiny. By virtue of the universal call of the Gospel and by virtue of the historical summons specific to the region in which the Latin American Church lives, it must be the Church of the poor. If it were to be that in truth, then it would give impetus to a new historical form of Christianity that should be transmitted to the Universal Church. And this new form will be transmitted, if it acquires the necessary drive and tension.[904]

In an interview given prior to his death in 1984, Karl Rahner stated: "If the Church is an *ecclesia semper reformanda* [a Church always to be reformed], as Vatican II emphasized, then it is quite clear that it is never exactly what it should be. I can therefore wish what the Church should be and at the same time fear that it will fail to be that sufficiently."[905] True to its pilgrim nature, the transformation of the Church necessitated a prolonged, ongoing process of renewal. One observer, British Vatican correspondent David Willey, expressed the critical view that while "the Catholic Church's decision to endorse what it calls its 'preferential option for the

---

[903] J. B. Metz, *The Emergent Church: The Future of Christianity in a Post-bourgeois World*, p. 18.
[904] Ignacio Ellacuría, S.J., *Freedom Made Flesh: The Mission of Christ and His Church* (Maryknoll, NY: Orbis Books, 1976), p. 146.
[905] Karl Rahner, S.J., "Tasks Facing the Church," in Harvey Egan, S.J. (ed.), *Faith in A Wintry Season: Conversions and Interviews with Karl Rahner in the Last Years of His Life* (NY: Crossroad, 1990), p. 187.

poor' sounded good, [it] seemed to mean little in practice."[906] Willey's candid observation failed to take into account that no institution can transform its paradigm into something entirely different overnight, especially one so deeply embedded in human history and culture as the Roman Catholic Church, which often must struggle within the constraints of the eschatological tension of the "now" and the "not yet" in which it finds itself. Donal Dorr's assessment struck a more balanced and accurate chord:

> The new Catholic ethos which developed as a result of the work of John XXIII and Vatican II prepared the ground for a truly remarkable shift in the relationship between Church and the dominant powers in society, a break from the Constantinian conception of the role of the Church. This shift is summed up in the term "option for the poor." The first full-fledged commitment to such an option came at Medellín, when Latin American leaders pledged themselves to side with the poor in the struggle for justice.[907]

The winds of change that blew in Latin America in the wake of Vatican II brought about a deep struggle over what it meant to be an individual believer, and how to be Church in the socio-cultural context in which the faithful found themselves. For the first time in centuries, the Latin American Church came to full stature and manifested itself as fully indigenous and Christian. The indigenous Church's reclaimed Latin American identity led it to understand better the Gospel and its application within the Latin American context, and to strive to put Christian values into practice more effectively. After Medellín, for the first time since the colonial era of Bartolomé de las Casas and Antonio de Montesinos the Latin American Church made significant strides to be socially relevant in a way consistent

---

[906]David Willey, *God's Politician: Pope John Paul II, The Catholic Church, and The New World Order*, p. 234.
[907]Donal Dorr, *Option for the Poor* (1992 edition), p. 357.

with the Gospel. This paradigm shift yielded both a burst of creativity and a shockwave of conflict, both at the grassroots and within official church circles. The option for the poor proved to be divisive and controversial within the Church, since for some it represented a movement away from the long-established status quo. It caused some church leadership and membership to respond with contempt or suspicion, since they feared a disruption in social order or in the maintenance of an established lifestyle.

The option for the poor also sought to empower the oppressed as agents of social change and as proclaimers of the Gospel. In the course of time, the framers of the option for the poor departed from an earlier phase that dabbled in Marxist analysis to a later one that directed its attention to more directly church-related concerns. As Gustavo Gutiérrez pointed out:

> Liberation theology is in fact a "new stage" and, as such, strives to be in continuity with the teaching of the Church. This theology, in my understanding of it, does indeed seek to be "closely connected" with the Church's teaching... its power and importance are due to a *freshness* or newness that derives from attention to the historical vicissitudes of our peoples, for these are authentic signs of the times through which the Lord continually speaks to us. At the same time, its power and importance are due to the *continuity* that leads it to sink its roots deep in Scripture, Tradition, and the Magisterium. These factors play a determining role in the continuing evolution of a theology that aims at being "a reflection on praxis in the light of faith."[908]

Although Gustavo Gutiérrez asserted that the option for the poor constituted "the nub and core of a new way of being human and Christian in Latin America,"[909] it soon came to be perceived as more than a mere regional and pastoral entity.

---

[908]Gustavo Gutiérrez, "Expanding the View," pp. 31-32.
[909]Gustavo Gutiérrez, "From Medellín to Puebla," in *The Power of the Poor in History*, p. 44.

Gutiérrez asserted that the "preferential option for the poor is not a Latin American issue. It is a biblical, evangelical question. All of us in the Church must find our way in this preferential option for the poor."[910] The place of life that the option for the poor gained in the Universal Church was captured in Leonardo Boff's assessment of the second instruction of the Congregation for the Doctrine of the Faith on liberation theology, the "Instruction on Christian Freedom and Liberation" issued by the Congregation for the Doctrine for the Faith in March, 1986 that gave the Church "a newly universal dimension [to] values that were initially only those of the Third World."[911] The scrutiny accorded to the option for the poor within the two Vatican instructions on liberation theology at the same time provided it with a measure of institutional legitimization. As Alfred Hennelly observed: "[W]e now have a formal Vatican endorsement (with all the necessary caveats and provisos) of the liberation approach, not merely for Latin America or other parts of the Third World, but for the Universal Church."[912] The inclusion of the option for the poor within the text of the "Final Report" of the 1985 Synod demonstrated the measure of acceptance it achieved within the body of official Catholic social teaching:

> After Vatican II, the Church became more aware of her Mission for service of the poor, the oppressed, and the marginalized. In this preferential option, which is not to be understood as exclusive, the true spirit of the Gospel shines out... The Church must in prophetic fashion denounce every form of poverty and oppression and support everywhere the fundamental and inalienable rights of the human person (no. 11).[913]

---

[910]Gustavo Gutiérrez, "Church of the Poor," pp. 19, 24.
[911]Cited in Harvey Cox, *The Silencing of Leonardo Boff*, p. 115.
[912]Alfred T. Hennelly, S.J., "The Red-Hot Issue: Liberation Theology," p. 425.
[913]"The Final Report," in Xavier Rynne, *John Paul II's Extraordinary Synod: A Collegial Achievement*, p. 130.

This statement of the Synod's "Final Report" represented a further amplification of the text of the Synod's working draft, which stated: "The preferential option for the poor, the oppressed, the outcast has entered into the Church's thought and practice."[914] As Gustavo Gutiérrez pointed out, the outlook on the "preferential option for the poor" became "to core of the 'new evangelization,' which got underway in Latin America two decades [before], but which is so important to keep fresh and up to date. The novelty we cite was acknowledged, in a certain way, by the Synod held on the twentieth anniversary of the close of Vatican II."[915] "The ensuing theological reflection that energized the option for the poor spread from beyond Latin America to gain ground elsewhere. The former Archbishop of Milwaukee, Rembert George Weakland, in a discussion of the U.S. Bishops' pastoral letters on nuclear arms and the economy, remarked: "I wonder if we would have had the courage to write [these pastoral letters] if it had not been for the Medellín and Puebla documents."[916] In fact, in the United States Catholic Bishops' 1986 pastoral letter, "Economic Justice for All," utilizes the specific term "preferential option for the poor" four times (cf. nos. 16, 52, 87).[917]

In the final analysis, the preferential option for the poor loomed as an option for the God of the Kingdom proclaimed by Jesus (cf. MT 25: 31-46). It served as a call to conversion and to redefine the Mission of the Church in history. This shift required a break with the prior historical alliances with the powerful, and a decision to side with the oppressed masses. In the last resort, the option for the poor was not a question of the Church being poor *per se*, but of its desire to include the poor of this

---

[914]Cited in Peter Hebblethwaite, *Synod Extraordinary*, p. 112.

[915]Gustavo Gutiérrez, "Option for the Poor," in *Mysterium Liberationis*, p. 250.

[916]Cited in Alfred T. Hennelly, S.J., "The Influence of Liberation Theology," in Edward L. Cleary, O.P., *Born of the Poor*, p. 29.

[917]National Conference of Catholic Bishops, *Economic Justice For All: Pastoral Letter on Catholic Social Teaching and the U. S. Economy* (Washington, DC: United States Catholic Conference, 1986), pp. x, xi, 28, 45.

world in a privileged way among the People of God. This shift required a profound transformation on the part of the Church. As Cardinal Paulo Evaristo Arns pointed out: "The first consequence of the option for the poor is the conversion of the Church in its totality."[918] Gustavo Gutiérrez stressed similarly that the essence of the option for the poor required "personal conversion."[919] The bishops at Puebla expressed this goal of conversion in Part 4, Chapter 1 of the "Final Document" in the section entitled "The Preferential Option for the Poor":

> Despite the distortions and interpretations of some, who vitiate the spirit of Medellín, and despite the disregard and even hostility of others, we affirm the need for conversion on the part of the whole Church to a preferential option for the poor, and option aimed at their integral liberation (no. 1134).

The Puebla "Final Document" reflected the ongoing nature of this task, which requires "a constant conversion and purification in all Christians with the aim of identifying more fully day by day with the poor Christ and with the poor" (no. 1140). The fourth general meeting of the joint Latin American episcopates [CELAM IV] at Santo Domingo, in 1992, forcefully made the same point: "New evangelization demands that the Church undergo a pastoral conversion. Such a conversion must be in keeping with the [Second Vatican] Council" (no. 30).[920]

The option for the poor carried with it many implications for both the established, "First World" churches, and for the developing churches at the margins. It necessitated a genuine, ongoing conversion that featured several key elements: a).

---

[918]Paolo Evaristo Cardinal Arns, "The Church of the Poor: A Persecuted Church," in *Center Focus: News from the Center of Concern* 44 (July, 1981), p. 2.

[919]Gustavo Gutiérrez, *A Theology of Liberation* (1988 revision), p. 118.

[920]For the text and commentary, see Alfred T. Hennelly, S.J. (ed.), *Santo Domingo and Beyond: Documents and Commentaries From the Historic Meeting of the Latin American Bishops' Conference* (Maryknoll, NY: Orbis Books, 1993), especially pp. 29, 174,187, and 219.

a desire to view the lot of the poor through their own eyes; b). a willingness, as individuals, and as a body of believers, to take up the cause of the poor and become engaged in their struggle; c). an openness to take up the life of the poor and share in it, to whatever extent possible, in solidarity with them; d). a commitment to identify the mechanisms that produce poverty, and to work to overcome causes of structural poverty and injustice; e). finally, a pledge to work in order to produce a more authentic and integral theology, a reflection on praxis in the light of faith. As Jon Sobrino remarked

> This option can have various expressions. One of them is to live with the poor, but there are few who do that and it isn't what the poor most need. The option for the poor means to make an effort to see reality from their perspective, from where they are. Concretely, we must put our talents and resources at the service of the poor.[921]

The central thrust of the social teaching of the post-conciliar Latin American Church placed ethical demands that sought the historical enactment of the total liberation of the whole person and of all people, without exclusion. Such solidarity with the poor and oppressed was presented as a matter of moral obligation (cf. the Puebla "Final Document," nos. 480-490, and *Evangelii Nuntiandi*, nos. 29-36). While the task of seeking to transform history enjoined the believer to disavow "any kind of violence or the dialectic of the class struggle" (Puebla "Final Document," no. 486; cf. *Evangelii Nuntiandi*, no. 37), the preferential option for the poor indisputably put forward a partiality that was both justified and required, since it was based on biblical imperatives and on the level of need of the poor and vulnerable, not derived on the basis of anyone's personal merit or lack of the same. In the best Catholic

---

[921]Jon Sobrino, S.J., "Walk Humbly With God," in *Maryknoll* (February, 1994), p. 30.

sense, the option for the poor sought especially to be grounded in a movement towards community and the common good.

In spite of its rocky rise to prominence, by the mid-1980's even conservative theologians such as Hans Urs von Balthasar readily accepted the option for the poor as "something absolutely central to Christianity... that is now part and parcel of Christianity."[922] During his first trip to Brazil in 1980, John Paul II told the assembled workers at Morumbi Stadium: "The option for the poor is a Christian option; it is also the option of a society that is concerned with the common good" (no. 4).[923] In this respect, the option for the poor formed a summons to the believing community with a meaning for all, and served as a call to solidarity with the oppressed. John Paul II reiterated this point in his address to curial prelates in Rome in December, 1981:

> The option which is emphasized today with particular force by the bishops of Latin America, I have repeatedly confirmed... I have made and I do make this option. I identify myself with it. I feel it could not be otherwise, since it is the eternal message of the Gospel. That is the option Christ made, the option made by the Apostles, the option of the Church throughout its two thousand year history.[924]

Prior to the inclusion of the option for the poor in John Paul II's 1991 social encyclical *Centesimus Annus* (nos. 11, 57), one of his most unqualified uses of it to date came in an address to an Italian Catholic lay movement at Castelgondolfo, in December, 1986:

---

[922]"An Interview With Hans Urs von Balthasar," in *30 Giorni* (June, 1984), p. 78. The influence of this remark upon John Paul II was profound and he referred directly to von Balthasar's comments in his first Wednesday audience, upon his return from Puebla. See Pope John Paul II, "Liberation Theology Involves 'That Truth Which Makes Us Free,'" p. 12.

[923]John Paul II, "Address to the Workers of Brazil at Morumbi Stadium," in *A.A.S.* 72 (1980), p. 891.

[924]John Paul II, "Discourse to the Cardinals and Prelates of the Roman Curia," in *Osservatore Romano* (January 21, 1985), p. 9.

> Today this option is discussed above all in Latin America. But it is also discussed with regard to the Universal Church, as the [1985] Synod of Bishops confirmed. But today this option is discussed and reaffirmed in a new context. The option for the poor is the choice of the Gospel: It is the option of Christ and for Christ. His own choice was exactly that: an option for the poor. And the option for the poor is at the same time an option for Christ, in whatever century, whatever situation, in whatever country it is made.[925]

In his Apostolic Exhortation, *Ecclesia in America* ("The Church in America," based on the 1997 "Special Assembly for America" of the Synod of Bishops), John Paul II again returned to the theme of the option for the poor, though this time with even greater refinement and nuance. On January 22, 1999, he displayed this certain flourish as he signed the post-Synodal document[926] in which he reinforced the text of his prior Apostolic Exhortation *Tertio Millenio Adveniente* ("Preparing for the Year 2000") concerning the problems of the "New Evangelization" and "the enormous gap between the North and South" (no. 2). Pope John Paul II again warned that, "love for the poor must be preferential but not exclusive," and added that this reality concerned the Synod Fathers who observed that in part "because of an approach to the pastoral care of the poor marked by a certain exclusiveness that pastoral care for the leading sectors of society has been neglected and many people have been estranged from the Church" (no. 67). In the same document, John Paul affirmed that in its attitude towards the poor, the Church "needs to be of assistance, promotion, liberation, and fraternal openness. The goal of the Church is to ensure that no one is marginalized" (no. 58). In light of this solidarity, John Paul professed that, "The globalized economy must be analyzed in light of the principles of social justice, respecting the preferential option for the poor" (no. 55), and that the

[925]John Paul II, "Address to the *Comunità di Sant' Egidio*," in *Osservatore Romano* (December 14, 1986), pp. 6-8.
[926]John Paul II, "*Ecclesia in America*" (no. 2), in *Origins* (February 4, 1999), p. 567.

"preferential love for the poor which the Church in American nurtures… [exists] because of her love for the Lord and because she is aware that 'Jesus identified himself with the poor (cf. MT 25: 31-46).'"[927] Donal Dorr correctly pointed out that: "The Vatican has slowly and cautiously accepted the phrase. There was concern in Rome that an option for the poor would be understood either as an exclusion of the rich or (worse still) a 'class option'[928] in the Marxist sense, that is, an invitation to class struggle."

An example of this trajectory is seen in the progression and refinement of John Paul II's social thought on this issue. During his 1980 pastoral visit to Brazil, he endorsed the "preferential option for the poor."[929] During an address to the Roman Curia in 1984, Pope John Paul II adverted to the "preferential option for the poor" and said: "I have made and continue to make this 'option' my own. I identify with it… It is an option which is unwavering and irreversible."[930] In an address to laity, religious and priests in Mexico City on May 12, 1990, Pope John Paul II stated: "… no one must be excluded… the preferential option for the poor… is not an

---

[927]John Paul makes a similar point elsewhere in *Tertio Millenio Adveniente* (1996), explicitly invoking the term, "the preferential option for the poor": "If we recall that 'Jesus came to preach the good news to the poor,' (MT 11:5; Lk 7:22), how can we fail to lay greater emphasis on the *Church's preferential option for the poor and outcast?*" (no. 51), cited in *Preparing for the Year 2000* (Rome: Urbi et Orbi Communications, 1997 edition), p. 57. In this same text, authorized commentators such as theologian Paul O'Callaghan suggested that "among the range of pastoral challenges selected by the Holy Father" is "a renewed insistence on the Church's preferential love of the poor and the marginalized…", p. 207, while Camillo Cardinal Ruini concluded that: "The Pope lays great stress upon the Church's preferential option for the poor and marginalized," p. 257. Nevertheless, the concept has assumed a different application in practice when John Paul appointed archbishops with strong ties to *Opus Dei* to primatial sees such as Lima and Mexico City in the late 1990's.

[928]Donal Dorr, "Preferential Option for Poor," in Judith A. Dwyer (ed.), *The New Dictionary of Catholic Social Thought* (Collegeville, MN: Liturgical Press/A Michael Glazier Book, 1994), p. 757.

[929]See *Osservatore Romano* (July 4, 1980), p. 1.

[930]See *Osservatore Romano* (July 12, 1980), p. 2.

ideological option; neither is it a matter of letting oneself be trapped by a false theory of class struggle."[931]

Various authors have described the present time as "the Catholic Moment," a phrase coined by the Reverend Richard John Neuhaus to depict the present phase in history, "in which the Roman Catholic Church can and should be the lead Church in proclaiming and exemplifying the Gospel."[932] The option for the poor represented an undeterred retrieval of a core element of the Christian tradition that aimed to restore the Church to its vitality as the "sacrament of liberating evangelization," in the phrase of Gustavo Gutiérrez.[933] Karl Rahner similarly indicated:

> ...if Christianity really possessed that degree of radical consistency which by nature it demands, then it would be springtime in the Church... Each one of us should see these times as a personal challenge to work so that the inner core of faith comes alive. Then of course the Church will again shine radiantly, and it will again become clear that the Church is intended to be the sacramental sign of the world's salvation.[934]

---

[931]See *Osservatore Romano* (May 14, 1990), p. 3. Note that Pope Paul VI raised a similar concern in *Octogesima Adveniens*:"... the Christian who wishes to live his faith in political activity... cannot without contradicting himself adhere to ideological systems which radically or substantially go against his faith and his concept of man. He cannot adhere to the Marxist ideology... [I]t would be illusory and dangerous... to accept the elements of Marxist analysis without recognizing their relationships with ideology, and to enter into practice with class struggle and its Marxist interpretations, while failing to note the kind of totalitarian and violent society to which this process leads" (nos. 26, 34).

[932]Richard John Neuhaus, who was a Lutheran pastor for thirty years before converting to Catholicism, became a favorite among "neo-conservative" circles in American Catholicism in the 1990s and into the new millennium. Cited in Avery Dulles, S.J., "John Paul II and the New Evangelization," in *America* (February 1, 1992), p. 72. See also Richard John Neuhaus, "Introduction," in Kenneth A. Myers (ed.), *Aspiring to Freedom: Commentaries on John Paul II's Encyclical, The Social Concerns of the Church* (Grand Rapids, MI: Eerdmans, 1988), p. xiii.

[933]Gustavo Gutiérrez, *The Truth Shall Set You Free*, p. 148

[934]Carl Rahner, S.J., "A 'Wintry' Church and the Opportunities for Christianity," in Harvey D. Egan, S.J. (ed.), *Faith in a Wintry Season: Conversions and Interviews With Karl Rahner in the Last Years of His Life*, p. 200.

The question of the application of the preferential option for the poor and marginalized within the context of the more affluent, developed nations above the Tropic of Cancer lingers as one of the great Christian challenges to be confronted into the New Millennium. As Rembert Weakland once remarked: "What is important for North America now is to intensify its option for the poor in concrete ways. What is important for both Latin America and North America is not to lose heart in the renewal – the liberating renewal – that Vatican II brought about and of which we have all been the beneficiaries."[935]

The preferential option for the poor, with its limitations and attendant pastoral and theological implications, emerged as one of the most significant contributions that arose from the post-conciliar, Latin American Church and took hold in world Catholicism. While deeply rooted in the ancient biblical[936] and patristic witness, in the present age the option for the poor displayed particular, fresh characteristics, owing to the Church's contemporary encounter with the depth and complexity of the mechanisms of poverty and oppression that marred the contemporary world. The degree of acceptance eventually accorded to the option for the poor within the body of official Catholic social teaching derived from a deeper awareness of the sociological, economic, cultural and political mechanisms that conspired to produce and perpetuate the cycle of poverty. But most especially, the preferential option for the poor took root on account of the light that a new reading of the Word of God shed on the pernicious hold of poverty within the contemporary world.

The preferential option for the poor surged to prominence to remind the Church of the biblical mandate that the believer or community that does not choose

---

[935]Archbishop Rembert George Weakland, "How Medellín and Puebla influenced North America," in *Origins* (April 13, 1989), p. 760.
[936]Donal Dorr comments, "The notion of a preferential option for the poor is solidly rooted in the Bible," in "Preferential Option for Poor," *The New Dictionary of Catholic Social Thought*, p. 755.

to live the challenges imposed by this commitment are not worthy of the name Christian[937] since the poor occupy so much of the world and define what response the Church must render to the world. The progressive movement of the Catholic faith community in its embrace of this social teaching reflects the observation of Cardinal Suenens that "it had become necessary to free ourselves from a theology that limited and restricted the mystery of the Church. What we were about to experience was not a 'theology of liberation,' but rather 'liberation from a particular theology.'[938]

In the late Twentieth Century, the concept of the option for the poor gained currency within worldwide Catholicism. It became less of a partisan slogan or focal point for a regional form of liberation theology than a catalyst for social change that became incorporated into the universal currents of official Catholic social teaching. The notion of the preferential option for the poor emerged in the latter third of the Twentieth Century as a vision, a moral concern and a call to the liberation and empowerment of the poor.[939] The preferential option for the poor emerged as a distinctive contribution to the world Church, a concept "open to all theology and conscious of the fact that its final destiny is to disappear as [reflective of] a particular theology and become simply theology,"[940] grounded as a fundamental precept of the social teaching of the Universal Church, with the appropriate proviso of Pope John Paul II that it be grounded in "a deep and solid Christology... a healthy anthropology... and a clear and correct ecclesial vision".[941] While the 1994

---

[937]See Oscar Romero, "Sermon of February 17, 1980," in James Brockman, S.J. (ed.), *The Violence of Love*, p. 195.

[938]Leo-Josef Suenens, *Memories and Reflections* (Dublin: Veritas Publications, 1992), p. 75.

[939]For a succinct analysis of these three categories, see Kenneth R. Himes, O.F.M., *Responses to 101 Questions on Catholic Social Teaching* (NY: Paulist Press, 2001), pp. 39-40.

[940]Leonardo Boff and Clodovis Boff, *Introducing Liberation Theology* (Maryknoll, NY: Orbis Books, 1987), p. 83.

[941]John Paul II, "Opening Address of the Holy Father," Part IV, at CELAM IV, Santo Domingo (1992), cited in Alfred T. Hennelly, S.J., *Santo Domingo and Beyond*, pp. 53 – 56. Here, Pope John Paul clearly echoed Puebla's analysis and methodology that centered on "the truth about Jesus

Catechism of the Catholic Church avoided explicit use of the term, the "preferential option for the poor," it retained the phrase "*a preferential love* on the part of the Church... [that] has not ceased to work for [the poor's] relief, defense and liberation through numerous works of charity, which remain indispensable always and everywhere."[942]

The term, "the preferential option for the poor," took form only in the aftermath of the Medellín conference in 1968. Despite the controversies that it engendered over the course of its development and refinement, it became ensconced as a cornerstone of contemporary Catholic social teaching. The Administrative Committee of the United States Conference of Catholic Bishops reiterated this point in its quadrennial call to political responsibility prior to the 2004 U.S. presidential election, *Faithful Citizenship*, referencing Pope John Paul's apostolic exhortation, *Novo Millennio Ineunte*[943]:

> Scripture teaches that God has a special concern for the poor and vulnerable... The Church calls on all of us to embrace this *preferential option for the poor* [my emphasis] and vulnerable, to embody it in our lives, and to work to have it shape public policies

---

Christ... about the mission of the Church... [and] about human beings" (Nos. 1.2-1.9).

[942]*Catechism of the Catholic Church*, p. 648, citing directly the 1986 Instruction of the C.D.F., Libertatis Conscientia (no.68). Interestingly, the Catechism eschews the term the "preferential option for the poor," whereas it appeared with increasing frequency and without qualification in Pope John Paul II's writings and allocutions during his later pontificate. The catechism stresses that the understanding of poverty ought to extend "not only to material poverty, but also to the many forms of cultural and religious poverty" (no. 2444), p. 647. Avery Dulles pointed out this lacuna: "A stronger case for evangelization and for the social mission of the Church would be desirable" in the Catechism, in "The Church in the Catechism," in Thomas J. Reese, S.J. (ed.), *The Universal Catechism Reader: Reflections and Responses* (San Francisco, CA: Harper & Row, 1990), p. 92. See Peter C. Phann, "What is Old and New in the Catechism?", in Berard L. Marthaler (ed.), *Introducing the Catechism of the Catholic Church* (NY: Paulist Press, 1994), p. 68: "... the option for the poor is somewhat muted; it is not made into the leitmotif of the section on social justice. Instead, the expression is not used in the CCC."

[943]John Paul II, *Novo Millennio Ineunte* [January 6, 2001] (no. 49), in *A.A.S.* 84 (1992), p. 781.

> and priorities. A fundamental measure of our society is how we care for and stand with the poor and vulnerable.[944]

Pope John Paul reiterated this stance in his apostolic exhortation on the role of the bishop, *Pastores Gregis*, dated October 16, 2003:

> The bishop who wishes to be an authentic witness and minister of the Gospel of hope must be a *vir pauper*... It is also demanded by the Church's concern for the poor, who must be the object of a preferential option... The title *procurator pauperum* has always been applied to the Church's pastors. This must also be the case today, so that the Gospel of Jesus Christ can become present and heard as a source of hope for all, but especially for those who can expect from God alone a more dignified life and a better future. Encouraged by the example of their pastors, the Church and churches must practice that 'preferential option for the poor' which I have indicated as programmatic for the third millennium (nos. 20, 21).[945]

The concept of the "preferential option for the poor" emerged as a new paradigm within a generation of being coined by Gustavo Gutiérrez to be encapsulated as one of the seven "key themes at the heart of our Catholic social teaching tradition."[946] John Paul II applied this lens to the global economy in his Apostolic Exhortation, *Ecclesia in America*: "[T]he globalized economy must be analyzed in light of the principles of social justice, respecting the preferential option for the poor who must be allowed to take their place in such an economy, and the requirements of the international common good."[947] This dramatic shift, identified by Pope John Paul II as programmatic of the New Millennium, represents one of the

---

[944]Administrative Committee of the United States Catholic Conference, *Faithful Citizenship: A Catholic Call to Responsibility* (Washington, DC: USCCB Publications Office, 2003), p. 15.
[945]Citing John Paul II, *Novo Millennio Ineunte* [January 6, 2001], no. 49. in *A.A.S.* 84 (1992), p. 781.
[946]Ibid.
[947]John Paul II, Post-Synodal Apostolic Exhortation "*Ecclesia in America* (January 22, 1999) (no. 55); *A.A.S.* 91 (1999), pp. 790-791.

most amazing paradigm shifts involving the worldwide social question in post-Vatican II Roman Catholicism. Indeed, within a generation, a profound shift occurred in which "the option for the poor [became] and integral part of Catholic social teaching."[948]

The main lines of this profound shift were enunciated with great clarity in the 1986 pastoral letter on Catholic social teaching and the U.S. Economy, "Economic Justice for All":

> *All members of society have a special obligation to the poor and vulnerable.* From the Scriptures and church teaching, we learn that the justice of a society is tested by the treatment of the poor... We are challenged to make a 'fundamental option for the poor' – to speak for the voiceless, to defend the defenseless, to assess lifestyles, policies and social institutions in terms of their impact on the poor. This 'option for the poor' does not mean pitting one group against another, but rather, strengthening the whole community by assisting those who are most vulnerable. As Christians, we are called to respond to the needs of *all* our brothers and sisters, but those with the greatest needs require the greatest response (no. 16).
>
> Such perspectives provide a basis today for what is called a 'preferential option for the poor'(no. 52).
>
> As individuals and as a nation, therefore, we are called to make a fundamental 'option for the poor'... Those who are marginalized and whose rights are denied have privileged claims if society is to provide justice for *all* (no. 87).
>
> The prime purpose of this special commitment to the poor is to enable them to become active participants in the life of society. It is to enable *all* persons to share in and contribute to the common good. The 'option for the poor,' therefore, is not an adversarial slogan that

---

[948]David Boileau, "Some Reflections on the Historical Perspectives of Catholic Social Teaching," in David Boileau, *Roger Aubert: Catholic Social Teaching/An Historical Perspective* (Milwaukee, WI: Marquette University Press, 2003), p. 259.

> pits one group or class against another. Rather it states that the deprivation and powerlessness of the poor wounds the whole community. The extent of their suffering is a measure of how far we are from being a true community of believers. These wounds will be healed only be greater solidarity with the poor and among the poor themselves (no. 88).[949]

During the latter phase of the pontificate of Pope John Paul II, the "preferential option for the poor" gained widespread acceptance as an undergirding principal theme of official Roman Catholic social teaching. Recall that even so conservative theologian as Hans Urs Von Balthasar noted that in Latin America "something absolutely central for Christianity is making its appearance: the option for the poor. Henceforth, this may never be renounced."[950] As the Roman Synod on Evangelization concluded: "Since the Second Vatican Council, the Church has become more aware of its Mission to serve the poor, the oppressed and the outcast"[951] As Juan José Tamayo points out, "The option for the poor has ceased to function as a mere slogan for action. Its place is no longer merely the field of ethics or pastoral theology. It constitutes the hermeneutic and epistemological locus of faith and theology."[952] As Ignacio Ellacuría concluded: "The option for the poor, with all of the pastoral and theological consequences of that option, is one of the most important contributions to the life of the Church Universal to have emerged from the theology of liberation and the Church on our [Latin American] continent."[953] Indeed, it

---

[949]National Conference of Catholic Bishops, "Economic Justice for All": *Pastoral Letter on Catholic Social Teaching and the U.S. Economy* (Washington, DC: USCC Publications Office, 1986), pp. x-xi, 28, 45, 46.
[950]Interviewed in *30 Giorni* (June, 1984), p. 78.
[951]Cited in Ignacio Ellacuría, "The Historicity of Christian Salvation," in Ignacio Ellacuría and Jon Sobrino (eds.), *Mysterium Liberationis*, p. 250.
[952]Juan José Tamayo, "Reception of the Theology of Liberation," in Ellacuría and Sobrino (eds.), *Mysterium Liberationis*, p. 53.
[953]Ignacio Ellacuría, S.J., "The Historicity of Christian Salvation," in Ignacio Ellacuría and Jon Sobrino (eds.), *Mysterium Liberationis*, p. 250.

emerges as the distinctive contribution of the Latin American faith community to the life of the Universal Church.

Walter J. Burghardt, S.J., in a magisterial treatment on the virtue of justice, asserted that at this moment in the Roman Catholic tradition, the "preferential option for the poor" has become one of six fundamental facets of Catholic social teaching: "Not because they are necessarily holier; only because they stand in greater need... The expression may be recent; the reality is an ancient as Exodus."[954] In a summary statement concerning the option for the poor, the sage Father Burghardt concluded:

> The formula did indeed originate within Latin American liberation theology, but it has put its stamp on various levels of the Catholic magisterium. Suggested at the second meeting of the Latin American episcopate at Medellín, Colombia, in 1968, and explicitly adopted during its third meeting in Puebla, Mexico, in 1979, it has been solidly endorsed by John Paul II. It does not glorify poverty, does not canonize the poor. It does involve a new way of viewing reality wherein we live, seeing it not from the standpoint of the powerful and the comfortable but from the perspective of the powerless and the pressured; a new way of reading Scripture, with a preference for those whom Jesus himself favored.[955]

Despite its early contentious history, by the twilight of the Papacy of John Paul II, the preferential option for the poor became solidly ensconced as a pivotal aspect of Catholic social teaching, reaffirming and embodying a love of preference for those most favored by Jesus himself. As such, it can be readily concluded that

---

[954]Walter J. Burghardt, S.J., "Justice Analyzed," in Walter J. Burghardt, S.J., *Justice: A Global Adventure* (Maryknoll, NY: Orbis Books, 2004), p. 26.

[955]Ibid., p. 32. Note that Franciscan moral theologian Kenneth Himes, in an address on "Globalization and Inequality: Perspectives from Catholic Social Teaching" delivered at Boston College on April 18, 2002, indicated: "Catholic Social Teaching identifies four essential elements of a code of ethics for the present globalization: the preferential option for the poor, solidarity, participation and basic human rights." This address was reprinted as "Globalization's Next Phase," in *Origins* 32, no. 2 (May 23, 2002), pp. 17, 19-22.

the distinctive contribution of Latin American theology to the Universal Church and to the world at large is its theological reflection upon the preferential option for the poor, since, as Father Burghardt asserted: "This is what the God of Israel demanded of kings (see Psalm 72); what Jesus persistently preached in his preference for the sinner and the sufferer, the outcast and the oppressed; what Fathers of the Church like Basil and Chrysostom proclaimed to powerful princes and powerless people."[956] By appropriating this remarkable insight, a new vision has been claimed to illumine Catholic Social Teaching in the Third Millennium. In the words of Brazilian Bishop Pedro Casadáliga, "Today the option for the poor is more timely than ever. There are two reasons: There are more of them, both in Latin America, and in all the Third World; and they are ever poorer."[957] Although its acceptance within Roman Catholic social teaching took an arduous path,[958] as its "godfather," Gustavo Gutiérrez, concluded: "The preferential option for the poor has gradually become a central tenet of the Church's teaching."[959] Pope John Paul II, in *Pastores Gregis*, embraced and lent approbation to this remarkable paradigm shift: "... the Church and churches must practice that 'preferential option for the poor' which I have indicated as programmatic for the Third Millennium" (no. 21).[960] As he stated elsewhere: "I have made and I do make this option... I feel it could not be otherwise, since it is the eternal message of the Gospel."[961] Pope John Paul II definitively concluded: "Today

---

[956]Walter J. Burghardt, S.J., "Justice Analyzed," in Burghardt, *Justice*, p. 26.

[957]Cited in Jon Sobrino, S.J., "Preface," *Mysterium Liberationis*, p. xiv.

[958]See, especially, Alfred T. Hennelly, S.J., "The Red-Hot Issue: Liberation Theology," in *America* (January 28, 1986) pp. 425-428, for some of the testier moments experienced in this struggle n the mid-1980's.

[959]Daniel Hartnett, "Remembering the Poor: An Interview with Gustavo Gutiérrez," p. 14.

[960]See also p. 291, n. 945 for the fuller excerpt of the original text, dated October 16, 2003, most readily accessible at the Vatican website, `www.vatican.va`, under "Pope John Paul II/Apostolic Exhortations."

[961]John Paul II, "Discourse to the Cardinals and Prelates of the Roman Curia," in *Osservatore Romano* (January 21, 1985), p. 9. Similarly, in the Apostolic Constitution *Tertio Millennio Adveniente* (10/11/94), John Paul II noted: "How can we not emphasize more decisively the preferential option

this option is discussed and reaffirmed in a new context. The option for the poor is the choice of the Gospel: It is the option of Christ and for Christ… And the option for the poor is at the same time an option for Christ, in whatever century, whatever situation, in whatever country it is made."[962]

---

for the poor and marginalized?" (no. 51), in *Preparing for the Year 2000* (Rome: Orbi et Urbi Communications, 1997 edition), p. 57.

[962]John Paul II, "Address to the '*Comunità di Sant' Egidio*,' in *Osservatore Romano* (December 14, 1986), p. 6. In his Apostolic Letter, *Mane Nobiscum Domine* (10/7/04), Pope John Paul II made the explicit link between the liturgy and social justice. He stressed that faith communities ought to "respond with fraternal solicitude to one of the many forms of poverty in our present world... I think, for example, of the tragedy of hunger which plagues hundreds of millions of human beings, the diseases which afflict developing countries, the loneliness of the elderly, the hardships faced by the unemployed, the struggles of immigrants. These are evils which are present – albeit to a different degree – even in areas of immense wealth. We cannot delude ourselves: by our mutual love and, in particular, by our concern for those in need we will be recognized as the true followers of Christ (cf. JN 13:35; MT 25:41-46). This will be the criterion by which the authenticity of our Eucharist celebrations is judged" (no. 28). The full text of the "Apostolic Letter *Mane Nobiscum Domine* of the Holy Father John Paul II to the Bishops, Clergy and Faithful for the Year of the Eucharist" is accessible at: www.vatican.va/john_paulii/apost_letters/documents.

Bibliography

Books

A Century of Catholic Social Teaching: A Common Heritage, A Continuing Challenge. Washington, DC: United States Catholic Conference, 1990.

André-Vincent, Ph.-I. *La Doctrine Sociale de Jean Paul II*. Paris: Editions France-Empire, 1983.

Abbott, S.J., Walter, ed. *The Documents of Vatican II.* NY: Herder & Herder, 1966.

Abell, Aaron I. *American Catholic Thought on Social Questions*. Indianapolis, IN: Bobbs-Merrill, 1962.

Administrative Board, United States Catholic Conference. *Political Responsibility: Revitalizing American Democracy*. Washington, DC: United States Catholic Conference, 1991.

Administrative Board, United States Catholic Conference. *Putting Children and Family First: A Challenge for Our Church, Nation and World.* Washington, DC: United States Catholic Conference, 1992.

Adriance, Madeleine. *The Option for the Poor in Brazilian Catholicism: A Sociological Analysis*. Kansas City, MO: Sheed & Ward, 1986.

Aland, Kurt. *A History of Christianity From the Reformation the Present.* Philadelphia: Fortress Press, 1986 revision.

Alberigo, Giuseppe, ed. *Les Eglises aprés Vatican II.* Paris: Beauchesne, 1981.

Alberigo, Giuseppe, Jossua, Jean-Pierre, and Komonchak, Joseph A. eds. *The Reception of Vatican II.* Washington, DC: Catholic University of America Press, 1987.

Alberigo, Angelina and Giuseppe, eds. *Giovanni XXIII, Profezia nella Fedelta.* Brescia: Editrice Queriniana, 1978.

Alberigo, Giuseppe and Melloni, Alberto. *Fede Profezia: Studi du Giovanni XXIII e sul Vaticano*. Brescia: Editrice Queriniana, 1984.

Alfaro, S.J., Juan. *Theology of Justice in the World.* Rome: Pontifical Commission on Justice and Peace, 1973.

Anderson, Frank, ed. *Council Daybook, Vatican II, Sessions I and II.* Washington, DC: United States Catholic Conference, 1965.

Antoncich, Ricardo. *Christians in the Face of Injustice: A Latin American Reading of Catholic Social Teaching*. Maryknoll, NY: Orbis Books, 1987.

______. *El tema de la liberación en Medellín y el Sinodo de 1974*. Lima: Comisión Episcopal de Acción Social, 1975.

Araya, Victorio. *God of the Poor: The Mystery of God in Latin American Liberation Theology*. Maryknoll, NY: Orbis Books, 1988.

Arns, Paulo Evaristo, *et al*. *Opçao pelos pobres: educaçao e nova sociedade*. São Paulo: Loyola, 1983.

Aubert, Roger and John Dolan, eds. *The Church Between Revolution and Restoration.* NY Crossroad, 1989.

Aubert, Roger, *et al.*, eds. *The Church in a Secularized Society*. NY: Paulist Press, 1978.

Aubert, Roger, and John Dolan, eds. *The Church in the Age of Liberalism*. NY: Crossroad, 1989.

Azzi, Riolando. *O Catolicismo Popular no Brasil: Aspectos Historicos*. Petropolis, Brazil Editorial Vozes, 1978.

Balasuriya, O.M.I., Tissa. *The Eucharist and Human Liberation*. Maryknoll, NY: Orbis Books, 1979.

Barriero, A. *Os pobres e o Reino. Do Evangelho at Joaõ Paulo II.* São Paulo: Loyola, 1983.

Baruana, O.F.M., Guillermo, ed. *La Iglesia del Vaticano II: Estudios en torno a la Constitución conciliar sobre la Iglesia.* Barcelona: Juan Flors, 1966.

Baum, Gregory. *The Priority of Labor: A Commentary on Laborem Excercens.* NY: Paulist Press, 1986.

Baum, Gregory and Cameron, Donald, eds. *Ethics and Economics: Canada's Catholic Bishops on the Economic Crisis.* Toronto: Lorimer, 1984.

Baum, Gregory and Ellsberg, Robert, eds. *The Logic of Solidarity: Commentaries on John Paul II's Encyclical "On Social Concern".* Maryknoll, New York: Orbis Books, 1989.

Benigni, Mario and Zanchi, Goffredo. *John XXIII: The Biography.* Boston, MA: Pauline Books & Media, 2001.

Bernadin, Joseph L. *John Paul II: A Panaroma of His Teachings.* NY: New City Press, 1989.

Bernstein, Carl and Politi, Marco. *His Holiness: John Paul II the Hidden History of Our Time.* NY: Doubleday, 1996.

Berryman, Phillip. *Liberation Theology: Essential Facts About the Revolutionary Movement in Latin America – And Beyond.* NY: Pantheon Books, 1987.

Betto, Frei. *17 días de la Iglesia latinoamericana: diaro de Puebla.* Mexico City: Centro de Reflexión Teológica, 1979.

Between Honesty and Hope: Documents From and About the Church in Latin America, issued by the Peruvian Bishops' Commission for Social Action. Maryknoll, NY: Maryknoll Publications, 1970.

Blardone, Georges, *et al.* *L'Eglise des Pauvres: des Riches.* Paris: Editions du Cerf, 1965.

Boff, Clodovis. *Agente Pastoral e Povo.* Petropolis, Brazil: Editorial Vozes, 1980.

________. *Theology and Praxis: Epistemological Foundations.* Maryknoll, NY: Orbis Books, 1987.

Boff, Clodovis and Pixley, George. *The Bible, the Church, and the Poor.* Maryknoll, NY: Orbis Books, 1989.

Boff, Leonardo. *New Evangelization: Good News to the Poor.* Maryknoll, NY: Orbis Books, 1991.

________. *Church: Charism and Power.* NY: Crossroad, 1985.

_______. *Faith on the Edge: Religion and Marginalized Existence.* San Francisco: Harper & Row, 1989.

_______. *Liberating Grace.* Maryknoll, NY: Orbis Books, 1979.

_______. *New Evangelization.* Maryknoll, NY: Orbis Books, 1991.

_______. *When Theology Listens to the Poor.* San Francisco: Harper & Row, 1988.

Boff, Leonardo and Boff, Clodovis. *Introducing Liberation Theology.* Maryknoll, NY: Orbis Books, 1987.

_______. *Liberation Theology: From Confrontation to Dialogue.* San Francisco: Harper & Row, 1986.

Boff, Leonardo and Elizondo, Virgil, eds. *1492-1992: The Voice of the Victims.* London: S.C.M. Press, 1990.

______. *Option for the Poor: Challenge for the Rich Countries.* Edinburgh: T. & T. Clark, Ltd., 1986.

Boff, Leonardo and Boff, Clodovis. *Salvation and Liberation.* Maryknoll, NY: Orbis Books, 1984.

Boff, Leonardo and Elizondo, Virgil, eds. *The People of God Amidst the Poor.* Edinburgh: T. & T. Clark, 1984.

Bonino, José Míguez. *Towards a Christian Political Ethics.* London: SCM Press, 1983.

Bonnot, Bernard R. *Pope John XXIII: Model and Mentor for Leaders.* Staten Island, NY. St. Paul's Media, 2003.

Bottenkotter, Thomas. *A Concise History of the Catholic Church.* NY: Doubleday Image Books, 1990 revision.

Brazilian Bishops and Religious Superiors of the Northeast. *Eu Ouvi os Clamores do Meu Povo.* Salvador, Brazil: Editora Beneditina, 1973.

Bravo, Rubén Sierra. *Doctrina Social y Economica de los Padres de la Iglesia.* Madrid: Compi, 1967.

Brockman, S.J., James R. *Romero: A Life.* Maryknoll, NY: Orbis Books, 1989.

Brockman, S.J., James R., ed. *The Violence of Love: The Pastoral Wisdom of Archbishop Romero.* San Francisco: Harper & Row, 1988.

Brown, Robert McAfee. *Gustavo Gutiérrez: An Introduction to Liberation Theology.* Maryknoll, NY: Orbis Books, 1990.

Bruneau, Thomas. *The Political Transformation of the Brazilian Church.* London: Cambridge University Press, 1974.

Burghardt, S.J., Walter J., *Justice: A Global Adventure.* Maryknoll, NY: Orbis Books, 2004.

Bühlmann, Walbert, O.F.M. Cap. *Dreaming About the Church.* Kansas City, MO: Sheed & Ward, 1987.

_________. *The Coming of the Third Church.* Maryknoll, NY: Orbis Books, 1977.

Butler, O.S.B., Christopher. *The Theology of Vatican II.* Westminster, MD: Christian Classics, 1981.

Cabestrero, Teofilo. *Los teologos de la liberación en Puebla.* Madrid: PPC Editorial, 1979.

Calvez, S.J., Jean Yves. *Faith and Justice: The Social Dimension of Evangelization.* St. Louis Institute of Jesuit Sources, 1991.

_________. *The Social Thought of John XXIII: Mater et Magistra.* London: Burns & Oates, 1964.

Calvez, S.J., Jean Yves and Perrin, S.J., Jacques. *The Church and Social Justice: The Social Teaching of the Popes From Leo XIII to Pius XII.* Chicago: Henry Regnery Company, 1961.

Câmara, Helder. *The Church and Colonialism.* London: Geoffrey Chapman, 1969.

Camp, Richard L. *The Papal Ideology of Social Reform: A Study in Historical Development, 1878-1967.* Leiden: E. J. Brill, 1969.

Caramuru de Barros, Raimundo. *Brasil: Uma Igreja em Renovaçao.* Petropolis, Brazil: Editorial Vozes, 1968.

Capovilla, Loris Francesco, ed. *Pope John XXIII: Letters to His Family.* London: Geoffrey Chapman, 1970.

Capovilla, Loris Francesco, ed. *Vent' Anni dalla Elezione di Giovanni XXIII.* Rome: Storia e Letteratura, 1978.

Caprile, S. J. *Paulo VI, Discorsi e Documenti sul Concilio.* Brescia: *Instituto Paulo VI,* 1986.

Carlen, I.H.M., Claudia, ed. *The Papal Encyclicals*, 5 vols. Wilmington, NC: McGrath, 1981.

Carrier, Harvé. *Gospel Message and Human Cultures: From Leo XIII to John Paul II.* Pittsburgh Duquesne University Press, 1989.

________. *The Social Doctrine of the Church Revisited: A Guidefor Study.* Vatican City Pontifical Council for Justice and Peace, 1990.

Casaldáliga, Pedro. *In Pursuit of the Kingdom: Writings 1968 – 1988.* Maryknoll, NY: Orbis Books, 1990.

________. *Prophets in Combat: The Nicaraguan Journal of Bishop Pedro Casaldáliga.* Oak Park, IL: Myer Stone Books, 1987.

Catechism of the Catholic Church. NY: Doubleday Image. 1995 edition.

Charles, Roger with Maclaren, Drostan. *The Social Teaching of Vatican II: Its Origin and Development.* San Francisco: Ignatius Press, 1982.

Chenu, O.P., Marie Dominique. *La dottrina sociale della Chiesa: origine e sviluppo, 1891- 1971*. Brescia: Editrice Queriniana, 1977.

_______. *La "Doctrine Sociale" du l'Eglise comme Idéologie*. Paris: Editions du Cerf, 1979.

Chopp, Rebecca. *The Power to Speak.* NY: Crossroad, 1989.

Cleary, O.P., Edward L. *Crisis and Change: The Church in Latin America Today.* Maryknoll, NY: Orbis Books, 1985.

Cleary, O.P., Edward L., ed. *Born of the Poor: The Latin American Church Since Medellín.* Notre Dame: University of Notre Dame Press, 1990.

Cleary, O.P., Edward L., ed. *Path from Puebla: Significant Documents of the Latin American Bishops Since 1979.* Washington, D.C.: United States Catholic Conference, 1989.

Coleman, S.J., John A., ed. *One Hundred Years of Catholic Social Thought.* Maryknoll, NY: Orbis Books, 1991.

Coleman, John and Baum, Gregory. *Rerum Novarum: A Hundred Years of Catholic Social Teaching.* London: SCM Press, 1991.

Colonnese, Louis Michael, ed. *The Church in the Present-Day Transformation of Latin America in the Light of the Council* [Medellín Documents]. Washington, DC: Latin American Bureau, United States Catholic Conference, 1969.

Conferencia Nacional dos Bispos do Brasil (CNBB). *Comunicaçao Pastoral ao Povo de Deus*. Sao Paulo: Edicoes Paulinas, 1977.

Congar, O.P., Yves. *Le Concile Vatican II. Son Eglise, Peuple de Dieu et Corps du Christ.* Paris Editions du Cerf, 1984.

_______. *Power and Poverty in the Church.* Baltimore: Helicon, 1965.

_______. *Report From the Council: The First Session of Vatican II.* London: Geoffrey Chapman, 1963.

Congregation for Catholic Education. *Guidelines for the Study and Teaching of the Church's Social Doctrine in the Formation of Priests.* Washington, DC: United States Catholic Conference, 1988.

Cooke, Bernard, ed. *The Papacy and the Church in the United States.* NY: Paulist Press, 1989.

Contemporary Catholic Social Teaching. Washington, DC: United States Catholic Conference, 1991.

Cox, Harvey. *The Silencing of Leonardo Boff: The Vatican and the Future of World Christianity.* Oak Park, IL: Meyer Stone Books, 1988.

Cottier, Georges, *et al.* *Eglise et Pauvreté.* Paris: Editions du Cerf, 1965.

Cronin, S.S., John F. *Catholic Social Action.* Milwaukee: Bruce, 1948.

_______. *Catholic Social Principles.* Milwaukee: Bruce, 1950.

Cronin, S.S., John F., *et al.*, eds. *The Encyclicals and Other Messages of John XXIII.* Washington, DC: T.P.S. Press, 1964.

Curran, Charles E. *Directions in Catholic Social Ethics.* Notre Dame, IN: University of Notre Dame Press, 1985.

______. *Tensions in Moral Theology.* Notre Dame, IN: University of Notre Dame Press, 1988.

Curran, Charles E. and McCormick, S.J., Richard A. (eds.). *John Paul II and Moral Theology.* NY: Paulist Press, 1998.

_____. *Readings in Moral Theology No. 5, Official Catholic Teaching.* NY: Paulist Press, 1986.

Daniel-Rops, Henri. *The Church in an Age of Revolution: 1789 – 1870.* NY: Doubleday Image Books, 1967.

DeBroucker, José. *Dom Helder Câmara: The Violence of a Peacemaker.* Maryknoll, NY: Orbis Books, 1970.

________. *Dom Helder Câmara: The Conversions of a Bishop*. NY: Collins, 1979.

Delgado, Jesús. *Oscar A. Romero: Biografia*. Madrid: Ediciones Paulinas, 1986.

Los Derechos humanos hoy en Latinoamerica: las declaraciones y documentos de las iglesias latinoamericanas, de la Iglesia Universal, y de las Naciones Unidas. Lima: Centro de Proyección Cristiana, 1980.

Deretz, J. and Nocent, O.S.B., Adrian. *Dictionary of the Council*. Washington, DC: Corpus Books, 1968.

Documents of the Thirty-Second General Congregation of the Society of Jesus. Washington, DC The Jesuit Conference, 1975.

Dorr, Donal. *Option for the Poor: A Hundred Years of Vatican Teaching.* Maryknoll, NY: Orbis Books, 1992 revision.

_______. *The Social Justice Agenda: Justice, Ecology, Power and the Church.* Maryknoll, NY: Orbis Books, 1991.

Douglas, R. Bruce, ed. *The Deeper Meaning of Economic Life: Critical Essays on the U.S. Catholic Bishops' Pastoral Letter on the Economy*. Washington, DC: Georgetown University Press, 1986.

Drummond, William. *Social Justice.* Milwaukee: Bruce Publishing Company, 1955.

Dulles, S.J., Avery. *A Church to Believe In*. NY: Crossroad, 1982.

_____. *The Splendor of Faith: Theological Vision of Pope John Paul II*. NY: Herder & Herder, 2003 revision.

______. *The Reshaping of Catholicism: Current Challenges in the Theology of the Church*. San Francisco: Harper & Row, 1988.

Dussel, Enrique. *De Medellín a Puebla: Una decada de sangre y esperanza.* Mexico City: CEE-Edicol, 1979.

_____. *Hipotesis para una historia de la teologia en América Latina*. Bogotá: Indo-American Press, 1985.

______. *Historia de la Iglesia en America Latina: coloniaje y liberación (1492-1983)*. Madrid: Esquila Missional, 1983.

_____. *History and the Theology of Liberation: A Latin American Perspective*. Maryknoll, NY: Orbis Books, 1976.

Eagleson, John and Sharper, Philip, eds. *Puebla and Beyond*. Maryknoll, NY: Orbis Books, 1979.

Echegaray, Hugo. *The Practice of Jesus*. Maryknoll, NY: Orbis Books, 1984.

Economic Justice for All: Pastoral Letter on Catholic Social Teaching and the U.S. Economy. Washington, DC: United States Catholic Conference, 1986.

Ellacuría, Ignacio, S.J. and Sobrino, Jon, S.J. (eds.). *Mysterium Liberationis: Fundamental Concepts of Liberation Theology*. Maryknoll, NY: Orbis Books, 1993.

Ellis, Marc H. and Maduro, Otto, eds. *The Future of Liberation Theology: Essays in Honor of Gustavo Gutiérrez*. Maryknoll, NY: Orbis Books, 1989.

____. *Expanding the View: Gustavo Gutiérrez and the Future of Liberation Theology*. Maryknoll, NY: Orbis Books, 1990.

Erdozaín, Plácido. *Archbishop Romero: Martyr of Salvador*. Maryknoll, NY: Orbis Books, 1981.

Erhueh, Anthony. *Vatican II: Image of God in Man: An Inquiry Into the Theological Foundations and Significance of Human Dignity in the Pastoral Constitution on the Church in the Modern World, "Gaudium et Spes"*. Rome: Urbaniana University Press, 1987.

Fabella, Virginia, ed. *Asia's Struggle for Full Humanity*. Maryknoll, NY: Orbis Books, 1980.

Fabella, Virginia and Torres, Sergio, eds. *Irruption of the Third World*. Maryknoll, NY: Orbis Books, 1983.

_____. *Doing Theology in a Divided World*. Maryknoll, NY: Orbis Books, 1985.

Fagin, S.J., Gerald M. *Vatican II: Open Questions and New Horizons*. Wilmington, DE: Michael Glazier, 1984.

Falconi, Carlo. *Pope John and His Council*. London: Weidenfeld and Nicolson, 1964.

Fanfani, Amintore. *Catechism of Catholic Social Teaching*. Westminster, MD: Newman Press, 1960.

Farrell, Gerardo T. *Doctrina Social de la Iglesia*. Buenos Aires: Editorial Guadalupe, 1982.

Ferm, Deane William. *Third World Liberation Theologies: An Introductory Survey*. Maryknoll, NY: Orbis Books, 1986.

Fesquet, Henri. *The Drama of Vatican II: The Ecumenical Council/ June 1962 – December 1965*. New York: Random House, 1967.

Filowski, Julian and McDonagh, Francis, eds. *Reflections on Puebla*. London: Catholic Institute for International Relations, 1980.

Flannery, O.P., Austin. *Vatican II: More Post-Documents*. Northport, NY: Costello Publishing Co., 1982.

Flannery, O.P., Austin, ed. *Evangelization Today*. Northport, NY: Costello Publishing Co., 1977.

Fremantle, Anne, ed. *The Papal Encyclicals in Their Historical Context*. NY: Mentor-Omega Books, 1963 revision.

Freire, Paulo. *Concientizacíon*. Bogotá, Colombia: Ediciones Paulinas, 1974.

________. *Pedagogy of the Oppressed*. NY: Herder & Herder, 1970.

Fuechtman, Thomas, ed. *Joseph Cardinal Bernardin/Consistent Ethic of Life*. Chicago: Loyola University Press, 1988.

Fülöp-Miller, René. *Leo XIII and Our Times*. London: Longmans, Green & Company, 1937.

Galdámez, Pablo. *Faith of a People: The Story of a Christian Community in El Salvador, 1970-1980*. Maryknoll, NY: Orbis Books, 1986.

Galilea, Segundo. *La teologia de la liberación después de Puebla*. Bogotá: Indo-American Press Service, 1979.

Galli, Mario von. *The Council and the Future*. NY: McGraw-Hill, 1966.

Garcia, Ismael. *Justice in Latin American Theology of Liberation*. Atlanta: John Knox Press, 1987.

Gauthier, Paul. *Christ, the Church, and the Poor*. Westminster, MD: Newman Press, 1965.

______. *Nazareth Diary*. London: Geoffrey Chapman, 1966.

Geffré, Claude and Jossua, Jean-Pierre, eds. *1789: The French Revolution and the Church*. Edinburgh: T. & T. Clark, Ltd., 1989.

Geffré, Claude and Gutiérrez, Gustavo, eds. *The Mystical and Political Dimension of the Christian Faith*. NY: Herder & Herder, 1974.

Gelin, Albert. *The Poor of Yahweh*. Collegeville, MN: Liturgical Press, 1964.

Gheddo, Peter. *Why Is the Third World Poor?* Maryknoll, NY: Orbis Books, 1973.

Gibbons, S.J., William J., ed. *Seven Great Encyclicals*. NY: Paulist Press, 1963 revision.

Gibellini, Rosino. *The Liberation Theology Debate*. Maryknoll, NY: Orbis Books, 1988.

Gibellini, Rosino, ed. *Frontiers of Theology in Latin America*. Maryknoll, NY: Orbis Books, 1979.

Gilson, Etienne. *The Church Speaks to the Modern World: The Social Teachings of Leo XIII*. NY: Doubleday Image Books, 1954.

Gonzalez Ruíz, José María. *Pobreza y Promoción Humana*. Madrid: Nova Terra, 1966.

Greeley, Andrew M. *The Making of the Popes 1978.* Kansas City, MO: Andrews & McMeel, 1979.

Greinbäch, Norbert and Müller, Alois, eds. *The Poor and the Church.* NY: Seabury Press, 1977.

Gremillion, Joseph, ed. *The Gospel of Peace and Justice: Catholic Social Teaching Since Pope John.* Maryknoll, NY: Orbis Books, 1976.

Grootaers, Jan. *De Vatican II a Jean Paul II, Le Grand Tournant de l'Eglise Catholique.* Paris: le Centurion, 1981.

Group 2000, eds. *The Church Today: Commentaries on the Pastoral Constitution on the Church in the Modern World.* NY: Paulist/Newman Press, 1968.

Guitton, Jean. *The Pope Speaks: Dialogues of Paul VI.* NY: Meredith Press, 1968.

Gutiérrez, Gustavo. *A Theology of Liberation: History, Politics, and Salvation.* Maryknoll, NY: Orbis Books, 1988 revision.

_____. *Los pobres y la liberación en Puebla.* Bogotá: Indo-American Press Service, 1979.

_____. *The God of Life.* Maryknoll, NY: Orbis Books, 1991.

_____. *The Power of the Poor in History.* Maryknoll, NY: Orbis Books, 1983.

_____. *The Truth Shall Make You Free.* Maryknoll, NY: Orbis Books, 1990.

Gutiérrez, Gustavo and Shaull, Richard. *Liberation and Change.* Atlanta: John Knox Press, 1977.

Habiger, Matthew. *Papal Teaching on Private Property, 1891 to 1981.* Lanham, MD: University Press of America, 1990.

Hacala, S.J., Joseph R. and Jennings, James R. *Principles, Prophecy and a Pastoral Response: An Overview of Modern Catholic Social Teaching.* Washington, DC: Campaign for Human Development, United States Catholic Conference, 1991.

Haight, S.J., Roger. *An Alternative Vision: An Interpretation of Liberation Theology*. NY: Paulist Press, 1985.

Hales, E. E. Y. *The Catholic Church in the Modern World: A Survey From the French Revolution to the Present*. Garden City, NY: Hanover House, 1958.

______. *Pio Nono: A Study in European Politics and the Nineteenth Century*. NY: P. J. Kenedy & Sons, 1954.

_____. *Pope John and His Revolution*. London: Eyre and Spottiswoode, 1965.

Harte, C.Ss.R., Thomas J. *Papal Social Principles: A Guide and Digest*. Milwaukee: Bruce Publishing Co., 1956.

Hastings, Adrian. *Modern Catholicism: Vatican II and After*. NY: Oxford University Press, 1991.

Hatch, Alden. *A Man Named John: The Life of Pope John XXIII*. NY: Hawthorn Books, 1963.

Haughey, S.J., John C., ed. *The Faith That Does Justice: Examining the Christian Sources for Social Change*. NY: Paulist Press, 1977.

Hebblethwaite, Peter. *Pope John XXIII: Shepherd of the Modern World*. Garden City, NY: Doubleday, 1985.

_______. *Paul VI: The First Modern Pope*. NY: Paulist Press, 1993.

________. *The Christian-Marxist Dialogue: Beginnings, Present Status, and Beyond.* NY: Paulist Press, 1977.

________. *Synod Extraordinary*. Garden City, NY: Doubleday & Co., 1986.

________. *The Year of Three Popes*. Cleveland, OH: Collins, 1979.

Hebblethwaite, Peter and Kaufmann, Ludwig. *John Paul II: A Pictorial Biography*. NY: McGraw-Hill, 1979.

Heckel, Roger. *The Theme of Liberation*. Rome: Pontifical Commission on Justice and Peace, 1980.

_____. *The Social Teaching of John Paul II.* Vatican City: Pontifical Commission *Iustitia et Pax*, 1980.

_____. *The Social Teaching of John Paul II: The Use of the Expression "Social Doctrine" of the Church.* Vatican City: Pontifical Commission *Iustitia et Pax*, 1980.

Hegy, Pierre, ed. *The Church in the Nineties: Its Legacy, Its Future*. Collegeville, MN: Liturgical Press, 1993.

Hengel, Martin. *Property and Riches in the Early Church.* Philadelphia: Fortress Press, 1974.

Hennelly, S.J., Alfred T. *Theology for a Liberating Church: The New Praxis of Freedom.* Washington, DC: Georgetown University Press, 1989.

Hennelly, S.J., Alfred T., ed. *Liberation Theology: A Documentary History.* Maryknoll, NY: Orbis Books, 1990.

_____. *Santo Domingo and Beyond Documents and Commentaries From The Fourth Conference of Latin American Bishops.* Maryknoll, NY: Orbis Books, 1993.

Hennelly, S.J., Alfred T. and Langan, S.J., John, eds. *Human Rights in the Americas: The Struggle for Consensus.* Washington, DC: Georgetown University Press, 1982.

Henriot, S.J., Peter J. *Catholic Social Teaching: Our Best Kept Secret.* Maryknoll, NY: Orbis Books, 1992 revision.

________. *Opting for the Poor: A Challenge for North Americans.* Washington, DC: Center for Concern, 1990.

Hollenbach, S.J., David. *Claims in Conflict: Retreiving and Renewing the Catholic Human Rights Tradition.* NY: Paulist Press, 1979.

_______. *Justice, Peace, and Human Rights: American Catholic Social Ethics in a Pluralistic World.* NY: Crossroad, 1988.

Hollis, Christopher. *Christianity and Economics.* NY: Hawthorne Books, 1961.

Holmes, J. Derek and Bernard W. Bickers. *A Short History of the Catholic Church.* London: Burns & Oates, 1987 edition.

Holmes, J. Derek. *The Papacy in the Modern World.* NY: Crossroad, 1981.

_____. *The Triumph of the Holy See: A Short History of the Papacy in Nineteenth Century Europe.* London: Burns & Oates, 1978.

Hoppe, O.F.M., Leslie J. *Being Poor: A Biblical Study.* Wilmington, DE: Michael Glazier, 1987.

Houck, John W. and Williams, C.S.C., Oliver F. *Co-Creation and Capitalism: John Paul II's Laborem Exercens.* Washington, DC: University Press of America, 1983.

Irupción y caminar de la Iglesia de los pobres: presencia de Medellín. Lima: Instituto Bartolomé de las Casas, 1989.

Jarlot, Georges, *Doctrine Pontificale et Histoire: L'ensiegnement social de Léon XIII, Pie X et Benoit XV vu dans son ambiance historique (1878-1922).* Rome: Presses de L'Université Grégorienne, 1964.

Jedin, Hubert and Dolan, John, eds. *History of the Church: The Church in the Modern Age*, Vol. 10. NY: Crossroad, 1981.

Jennings, Anthony. *Our Response to the Poorest of the World.* Oxford: Pergamon Press, 1984.

Jaén, S.J., Nestor. *Toward a Liberation Spirituality* Chicago: Loyola University Press, 1991.

John Paul II For Peace in the Middle East. Vatican City: Libreria Editrice Vaticana, 1991.

John Paul II. *Addresses and Homilies in Brazil.* Washington, DC: United States Catholic Conference, 1980.

______. *Brazil: Journey in Light of the Eucharist.* Boston, MA: St. Paul Editions, 1980.

_____. *Catechesi Tradendae/ On Catechesis in Our Time*. Boston: St. Paul Editions, 1980.

_____. *Centesimus Annus*. Dublin: Veritas Publications, 1991.

_____. *Pilgrim of Peace: The Collected Speeches of John II in Ireland and the United States*. NY: Farrar, Strauss, Giroux, 1980.

______. *Pronunciamentos do Papa no Brasil*. Sao Paulo: Loyola, 1980.

_____. *Redemptoris Mater*. Washington, DC: United States Catholic Conference, 1987.

John Paul II, *et al*. *Reflections on Puebla*. London: CIIR, 1980.

Johnson, Paul. *Pope John XXIII*. Boston: Little, Brown, 1974.

Justice in the World. Washington, DC: United States Catholic Conference, 1972.

Kaiser, Robert. *Inside the Council*. London: Burns & Oates, 1963.

Keogh, Dermot, ed. *Church and Politics in Latin America*. NY: St. Martin's Press, 1990.

Kirby, Peadar. *Lessons in Liberation: The Church in America*. Dublin: Dominican Publications, 1981.

Kirwan, Joseph. *Rerum Novarum: Centenary Study Edition*. London: Catholic Truth Society, 1991.

______. *The Social Thought of John XXIII*. Oxford: Catholic Social Guild, 1964.

Klaiber, S.J., Jeffrey. *The Catholic Church in Peru*. Washington, DC: Catholic University of America Press, 1992.

Kloppenburg, O.F.M., Boavantura. *Concilio Vaticano II* 5 vols. Petropolis, Brazil: Editorial Vozes, 1966.

____. *Puebla: Opción Preferencial por los Pobres*. Bogotá, Colombia: Ediciones Paulinas, 1979.

________. *The Ecclesiology of Vatican* II. Chicago: Franciscan Herald Press, 1974.

Küng, Hans. *The Council in Action: Reflections on the Second Vatican Council.* NY: Sheed & Ward, 1963.

Küng, Hans, Congar, O.P., Yves and O'Hanlon, S.J., Daniel, eds. *Council Speeches of Vatican II.* Glen Rock, NJ: Paulist Press, 1964.

Land, Philip S. *An Overview: Justice in the World.* Vatican City: Pontifical Commission Justice & Peace, 1975.

Lane, Dermot. *Foundations for a Social Theory: Praxis, and Salvation.* NY: Paulist Press, 1984.

Lange, Martin and Iblacker, Reinhold. *Witnesses of Hope: The Persecution of Christians in Latin America.* Maryknoll, NY: Orbis Books, 1981.

Larrain, Manuel. *Desarollo. Exito o Fracaso en Amèrica Latina.* Santiago de Chile: Ediciones Mundo, 1965.

_____. *Lettre Pastorale sur le Développement et la Paix.* Paris: Pax Christi, 1965.

Latourelle, René, ed. *Vatican II: Assessments and Perspectives/ Twenty-Five Years After (1962-1987)* Vol. 2. NY: Paulist Press, 1989.

Latourelle, René, ed. *Vatican II: Assessments and Perspectives/ Twenty-Five Years After (1962-1987)* Vol. 3. NY: Paulist Press, 1989.

Latourette, Kenneth Scott. *A History of Christianity: Volume II/ A.D. 1500 – A.D. 1975.* San Francisco: Harper & Row, 1975 revision.

______. *The Nineteenth Century in Europe: Background and the Roman Catholic Phase.* Grand Rapids, MI: Zondervan Publishing House, 1969 edition.

Laurentin, René. *Liberation, Development and Salvation.* Maryknoll, NY: Orbis Books, 1972.

Lercaro, Giacomo. *Per la forza dello Spirito. Conciliari.* Bologna: Edizio di Dehoniane, 1984.

Lercaro, Giacomo and DeRosa, Gabrielle. *John XXIII: Simpleton or Saint?* Chicago: Regnery, 1967.

Lernoux, Penny. *Cry of the People: The Struggle for Human Rights in Latin America.* NY: Penguin Books, 1982.

_____. *People of God: The Struggle for World Catholicism.* NY: Penguin Books, 1989.

Levine, Daniel. *Religion and Politics in Latin America: The Catholic Church in Venezuela and Colombia.* Princeton: Princeton University Press, 1981.

Levine, Daniel, ed. *Churches and Politics in Latin America.* Beverly Hills: SAGE Publications, 1980.

_____. *Religion and Political Conflict in Latin America.* Chapel Hill, NC: University of North Carolina Press, 1986.

Lofink, S.J., Norbert. *Option for the Poor: the Basic of Liberation Theology on the Light of the Bible.* Berkeley, CA: BIBAL Press, 1987.

Lopez Trujillo, Alfonso. *Opciones e interpretaciones a la luz de Puebla.* Medellín: Consejo Episcopal Latinoamericano, 1980.

Los Episcopos Latinoamericanos entre Medellín y Puebla: documentos episcopales 1968-1978. San Salvador: UCA Editores, 1978.

MacEoin, Gary. *Central America's Options: Death or Life.* Kansas City, MO: Sheed & Ward, 1988.

MacEoin, Gary and Riley, Nivita. *Puebla: A Church Being Born.* NY: Paulist Press, 1980.

Mainwaring, Scott. *The Catholic Church and the Politics of Brazil, 1916-1965.* Stanford, CA: Stanford University Press, 1986.

Maríns, José. *Realidad y praxis en las pastoral latinoamericana.* Bogotá: Ediciones Paulinas, 1976.

Masse, Benjamin L. *Justice for All: An Introduction to the Social Teaching of the Catholic Church.* Milwaukee: Bruce, 1964.

McCool, S.J., Gerald A. *Catholic Theology in the Nineteenth Century The Quest for a Unitary Method.* NY: Seabury Press, 1977.

McGovern, S.J., Arthur F. *Liberation Theology and Its Critics: Towards and Assessment.* Maryknoll, NY: Orbis Books, 1989.

______. *Marxism: An American Christian Perspective.* Maryknoll, NY: Orbis Books, 1980.

McLaughlin, C.S.B., Terence P., ed. *The Church and the Reconstruction of the Modern World: The Social Encyclicals of Pope Pius XI.* Garden City, NY: Doubleday Image Books, 1957.

Meléndez, Guillermo. *Seeds of Promise: The Prophetic Church in Central America.* NY: Friendship Press, 1990.

Metraux, Guy and Crouzet, François, eds. *Religion and the Promise of the Twentieth Century.* NY: New American Library/Mentor Books, 1965.

Metz, Johannes Baptist. *Faith in History and Society.* NY: Crossroad, 1980.

____. *The Church in the World.* London: SCM Press, 1968.

____. *The Emergent Church.* NY: Crossroad, 1985.

Metz, Johannes Baptist, ed. *Foundational Theology: Faith and the World of Politics.* Edinburgh: T. & T. Clark, 1968.

Mieth, Dietmar, and Jacques Pohier, eds. *Christian Ethics and Economics: The North – South Conflict.* Edinburgh: T. & T. Clark, Ltd., 1980.

Miller, I.H.M., Amata. *Shaping a New World: The Catholic Social Justice Tradition, 1891-1991.* Washington, DC: NETWORK, 1991.

Miller, C.S.C., John H., ed. *Vatican II: An Interfaith Appraisal.* Notre Dame, IN: University of Notre Dame Press, 1966.

Misner, Paul. *Social Catholicism in Europe: From the Onset of Industrialization to the First World War*. NY: Crossroad, 1991.

Mohler, Dorothy A., ed. *The Social Teachings of Pope John II.* Washington, DC: Catholic University of America Press, 1987.

Moody, Joseph N. and Lawlor, Justus George, eds. *The Challenge of Mater et Magistra*. NY: Herder & Herder, 1963.

Moser, Mary Theresa. *The Church, the Sect, and the Poor France, 1880-1965.* Ann Arbor, MI: UMI Dissertation Services, 1983.

Mott, S. C. *Biblical Ethics and Social Change*. NY: Oxford University Press, 1982.

Mueller, Franz H. *The Church and the Social Question*. Washington, DC: American Enterprise Institute for Public Policy Research, 1984.

Myers, Kenneth A., ed. *Aspiring to Freedom: Commentaries on John Paul II's Encyclical "The Social Concerns of the Church"*. Grand Rapids, MI: Eerdmans, 1988.

Neal, Marie Augusta. *The Just Demands of the Poor*. NY: Paulist Press, 1986.

von Nell-Bruening, S.J., Oswald. *Reorganization of Social Economy*. Milwaukee: Bruce, 1936.

Nelson, Jack A. *Hunger for Justice: The Politics of Food and Faith*. Maryknoll, NY: Orbis Books, 1981.

Nelson-Pallmeyer, Jack. *War Against the Poor: Low Intensity Conflict and Christian Faith*. Maryknoll, NY: Orbis Books, 1989.

Neuhaus, Richard John, ed. *The Preferential Option for the Poor*. Grand Rapids, MI: Eerdmans, 1988.

Neuhaus, Richard John and Weigel, George, eds. *Being Christian Today: An American Conversation*. Washington: Ethics and Public Policy Center, 1992.

Nickoloff, James B, ed. *Gustavo Gutierrez: Essential Writings*. Minneapolis, MN: Fortress Press, 1996.

Novak, Michael. *Catholic Social Thought and Liberal Institutions: Freedom With Justice*. New Brunswick, NJ: Transaction Publishers, 1989 revision.

____. *Freedom With Justice: Catholic Social Thought and Liberal Institutions*. San Francisco: Harper & Row, 1984.

____. *The Open Church*. NY: Macmillan, 1964.

____. *Will It Liberate?: Questions About Liberation Theology*. NY: Paulist Press, 1986.

O'Brien, Darcy, *The Hidden Pope: The Untold Story of a Friendship That is Changing the Relationship Catholics and Jews*. NY: Daybreak Books, 1998.

O'Brien, David J. and Shannon, Thomas A., eds., *Catholic Social Thought: The Documentary Heritage*. Maryknoll, NY: Orbis Books, 1992.

____. *Renewing Earth: Catholic Documents on Peace, Justice and Liberation*. Garden City, NY: Doubleday Image Books, 1977.

O'Brien, John. *Theology and the Option for the Poor*. Collegeville, MN: Liturgical Press, 1992.

O'Collins, S.J., Gerald and Farrugia, S.J., Edward G. *A Concise Dictionary of Theology*. NY: Paulist Press, 1991.

O'Dea, Thomas. *The Catholic Crisis*. Boston: Beacon Press, 1968.

Oliveros, Roberto. *Liberación y teologia: genesís y crecimiento de una reflexión (1966-1976)*. Lima: CEP, 1977.

O'Malley, S.J., William J. *The Voice of Blood: Five Christian Martyrs for Our Time*. Maryknoll, NY: Orbis Books, 1983.

Overberg, Kenneth R. *An Inconsistent Ethic?: Teachings of the American Catholic Bishops*. Lanham, MD: University Press of America, 1980.

Padberg, S.J., John W. *Documents of the 31st and 32nd General Congregations of the Society of Jesus*. St. Louis: Institute of Jesuit Sources, 1977.

_____. *Documents of the 33rd General Congregation of the Society of Jesus*. St. Louis: Institute of Jesuit Sources, 1984.

Parada, Hernán. *Crónica de Medellín: segunda Conferencia del Episcopado Latinamericano*. Bogotá: Indo-American Press Service, 1975.

Path from Puebla: Significant Documents of the Latin American Bishops Since 1979. Washington, DC: United States Catholic Conference, 1988.

Paths to Peace: A Contribution/ Documents of the Holy See to the International Community. Brookfield, WI: Liturgical Publications, 1987.

Paul VI, A *Call to Action: Apostolic Letter on the Eightieth Anniversary of Rerum Novarum*. Washington, DC: United States Catholic Conference, 1971.

_______. *On Evangelization in the Modern World*. Washington, DC: United States CatholicConference, 1976.

______. *On the Development of Peoples*, Commentary by Ward, Barbara. NY: Paulist Press, 1977.

_______. *Paths of the Church*. Washington, DC: National Catholic Welfare Conference, 1964.

Perdiguerra, Sonia, ed. *Liberation Theology and the Vatican*. Quezon City, Philippines: Claretian Publications, 1986.

_____. *Liberation Theology and the Vatican Document: A Philippine Perspective.* Quezon City, Philippines: Claretian Publications, 1986.

Perdiguerra, Sonia, ed., *Liberation Theology and the Vatican Document: Perspectives From the Third World*. Quezon City, Philippines: Claretian Publications, 1987.

Peruvian Bishops' Commission for Social Action, *Between and Hope: Documents For and About the Church in America*. Maryknoll, NY: Maryknoll Publications, 1970.

Phan, Peter C. *Social Thought [Message of the Fathers of the Church 20]*. Wilmington, DE: Michael Glazier, 1984.

Philip, Peter. *Journey With the Poor*. Blackbourne, Australia: Collins Dove, 1988.

Pires, José María. *Do Centro para a Margem*. Joað Pessoa, Brazil: Editora Acaua, 1979.

Pironio, Eduardo F. *En el espíritu de Medellín*. Buenos Aires: Editora Patria Grande, 1976.

Planas, Ricardo. *Liberation Theology: The Political Expression of Religion*. Kansas City, MO: Sheed & Ward, 1986.

Pohier, Jacques and Mieth, Dietmar, eds. *Christian Ethics: Uniformity, Universality, Pluralism*. Edinburgh: T. & T. Clark, 1981.

Pontifical Commission *Iustitia et Pax*, *At the Service of the Human Community: An Ethical Approach to the International Debt Question*. Vatican City: Vatican Polyglot Press, 1986.

Pratt, Cranford and Hutchinson, Roger. *Christian Faith and Economic Justice: Toward a Canadian Perspective*. Burlington, Ontario: Trinity, 1988.

Praxis de los padres de América Latina: documentos de las conferencias episcopales de Medellín a Puebla, 1968-1978. Bogotá: Ediciones Paulinas, 1978.

Puebla: La Evangelización en el presente y en la futura de América Latina. Santo Domingo: Amigo del Hogar, 1979.

Quade, Quentin L., ed. *The Pope and Revolution: The Confronts Liberation Theology*. Washington, DC: Ethics and Public Policy Center, 1984.

Quinn, Bishop Alban. *The Church and the Option for the Poor Peru*. London: Catholic Institute for International Relations, 1984.

Rahner, S.J., Karl. *Concern for the Church*. NY: Crossroads, 1981.

_____. *The Shape of the Church to Come*. NY: Seabury, 1974.

Rahner, S.J., Karl, *et al.*, eds. *Gaudium et Spes, l'Eglise dans le Monde de çe Temps*. Paris Editions du Cerf, 1967.

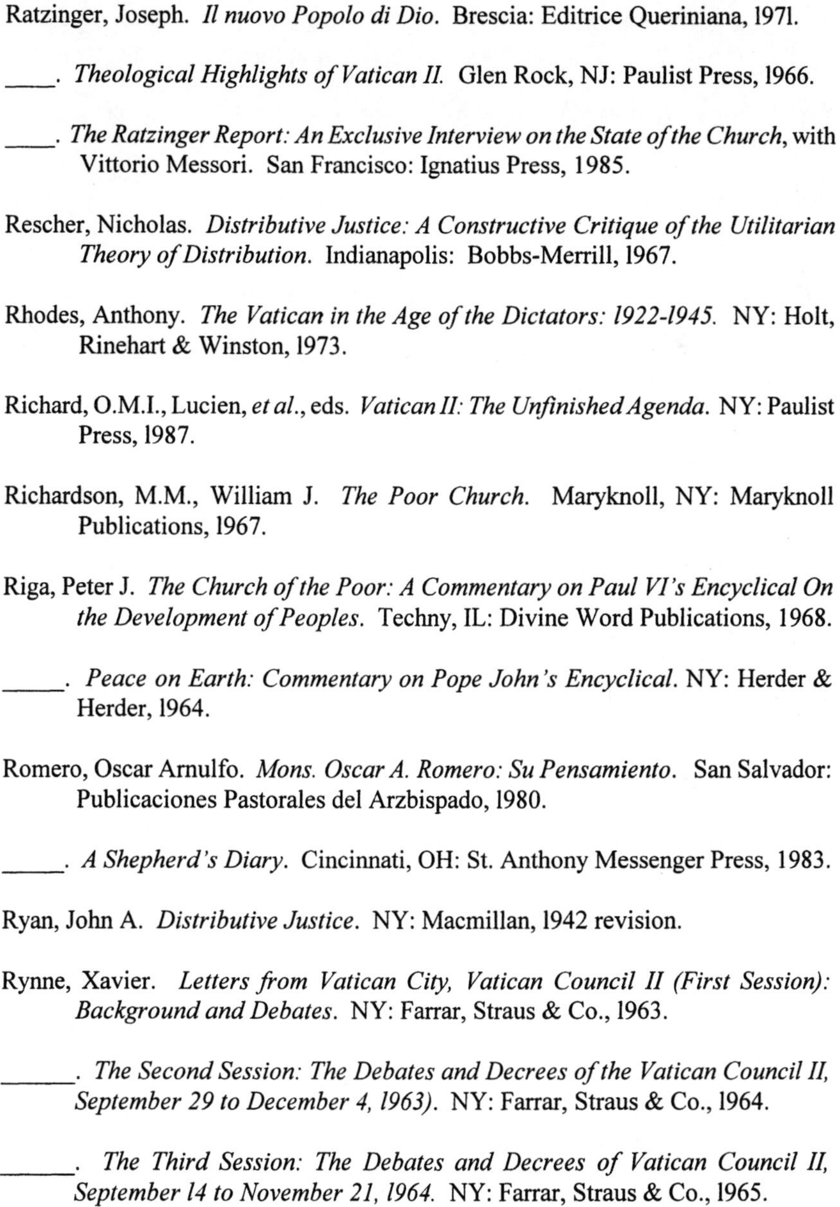

Ratzinger, Joseph. *Il nuovo Popolo di Dio*. Brescia: Editrice Queriniana, 1971.

____. *Theological Highlights of Vatican II.* Glen Rock, NJ: Paulist Press, 1966.

____. *The Ratzinger Report: An Exclusive Interview on the State of the Church*, with Vittorio Messori. San Francisco: Ignatius Press, 1985.

Rescher, Nicholas. *Distributive Justice: A Constructive Critique of the Utilitarian Theory of Distribution*. Indianapolis: Bobbs-Merrill, 1967.

Rhodes, Anthony. *The Vatican in the Age of the Dictators: 1922-1945.* NY: Holt, Rinehart & Winston, 1973.

Richard, O.M.I., Lucien, *et al.*, eds. *Vatican II: The Unfinished Agenda*. NY: Paulist Press, 1987.

Richardson, M.M., William J. *The Poor Church*. Maryknoll, NY: Maryknoll Publications, 1967.

Riga, Peter J. *The Church of the Poor: A Commentary on Paul VI's Encyclical On the Development of Peoples*. Techny, IL: Divine Word Publications, 1968.

_____. *Peace on Earth: Commentary on Pope John's Encyclical*. NY: Herder & Herder, 1964.

Romero, Oscar Arnulfo. *Mons. Oscar A. Romero: Su Pensamiento*. San Salvador: Publicaciones Pastorales del Arzbispado, 1980.

_____. *A Shepherd's Diary*. Cincinnati, OH: St. Anthony Messenger Press, 1983.

Ryan, John A. *Distributive Justice*. NY: Macmillan, 1942 revision.

Rynne, Xavier. *Letters from Vatican City, Vatican Council II (First Session): Background and Debates*. NY: Farrar, Straus & Co., 1963.

______. *The Second Session: The Debates and Decrees of the Vatican Council II, September 29 to December 4, 1963)*. NY: Farrar, Straus & Co., 1964.

______. *The Third Session: The Debates and Decrees of Vatican Council II, September 14 to November 21, 1964*. NY: Farrar, Straus & Co., 1965.

__________. *The Fourth Session: The Debates and Decrees of Vatican Council II, September 14 to December 8, 1965.* NY: Farrar, Straus & Giroux, 1966.

de Santa Ana, Julio. *Good News to the Poor*. Geneva: World Council of Churches, 1977.

Scannone, Juan Carlos. *Teologia de la liberación y social de la Iglesia*. Madrid: Ediciones Cristianidad, 1987.

Schillebeeckx, O.P., Edward. *Church: The Human Story of God.* NY: Crossroad, 1990.

_____. *For the Sake of the Gospel.* NY: Crossroad, 1990.

_____. *The Real Achievement of Vatican II.* NY: Herder & Herder, 1967.

Schuck, Michael J. *That They May Be One: The Social Teaching of the Papal Encyclicals, 1740-1989*. Washington, DC: Georgetown University Press, 1991.

Secretariat, Bishops' Committee for the Church in Latin America, *Santo Domingo: Conclusions*. Washington, DC: United States Catholic Conference, 1993.

Segundo, S.J., Juan Luís. *Las Etapas precristianas de fe*. Montevideo, Uruguay: Cursos de Complementación Cristiana, 1960.

____. *The Human Motives of Pastoral Action: Latin American Reflections*. Maryknoll, NY: Orbis Books, 1978.

____. *The Liberation of Theology*. Maryknoll, NY: Orbis Books, 1977.

____. *Theology and the Church: A Response to Cardinal Ratzinger and a Warning to the Whole Church.* Minneapolis, MN: Winston Press, 1985.

Schall, S.J., James V. Liberation Theology in Latin America. San Francisco: Ignatius Press, 1982.

Sharing the Tradition, Shaping the Future: A Christian Community Sharing Experience. Washington, DC: Campaign for Human Development, United States Catholic Conference, 1991.

Sherman, Amy. *Preferential Option: Neo-Liberal Strategy and Latin America's Poor.* Grand Rapids, MI: Eerdmans, 1992.

Sierra Bravo, Rubén. *Doctrina Social y Economica de los Padres de la Iglesia.* Madrid: Compi, 1967.

Sigmund, Paul E. *Liberation Theology at the Crossroads: Democracy or Revolution?.* NY: Oxford University Press, 1990.

Simoes, Jorge J. *Puebla: libertaçao do homem pobre.* Sao Paulo: Edicoes Loyola, 1981.

Smith, Christian. *The Emergence of Liberation Theology: Radical Religion and Social Movement Theory.* Chicago: University of Chicago Press, 1991.

Sobrino, S.J., Jon. *Christology at the Crossroads.* Maryknoll, NY: Orbis Books, 1978.

_____. *Jesus in Latin America.* Maryknoll, NY: Orbis Books, 1987.

_____. *Serena afirmación de Medellín cristologia.* Bogotá: Indo-American Press Service, 1979.

_____. *Spirituality of Liberation: Toward Political Wholeness.* Maryknoll, NY: Orbis Books, 1988.

_____. *The True Church and the Poor.* Maryknoll, NY: Orbis Books, 1984.

Sobrino, Jon, Ellacuría, Ignacio, *et al. Companions of Jesus: The Jesuit Martyrs of El Salvador.* Maryknoll, NY: Orbis Books, 1991.

Lo Social en Puebla: comentarios. Santiago de Chile: Editorial Salesiana, 1980.

Stacpoole, O.S.B., Alberic, ed. *Vatican II Revisited: By Who Were There.* Minneapolis, MN: Winston Press, 1986.

Tabb, William K., ed. *Churches in Struggle: Liberation Theologies and Social Change in North America.* NY: Monthly Review Press, 1986.

Torres, Sergio and Eagleson, John, eds. *The Challenge of Basic Christian Communities*. Maryknoll, NY: Orbis Books, 1981.

Torres, Sergio and Fabella, Virginia, eds. *The Emergent Gospel: Theology from the Underside of History*. Maryknoll, NY: Orbis Books, 1978.

Trevor, Meriol. *Pope John*. Garden City, NY: Doubleday & Co., 1967.

Troeltsch, Ernst. *The Social Teaching of the Christian Churches*. NY: Harper Torchbooks Edition, 1960.

Vallier, Ivan, *Catholicism, Social Control, and Modernization in Latin America*. Englewood Cliffs, NJ: Prentice-Hall, 1970.

Vidler, Alexander Roper, *A Century of Social Catholicism: 1820*-1920. London: SPCK, 1964.

______. *The Church in an Age of Revolution: 1989 to the Present Day*. Baltimore, MD: Penguin Books, 1974 revision.

Vinatier, Jean. *Le Cardinal Liènart et la Mission de France*. Paris: Editions du Centurion, 1978.

Vorgrimmler, Herbert, ed. *Commentary on the Documents of Vatican II*, Volume I. NY: Herder & Herder, 1967.

Walsh, S.J., James. *The Mind of Paul VI: On the Church and on the World.* Milwaukee: Bruce, 1964.

Walsh, Michael and Davies, Brian. *Proclaiming Justice and Peace: Papal Documents From Rerum novarum Through Centesimus Annus*. Mystic, CT: XXXIII Publications, 1991 revision.

Ward-Jackson, Barbara. *The Angry Seventies: The Second Development Decade: A Call to the Church*. Vatican City: Pontifical Commission *Iustitia et Pax*, 1970.

_____. *The Rich Nations and the Poor Nations*. NY: W.W. Norton, 1962.

Weigel, George and Royal, Robert, eds. *A Century of Catholic Social Thought: Essays on "Rerum novarum" and Nine Other Key Documents*. Washington, DC: Ethics and Public Policy Center, 1991.

Whale, John, Hebblethwaite, Peter, *et al*. *The Man Who Leads the Church: An Assessment of Pope John Paul II.* San Francisco: Harper & Row, 1980.

Willey, David. *God's Politician: Pope John Paul II, The Catholic Church, and the New World Order*. NY: St. Martin's Press, 1992.

Williams, George Huntston. *The Mind of John Paul II: Origins of His Thought and Action*. NY: Seabury Press, 1981.

Williams, Melvin J. *Catholic Social Thought: Its Approach to Contemporary Problems*. NY: The Ronald Press Company, 1950.

Wynn, Wilton. *Keepers of the Keys*. NY: Random House, 1988.

Yzermans, Vincent A., ed. *The Major Addresses of Pope Pius XII* (2 Vols.) St. Paul, MN: North Central Publishing Company, 1961.

Zimmerman, Michel. *Structure Social de l'Eglise: Doctrines et Praxis des Rapports Eglise-Etât du XVIIIe Siecle a Jean-Paul II.* Strausbourg: Centre de Recherche et de Documentation et des Institutions Chrètiennès, 1981.

Articles

Acerbi, A. "Receiving Vatican II in a Changed Historical Context," in *Concilium* 146 (1981): 77-84.

Alberigo, Giuseppe and Melloni, A. "*L'allocuzione Gaudet Mater Ecclesia di Giovanni XXIII (11 ottobre 1962)*." In *Fede Tradizione Profezia. Studi su Giovanni XXIII e sul Vaticano II*, 185-283. Brescia: Editrice Queriniana, 1984.

Alves, Rubém. "Theology and the Liberation of Man." In *New Theology No. 9*, ed. Martin Marty, 230-250. NY: Macmillan, 1972.

André-Vincent, Ph.-I. "*A Propos de l'Enseignement Pontifical et des Droits de l'Homme*," in *La Pensee Catholique* 185 (March/April, 1980): 91-102.

____. "*Pour le Centenaire de 'Rerum Novarum,'*" in *Esprit et Vie* 91 (1981): 509-511.

Alfaro, S.J., Juan. "Reflections on the Eschatology of Vatican II." In *Vatican II: Assessment and Perspectives/ Twenty-five Years After (1962-1987)*, ed. René Latourelle, S.J., 501-514. NY: Paulist Press, 1989.

Antoncich, S.J., Ricardo. "Liberation Theology and the Social Teaching of the Church," In *Rerum novarum*: *A Hundred Years of Catholic Social Teaching*, ed. John Coleman and Gregory Baum, 23-46. London: SCM Press, 1991.

____. "The Creed of a Liberation Theologian." In *Liberation Theology and the Vatican Document/ Volume III*, ed. Sonia Perdiguerra, 3-20. Quezon City, Philippines: Claretian Publications, 1987.

Arns, Paulo Evaristo. "The Church of the Poor: A Persecuted Church," in *Center Focus* (July, 1981) pp. 1-9.

Azzi, Riolando. "*A Igreja do Brasil na defesa dos Direitos Humanos*," in *Revista Eclesiasticas Brasiliera* 37 (1977): 106-142.

______. "*A Ingreja Catolica no Brasil no Periodo de 1950 a 1975: Relaçao cronologica de fatos, episodios, e declaraçoes relevantes*," in *Religiao e Sociedade* 1 (1977): 79-109.

Bandeira, Marina. "*Dom Helder Câmara e o Vaticano II*," in *Vozes* 72 (1978): 793-796.

Baum, Gregory. "Canadian Bishops Adapt Liberation Theology," in *Cross Currents* (Spring, 1978): 97-103.

_______. "Liberation Theology and 'The Supernatural,'" in *The Ecumenist* 19 (1981): 80-87.

_____. "The Social Context of American Catholic Theology," in *Proceedings of the Catholic Theological Society of America* 41 (1986): 83-100.

Bernardin, Joseph. "The U.S. Bishops and the *Constitution on the Church in the Modern World*, in *Origins* 15, October 17, 1985: 306-308.

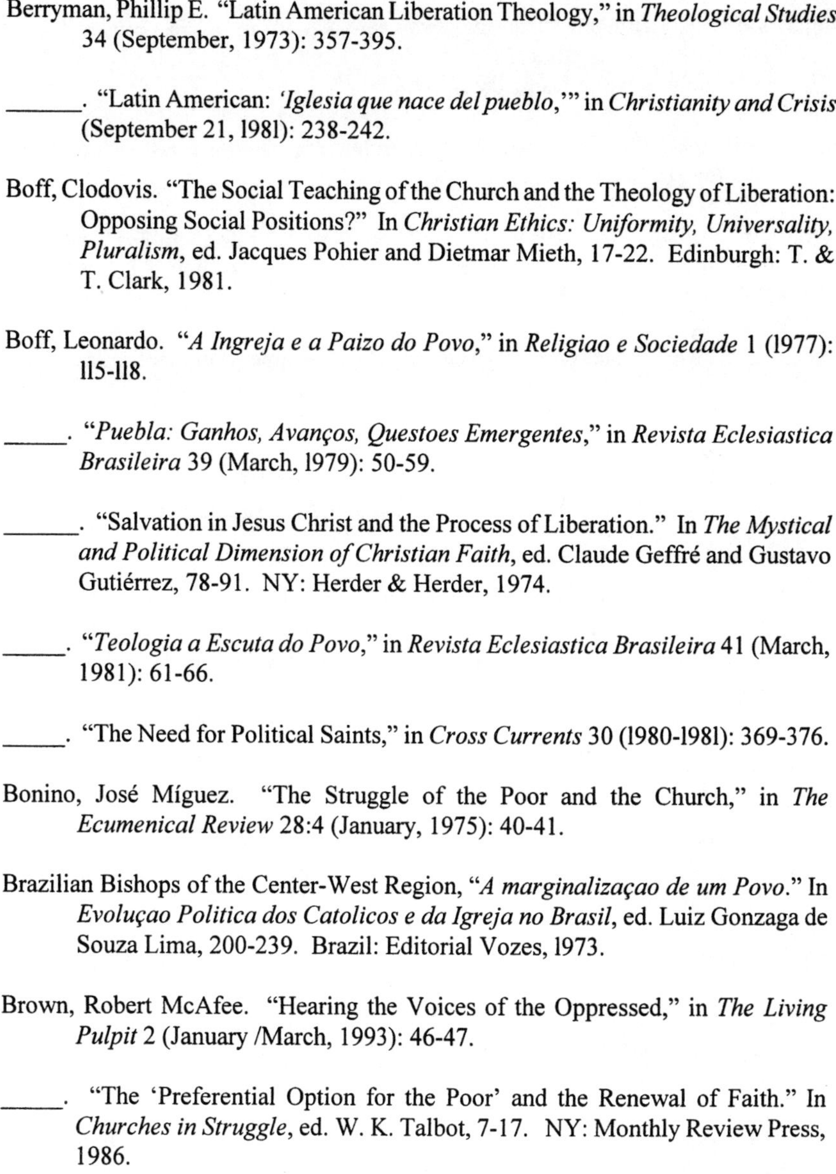

Berryman, Phillip E. "Latin American Liberation Theology," in *Theological Studies* 34 (September, 1973): 357-395.

______. "Latin American: *'Iglesia que nace del pueblo,'*" in *Christianity and Crisis* (September 21, 1981): 238-242.

Boff, Clodovis. "The Social Teaching of the Church and the Theology of Liberation: Opposing Social Positions?" In *Christian Ethics: Uniformity, Universality, Pluralism*, ed. Jacques Pohier and Dietmar Mieth, 17-22. Edinburgh: T. & T. Clark, 1981.

Boff, Leonardo. "*A Ingreja e a Paizo do Povo*," in *Religiao e Sociedade* 1 (1977): 115-118.

_____. "*Puebla: Ganhos, Avanços, Questoes Emergentes*," in *Revista Eclesiastica Brasileira* 39 (March, 1979): 50-59.

______. "Salvation in Jesus Christ and the Process of Liberation." In *The Mystical and Political Dimension of Christian Faith*, ed. Claude Geffré and Gustavo Gutiérrez, 78-91. NY: Herder & Herder, 1974.

_____. "*Teologia a Escuta do Povo*," in *Revista Eclesiastica Brasileira* 41 (March, 1981): 61-66.

_____. "The Need for Political Saints," in *Cross Currents* 30 (1980-1981): 369-376.

Bonino, José Míguez. "The Struggle of the Poor and the Church," in *The Ecumenical Review* 28:4 (January, 1975): 40-41.

Brazilian Bishops of the Center-West Region, "*A marginalizaçao de um Povo*." In *Evoluçao Politica dos Catolicos e da Igreja no Brasil*, ed. Luiz Gonzaga de Souza Lima, 200-239. Brazil: Editorial Vozes, 1973.

Brown, Robert McAfee. "Hearing the Voices of the Oppressed," in *The Living Pulpit* 2 (January /March, 1993): 46-47.

_____. "The 'Preferential Option for the Poor' and the Renewal of Faith." In *Churches in Struggle*, ed. W. K. Talbot, 7-17. NY: Monthly Review Press, 1986.

Butler, O.S.B., Christopher. "The *Aggiornamento* of Vatican II." In *Vatican II: An Interfaith Appraisal*, ed. John H. Miller, C.S.C., 3-13. Notre Dame, IN: University of Notre Dame Press, 1966.

Byrne, Patrick H. "*Ressentiment* and the Preferential Option for the Poor," in *Theological Studies* 54 (June, 1993): 213-241.

Byron, S.J., William. "The Bishops' Letter and Everyday Life." In *The Catholic Challenge to the American Economy*, ed. Thomas M. Gannon, S.J., 246-255. NY: Macmillan, 1987.

Cahill, Lisa Sowle. "Notes on Moral Theology: 'The Seamless Garment': Life in Its Beginnings," in *Theological Studies* 46 (March, 1985): 64-74.

Calvez, S.J., Jean-Yves. "Economic Policy Issues in Roman Catholic Social Teaching: An International Perspective." In *The Catholic Challenge to the American Economy,* ed. Thomas M. Gannon, S.J., 15-27. NY: Macmillan, 1987.

___. "Medellín and Puebla in the Perspective of the World Church." In *Born of the Poor: The Latin American Church Since Medellín*, ed. Edward L. Cleary, O.P., 183-196. Notre Dame, IN: University of Notre Dame Press, 1990.

___. "The Preferential Option for the Poor: Where Does It Come From For Us?," in John W. Padberg, S.J. (ed.), *Studies in the Spirituality of the Jesuits* 21:2 (March, 1989): pp. 2-35.

Capovilla, Loris F. "Reflections on the Twentieth Anniversary." In *Vatican II Revisited: By Those Who Were There*, ed. Alberic Stackpoole, O.S.B., 106-128. Minneapolis, MN: Winston Press, 1986.

Cardonnel, Jean. "The Council of Poverty," in *Esprit* (June, 1963): 1119-1131.

Carrier, S.J., Hervé. "The Contribution of the Council to Culture." In *Vatican II: Assessment and Perspectives Twenty-Five Years After (1962-1987)* Vol. III, ed. René Latourelle, S.J., 442- 465. NY: Paulist Press, 1989.

Chenu, O.P., Marie-Dominique. "*Les Signes des Temps: Reflexion Théologique.*" In *L'Eglise dans le Monde de çe Temps: Constitution Pastorale 'Gaudium et*

Spes' Tome 2, ed. Yve-Marie Congar, O.P., *et al.*, 205-225. Paris: Cerf, 1967.

______. "The Church's 'Social Doctrine." In *Christian Ethics and Economics: The North-South Conflict*, ed. Dietmar Meith and Jacques Pohier, 72-74. Edinburgh: T. & T. Clark, 1980.

Christiansen, S.J., Drew. "Basic Needs: Criterion for the Legitimacy of Development." In *HumanRights in the Americas: The Struggle for Consensus*, ed. Alfred T. Hennelly, S.J. and John Langan, S.J., 260-262. Washington, DC: Georgetown University Press, 1982.

Coleman, S.J., John. "Development of Church Social Teaching," in *Origins* 11: 33-41.

_______. "Mission of the Church and Justice." In *The Church as Mission*, ed. James Provost, 178-192. Washington, DC: Canon Law Society of America, 1984.

Congar, O.P., Yves. "A Last Look at the Council." *In Vatican II Revisited: By Those Who Were There*, ed. Alberic Stackpoole, O.S.B., 337-356. Minneapolis, MN: Winston Press, 1986.

_____. *"La 'Reception' comme Réalité Ecclesiastique," in Revue des Sciences Philosophiques et Theologiques* ." (1972): 369-403.

_____. "Moving Toward a Pilgrim Church." *In Vatican II Revisited: By Those Who Were There*, ed. Alberic Stacpoole, O.S.B., 129-154. Minneapolis, MN: Winston Press, 1986.

Cosmao, Vincent. "*Le tournant de Puebla*," in *Foi et Developpent*, nos. 65, 66, 67 (*mars-mai*, 1979): 1-7.

Cronin, S.S., John F. "Significance of John XXIII." In *Church and Social Progress: Background Readings for John's Mater et Magistra*, ed. Benjamin Masse, 40-48. Milwaukee: Bruce, 1966.

Donahue, S.J., John R. "Biblical Perspectives on Justice." In *The Faith That Does Justice*, ed. John Haughey, S.J., 68-112. NY: Paulist Press, 1977.

Dorr, Donal. “John XXIII and the Option for the Poor,” in *Irish Theological Quarterly* 47 (1980): 247-271.

Dulles, S.J., Avery. “John Paul II and the New Evangelization,” in *America*, February 1, 1992, pp. 52-59; 69-72.

_____. “The Meaning of Faith Considered in Relation to Justice.” In *The Faith that Does Justice*, ed. John Haughey, S.J., 10-46. NY: Paulist Press, 1977.

Dupont, J. “*La Iglesia y la Pobreza.*” In *La Iglesia del Vaticano II: Estudios en torno a la Constitución conciliar sobre la Iglesia*, ed. Guillermo Baruana, O.F.M., 401-432. Barcelona: Juan Flors, 1966.

Ellacuría, S.J., Ignacio. “*La Iglesia de los pobres, sacramento histórico de la liberación,*” in *Estudios Centroamericanos* (*octobre-noviembre*, 1977): 710-721.

_____. “*Iglesia de los pobres: Presencia y anuncio de una Iglesia nueva.*” In *Cruz y Resurrección*, 47-273. Mexico City: CRT, 1978.

_____. “*Possibilidad, necessidad, y sentido de una teologia latinoamericana,*” in *Christus* (*febrero*, 1975): 12-16; (*marzo*, 1975): 17-23.

Gaillot, Jacques, “Opting for the Poor.” In *Synod 85 – An Evaluation*, eds. Giuseppe Alberigo and James Provost, 124- 30. Edinburgh: T. & T. Clark, Ltd., 1986.

Freire, Paulo. “Conscientization, ” in Cross Currents 23:1 (1974): 23-31.

Galilea, Segundo. “Between Medellín and Puebla,” in *Cross Currents* 28 (1978/1979): 71-78.

_____. “Liberation Theology Began With Medellín,” in *LADOC* (May, 1975): pp. 1-6.

_____. “Spiritual Awakening and Movements of Liberation in Latin America.” In *Spiritual Renewals*, ed. Christian Duquoc and Casiano Floristan, 129-138. NY: Herder & Herder, 1973.

Gérard, S.J., Marcel. "Documentation to Direct Religious Education Towards the Service of the Poor and of Mankind: Words and Actions of the Church in Council," in *Lumen Vitae*, vol. XVIII, no. 4 (December, 1963): 679-718.

______. "Documentation to Direct Religious Education Towards the Service of the Poor and of Mankind: Words and Actions of the church in Council," in *Lumen Vitae*, Vol. XIX, no. 1 (March, 1964): 5-78.

"The Greatest Love: El Salvador's Sacrament of Salvation/ An Interiew with Jon Sobrino," in *Sojourners*, April, 1990, pp. 16-21.

Gremillion, Joseph. "The Significance of Puebla for the Catholic Church in North America." In *Puebla and Beyond*, ed. John Eagleson and Philip Sharper, 310-329. Maryknoll, NY: Orbis Books, 1979.

Grondelski, John M. "The Social Thought of Karol Wojtyla/Pope John Paul II: A Bibliographical Essay," in *Social Thought* XIII (Spring/Summer, 1987): 151-165.

Gudorf, Christine E. "Major Differences: Liberation Theology and Current Church Teaching." In *Readings in Moral Theology No. 5: Official Catholic Social Teaching*, ed. Charles E. Curran and Richard A. McCormick, S.J., 442-447. NY: Paulist Press, 1986.

Gutiérrez, Gustavo. "Church of the Poor." In *Born of the Poor: The Latin American Church Since Medellín*, ed. Edward L. Cleary, O.P., 9-25. Notre Dame, IN: University of Notre Dame Press, 1990.

____. "Faith as Freedom: Solidarity With the Alienated and Confidence in the Future," in *Horizons* (Spring, 1975): 25-30.

_____. "*Itinerario eclesial: De Medellín a Puebla*," in *Moralia* 314 (1982): 51-66.

_____. "Liberation and Development," in *Cross Currents* (Summer, 1971), pp. 243-256.

_____. "Liberation Movements in Theology." In *Jesus Christ and Human Freedom*, ed. Edward Schillebeeckx and Bas van Iersel, pp. 135-146. NY: Herder & Herder, 1974.

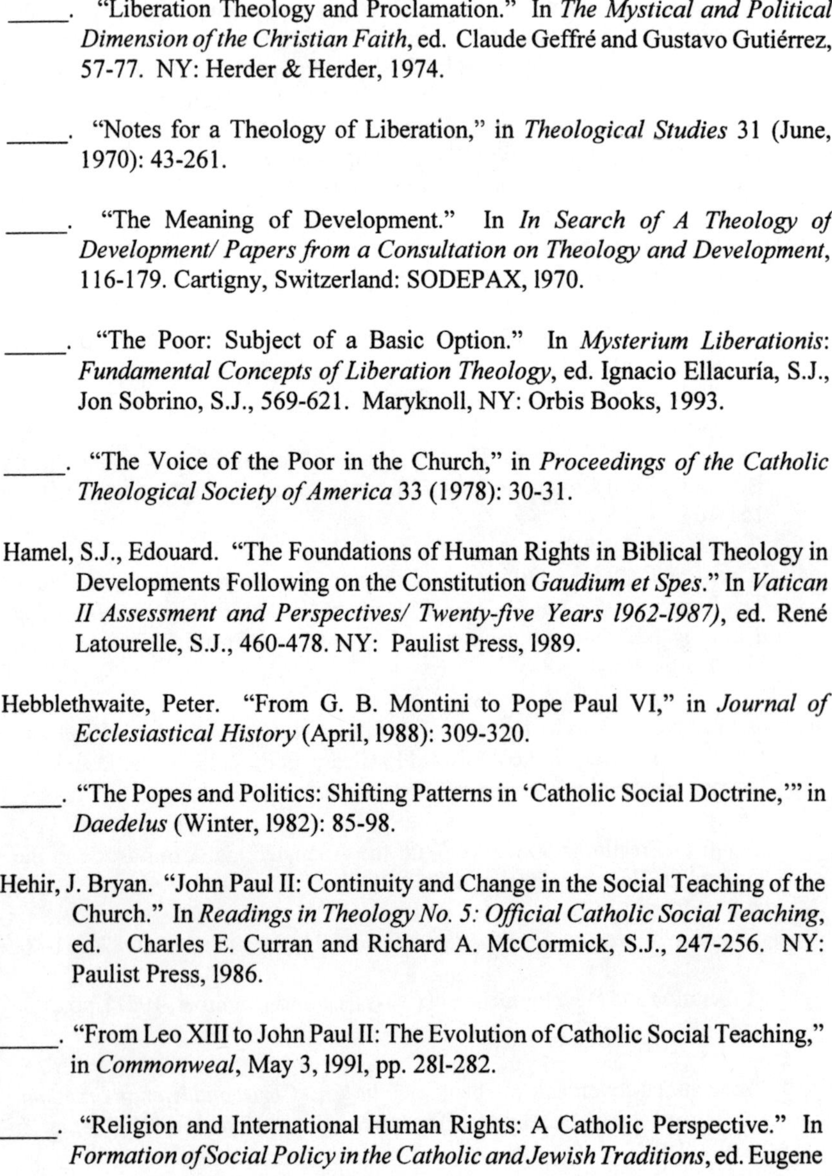

_____. "Liberation Theology and Proclamation." In *The Mystical and Political Dimension of the Christian Faith*, ed. Claude Geffré and Gustavo Gutiérrez, 57-77. NY: Herder & Herder, 1974.

_____. "Notes for a Theology of Liberation," in *Theological Studies* 31 (June, 1970): 43-261.

_____. "The Meaning of Development." In *In Search of A Theology of Development/ Papers from a Consultation on Theology and Development*, 116-179. Cartigny, Switzerland: SODEPAX, 1970.

_____. "The Poor: Subject of a Basic Option." In *Mysterium Liberationis: Fundamental Concepts of Liberation Theology*, ed. Ignacio Ellacuría, S.J., Jon Sobrino, S.J., 569-621. Maryknoll, NY: Orbis Books, 1993.

_____. "The Voice of the Poor in the Church," in *Proceedings of the Catholic Theological Society of America* 33 (1978): 30-31.

Hamel, S.J., Edouard. "The Foundations of Human Rights in Biblical Theology in Developments Following on the Constitution *Gaudium et Spes*." In *Vatican II Assessment and Perspectives/ Twenty-five Years 1962-1987)*, ed. René Latourelle, S.J., 460-478. NY: Paulist Press, 1989.

Hebblethwaite, Peter. "From G. B. Montini to Pope Paul VI," in *Journal of Ecclesiastical History* (April, 1988): 309-320.

_____. "The Popes and Politics: Shifting Patterns in 'Catholic Social Doctrine,'" in *Daedelus* (Winter, 1982): 85-98.

Hehir, J. Bryan. "John Paul II: Continuity and Change in the Social Teaching of the Church." In *Readings in Theology No. 5: Official Catholic Social Teaching*, ed. Charles E. Curran and Richard A. McCormick, S.J., 247-256. NY: Paulist Press, 1986.

_____. "From Leo XIII to John Paul II: The Evolution of Catholic Social Teaching," in *Commonweal*, May 3, 1991, pp. 281-282.

_____. "Religion and International Human Rights: A Catholic Perspective." In *Formation of Social Policy in the Catholic and Jewish Traditions*, ed. Eugene

Fisher and Daniel Polish, 111-124. Notre Dame, IN: University of Notre Dame Press, 1980.

Hellwig, Monika. "Liberation Theology: An Emerging School," in *Scottish Journal of Theology* 30 (1976): 137-151.

Hennelly, S.J., Alfred T. "Apprentices in Freedom: Theology Since Medellín," in *America*, May 27, 1988, pp. 418-421.

_____. "The Influence of Liberation Theology." In *Born of the Poor: The Latin American Church Since Medellín*, ed. Edward L. Cleary, O.P., 26-44. Notre Dame, IN: University of Notre Dame Press, 1990.

____. "The Red-Hot Issue: Liberation Theology," in *America*, May 24, 1986, pp. 425-428.

____. "Today's New Task: Geotheology," in *America*, January 18, 1975, pp. 27-29.

Henriot, S.J., Peter. "A Theology of Action for Social Justice: Applications in the Global Context," in *Catholic Mind* (December, 1973): 31-45.

_____. "The Concept of Social Sin," in *Catholic Mind* (October, 1973): 38-53.

Himes, Kenneth, O.F.M., "Globalization's Next Phase," in *Origins* 32, no. 2 (May 23, 2002), pp. 17, 19-22.

Hollenbach, S.J., David. "Modern Catholic Teachings Concerning Justice." In *The Faith That Does Justice*, ed. John Haughey, S.J., 207-233. NY: Paulist Press, 1977.

Hoornaert, Eduardo. "*A Igreja Diante de uma Nova Situaçao,*" *in Revista Eclesiastica Brasileira* 26:4 (1966): 872-884.

_____. "*O Concilio Vaticano II e a Igreja no Brasil,*" in *Revista Eclesiastica Brasileira* 27:1(1967): 43-45.

Kamphaus, Franz. "*Die Verantwortung des Galubens angesicht erfahrener Ungerechtigkeit. Zum Verhaltnis von katholischer Soziallehre und Theologie der Befreiung,*" in *Herder-Korrespondence* 6 (1986): 282-286.

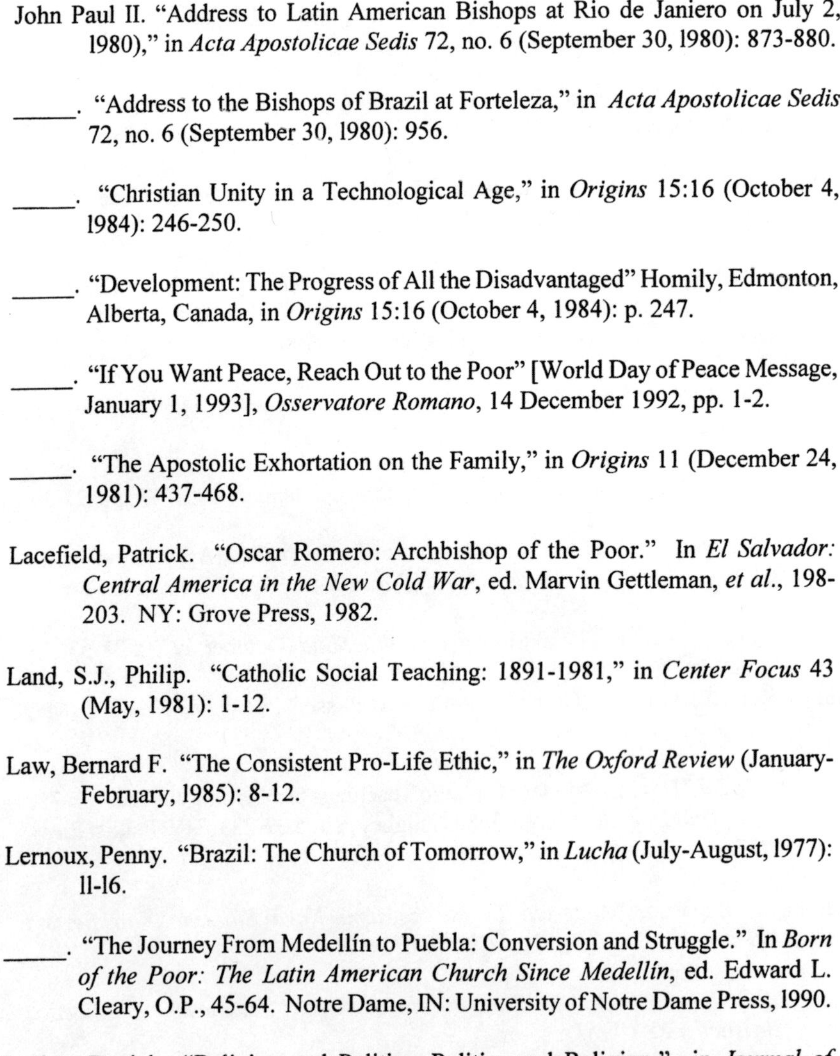

John Paul II. "Address to Latin American Bishops at Rio de Janiero on July 2, 1980)," in *Acta Apostolicae Sedis* 72, no. 6 (September 30, 1980): 873-880.

_____. "Address to the Bishops of Brazil at Forteleza," in *Acta Apostolicae Sedis* 72, no. 6 (September 30, 1980): 956.

_____. "Christian Unity in a Technological Age," in *Origins* 15:16 (October 4, 1984): 246-250.

_____. "Development: The Progress of All the Disadvantaged" Homily, Edmonton, Alberta, Canada, in *Origins* 15:16 (October 4, 1984): p. 247.

_____. "If You Want Peace, Reach Out to the Poor" [World Day of Peace Message, January 1, 1993], *Osservatore Romano*, 14 December 1992, pp. 1-2.

_____. "The Apostolic Exhortation on the Family," in *Origins* 11 (December 24, 1981): 437-468.

Lacefield, Patrick. "Oscar Romero: Archbishop of the Poor." In *El Salvador: Central America in the New Cold War*, ed. Marvin Gettleman, *et al.*, 198-203. NY: Grove Press, 1982.

Land, S.J., Philip. "Catholic Social Teaching: 1891-1981," in *Center Focus* 43 (May, 1981): 1-12.

Law, Bernard F. "The Consistent Pro-Life Ethic," in *The Oxford Review* (January-February, 1985): 8-12.

Lernoux, Penny. "Brazil: The Church of Tomorrow," in *Lucha* (July-August, 1977): 11-16.

_____. "The Journey From Medellín to Puebla: Conversion and Struggle." In *Born of the Poor: The Latin American Church Since Medellín*, ed. Edward L. Cleary, O.P., 45-64. Notre Dame, IN: University of Notre Dame Press, 1990.

Levine, Daniel. "Religion and Politics, Politics and Religion," in *Journal of Interamerican Studies and World Affairs* 21:1 (1979): 5-29.

_____. "The Impact and Lasting Influence of Medellín and Puebla." In *Born of the Poor: The Latin American Since Medellín*, ed. Edward L. Cleary, O.P., 64-74. Notre Dame, IN: University of Notre Dame Press, 1990.

Libanio, Joaõ B. "Igreja, Povo que se Liberta: III Encontro Intereclesial de Comunidades de *Base*," in *Sintese* 5: (1979): 93-110.

Lofink, S.J., Norbert. "*Reino de Dios y economia en la Biblia*," in *Communio* (March-April, 1986): 112-119.

Mara, Gerald. "Poverty and Justice: The Bishops and Contemporary Liberalism." In *The Deeper Meaning of Economic Life*, ed. R. Bruce Douglas, 157-178. (Washington, DC: Georgetown University Press, 1986.

McCann, Dennis P. "Option for the Poor: Rethinking a Catholic Tradition." In *The Preferential Option for the Poor*, ed. Richard John Neuhaus, 35-52. Grand Rapids, MI: Eerdmans, 1988.

McCarthy, Gerald. "Puebla in Retrospect," in *The Month*, September, 1979, pp. 306-309.

McCormack, Arthur. "*La commission pontificale 'Iustitia et Pax'*," in *Justitia Monde* (1966/67): 435-455.

McGovern, S.J., Arthur F. "A 500th Anniversary: The Church in Latin America," in *America*, May 16, 1992, pp. 426-431.

McGrath, C.S.C., Marcos. "The Medellín and Puebla Conferences and Their Impact on the Latin American Church." In *Born of the Poor: The Latin American Church Since Medellín*, ed. Edward L. Cleary, O.P., 75-93. Notre Dame, IN: University of Notre Dame Press, 1990.

_____. "Social Teaching Since the Council: A Response From Latin America." In *Vatican II Revisited: By Those Who Were There*, ed. Alberic Stackpoole, O.S.B., 324-336. Minneapolis, MN: Winston Press, 1986.

McKeown, Elizabeth. "The Seamless Garment: The Bishops' Letter in the Light of the American Catholic Pastoral Tradition." In *The Deeper Meaning of Economic Life*, ed. R. Bruce Douglas, 117-138. Washington, DC: Georgetown University Press, 1986.

Metz, Johannes Baptist. "The Church's Social Function in Light of a 'Political' Theology." In *Foundational Theology: Faith and the World of Politics*, ed. Johannes B. Metz, 4-16. Edinburgh: T. & T. Clark, 1968.

Mueller, Franz H. "The Church and the Social Question." In *The Challenge of Mater et Magistra*, ed. Joseph N. Moody and Justus George Lawlor, 13-33. NY: Herder & Herder, 1963.

Murphy, Charles M. "Action for Justice as Constitutive of Preaching of the Gospel: What Did the 1971 Synod Mean?" In *Readings in Moral Theology No. 5: Official Catholic Social Teaching*, ed. Charles E. Curran, and Richard A. McCormick, S.J., 150-168. NY: Paulist Press, 1986.

Neal, Marie Augusta. "The Context of Medellín and Puebla: World Church Movement Towards Social Justice." In *Born of the Poor: The Latin American Church Since Medellín*, ed. Edward L. Cleary, O.P., 171-182. Notre Dame, IN: University of Notre Dame Press, 1990.

Novak, Michael. "Liberation Theology and the Pope." In *The Pope and Revolution: John Paul II Confronts Liberation Theology*, ed. Quentin L. Quade, 73-85. Washington, DC: Ethics and Public Policy Center, 1982).

O'Grady, Desmond. "Towards a Church of the Poor," vol. 10, no. 2. *Perspectives* X (March-April, 1964): 36-44.

de Oliveira, Pedro Riveiro. "*Presenca da Igreja Catholica na Sociedade Brasileira*," in *Religiao e Sociedade* (1977): 111-113.

_____. "*Opçao pelos Pobres: Criterios Praticos*," in *Revista Eclesiastica Brasileira* 40:158 (1980): 211-215.

_____. "*Oprimidos: A Opçao Pela Igreja*," in *Revista Eclesiastica Brasiliera* 41:164 (1981): 654-659.

O'Malley, S.J., John W. "Reform, Historical Consciousness, and Vatican II's Aggiornamento," in *Theological Studies* 32 (1971): 573-601.

Peruvian Theologians, "Our Martyrs Give Hope of Resurrection," in *Cross Currents* (Spring, 1978): 47-53.

O'Riordan, C.Ss.R., Sean. "The Teaching of the Papal Encyclicals as a Source and Norm of Moral Theology," in *Studia Moralia* 14 (1976): 135-157.

Pawlikowski, O.S.M., John T. "Catholicism and the Public Church: Recent U.S. Developments," in *The Annual of the Society of Christian Ethics* (1989): 148-165.

Piehl, Mel. "A Wealth of Nations: *'Rerum Novarum'* and Its Offspring in America," in *Commonweal*, May 3, 1991, pp. 283-288.

Poelman, Roger. "The Poor, Christ, and the Church," in *La Revue Nouvelle* (June, 1963): 688-671.

Pollock, S.J., James R. "Horizons in Moral Theology," in *Chicago Studies* 26 (August, 1987): 216-237.

Pope, Stephen J. "Proper and Improper Partiality and the Preferential Option for the Poor," in *Theological Studies* 54 (June, 1993): 242-271.

Quigley, Thomas E. "Latin America's Church: No Turning Back," in *Cross Currents* (Spring, 1978): 79-89.

Riccardi, A. "*Dalla Chiesa di Pio XII alla Chiesa Giovannea*." In *Papa Giovanni*, ed. Giuseppe Alberigo, 153-174. Rome: storia e litteratura, 1987.

Richard, Pablo. "The Latin American Church: 1959-1978," in *Cross Currents* (Spring, 1978): 34-46.

Ryle, Edward J. "Option for the Poor in Catholic Charities – Policy and the Social Teaching of Pope John Paul II," in *Social Thought XIII* (Spring, 1987): 139-150.

Scannone, Juan Carlos. "The Theology of Liberation: Evangelic or Ideological?" In *Jesus Christ and Human Freedom*, ed. Edward Schillebeeckx and Bas van Iersel, 147-156. NY: Herder & Herder, 1974.

_____. "Various Latin American Interpretations of the Puebla Document," in *Lumen Vitae* (1980): 353-369.

Schuck, Michael. "Encyclical Social Teaching Since Vatican II: Contradiction or Coherence." In *The Church in the Nineties: Its Legacy, Its Future*, ed. Pierre Hegy, 139-146. Collegeville, MN: Liturgical Press, 1993.

Segundo, S.J., Juan Luís. "Capitalism – Socialism: A Theological Crux." In *The Mystical and Political Dimension of the Christian Faith*, ed. Claude Geffré and Gustavo Gutiérrez, 105-126. NY: Herder & Herder, 1974.

Sharper, Philip. "The Theology of Liberation: Some Reflections," in *The Catholic Mind* (April, 1976): 44-51.

Sobrino, S.J., Jon. "*La promoción de la justicia come exigencia esencial del mensaje evangélico*," in *Diakonia* 12 (December, 1979): 45-48.

_____. "*Los documentos de Puebla: serena afirmación de Medellín*," in *Puebla* 4 (1979): 197-217.

_____. "Poverty Means Death to the Poor," in *Cross Currents* 36 (1986/1987): 267-276.

_____. "The Significance of Puebla for the Catholic Church in Latin America." In *Puebla and Beyond*, ed. John Eagleson and Philip Sharper, 289-309. Maryknoll, NY: Orbis Books, 1979.

Steinfels, Peter. "CELAM and the Vatican: A Preferential Option for Dickering," in *Commonweal*, November 20, 1992, pp. 5-6.

_____. "Latin Bishops Set No New Directions," in *The New York Times*, 1 November 1992, p. 15.

Surlis, Paul, "Option for the Poor." In *The New Catholic Encyclopedia Supplementary* Vol. 18, 339-340. NY: McGraw-Hill, 1989.

_____. "The Relation Between Social Justice and Enculturation in the Papal Magisterium," in *Irish Theological Quarterly* 52 (1986): 245-267.

Tambasco, Anthony. "Option for the Poor." In *The Deeper Meaning of Economic Life*, ed. R. Bruce Douglas, 37-96. Washington, DC: Georgetown University Press, 1986.

Tripole, Martin. "A Church for the Poor and the World: At Issue with Ecclesiology," in *Theological Studies* 42 (December, 1981): 645-659.

Ward, Barbara. "Looking Back on *Populorum Progressio*," in *Readings in Moral Theology* No. 5: Official Catholic Social Teaching, ed. Charles E. Curran and Richard A. McCormick, S.J., 130- 149. NY: Paulist Press, 1986.

Weakland, Rembert G. "How Medellín and Puebla Influenced North America," in *Origins* 18 (April 13, 1989): 758-760.

_____. "Where Does the Economics Pastoral Stand?," in *Origins* 13 (April 26, 1984): 758-759.

Wilmore, Gayraud. "Theological Ferment in the Third World," in *Christian Century* (February 15, 1978): 164-168.

"World Poverty and Vatican II," in *Catholic Charities Review* 48 (October, 1964): 2-3.

Index

ROMAN CATHOLIC STUDIES

1. L. Thomas Snyderwine (ed.), **Researching the Development of Lay Leadership in the Catholic Church Since Vatican II: Bibliographical Abstracts**
2. Frank Przetacznik, **The Catholic Concept of Genuine and Just Peace as a Basic Collective Human Right**
3. Andrew Cuschieri, **Introductory Readings in Canon**
4. Ernest Skublics, **How Eastern Orthodoxy Can Contribute to Roman Catholic Renewal: A Theological and Pastoral Proposition**
5. Robert J. Kaslyn, **"Communion with the Church" and the Code of Canon Law: An Analysis of the Foundation and Implications of the Canonical Obligation to Maintain Communion with the Catholic Church**
6. Patricia Voydanoff and Thomas M. Martin (eds.), **Using a Family Perspective in Catholic Social Justice and Family Ministries**
7. Michael Sundermeier and Robert Churchill (eds.), **The Literary and Educational Effects of the Thought of John Henry Newman**
8. Ross A. Shecterle, **The Theology of Revelation of Avery Dulles, 1980-1994: Symbolic Mediation**
9. Filippo Maria Toscano, **El Universalismo Del Pensamiento Cristiano De Don Luigi Sturzo**
10. James L. MacNeil, **A Study of Gaudium et Spes 19-22, The Second Vatican Council Response to Contemporary Atheism**
11. David B. Perrin, **The Sacrament of Reconciliation: An Existential Approach**
12. Stephen R. Duncan, **A Genre in Hindusthani Music (Bhajans) as Used in the Roman Catholic Church**
13. Maria G. McClelland, **The Sisters of Mercy, Popular Politics and the Growth of the Roman Catholic Community in Hull, 1855-1930**
14. Robert Berchmans, **A Study of Lonergan's Self-Transcending Subject and Kegan's Evolving Self: A Framework for Christian Anthropology**
15. Larry Hostetter, **The Ecclesial Dimension of Personal and Social Reform in the Writings of Isaac Thomas Hecker**
16. Patricia Smith, **Theoretical and Practical Understanding of the Integral Reordering of Canon Law**
17. Kevin E. Schmiesing, **American Catholic Intellectuals and the Dilemma of Dual Identities, 1895-1955**
18. John Langlois, **A Catholic Response in Sixteenth-Century France to Reformation Theology–The Works of Pierre Doré**
19. Ericka Kim Verba, **Catholic Feminism and the Social Question in Chile, 1910-1917: The Liga de Damas Chilenas**
20. Anthony J. Blasi with Joseph F. Zimmerman, **Transition from Vowed to Lay Ministry in American Catholicism**
21. Peter M. Batts, **Henri-Dominique Lacordaire's Re-Establishment of the Dominican Order in Nineteenth-Century France**
22. Gerald S. Twomey, **The "Preferential Option for the Poor" in Catholic Social Thought from John XXIII to John Paul II**